Undergraduate Topics in Computer Science

'Undergraduate Topics in Computer Science' (UTiCS) delivers high-quality instructional content for undergraduates studying in all areas of computing and information science. From core foundational and theoretical material to final-year topics and applications, UTiCS books take a fresh, concise, and modern approach and are ideal for self-study or for a one- or two-semester course. The texts are all authored by established experts in their fields, reviewed by an international advisory board, and contain numerous examples and problems, many of which include fully worked solutions.

The UTiCS concept relies on high-quality, concise books in softback format, and generally a maximum of 275–300 pages. For undergraduate textbooks that are likely to be longer, more expository, Springer continues to offer the highly regarded Texts in Computer Science series, to which we refer potential authors.

Gerard O'Regan

Concise Guide to Software Engineering

From Fundamentals to Application Methods

Second Edition

 Springer

Gerard O'Regan
University of Central Asia
Naryn, Kyrgyzstan

ISSN 1863-7310 ISSN 2197-1781 (electronic)
Undergraduate Topics in Computer Science
ISBN 978-3-031-07815-6 ISBN 978-3-031-07816-3 (eBook)
https://doi.org/10.1007/978-3-031-07816-3

This Springer imprint is published by the registered company Springer Nature Switzerland AG
The registered company address is: Gewerbestrasse 11, 6330 Cham, Switzerland

To
Past and present members of the Formal
Methods Group (Foundations and Methods
Group) at Trinity College Dublin, Ireland.

Preface

Overview

The objective of this book is to provide a concise introduction to the software engineering field to students and practitioners. The principles of software engineering are discussed, and the goal is to give the reader a grasp of the fundamentals of the software engineering field, as well as guidance on how to apply the theory in an industrial environment.

Organization and Features

Chapter 1 presents a broad overview of software engineering and discusses various software lifecycles and the activities in software development. We discuss requirements gathering and specification, software design, implementation, testing and maintenance. The lightweight Agile methodology is introduced, and it has become very popular in industry.

Chapter 2 discusses the professional responsibilities of software engineers. Engineers have a responsibility to ensure that the products that they design and develop are built to the highest possible standards and are safe for the public to use. Engineers must behave ethically in their dealings with their clients, and they need to adhere to the code of ethics of the professional engineering body.

Chapter 3 discusses ethical software engineering where the ethical software engineer needs to examine both the technical and the ethical dimensions of decisions that affect wider society. We discuss the Volkswagen emissions scandal where engineers installed a "defeat device" to enable cars to pass an emissions test.

Chapter 4 introduces project management for traditional software engineering, and we discuss project estimation, project planning and scheduling, project monitoring and control, risk management, managing communication and change, and managing project quality.

Chapter 5 discusses requirements engineering and discusses activities such as requirements gathering, requirements elicitation, requirements analysis, requirements management, and requirements verification and validation.

Chapter 6 discusses software design and development, where software design is the blueprint of the solution to be developed. It is concerned with the high-level architecture of the system, as well as the detailed design that describes the algorithms and functionality of the individual programs. The detailed design is then implemented in a programming language such as C++ or Java. We discuss software development topics such as software reuse, customized-off-the-shelf software (COTS), and open-source software development.

Chapter 7 discusses software inspections, which play an important role in building quality into a product. The well-known Fagan inspection process that was developed at IBM in the 1970s is discussed, as well as lighter review and walk-through methodologies.

Chapter 8 is concerned with software testing and discusses the various types of testing that may be carried out during the project. We discuss test planning, test case definition, test environment set-up, test execution, test tracking, test metrics, test reporting, and testing in an e-commerce environment.

Chapter 9 discusses ethics and privacy where professional ethics are a code of conduct that governs how members of a profession deal with each other and with third parties. It expresses ideals of human behaviour, and the fundamental values of the organization, and is an indication of its professionalism. Privacy is defined as "the right to be left alone," and specifies there should be no intrusion upon seclusion, and no public disclosure of private facts or false information.

Chapter 10 is concerned with metrics and problem-solving, and this includes a discussion of the balanced score card which assists in identifying appropriate metrics for the organization. The goal, question, metrics (GQM) approach is discussed, and this allows appropriate metrics related to the organization goals to be defined. A selection of sample metrics for an organization is presented, and problem-solving tools such as fishbone diagrams, Pareto charts, trend charts are discussed.

Chapter 11 is concerned with the selection and management of a software supplier. It discusses how candidate suppliers may be identified, formally evaluated against defined selection criteria, and how the appropriate supplier is selected. We discuss how the selected supplier is managed during the project.

Chapter 12 discusses software configuration management and discusses the fundamental concept of a baseline. Configuration management is concerned with identifying those deliverables that must be subject to change control and controlling changes to them.

Chapter 13 discusses software quality assurance and the importance of process quality. It is a premise in the quality field that good processes and conformance to them is essential for the delivery of high-quality product, and this chapter discusses audits, and describes how they are carried out.

Chapter 14 discusses the Agile methodology which is a popular lightweight approach to software development. Agile provides opportunities to assess the direction of a project throughout the development lifecycle and ongoing changes to requirements are considered normal in the Agile world. It has a strong collaborative style of working, and it advocates adaptive planning and evolutionary development.

Chapter 15 discusses software reliability and dependability and covers topics such as software reliability and software reliability models; the cleanroom methodology, system availability; safety and security critical systems; and dependability engineering.

Chapter 16 discusses formal methods, which consist of a set of mathematical techniques to specify and derive a program from its specification. Formal methods may be employed to rigorously state the requirements of the proposed system. They may be employed to derive a program from its mathematical specification, and they may be used to provide a rigorous proof that the implemented program satisfies its specification. They have been mainly applied to the safety critical field.

Chapter 17 presents the Z specification language, which is one of the more popular formal methods. It was developed at the Programming Research Group at Oxford University in the early 1980s. Z specifications are mathematical, and the use of mathematics ensures precision and allows inconsistencies and gaps in the specification to be identified. Theorem provers may be employed to demonstrate that the software implementation meets its specification.

Chapter 18 presents the unified modelling language (UML), which is a visual modelling language for software systems, and I used to present several views of the system architecture. It was developed at Rational Corporation as a notation for modelling object-oriented systems. We present various UML diagrams such as use case diagrams, sequence diagrams, and activity diagrams.

Chapter 19 discusses software process improvement. It begins with a discussion of a software process and discusses the benefits that may be gained from a software process improvement initiative. Various models that support software process improvement are discussed, and these include the Capability Maturity Model Integration (CMMI), ISO 9000, Personal Software Process (PSP), and Team Software Process (TSP).

Chapter 20 gives an overview of the CMMI model and discusses its five maturity levels and their constituent process areas. We discuss both the staged and continuous representations of the CMMI and SCAMPI appraisals that indicate the extent to which the CMMI has been implemented in the organization, as well as identifying opportunities for improvement.

Chapter 21 discusses various tools to support the various software engineering activities. The focus is first to define the process, and then to find tools to support the process. Tools to support project management are discussed as well as tools to support requirements engineering, configuration management, design and development activities, and software testing.

Chapter 22 discusses innovation in the software field including miscellaneous topics such as distributed systems, service-oriented architecture, software as a service, cloud computing and embedded systems. We discuss the need for innovation in software engineering and discuss some recent innovations such as aspect-oriented software engineering.

Chapter 23 is concerned with the application of the legal system to the computing field. This includes the protection of intellectual property such as patents, copyright, trademarks and trade secrets, and the resolution of disputes between parties.

Chapter 24 discusses cybersecurity and cybercrime. Cybercrime is a crime that involves a computer and a network. The computer may be the vehicle by which the crime was conducted, or it may be the target of the crime. Cybersecurity is concerned with the ability of a computer system to protect itself from attacks, and there are several characteristics of security such as confidentiality, integrity, and availability.

Chapter 25 is the concluding chapter in which we summarize the journey that we have travelled in this book.

Audience

The main audience of this book is computer science students who are interested in learning about software engineering and in learning on how to build high-quality and reliable software on time and on budget. It will also be of interest to industrialists including software engineers, quality professionals and software managers, as well as the motivated general reader.

Acknowledgments

I am deeply indebted to family and friends who supported my efforts in this endeavour, and my thanks, as always, to the team at Springer. This book is dedicated to present and past members of the Formal Methods Group (Foundations and Methods Group) at Trinity College Dublin where the author spent several happy years. I would especially like to thank Dr. Mícheál Mac An Airchinnigh, Dr. Andrew Butterfield, Dr. Hugh Gibbons, Dr. Arthur Hughes, Alexis Donnelly, Dara Gallagher, Eoin McDonnell, Gradamir Starovic, and Glenn Strong.

Cork, Ireland   Gerard O'Regan

Contents

List of Figures

List of Tables

Fundamentals of Software Engineering

1

Abstract

This chapter presents a broad overview of software engineering and discusses various software lifecycles and the phases in software development. We discuss requirements gathering and specification, software design, implementation, testing and maintenance. The lightweight Agile methodology is introduced, and it has become very popular in industry. Mathematics may potentially assist software engineers in delivering high-quality software products that are safe to use, and the extent to which mathematics should be employed remains a topic of active debate.

Keywords

Standish chaos report · Software lifecycles · Waterfall model · Spiral model · Rational unified process · Agile development · Software inspections · Software testing · Project management

1.1 Introduction

The approach to software development in the 1950s and 1960s has been described as the *"Mongolian Hordes Approach"* by Fred Brooks [1].[1] The "method" or lack of method was applied to projects that were running late, and it involved adding many inexperienced programmers to the project, with the expectation that this

---

[1] The "Mongolian Hordes" management myth is the belief that adding more programmers to a software project that is running late will allow catch-up. In fact, as Brooks says adding people to a late software project makes it later.

© Springer Nature Switzerland AG 2022
G. O'Regan, *Concise Guide to Software Engineering*,
Undergraduate Topics in Computer Science,
https://doi.org/10.1007/978-3-031-07816-3_1

would allow the project schedule to be recovered. However, this approach was deeply flawed as it led to programmers with inadequate knowledge of the project attempting to solve problems, and they inevitably required significant time from the other project team members.

This resulted in the project being delivered even later, as well as subsequent problems with quality (i.e., the approach of throwing people at a problem does not work). The philosophy of software development back in the 1950/60s was characterized by:

> The completed code will always be full of defects.
> The coding should be finished quickly to correct these defects.
> Design as you code approach.

This philosophy accepted defeat in software development, and suggested that irrespective of a solid engineering approach, that the completed software would always contain lots of defects, and that it therefore made sense to code as quickly as possible, and to then identify the defects that were present, and to correct them as quickly as possible to solve a problem.

In the late 1960s it was clear that the existing approaches to software development were deeply flawed, and that there was an urgent need for change. The NATO Science Committee organized two famous conferences to discuss critical issues in software development [2]. The first conference was held at Garmisch, Germany, in 1968, and it was followed by a second conference in Rome in 1969. Over fifty people from eleven countries attended the Garmisch conference, including Edsger Dijkstra, who did important theoretical work on formal specification and verification. The NATO conferences highlighted problems that existed in the software sector in the late 1960s, and the term "*software crisis*" was coined to refer to these. There were problems with budget and schedule overruns, as well as the quality and reliability of the delivered software.

The conference led to the birth of *software engineering* as a discipline in its own right, and the realization that programming is quite distinct from science and mathematics. Programmers are like engineers in that they build software products, and they therefore need education in traditional engineering as well as the latest technologies. The education of a classical engineer includes product design and mathematics. However, often computer science education places an emphasis on the latest technologies, rather than on the important engineering foundations of designing and building high-quality products that are safe for the public to use.

Programmers therefore need to learn the key engineering skills to enable them to build products that are safe for the public to use. This includes a solid foundation on design and on the mathematics required for building safe software products. Mathematics plays a key role in classical engineering, and in some situations, it may also assist software engineers in the delivery of high-quality software products. Several mathematical approaches to assist software engineers are described in [3].

There are parallels between the software crisis in the late 1960s, and serious problems with bridge construction in the nineteenth century. Several bridges collapsed, or were delivered late or over-budget, since people involved in their design

Fig. 1.1 Standish report—
Results of 1995 and 2009
survey

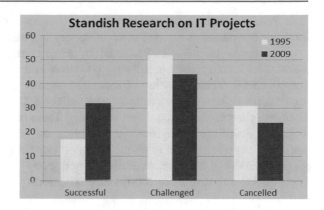

and construction did not have the required engineering knowledge. This led to bridges that were poorly designed and constructed, leading to their collapse and loss of life, as well as endangering the lives of the public.

This led to legislation requiring engineers to be licensed by the Professional Engineering Association prior to practising as engineers. This organization specified a core body of knowledge that the engineer is required to possess, and the licensing body verifies that the engineer has the required qualifications and experience. This helps to ensure that only personnel competent to design and build products do so. Engineers have a professional responsibility to ensure that the products are properly built and are safe for the public to use.

The Standish group has conducted research (Fig. 1.1) on the extent of problems with IT projects since the mid-1990s. These studies were conducted in the United States, but there is no reason to believe that European or Asian companies perform any better. The results indicate serious problems with on-time delivery of projects, and projects being cancelled prior to completion.[2] However, the comparison between 1995 and 2009 suggests that there have been some improvements with a greater percentage of projects being delivered successfully, and a reduction in the percentage of projects being cancelled.

Fred Brooks argues that software is inherently complex, and that there is no *silver bullet* that will resolve all the problems associated with software development such as schedule or budget overruns [1, 4]. Poor software quality can lead to defects in the software that may adversely impact the customer, and even lead to loss of life. It is therefore essential that software development organizations place sufficient emphasis on quality throughout the software development process.

The Y2K problem was caused by a two-digit representation of dates, and it required major rework to enable legacy software to function for the new millennium. Clearly, well-designed programs would have hidden the representation of the

---

[2] These are IT projects covering diverse sectors including banking, telecommunications, etc., rather than pure software companies. Software companies following maturity frameworks such as the CMMI generally achieve more consistent results.

date, which would have required minimal changes for year 2000 compliance. Instead, companies spent vast sums of money to rectify the problem.

The quality of software produced by some companies is impressive.[3] These companies employ mature software processes and are committed to continuous improvement. There is a lot of industrial interest in software process maturity models for software organizations, and various approaches to assess and mature software companies are described in [5, 6].[4] These models focus on improving the effectiveness of the management, engineering and organization practices related to software engineering, and in introducing best practice in software engineering. The disciplined use of the mature software processes by the software engineers enables high-quality software to be consistently produced.

1.2 What is Software Engineering?

Software engineering involves the multi-person construction of multi-version programs. The IEEE 610.12 definition of Software Engineering is:

> Software engineering is the application of a systematic, disciplined, quantifiable approach to the development, operation, and maintenance of software; that is, the application of engineering to software, and the study of such approaches.

Software engineering includes:

1. Methodologies to design, develop, and test software to meet customers' needs.
2. Software is engineered. That is, the software products are properly designed, developed, and tested in accordance with engineering principles.
3. Quality and safety are properly addressed.
4. Mathematics may be employed to assist with the design and verification of software products. The level of mathematics employed will depend on the safety critical nature of the product. Systematic peer reviews and rigorous testing will often be sufficient to build quality into the software, with heavy mathematical techniques reserved for safety and security critical software.
5. Sound project management and quality management practices are employed.
6. Support and maintenance of the software is properly addressed.

---

[3] I recall projects at Motorola that regularly achieved 5.6σ-quality in a L4 CMM environment (i.e., approx. 20 defects per million lines of code. This represents very high quality).
[4] Approaches such as the CMM or SPICE (ISO 15504) focus mainly on the management and organizational practices required in software engineering. The emphasis is on defining software processes that are fit for purpose and consistently following them. The process maturity models focus on what needs to be done rather how it should be done. This gives the organization the freedom to choose the appropriate implementation to meet its needs. The models provide useful information on practices to consider in the implementation.

Software engineering is not just programming. It requires the engineer to state precisely the requirements that the software product is to satisfy, and then to produce designs that will meet these requirements. The project needs to be planned and delivered on time and budget. The requirements must provide a precise description of the problem to be solved: i.e., *it should be evident from the requirements what is and what is not required*.

The requirements need to be rigorously reviewed to ensure that they are stated clearly and unambiguously and reflect the customer's needs. The next step is then to create the design that will solve the problem, and it is essential to validate the correctness of the design. Next, the software code to implement the design is written, and peer reviews and software testing are employed to verify and validate the correctness of the software.

The verification and validation of the design is rigorously performed for safety critical systems, and it is sometimes appropriate to employ mathematical techniques for these systems. However, it will usually be sufficient to employ peer reviews or software inspections as these methodologies provide a high degree of rigour. This may include approaches such as Fagan inspections [7], Gilb inspections [8], or Prince 2's approach to quality reviews [9].

The term *"engineer"* is a title that is awarded on merit in classical engineering. It is generally applied only to people who have attained the necessary education and competence to be called engineers, and who base their practice on classical engineering principles. The title places responsibilities on its holder to behave professionally and ethically. Often in computer science the term *"software engineer"* is employed loosely to refer to anyone who builds things, rather than to an individual with a core set of knowledge, experience, and competence.

Several computer scientists (such as Parnas[5]) have argued that computer scientists should be educated as engineers to enable them to apply appropriate scientific principles to their work. They argue that computer scientists should receive a solid foundation in mathematics and design, to enable them to have the professional competence to perform as engineers in building high-quality products that are safe for the public to use. The use of mathematics is an integral part of the engineer's work in other engineering disciplines, and so the *software engineer* should be able to use mathematics to assist in the modelling or understanding of the behaviour or properties of the proposed software system.

Software engineers need education[6] on specification, design, turning designs into programs, software inspections, and testing. The education should enable the software engineer to produce well-structured programs that are fit for purpose.

---

[5] Parnas has made important contributions to computer science. He advocates a solid engineering approach with the extensive use of classical mathematical techniques in software development. He also introduced information hiding in the 1970s, which is now a part of object-oriented design.

[6] Software Companies that are following approaches such as the CMM or ISO 9001 consider the education and qualification of staff prior to assigning staff to performing specific tasks. The appropriate qualifications and experience for the specific role are considered prior to appointing a person to carry out the role. Many companies are committed to the education and continuous

Parnas has argued that software engineers have responsibilities as professional engineers.[7] They are responsible for designing and implementing high-quality and reliable software that is safe to use. They are also accountable for their decisions and actions,[8] and have a responsibility to object to decisions that violate professional standards. Engineers are required to behave professionally and ethically with their clients. The membership of the professional engineering body requires the member to adhere to the code of ethics[9] of the profession. Engineers in other professions are licensed, and therefore Parnas argues that a similar licensing approach be adopted for professional software engineers[10] to provide confidence that they are competent for the assignment. Professional software engineers are required to follow best practice in software engineering and the defined software processes.[11]

Many software companies invest heavily in training, as the education and knowledge of its staff are essential to delivering high-quality products and services. Employees receive professional training related to the roles that they are performing, such as project management, software design and development, software testing, and service management. The fact that the employees are professionally qualified increases confidence in the ability of the company to deliver high-quality products and services. A company that pays little attention to the competence and continuous development of its staff will obtain poor results and suffer a loss of reputation and market share.

---

development of their staff, and on introducing best practice in software engineering into their organization.

[7] The ancient Babylonians used the concept of accountability, and they employed a code of laws (known as the Hammurabi Code) c. 1750 B.C. It included a law that stated that if a house collapsed and killed the owner then the builder of the house would be executed.

[8] However, it is unlikely that an individual programmer would be subject to litigation in the case of a flaw in a program causing damage or loss of life. A comprehensive disclaimer of responsibility for problems rather than a guarantee of quality accompanies most software products. Software engineering is a team-based activity involving many engineers in various parts of the project, and it would be potentially difficult for an outside party to prove that the cause of a particular problem is due to the professional negligence of a particular software engineer, as there are many others involved in the process such as reviewers of documentation and code and the various test groups. Companies are more likely to be subject to litigation, as a company is legally responsible for the actions of their employees in the workplace, and a company is a wealthier entity than one of its employees. The legal aspects of licensing software may protect software companies from litigation. However, greater legal protection for the customer can be built into the contract between the supplier and the customer for bespoke-software development.

[9] Many software companies have a defined code of ethics that employees are expected to adhere. Larger companies will wish to project a good corporate image and to be respected worldwide.

[10] The British Computer Society (BCS) has introduced a qualification system for computer science professionals that it used to show that professionals are properly qualified. The most important of these is the BCS Information Systems Examination Board (ISEB) which allows IT professionals to be qualified in service management, project management, software testing, and so on.

[11] Software companies that are following the CMMI or ISO 9001 standards will employ audits to verify that the processes and procedures have been followed. Auditors report their findings to management and the findings are addressed appropriately by the project team and affected individuals.

1.3 Challenges in Software Engineering

The challenge in software engineering is to deliver high-quality software on time and on budget to customers. The research done by the Standish Group was discussed earlier in this chapter, and the results of their 1998 research (Fig. 1.2) on project cost overruns in the US indicated that 33% of projects are between 21 and 50% overestimate, 18% are between 51 and 100% over estimate, and 11% of projects are between 101 and 200% overestimate.

The accurate estimation of project cost, effort and schedule is a challenge in software engineering. Therefore, project managers need to determine how good their estimation process actually is and to make appropriate improvements. The use of software metrics is an objective way to do this, and improvements in estimation will be evident from a reduced variance between estimated and actual effort (see Chap. 10). The project manager will determine and report the actual versus estimated effort and schedule for the project.

Risk management is an important part of project management, and the objective is to identify potential risks early and throughout the project, and to manage them appropriately. The probability of each risk occurring, and its impact is determined, and the risks are managed during project execution.

Software quality needs to be properly planned to enable the project to deliver a quality product. Flaws with poor quality software may lead to a negative perception of the company and may potentially lead to damage to the customer relationship with a subsequent loss of market share.

There is a strong economic case to building quality into the software, as less time is spent in re working defective software. The cost of poor quality (COPQ) should be measured, and targets set for its reductions. It is important that lessons are learned during the project and acted upon appropriately. This helps to promote a culture of continuous improvement.

Several high-profile software failures are discussed in [6]. These include the millennium bug (Y2K) problem; the floating-point bug in the Intel microprocessor; the European Space Agency Ariane-5 disaster, and so on. These failures led to

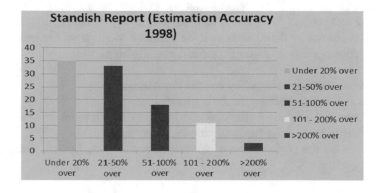

Fig. 1.2 Standish 1998 report—Estimation accuracy

embarrassment for the organizations, as well as the associated cost of replacement and correction.

The millennium bug was due to the use of two digits to represent dates rather than four digits. The solution involved finding and analysing all code that that had a Y2K impact; planning and making the necessary changes; and verifying the correctness of the changes. The worldwide cost of correcting the millennium bug is estimated to have been in billions of dollars.

The Intel Corporation was slow to acknowledge the floating-point problem in its Pentium microprocessor, and in providing adequate information on its impact to its customers. It incurred a large financial cost in replacing microprocessors for its customers. The Ariane-5 failure caused major embarrassment and damage to the credibility of the European Space Agency (ESA). Its maiden flight ended in failure on June 4, 1996, after a flight time of just 40 s.

These failures indicate that quality needs to be carefully considered when designing and developing software. The effect of software failure may be large costs to correct the software, loss of credibility of the company, or even loss of life.

1.4   Software Processes and Lifecycles

Organizations vary by size and complexity, and the processes employed will reflect the nature of their business. The development of software involves many processes such as those for defining requirements; processes for project estimation and planning; processes for design, implementation, testing, and so on.

It is important that the processes employed are fit for purpose, and a key premise in the software quality field is that the quality of the resulting software is influenced by the quality and maturity of the underlying processes, and compliance to them. Therefore, it is necessary to focus on the quality of the processes as well as the quality of the resulting software.

There is, of course, little point in having high-quality processes unless their use is institutionalized in the organization. That is, all employees need to follow the processes consistently. This requires that the employees are trained on the processes, and that process discipline is instilled with an appropriate audit strategy that ensures compliance to them. Data will be collected to improve the process. The software process assets in an organization generally consist of:

- A software development policy for the organization,
- Process maps that describe the flow of activities,
- Procedures and guidelines that describe the processes in more detail,
- Checklists to assist with the performance of the process,
- Templates for the performance of specific activities (e.g., Design, Testing),
- Training Materials.

The processes employed to develop high-quality software generally include:

- Project Management Process,
- Requirements process,
- Design Process,
- Coding Process,
- Peer Review Process,
- Testing Process,
- Supplier Selection and Management processes,
- Configuration Management process,
- Audit process,
- Measurement Process,
- Improvement Process,
- Customer Support and Maintenance processes.

The software development process has an associated lifecycle that consists of various phases. There are several well-known lifecycles employed such as the waterfall model [10]; the spiral model [11], the Rational Unified Process [12] and the Agile methodology [13] which has become popular in recent years. The choice of a particular software development lifecycle is determined from the needs of the specific project. The various lifecycles are described in more detail in the following sections.

1.4.1 Waterfall Lifecycle

The waterfall model (Fig. 1.3) starts with requirements gathering and definition. It is followed by the system specification (with the functional and non-functional requirements), the design and implementation of the software, and comprehensive testing. The testing generally includes unit, system, and user acceptance testing.

The waterfall model is employed for projects where the requirements can be identified early in the project lifecycle or are known in advance. We are treating the waterfall model as the "V" life cycle model, with the left-hand side of the "V" detailing requirements, specification, design, and coding and the right-hand side

Fig. 1.3 Waterfall V lifecycle model

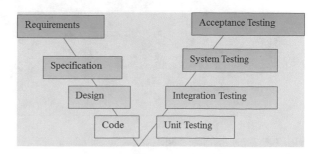

detailing unit tests, integration tests, system tests and acceptance testing. Each phase has entry and exit criteria that must be satisfied before the next phase commences. There are several variations to the waterfall model.

Many companies employ a set of templates to enable the activities in the various phases to be consistently performed. Templates may be employed for project planning and reporting; requirements definition; design; testing and so on. These templates may be based on the IEEE standards or industrial best practice.

1.4.2 Spiral Lifecycles

The spiral model (Fig. 1.4) was developed by Barry Boehm in the 1980s [11], and it is useful for projects where the requirements are not fully known at project initiation, or where the requirements evolve as a part of the development lifecycle. The development proceeds in several spirals, where each spiral typically involves objectives and an analysis of the risks, updates to the requirements, design, code, testing, and a user review of the iteration or spiral.

The spiral is, in effect, a re-usable prototype with the business analysts and the customer reviewing the current iteration and providing feedback to the development team. The feedback is analysed and used to plan the next iteration. This approach is often used in joint application development, where the usability and look and feel of

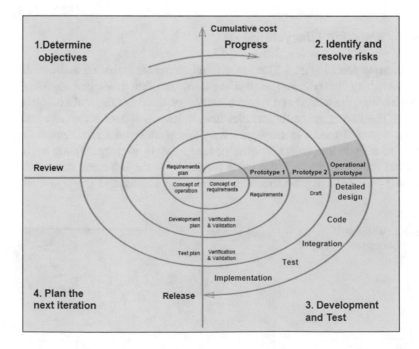

Fig. 1.4 Spiral lifecycle model … public domain

the application is a key concern. This is important in web-based development and in the development of a graphical user interface (GUI). The implementation of part of the system helps in gaining a better understanding of the requirements of the system, and this feeds into subsequent development cycles. The process repeats until the requirements and the software product are fully complete.

There are several variations of the spiral model including Rapid Application Development (RAD); Joint Application Development (JAD) models; and the Dynamic Systems Development Method (DSDM) model. The Agile methodology (discussed in Chap. 14) has become popular in recent years, and it employs sprints (or iterations) of 2–4 weeks duration to implement a number of user stories. A sample spiral model is shown in Fig. 1.4.

There are other life-cycle models such as the iterative development process that combines the waterfall and spiral lifecycle model. An overview of Cleanroom is presented in Chap. 11, and the methodology was developed by Harlan Mills at IBM. It includes a phase for formal specification, and its approach to software testing is based on the predicted usage of the software product, which allows a software reliability measure to be calculated. The Rational Unified Process (RUP) was developed by Rational, and it is discussed in the next section.

1.4.3   Rational Unified Process

The *Rational Unified Process* [12] was developed at the Rational Corporation (now part of IBM) in the late 1990s. It uses the Unified Modelling Language (UML) as a tool for specification and design, where UML is a visual modelling language for software systems that provides a means of specifying, constructing, and documenting the object-oriented system. It was developed by James Rumbaugh, Grady Booch, and Ivar Jacobson, and it facilitates the understanding of the architecture and complexity of the system.

RUP is *use case driven, architecture centric, iterative,* and *incremental,* and includes cycles, phases, workflows, risk mitigation, quality control, project management, and configuration control (Fig. 1.5). Software projects may be very complex, and there are risks that requirements may be incomplete, or that the interpretation of a requirement may differ between the customer and the project team. RUP is a way to reduce risk in software engineering.

Requirements are gathered as use cases, where the *use cases describe the functional requirements from the point of view of the user of the system.* They describe what the system will do at a high level and ensure that there is an appropriate focus on the user when defining the scope of the project. *Use cases also drive the development process,* as the developers create a series of design and implementation models that realize the use cases. The developers review each successive model for conformance to the use-case model, and the test team verifies that the implementation correctly implements the use cases.

The software architecture concept embodies the most significant static and dynamic aspects of the system. The architecture grows out of the use cases and

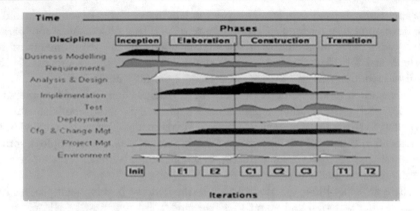

Fig. 1.5 Rational unified process

factors such as the platform that the software is to run on, deployment considerations, legacy systems, and the non-functional requirements.

RUP decomposes the work of a large project into smaller slices or mini-projects, and *each mini-project is an iteration that results in an increment to the product.* The iteration consists of one or more steps in the workflow, and generally leads to the growth of the product. If there is a need to repeat an iteration, then all that is lost is the misdirected effort of one iteration, rather that the entire product. Another words, RUP is a way to mitigate risk in software engineering.

1.4.4 Agile Development

There has been a massive growth of popularity among software developers in lightweight methodologies such as *Agile*. This is a software development methodology that is more responsive to customer needs than traditional methods such as the waterfall model. *The waterfall development model is similar to a wide and slow-moving value stream*, and halfway through the project 100% of the requirements are typically 50% done. *However, for agile development 50% of requirements are typically 100% done halfway through the project.*

This methodology has a strong collaborative style of working and its approach includes:

- Aims to achieve a narrow fast flowing value stream,
- Feedback and adaptation employed in decision making,
- User Stories and sprints are employed,
- Stories are either done are not done (no such thing as 50% done),
- Iterative and Incremental development is employed,
- A project is divided into iterations,
- An iteration has a fixed length (i.e., Time boxing is employed),

- Entire software development lifecycle is employed for the implementation of each story,
- Change is accepted as a normal part of life in the Agile world,
- Delivery is made as early as possible,
- Maintenance is seen as part of the development process,
- Refactoring and Evolutionary Design Employed,
- Continuous Integration is employed,
- Short Cycle Times,
- Emphasis on Quality,
- Stand Up Meetings,
- Plan regularly,
- Direct interaction preferred over documentation,
- Rapid conversion of requirements into working functionality,
- Demonstrate value early,
- Early decision making.

Ongoing changes to requirements are considered normal in the Agile world, and it is believed to be more realistic to change requirements regularly throughout the project rather than attempting to define all the requirements at the start of the project. The methodology includes controls to manage changes to the requirements, and good communication and early regular feedback is an essential part of the process.

A story may be a new feature or a modification to an existing feature. It is reduced to the minimum scope that can deliver business value, and a feature may give rise to several stories. Stories often build upon other stories and the entire software development lifecycle is employed for the implementation of each story. *Stories are either done or not done—i.e., there is such thing as a story being 80% done.* The story is complete only when it passes its acceptance tests. Stories are prioritized based on a number of factors including:

- Business Value of Story,
- Mitigation of risk,
- Dependencies on other stories.

The Scrum approach is an Agile method for managing iterative development, and it consists of an outline planning phase for the project followed by a set of sprint cycles (where each cycle develops an increment). *Sprint planning* is performed before the start of the iteration, and stories are assigned to the iteration to fill the available time. Each scrum sprint is of a fixed length (usually 2–4 weeks), and it develops an increment of the system. The estimates for each story and their priority are determined, and the prioritized stories are assigned to the iteration. *A short morning stand-up meeting is held daily* during the iteration, and attended by the scrum master, the project manager[12] and the project team. It discusses the progress made the previous day, problem reporting and tracking, and the work planned for the day ahead. A separate meeting is held for issues that require more detailed discussion.

Once the iteration is complete the latest product increment is demonstrated to an audience including the product owner. This is to receive feedback and to identify new requirements. The team also conducts a retrospective meeting to identify what went well and what went poorly during the iteration. This is for continuous improvement of future iterations. Planning for the next sprint then commences. The scrum master is a facilitator who arranges the daily meetings and ensures that the scrum process is followed. The role involves removing roadblocks so that the team can achieve their goals and communicating with other stakeholders.

Agile employs pair programming and a collaborative style of working with the philosophy that two heads are better than one. This allows multiple perspectives in decision making and a broader understanding of the issues.

Software testing is very important and Agile generally employs automated testing for unit, acceptance, performance, and integration testing. Tests are run frequently with the goal of catching programming errors early. They are generally run on a separate build server to ensure that all dependencies are checked. Tests are re-run before making a release. *Agile employs test driven development with tests written before the code.* The developers write code to make a test pass with ideally developers only coding against failing tests. This approach forces the developer to write testable code.

Refactoring is employed in Agile as a design and coding practice. The objective is to change how the software is written without changing what it does. Refactoring is a tool for evolutionary design where the design is regularly evaluated, and improvements are implemented as they are identified. It helps in improving the maintainability and readability of the code and in reducing complexity. The automated test suite is essential in showing that the integrity of the software is maintained following refactoring.

Continuous integration allows the system to be built with every change. Early and regular integration allows early feedback to be provided. It also allows all of the automated tests to be run thereby identifying problems earlier. Agile is discussed in more detail in Chap. 14.

1.4.5 Continuous Software Development

Continuous software development is in a sense the successor to Agile, and involves activities such as continuous integration, continuous delivery, continuous testing, and continuous deployment of the software. Its objective is to enable technology companies to accelerate the delivery of their products to their customers, thereby

---

[12] Agile teams are self-organizing, and the project manager role is generally not employed for small projects (<20 staff).

delivering faster business benefits as well as reshaping relationships with their customers.

Continuous integration is a coding philosophy with an associated set of practices where each developer submits their work as soon as it is finished, and several builds may take place during the day in response to the addition of significant change. The build has an associated set of unit and integration tests that are automated and are used to verify the integrity of the build, and this ensures that the addition of the new code is of a high-quality. Continuous integration ensures that the developers receive immediate feedback on the software that they are working on.

Continuous delivery builds on the activities in continuous integration, where each code that is added to the build has automated unit and system tests conducted. Automated functional tests, regression tests and possibly acceptance tests will be conducted, and once the automated tests pass the software is sent to a staging environment for deployment.

Continuous testing allows the test group to continuously test the most up to date version of the software, and it includes manual testing as well as user acceptance testing. It differs from conventional testing as the software is expected to change over time.

Continuous deployment allows changes to be delivered to end users quickly without human intervention, and it requires the completion of the automated delivery tests prior to deployment to production.

1.5 Activities in Software Development

There are various activities involved in software development including:

- Requirements Definition,
- Design,
- Implementation,
- Software Testing,
- Support and Maintenance.

These activities are discussed in the following sections and cover both traditional software engineering and Agile.

1.5.1 Requirements Definition

The user (business) requirements specify what the customer wants and define what the software system is required to do (*as distinct from how this is to be done*). The requirements are the foundation for the system, and if they are incorrect, then the implemented system will be incorrect. *Prototyping may be employed* to assist in the definition and validation of the requirements. The process of determining the requirements, analysing, and validating them and managing them throughout the project lifecycle is termed *requirements engineering*.

The *user requirements* are determined from discussions with the customer to determine their actual needs, and they are then refined into the *system requirements*, which state the *functional* and *non-functional* requirements of the system. The specification of the user requirements needs to be unambiguous to ensure that all parties involved in the development of the system share a common understanding of what is to be developed and tested.

There is no requirements document as such in Agile, and the product backlog (i.e., the prioritized list of functionality of the product to be developed) is the closest to the idea of a requirements document in a traditional project. However, the written part of a user story in Agile is incomplete until the discussion of that story takes place. It is often useful to think of the written part of a story as a pointer to the real requirement, such as a diagram showing a workflow or the formula for a calculation. The Agile software development methodology argues that as requirements change so quickly that a requirements document is unnecessary, since such a document would be out of date as soon as it was written.

Requirements gathering in traditional software engineering involve meetings with the stakeholders to gather all relevant information for the proposed product. The stakeholders are interviewed, and requirements workshops conducted to elicit the requirements from them. An early working system (prototype) is often used to identify gaps and misunderstandings between developers and users. The prototype may serve as a basis for writing the specification.

The requirements workshops are used to discuss and prioritize the requirements, as well as identifying and resolving any conflicting requirements. The collected information is consolidated into a coherent set of requirements. Changes to the requirements may occur during the project, and these need to be controlled. It is essential to understand the impacts (e.g., schedule, budget and technical) of a proposed change to the requirements prior to its approval.

Requirements verification is concerned with ensuring that the requirements are properly implemented (i.e., building it right) in the design and implementation. *Requirements validation* is concerned with ensuring that the right requirements are defined (building the right system), and that they are precise, complete, and reflect the actual needs of the customer.

The requirements are validated by the stakeholders to ensure that they are those desired, and to establish their feasibility. This may involve several reviews of the requirements until all stakeholders are ready to approve the requirements document. Other validation activities include reviews of the prototype and the design, and user acceptance testing.

The requirements for a system are generally documented in a natural language such as "English". Other notations that are employed include the visual modelling language UML [14], and formal specification languages such as VDM or Z for the safety critical field.

The specification of the system requirements of the product is essentially a statement of what the software development organization will provide to meet the business (user) requirements. That is, the detailed business requirements are a statement of what the customer wants, whereas the specification of the system requirements is a statement of what will be delivered by the software development organization.

It is essential that the system requirements are valid with respect to the user requirements, and they are reviewed by the stakeholders to ensure their validity. Traceability may be employed to show that the business requirements are addressed by the system requirements.

There are two categories of system requirements: namely, functional and non-functional requirements. The *functional requirements* define the functionality that is required of the system, and it may include screen shots, report layouts or desired functionality specified as use cases. The *non-functional requirements* will generally include security, reliability, availability, performance, and portability requirements, as well as usability and maintainability requirements.

1.5.2 Design

The design of the system consists of engineering activities to describe the architecture or structure of the system, as well as activities to describe the algorithms and functions required to implement the system requirements. It is a creative process concerned with how the system will be implemented, and its activities include architecture design, interface design, and data structure design. There are often several possible design solutions for a particular system, and the designer will need to decide on the most appropriate solution.

Refactoring is employed in Agile as a design and coding practice. The objective is to change how the software is written without changing what it does. Refactoring is a tool for evolutionary design where the design is regularly evaluated, and improvements are implemented as they are identified. It helps in improving the maintainability and readability of the code and in reducing complexity. The auto mated test suite is essential in demonstrating that the integrity of the software is maintained following refactoring.

The design may be specified in various ways such as graphical notations that display the relationships between the components making up the design. The notation may include flow charts, or various UML diagrams such as sequence diagrams, state charts, and so on. Program description languages or pseudo code may be employed to define the algorithms and data structures that are the basis for implementation.

Function-oriented design is historical, and it involves starting with a high-level view of the system and refining it into a more detailed design. The system state is centralized and shared between the functions operating on that state.

Object-oriented design is based on the concept of *information hiding* developed by Parnas [15]. The system is viewed as a collection of objects rather than functions, with each object managing its own state information. The system state is decentralized, and an object is a member of a class. The definition of a class includes attributes and operations on class members, and these may be inherited from super classes. Objects communicate by exchanging messages.

It is essential to verify and validate the design with respect to the system requirements, and this may be done by traceability of the design to the system requirements and design reviews.

1.5.3   Implementation

This phase is concerned with implementing the design in the target language and environment (e.g., C++ or Java), and it involves writing or generating the actual code. The development team divides up the work to be done, with each programmer responsible for one or more modules. The coding activities often include code reviews or walkthroughs to ensure that quality code is produced, and to verify its correctness. The code reviews will verify that the source code conforms to the coding standards and that maintainability issues are addressed. They will also verify that the code produced is a valid implementation of the software design.

The development of a new feature in Agile begins with writing a suite of test cases based on the requirements for the feature. The tests fail initially, and so the first step is to write some code that enables the new test cases to pass. This new code may be imperfect (it will be improved later). The next step is to ensure that the new feature works with the existing features, and this involves executing all new and existing test cases.

This may involve modification of the source code to enable all of the tests to pass, and to ensure that all features work correctly together. The final step is refactoring the code, and this involves cleaning up and restructuring the code, and improving its structure and readability. The test cases are re-run during the refactoring to ensure that the functionality is not altered in any way. The process repeats with the addition of each new feature.

Software reuse provides a way to speed up the development process. Components or objects that may be reused need to be identified and handled accordingly. The implemented code may use software components that have either being developed internally or purchased off the shelf. Open-source software has become popular in recent years, and it allows software developed by others to be used (*under an open-source license*) in the development of applications.

The benefits of software reuse include increased productivity and a faster time to market. There are inherent risks with customized-off-the shelf (COTS) software, as the supplier may decide to no longer support the software, or there is no guarantee that software that has worked successfully in one domain will work correctly in a different domain. It is therefore important to consider the risks as well as the benefits of software reuse and open-source software.

1.5.4   Software Testing

Software testing is employed to verify that the requirements have been correctly implemented, and that the software is fit for purpose, as well as identifying defects present in the software. There are various types of testing that may be conducted including *unit testing, integration testing, system testing, performance testing and user acceptance testing*. These are described below:

Unit and Integration Testing

Unit testing is performed by the programmer on the completed unit (or module), and prior to its integration with other modules. The programmer writes these tests, and the objective is to show that the code satisfies the design. The unit test case is generally documented, and it should include the test objective and the expected results.

Code coverage and branch coverage metrics are often generated to give an indication of how comprehensive the unit testing has been. These metrics provide visibility into the number of lines of code executed, as well as the branches covered during unit testing. The developer executes the unit tests; records the results; corrects any identified defects, and re-tests the software.

Test driven development (TDD) is employed in the Agile world, and this involves writing the unit test cases (and possibly other test cases) before the code, and the code is then written to pass the defined test cases. These tests are automated in the Agile world and are run with every build.

Integration testing is performed on the integrated system once all of the individual units work correctly in isolation. The objective is to verify that all of the modules and their interfaces work correctly together, and to identify and resolve any issues. Modules that work correctly in isolation may fail when integrated with other modules. The developers generally perform this type of testing. These tests are automated in the Agile world.

System and Performance Testing

The purpose of system testing is to verify that the implementation is valid with respect to the system requirements. It involves the specification of system test cases, and the execution of the test cases will verify that the system requirements have been correctly implemented. An independent test group generally conducts this type of testing, and the system tests are traceable to the system requirements.

The purpose of performance testing is to ensure that the performance of the system satisfies the non-functional requirements. It may include *load performance testing*, where the system is subjected to heavy loads over a long period of time, and *stress testing*, where the system is subjected to heavy loads during a short time interval. *Performance testing often involves the simulation of many users* using the system and involves measuring the response times for various activities.

Any system requirements that have been incorrectly implemented will be identified, and defects logged and reported to the developers. System testing may also include security and usability testing. The preparation of the test environment may involve ordering special hardware and tools, and needs to be set up early in the project.

User Acceptance Testing

UAT testing is usually performed under controlled conditions at the customer site, and its operation will closely resemble the real-life behaviour of the system. The customer will see the product in operation and will judge whether the system is fit for purpose. The objective is to demonstrate that the product satisfies the business requirements and meets the customer expectations. Upon its successful completion the customer is happy to accept the product.

1.5.5   Support and Maintenance

Software systems often have a long lifetime, and the software needs to be continuously enhanced over its lifetime to meet the evolving needs of the customers. This may involve regular new releases with new functionality and corrections to known defects.

Any problems that the customer identifies with the software are reported as per the customer support and maintenance agreement. The support issues will require investigation, and the issue may be *a defect in the software*, *an enhancement to the software*, or *due to a misunderstanding*. An appropriate solution is implemented to resolve, and testing is conducted to verify that the solution is correct, and that the changes made have not adversely affected other parts of the system. A post-mortem may be conducted to learn lessons from the defect,[13] and to take corrective action to prevent a re-occurrence.

The goal of building a correct and reliable software product the first time is difficult to achieve, and the customer is always likely to find some issues with the released software product. It is accepted today that quality needs to be built into each step in the development process, with the role of software inspections and testing to identify as many defects as possible prior to release and minimize the risk that serious defects will be found post-release.

The effective in-phase inspections of the deliverables will influence the quality of the resulting software, and lead to a corresponding reduction in the number of defects. The testing group plays a key role in verifying that the system is correct, and in providing confidence that the software is fit for purpose and ready to be released. The approach to software correctness involves testing and re-testing, until

---

[13] This is essential for serious defects that have caused significant inconvenience to customers (e.g., a major telecom outage). The software development organization will wish to learn lessons to determine what went wrong in its processes that prevented the defect from been identified during peer reviews and testing. Actions to prevent a reoccurrence will be identified and implemented.

the testing group believe that all defects have been eliminated. Dijkstra [16] comments on testing are well-known:

Testing a program demonstrates that it contains errors, never that it is correct.

That is, irrespective of the amount of time spent testing, it can never be said with absolute confidence that all defects have been found in the software. Testing provides increased confidence that the program is correct, and statistical techniques may be employed to give a measure of the software reliability.

Some mature organizations have a quality objective of three defects per million lines of code, which was introduced by Motorola as part of its six-sigma (6σ) program It was originally applied it to its manufacturing businesses and subsequently applied to its software organizations. The goal is to reduce variability in manufacturing processes and to ensure that the processes performed within strict process control limits.

1.6 Software Inspections

Software inspections are used to build quality into software products. There are a number of well-known approaches such as the Fagan Methodology [7]; Gilb's approach [8]; and Prince 2's approach.

Fagan inspections were developed by Michael Fagan of IBM It is a seven-step process that identifies and removes errors in work products. The process mandates that requirement documents, design documents, source code, and test plans are all formally inspected by experts independent of the author of the deliverable to ensure quality.

There are various *roles* defined in the process including the *moderator* who chairs the inspection. *The reader's* responsibility is to read or paraphrase the deliverable, and *the author* is the creator of the deliverable and has a special interest in ensuring that it is correct. The *tester* role is concerned with the test viewpoint.

The inspection process will consider whether the design is correct with respect to the requirements, and whether the source code is correct with respect to the design. Software inspections play an important role in building quality into software, and in reducing the cost of poor quality in the organization.

1.7 Software Project Management

The timely delivery of quality software requires good management and engineering processes. Software projects have a history of being delivered late or over budget, and good project management practices include the following activities:

- Estimation of cost, effort and schedule for the project,
- Identifying and managing risks,
- Preparing the project plan,
- Preparing the initial project schedule and key milestones,
- Obtaining approval for the project plan and schedule,
- Staffing the project,
- Monitoring progress, budget, schedule, effort, risks, issues, change requests and quality,
- Taking corrective action,
- Re-planning and re-scheduling,
- Communicating progress to affected stakeholders,
- Preparing status reports and presentations.

The project plan will contain or reference several other plans such as the project quality plan; the communication plan; the configuration management plan; and the test plan.

Project estimation and scheduling are difficult as often software projects are breaking new ground and may differ from previous projects. That is, previous estimates may often not be a good basis for estimation for the current project. Often, unanticipated problems can arise for technically advanced projects, and the estimates may often be optimistic. Gantt charts are often employed for project scheduling, and these show the work breakdown for the project, as well as task dependencies and allocation of staff to the various tasks.

The effective management of risk during a project is essential to project success. Risks arise due to uncertainty and the risk management cycle involves[14] risk identification; risk analysis and evaluation; identifying responses to risks; selecting and planning a response to the risk; and risk monitoring. The risks are logged, and the likelihood of each risk arising, and its impact is then determined. The risk is assigned an owner and an appropriate response to the risk determined. Project management is discussed in more detail in Chap. 4.

1.8 CMMI Maturity Model

The CMMI is a framework to assist an organization in the implementation of best practice in software and systems engineering. It is an internationally recognized model for software process improvement and assessment and is used world-wide by thousands of organizations. It provides a solid engineering approach to the development of software, and it supports the definition of high-quality processes for the various software engineering and management activities.

---

[14] These are the risk management activities in the Prince2 methodology.

It was developed by the Software Engineering Institute (SEI) who adapted the process improvement principles used in the manufacturing field to the software field. They developed the original CMM model and its successor the CMMI. The CMMI states *what the organization needs to do* to mature its processes rather than *how this should be done*.

The CMMI consists of five maturity levels with each maturity level consisting of several process areas. Each process area consists of a set of goals, and these goals are implemented by practices related to that process area. Level two is focused on management practices; level three is focused on engineering and organization practices; level four is concerned with ensuring that key processes are performing within strict quantitative limits; and level five is concerned with continuous process improvement. Maturity levels may not be skipped in the staged representation of the CMMI, as each maturity level is the foundation for the next level. The CMMI and Agile are compatible, and CMMI v1.3 supports Agile software development.

The CMMI allows organizations to benchmark themselves against other organizations. This is done by a formal SCAMPI appraisal conducted by an authorized lead appraiser. The results of the appraisal are generally reported back to the SEI, and there is a strict qualification process to become an *authorized lead appraiser*. An appraisal is useful in verifying that an organization has improved, and it enables the organization to prioritize improvements for the next improvement cycle. The CMMI is discussed in more detail in Chap. 20.

1.9 Formal Methods

Dijkstra and Hoare have argued that the way to develop correct software is to derive the program from its specifications using mathematics, and to employ *mathematical proof* to demonstrate its correctness with respect to the specification. This offers a rigorous framework to develop programs adhering to the highest quality constraints. However, in practice mathematical techniques have proved to be cumbersome to use, and their widespread use in industry is unlikely at this time.

The *safety–critical area* is one domain to which mathematical techniques have been successfully applied. There is a need for extra rigour in the safety and security critical fields, and mathematical techniques can demonstrate the presence or absence of certain desirable or undesirable properties (e.g., *"when a train is in a level crossing, then the gate is closed"*).

Spivey [17] defines a *"formal specification"* as the use of mathematical notation to describe in a precise way the properties which an information system must have, without unduly constraining the way in which these properties are achieved. It describes *what* the system must do, as distinct from *how* it is to be done. This abstraction away from implementation enables questions about what the system does to be answered, independently of the detailed code. Further, the unambiguous nature of mathematical notation avoids the problem of ambiguity in an imprecisely worded natural language description of a system.

The formal specification thus becomes the key reference point for the different parties concerned with the construction of the system and is a useful way of promoting a common understanding for all those concerned with the system. The term "*formal methods*" is used to describe a formal specification language, and a method for the design and implementation of computer systems.

The specification is written precisely in a mathematical language. The derivation of an implementation from the specification may be achieved via *stepwise refinement*. Each refinement step makes the specification more concrete and closer to the actual implementation. There is an associated *proof obligation* that the refinement be valid, and that the concrete state preserves the properties of the more abstract state. Thus, assuming the original specification is correct and the proofs of correctness of each refinement step are valid, then there is a very high degree of confidence in the correctness of the implemented software.

Formal methods have been applied to a diverse range of applications, including circuit design, artificial intelligence, specification of standards, specification and verification of programs, etc. They are described in more detail in Chap. 16.

1.10   Review Questions

1. Discuss the research results of the Standish Group the current state of IT project delivery?
2. What are the main challenges in software engineering?
3. Describe various software lifecycles such as the waterfall model and the spiral model.
4. Discuss the benefits of Agile over conventional approaches. List any risks and disadvantages?
5. Describe the purpose of the CMMI? What are the benefits?
6. Describe the main activities in software inspections.
7. Describe the main activities in software testing.
8. Describe the main activities in project management?
9. What are the advantages and disadvantages of formal methods?

1.11   Summary

The birth of software engineering was at the NATO conference held in 1968 in Germany. This conference highlighted the problems that existed in the software sector in the late 1960s, and the term "*software crisis*" was coined to refer to these. The conference led to the realization that programming is quite distinct from science and mathematics, and that software engineers need to be properly trained to enable them to build high-quality products that are safe to use.

The Standish group conducts research on the extent of problems with the delivery of projects on time and budget. Their research indicates that it remains a challenge to deliver projects on time, on budget and with the right quality.

Programmers are like engineers in the sense that they build products. Therefore, programmers need to receive an appropriate education in engineering as part of their training. The education of traditional engineers includes training on product design, and an appropriate level of mathematics.

Software engineering involves multi-person construction of multi-version programs. It is a systematic approach to the development and maintenance of the software, and it requires a precise statement of the requirements of the software product, and then the design and development of a solution to meet these requirements. It includes methodologies to design, develop, implement and test software as well as sound project management, quality management and configuration management practices. Support and maintenance of the software needs to be properly addressed.

Software process maturity models such as the CMMI have become popular in recent years. They place an emphasis on understanding and improving the software process to enable software engineers to be more effective in their work.

References

1. F. Brooks, *The Mythical Man Month* (Addison Wesley, 1975)
2. Petrocelli, Software engineering, in *Report on two NATO Conferences held in Garmisch, Germany (October1968) and Rome, Italy*, Oct 1969, ed. by P. Naur, B. Randell (Buxton, 1975)
3. G. O'Regan, *Mathematical Approaches to Software Quality* (Springer, London, 2006)
4. F. Brooks, No silver bullet. Essence and accidents of software engineering, in *Information Processing* (Elsevier, Amsterdam, 1986)
5. G. O'Regan, *Introduction to Software Process Improvement* (Springer, London, 2010)
6. G. O'Regan, *Introduction to Software Quality* (Springer, 2014)
7. M. Fagan, Design and code inspections to reduce errors in software development. IBM Syst. J. **15**(3) (1976)
8. T. Gilb, D. Graham (1994) *Software Inspections* (Addison Wesley, 1994)
9. *Managing Successful Projects with PRINCE2* (Office of Government Commerce, 2004)
10. W. Royce, The software lifecycle model (waterfall model), in *Proceedings of WESTCON*, Aug 1970
11. B. Boehm, A spiral model for software development and enhancement. Computer (1988)
12. J. Rumbaugh et al., *The Unified Software Development Process* (Addison Wesley, 1999)
13. K. Beck, *Extreme Programming Explained. Embrace Change* (Addison Wesley, 2000)
14. I.J.G. Booch, J. Rumbaugh, *The Unified Software Modelling Language User Guide* (Addison-Wesley, 1999)

15. D. Parnas, On the criteria to be used in decomposing systems into modules. Commun. ACM **15**(12) (1972)
16. E.W. Dijkstra, *Structured Programming* (Academic Press, 1972)
17. J.M. Spivey, *The Z Notation. A Reference Manual* (Prentice Hall International Series in Computer Science, 1992)

Professional Responsibility of Software Engineers

2

Abstract

This chapter discusses the professional responsibilities of software engineers. Engineers have a professional responsibility to build products properly and to ensure that they are safe for the public to use. They are required to behave ethically with their clients and to adhere to the code of ethics of the engineering profession.

Keywords

IEEE code of ethics · BCS code of ethics · ACM code of ethics · Whistle blower · Precautionary principle

2.1 Introduction

Software engineering involves multi-person construction of multi-version programs. It requires the engineer to state precisely the requirements that the software product is to satisfy, and to produce designs that will meet these requirements. It involves starting with a precise description of the problem to be solved; producing a design and validating the correctness of the design; finally, the implementation and testing are performed.

Parnas has argued that computer scientists need the right education to apply scientific and mathematical principles in their work. Software engineers need education on specification, design, turning designs into programs, software inspections and testing. This should enable the software engineer to produce well-structured programs using module decomposition and information hiding. He

© Springer Nature Switzerland AG 2022
G. O'Regan, *Concise Guide to Software Engineering*,
Undergraduate Topics in Computer Science,
https://doi.org/10.1007/978-3-031-07816-3_2

Table 2.1 Professional responsibilities of software engineers and testers

No.	Responsibility
1.	Honesty and fairness in dealings with Clients
2.	Responsibility for actions
3.	Continuous learning to ensure appropriate knowledge to serve the client effectively

argues that *"software engineers have individual responsibilities as professionals"*.[1] They are responsible for designing and implementing high-quality and reliable software that is safe to use. They are also accountable for their own decisions and actions,[2] and have a responsibility to object to decisions that violate professional standards.

Professional engineers have a duty to their clients to ensure that they are solving the real problem of the client. They need to precisely state the problem before working on its solution. Engineers need to be honest about current capabilities when asked to work on problems that have no appropriate technical solution, rather than accepting a contract for something that cannot be done.[3]

The *licensing of a professional engineer* provides confidence that the engineer has the right education, experience to build safe and reliable products. Otherwise, the profession gets a bad name because of poor work carried out by unqualified people. Professional engineers are required to follow rules of good practice and to object when rules are violated. The licensing of an engineer requires that the engineer completes an accepted engineering course and understands the professional responsibility of an engineer. The professional body is responsible for enforcing standards and certification. The term '*engineer*' is a title that is awarded on merit, but *it also places responsibilities on its holder*.

Engineers have a professional responsibility and are required to behave ethically with their clients. The membership of the professional engineering body requires the member to adhere to the code of ethics of the profession. The code of ethics[4] will detail the ethical behaviour and responsibilities including (Table 2.1).

---

[1] The concept of accountability for actions dates back thousands of years. The ancient Babylonians employed a code of laws c. 1750 B.C. known as 'The Hammarabi Code'. This included a law that if a house collapsed and killed the owner then the builder of the house would be executed.

[2] However, it is unlikely that an individual programmer would be subject to litigation in the case of a flaw in a program causing damage or loss of life, and instead it would be their employer that could potentially be sued. However, many software products are accompanied by a comprehensive disclaimer of responsibility for problems, rather than a guarantee of quality.

[3] Parnas applied this professional responsibility faithfully when he argued against the Strategic Defence Initiative (SDI), as he believed that the public (i.e., taxpayers) were being misled and that the goals of the project were not achievable.

[4] These are core values of most mature software companies, and many companies today have a code of ethics that employees are required to adhere to.

2.2 What is a Code of Ethics?

A professional code of ethics expresses ideals of human behaviour, and it defines the core principles of the organization . Several organizations such as the Association Computing Machinery (ACM), the Institute of Electrical and Electronic Engineers (IEEE), and the British Computer Society (BCS) have developed a code of conduct for their members. Violations of the code by members are taken seriously and are subject to investigations and disciplinary procedures. A professional code of conduct for a professional body or corporation includes:

1. Guidelines for responsible behaviour of its members.
2. The guidelines may be detailed and prescriptive or a broad statement of values.
3. Codes of conduct are an addendum to legal requirements.
4. Professional codes are formulated by Engineering bodies.
5. Corporate codes are formulated by companies.
6. Violations of codes are investigated where appropriate.
7. Members may be disciplined for violating the codes.

There are various types of codes of ethics including (Table 2.2).

A code of ethics places professional and ethical responsibility on computer professionals and software engineers to others and to society, and it includes ethical behaviour and responsibilities such as[6]:

1. Values of the profession
2. Behaving with integrity and honesty
3. Obligations to employer and to clients
4. Responsibility towards public and society.

Companies have a corporate social responsibility (CSR) including a responsibility to their stakeholders and to wider society, in addition to their traditional legal and commercial responsibilities to protect shareholder interest. CSR can help to promote

Table 2.2 Types of professional codes

Code	Responsibility
Aspirational codes	These are the values that the profession or company is committed to and aspires to achieve
Advisory codes	These values help professionals to make moral judgements in different situations, based on the values of the profession or company
Disciplinary codes	These include disciplinary procedures to ensure that the behaviour of professionals adheres to the values specified in the code of ethics

---

[5] These are core values of many mature software companies, and most companies operating today have a code of ethics that employees are expected to adhere to.

the corporation in the community where it operates, and to be seen as a socially responsible citizen in the community. It plays a role in ensuring that the corporation behaves ethically within society and has a positive impact on the environment.

Codes of conduct are values that members of a professional body or employees of a company are expected to adhere to, but may not be legally enforced as such. However, members of a particular profession or employees of a company that violate the codes may be subject to disciplinary procedures by the professional body or their employer. An effective code of ethics helps the corporation to achieve its corporate social responsibilities.

Unfortunately, codes of conduct may sometimes be just *window dressing*, where the aspirations expressed in the code of ethics does not reflect the reality on the ground. The code may give the appearance that work is carried out a certain way (e.g., emissions below certain thresholds), and that the engineers are ethical in their day-to-day work. However, the reality on the ground may be quite different with unethical work practices taking place but covered up. Further, codes of conduct have been criticized as being vague and contradictory, and this may create uncertainty for the employee or member of the professional as to what is the right action or behaviour is for a given situation.

Moral judgements and ethical decisions occur in various situations in a work environment, and so it would not be feasible for a code of ethics to cover all scenarios. In practice, a code of ethics expresses the moral principles of an organization, and so an employee or software professional needs a *moral compass*, and to recognize situations where ethical decisions need to be made to apply their ethical judgement to a particular case.

There may be conflicts between the loyalty that a person has to their employer and their duty to do the right thing such as protecting the public. No employee desires to be placed in a situation where there is a conflict between what is morally right and their loyalty to their employer, and it is important that organizations establish structures, where serious problems can be reported, discussed openly, and dealt with appropriately. In rare situations, an employee may have no choice but to become a *whistle-blower* to protect the public, where the organization is intent or proceeding with a very risky approach that potentially endangers life or the environment. However, every effort should be made to avoid this situation as it places the employee in a very difficult position with consequences to their career if he or she speaks out (Fig. 2.1).

Fig. 2.1 Whistle blower

An employee may have a *conflict of interest* that could affect her professional judgement in a certain situation. For example, suppose that an employee has responsibility for selecting a new software package, and her husband runs one of the firms tendering for the work. Then an ethical employee would inform management of the conflict of interest and remove herself from the selection process to remove any possibility of bias in the selection process.

That is, a conflict of interest is an interest which if pursued interferes or conflicts with the obligation of the employee to his/her employer or client. The conflict of interest may corrupt or interfere with the employee's professional judgement and could potentially lead to inappropriate or immoral behaviour. It potentially destroys the trustworthiness of an individual, and so it is important to disclose a potential conflict of interest as soon as it arises.

Bribery and corruption are endemic to some countries, and as these are illegal activities in most countries the employee needs to report such activities when they arise. For example, an employee such as a purchasing manager is in a position of influence in an organization and could potentially be offered a *bribe* by another individual or company to influence his/her decision-making. Often, individuals or companies may be subtle in their attempt to gain influence on decision makers, with gifts or invitations to all-expenses paid events such as golf outings used to build up relationships with decision makers.

It is important to be cautious with respect to corporate entertainment, and many companies have policies that prohibit or restrict gifts to employees from external organizations or individuals. This helps to prevent employees being inappropriately influenced by others in their decision-making.

2.2.1 Role of a Whistle Blower

The whistle-blower is a person who speaks out and informs the public on potentially unsafe or criminal acts in an organization. However, speaking out should be the very last step in the process as it could have serious consequences on the employee and her career. The first steps are to establish the facts to determine the extent of the danger and its potential impact on the public, communicating the perceived danger and evidence for the danger within the organization, and exhausting all internal procedures prior to acting by speaking out. The whistle blower should only speak out when:

1. The organization will do serious harm to the public.
2. The whistle blower has identified the threat, reported it to management, and concluded that management will not act.
3. The whistle blower has exhausted all internal procedures.
4. The whistle blower has convincing evidence that the threat is real.
5. The whistle blower believes that revealing the threat will prevent harm.

Table 2.3 describes the typical steps in whistle blowing.

Speaking out may be the ethical thing to do but often it comes at a serious cost to the employee, as he or she may be portrayed as being disloyal to the organization. Further, as the organization will wish to protect itself it may attempt to discredit the employee, and it may even terminate the employment of the employee. The organization may portray the issue as a disgruntled employee whose employment was terminated due to performance issues with the employee's work.

Whistle blowing can also place a lot of emotional strain on the employee, and even if the employee is not fired it may result in career termination in the organization, with zero prospects of further promotion in the company. It is important that the employee protects himself by gathering all evidence on the existence of danger, as this will be needed at a later stage. It may be prudent for the whistle blower to consider the consequences of speaking out and doing the right thing, both on themselves and on others, to ensure that they fully understand the implications of the serious steps that they are taking and can manage the difficult circumstances in the aftermath of speaking out.

It may seem reasonable to suggest that an employee is fulfilling his moral duty if he informs management of the danger, as management are the decision makers with all the pertinent facts and are thus best to make the final decision. However, such an approach can sometimes lead to loss of life, as with the Space Shuttle Challenger disaster back in 1986, which is discussed in Chap. 3. Robert Boisjoly, an engineer at Morton Thiokel was aware of the risks of erosion and failure when the 0-Rings of the Solid Rocket Booster (SRB) are exposed to low temperatures. He argued that the shuttle launch should not take place on the planned date due to the predicted temperatures and advised management of the situation. However, NASA placed pressure on Morton Thiokel to proceed with the launch, and it gave their go ahead to continue with the launch, which resulted in the death of the crew of the space shuttle.

Table 2.3 Steps in whistle blowing

No.	Responsibility
1.	Establish the facts and double (or triple check) to ensure that you are factually correct with respect to the danger and gather appropriate solid evidence that will convince any reasonable person of the danger
2.	Report the matter and present the factual information to your immediate superior and determine what action (if any) management will take
3.	In the case of inaction escalate as appropriate within the organization (organizations vary size/hierarchical structure and so escalation mechanism will differ) until all internal procedures are exhausted
4.	In the absence of a reasonable resolution to the situation, or the organization fails to act or find an appropriate solution there may be no alternative but to speak out
5.	The whistle blower reflects on the situation, weighs up the evidence and options, and decides that the only way to prevent harm is to speak out and reveal the danger to the public

The IEEE code of ethics highlights the importance of speaking out in the case of danger, and it includes the code: *"disclose promptly factors that might endanger the public or the environment"*. The IEEE codes are discussed in the next section.

2.3 IEEE Code of Ethics

The Institute of Electrical and Electronic Engineers (IEEE) is the world's largest technical professional organizations with over 400,000 members in over 160 countries, and it is dedicated to advancing technology for the benefit of mankind. It publishes over 30% of the world's technical literature in electrical engineering, computer science and electronics as well as technical books and monographs. It is a leading developer of international standards in telecommunications and information technology, and individuals who have made outstanding contributions to engineering and technology may receive the prestigious IEEE Medal.

IEEE has developed a code of ethics for its members designed to ensure that they adhere to the highest ethical standards, and that its members treat others fairly and ensure that they are not discriminated against on the grounds of gender, race, and so on (Table 2.4).

Table 2.4 IEEE code of ethics

No.	Description
Highest ethical standards	
1.	To hold paramount the safety, health, and welfare of the public, to strive to comply with ethical design and sustainable development practices, to protect the privacy of others, and to disclose promptly factors that might endanger the public or the environment
2.	To improve the understanding by individuals and society of the capabilities and societal implications of conventional and emerging technologies, including intelligent system
3.	To avoid real or perceived conflicts of interest whenever possible, and to disclose them to affected parties when they do exist
4.	To avoid unlawful conduct in professional activities, and to reject bribery in all its forms
5.	To seek, accept, and offer honest criticism of technical work, to acknowledge and correct errors, to be honest and realistic in stating claims or estimates based on available data, and to credit properly the contributions of others
6.	To maintain and improve technical competence and to undertake technological tasks for others only if qualified by training or experience, or after full disclosure of pertinent limitations
Treating people fairly	
7.	To treat all persons fairly and with respect, and to not engage in discrimination based on characteristics such as race, religion, gender, disability, age, national origin, sexual orientation, gender identity, or gender expression
8.	To not engage in harassment of any kind, including sexual harassment or bullying behaviour

(continued)

Table 2.4 (continued)

No.	Description
9.	To avoid injuring others, their property, reputation, or employment by false or malicious actions, rumours or any other verbal or physical abuses
Following the code	
10.	To support colleagues and co-workers in following this code of ethics, to strive to ensure the code is upheld, and to not retaliate against individuals reporting a violation

The IEEE Code of Ethics requires its members to promptly disclose any factors that might endanger the public or society, which shows that it recognizes the reality of whistle blowing and the need for members to speak out when there is danger to the public. The code mentions the importance of avoiding conflicts of interest and disclosing them when they occur, and stresses that unlawful activities such as bribery should be rejected. The code highlights the importance of carrying out roles only when one is qualified to do so, and to continue to improve one's technical competence. It emphasizes that people should be treated fairly and with respect, without discrimination on gender, ethnicity, etc., and that harassment and injury to others should be avoided.

2.4   British Computer Society Code of Conduct

The British Computer Society (BCS) is a professional organization for information technology and computer science that was founded by in 1957, and its first president was Sir Maurice Wilkes.[6] It has over 68,000 members in 150 countries, and it has played an important role in educating IT professionals. The BCS provides awards such as the Lovelace Medal[7] to individuals, who have made outstanding contributions to the computing field.

The BCS has developed a code of conduct that defines the standards expected of BCS members, and it applies to all grades of members during their professional work. Any known breaches of the BCS codes by a member are investigated by the BCS, and appropriate disciplinary procedures followed. The main parts of the BCS code of conduct are listed in Table 2.5.

The BCS Code of Ethics requires its members to be conscious of the public health and environment. It states that one should only carry out those roles that one is qualified to do so, and one should continue to improve one's technical competence. It states the importance of avoiding conflicts of interest and that unlawful activities such as bribery should be rejected. It emphasizes that members should seek to improve professional standards and support other members in their professional development.

---

[6] Sir Maurice Wilkes developed the EDSAC computer at Cambridge University, which was one of the earliest stored-program computers. It was operational from May 1949.
[7] Ada Lovelace was an English mathematician who collaborated with Babbage on applications for the Analytic Engine.

Table 2.5 BCS code of conduct

Area	Description
Public interest	Due regard to public health, privacy, security and environment Due regards to legitimate rights of third parties Conduct professional activities without discrimination Promote equal access to IT
Professional competence and integrity	Only do work within professional competence Do not claim competence that you do not possess Continuous development of knowledge/skills Understand/Knowledge/Comply with legislation Respect other viewpoints Avoid injuring others Reject bribery and unethical behaviour
Duty to relevant authority	Carry out professional responsibilities with due care and diligence Avoid conflicts of interest Accept professional responsibility for your work Do not disclose confidential information Accurate information on performance of products
Duty to the profession	Uphold reputation of profession and BCS Seek to improve professional standards Act with integrity Notify BCS if convicted of criminal offence Support other members in their professional development

2.5 ACM Code of Professional Conduct and Ethics

The Association of Computing Machinery (ACM) is the world's largest educational and scientific computing society, and it delivers resources that advance computing as a science. It has over 100,000 members around the world, and it includes several special interest groups (e.g., SIG AI is a special interest group on AI, and SIG SOFT is a special interest group on software engineering). The ACM has defined a code of ethics and professional conduct for its members, and the Code is summarized in Table 2.6.

The ACM Code of Ethics is comprehensive and requires its members to report any dangers that might cause damage or injury. The code mentions the importance of respecting intellectual property as well as privacy and confidentiality and carrying out roles only when one is qualified to do so. Conflicts of interest should be avoided, and their work should be to the highest professional standards. Members should seek to improve their technical competence, and people should be treated fairly and with respect. Finally, members should notify the ACM of any violations of the code.

We shall discuss the professional responsibilities of some specific roles (e.g., project management and software testing) in our discussion of ethical software engineering in Chap. 3.

Table 2.6 ACM code of conduct

No.	Area	Description
1. General principles		
1.1.	Contribute to society and human well-being	Computer professionals must strive to develop computer systems that will be used in socially responsible ways with minimal negative consequences
1.2.	Avoid harm to others	Computer professionals must follow best practice to ensure that they develop high-quality systems that are safe for the public. The professional has a responsibility to report any signs of danger in the workplace that could result in serious damage or injury
1.3.	Be honest and trustworthy	The computer professional will give an honest account of their qualifications and any conflicts of interest. The professional will make accurate statement on the system and the system design and will exercise care in representing ACM
1.4.	Be fair and act not to discriminate	Computer professionals are required to ensure that there is no discrimination in the use of computer resources, and that equality, tolerance and respect for others are respected
1.5.	Respect property rights/intellectual property	The professional must not violate copyright or patent law, and only authorized copies of software should be made. The integrity of intellectual property must be protected, and credit for another person's ideas or work must not be taken
1.6.	Respect the privacy of others	The professional must ensure that any personal information gathered for a specific purpose is not used for another purpose without the consent of the individuals. User data observed during normal system operation must be treated with the strictest confidentiality
1.7.	Respect confidentiality	The professional will respect all confidentiality obligations to employers, clients, and users
2. Professional responsibility		
2.1.	Quality of processes/Product	Computing professionals should strive to achieve the highest quality work throughout the process
2.2.	Maintain high standards	It is essential to maintain high standards of technical knowledge and competence, and to upgrade skills on an ongoing basis
2.3.	Respect rules	Computing professionals must adhere to rules including national and international laws and regulations
2.4.	Professional review	Peer reviews play an important role in building quality into a work product, and computing professions should seek reviews of their work as well as participating in reviews
2.5.	Comprehensive evaluations	Computing professionals are required to be thorough and comprehensive in their evaluation of computer systems including analysis and management of risk

(continued)

Table 2.6 (continued)

No.	Area	Description
2.6.	Areas of competence	Computing professionals should only undertake work for which they have the required competence
2.7.	Foster public awareness	Computing professionals should share technical knowledge with the public and foster public awareness and understanding of computing
2.8.	Authorzed use of resources	Computing professionals should only access computer systems and software unless they are authorzed to do so
2.9.	Secure systems	Computing professionals should develop robust and secure systems, as well as mitigation techniques and policies
3. Professional leadership		
3.1.	Public good	The leader should ensure that the public good is the central concern during all professional computing work
3.2.	Social responsibilities	Leaders should encourage computing professionals in meeting relevant social responsibilities
3.3.	Quality of working life	Leaders should enhance the quality of working life of workers
3.4.	Support principles of code	Leaders should pursue policies that are consistent with the Code and communicate them to the relevant stakeholders
3.5.	Support growth of professionals	Leaders should ensure that opportunities are available to computing professionals to improve their knowledge and skill
3.6.	Modifying/Retiring systems	Leaders should exercise care when modifying or retiring systems
3.7.	Special care	Leaders have a responsibility to be good stewards of systems that become part of the infrastructure of society
4. Compliance		
4.1.	Uphold code	Computing professionals should adhere to the principles in the Code and strive to improve them, and to express their concern to any individuals thought to be violating the code
4.2.	Violations of code	ACM members who recognze a breach in the Code should consider reporting the violation to the ACM

2.6   Precautionary Principle

The precautionary principle argues that if there is an identifiable risk of serious or irreversible harm, then it may be appropriate to place the burden of proof on the organization proposing the potentially risky activity to show that it is safe, and for inaction until a proof of safety has been provided.

The main problem with the precautionary principle is that it potentially forbids too much, and opponents have argued that several innovations used today would not have been implemented if the precautionary principle had been adhered to. Further, its opponents argue that its demands for incontrovertible proof of no damage or harm is impractical, and that it is more sensible to demand that there are reasonable grounds for believing that there is no harm.

The precautionary principle may also be applied to unknown threats, where the principle permits preventive measures to be taken prior to fully knowing the seriousness of the threat. That is,

1. There is a threat,
2. The threat is uncertain,
3. Action is required,
4. Action is taken.

2.7 Review Questions

1. Explain professional responsibility and accountability?
2. What is a code of ethics?
3. Describe the main features of the IEEE code of conduct.
4. Describe the main features of the BCS code of conduct.
5. Describe the main features of the ACM code of conduct.
6. What is the role of a whistle blower?
7. Give examples of conflicts of interest that could arise in the work place.
8. What is the precautionary principle?

2.8 Summary

Software engineers have responsibilities as computer professionals in that they are responsible for designing and implementing high-quality and reliable software that is safe for the public to use. They are also accountable for their own decisions and actions and have a responsibility to object to decisions that violate professional standards.

Professional engineers have a duty to their clients to ensure that they are solving the real problem of the client. They need to precisely state the problem before working on its solution. Engineers need to be honest about current capabilities when asked to work on problems that have no appropriate technical solution, rather than accepting a contract for something that cannot be done.

Professional engineers are required to follow rules of good practice and to object when rules are violated. The licensing of an engineer requires that the engineer completes an accepted engineering course and understands the professional responsibility of an engineer. The professional body is responsible for enforcing standards and certification. That is, the term '*engineer*' is award only to those that have achieved a certain minimum level of competence, and the term places responsibilities on its holder.

Several professional organizations such as the British Computer Society, IEEE and ACM have developed a code of ethics for their members to adhere to. These codes provide guidelines for the responsible behaviour of their members, and members may be disciplined for violating the code of ethics. A code of ethics places professional and ethical responsibilities on software engineers.

A whistle blower is a person who speaks out and informs the public on potentially unsafe or criminal acts in an organization. Speaking out may be the ethical thing to do but it often comes at a serious cost to the employee.

Ethical Software Engineering

3

Abstract

This chapter discusses ethical software engineering where the ethical software engineer needs to examine both the technical and the ethical dimensions of decisions that affect wider society. We discuss several case studies including the Volkswagen emissions scandal where engineers installed a "defeat device" to cheat on the emissions test, and we also discuss the infamous case of the Therac-25 radiation machine whose malfunction led to the deaths of several patients.

Keywords

Safety and ethics · Therac-25 · Space shuttle disaster · Volkswagen scandal · Ethical project management · Ethical software testing · Ethical design and development

3.1 Introduction

Software engineering is a discipline that is concerned with the development of software, and it includes activities such as requirements gathering and definition, software design and development, and software testing to verify the correctness of the software. It is a team-based activity with several roles involved such as project managers, system analysts, developers, and testers. Software engineering is much more than programming, and it involves rigorous engineering practices to define the right requirements, and to design and implement an appropriate solution that is fit for purpose and satisfies the requirements.

Technical decisions need to be made in software engineering, and often these decisions affect people's lives, with potential harmful impacts on others and society. This means that the ethical impacts of technical decisions need to be considered as part of the software engineering process, and so the ethical software engineer needs to examine both the technical and the ethical dimensions of decisions that affect wider society. At a minimum ethical, software engineers should:

- Do no harm,
- Do not take bribes,
- Be fair to others.

A fundamental principle of ethics is based on the Hippocratic Oath "Do *no harm*", which may be seen to be breached where there are violations of ethics. For example, the Volkswagen emissions scandal led to the deception of the public and harm to society, the company, and its employees. The actions of Volkswagen were unethical and illegal.

We discussed the professional responsibilities of software engineers in Chap. 2, as well as the code of ethics/conduct of several professional bodies such as IEEE, ACM and BCS. The codes of ethics provide guidance on the interaction of technology and values, and software engineers need to be aware of their ethical responsibilities throughout the software development process, and to act when ethical standards are in danger of being violated.

3.2   Safety and Ethics

The release of an unreliable software product may result in damage to property or injury (including loss of life) to a third party. Consequently, companies need to be confident that their software products are fit for purpose prior to their release. It is essential that software that is widely used is dependable, which means that the software is available whenever required, and that it operates safely and reliably without any adverse side effects.

Today, billions of devices and computers are connected to the Internet, and this has led to a growth in attacks on computers. It is essential that computer security is carefully considered, and that developers are aware of the threats facing a system, and techniques to eliminate them. The software developers need to be able to develop secure dependable systems that can deal with and recover from external attacks.

A safety critical system is a system whose failure could result in significant economic damage or loss of life. There are many examples of safety critical systems such as aircraft flight control systems, nuclear power stations and missile systems. It is essential to employ rigorous processes in the design and development of safety critical systems, and software testing alone is usually insufficient in verifying the correctness of these systems.

The safety critical industry takes the view that any change to safety critical software creates a new program. The new program is therefore required to demonstrate that it is reliable and safe to the public, and so extensive testing needs to be performed. Additional techniques such as formal verification and model checking may be employed to provide an extra level of assurance in the correctness of the system.

Safety critical systems need to be reliable, dependable, and available for use whenever required. The software must operate correctly and reliably without any adverse side effects. The consequence of failure (e.g., the failure of a weapons system) could be massive damage, leading to loss of life or endangering the lives of the public. We discuss two important case studies on disasters that occurred in the mid-1980s, and these are the Therac-25 disaster and the Space Shuttle Challenger Disaster.

3.2.1   Therac-25 Disaster

The Therac-25 was a computer-controlled radiation therapy machine that was developed by the Atomic Energy of Canada (AECL) in the early 1980s. This linear accelerator treated cancer patients by exposing them to a beam of particles that would destroy malignant tissue (Fig. 3.1).

The machine consisted of hardware and software, and whereas the role of software on the earlier Therac-20 machine was limited, software played a more important role in the Therac 25 machine. Its role was to perform many of the safety critical checks for the Therac-25, whereas this was performed by hardware on the earlier Therac-20 machine. The software on the Therac-25 radiation machine was responsible for:

- Monitoring the status of the machine,
- Accepting treatment input,
- Setting up the machine for the treatment,
- Turning on treatment beam,

Fig. 3.1 A radiotherapy machine

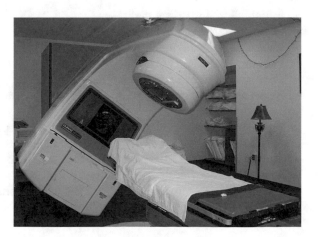

- Turning off treatment beam,
- Detecting hardware malfunction.

There were six major accidents with the machine in the mid-1980s (1985–1987), where patients were given massive overdoses of radiation. The machine malfunctioned, and several patients received doses that were hundreds of times more than the appropriate dose, resulting in the death of three people and serious injuries to three others.

The machine continued in use for over 18 months after the first accident, with AECL believing that an accident was impossible with the machine, and it took no action with respect to the first accident. The second accident occurred a month later, and AECL sent an engineer on site to investigate the incident. He was unable to reproduce the problem, but AECL made some hardware and software changes and claimed that this solved the problem, as well as increasing the reliability of the machine a multiple of times.

AECL's response to the third action was denial of the problem, where they stated that the malfunction could not have been caused by the Therac-25 machine. They claimed that the 4th accident was as the result of a wiring problem. Finally, because of the 5th accident, and FDA investigations into the operation of the Therac-25 machine, AECL finally launched a thorough investigation. The FDA ruled that the Therac-25 machines were defective, and advised AECL to prepare a corrective action plan, and to advise their customers of the problems with the machine.

The corrective action plan was prepared by AECL and presented to the FDA. It led to serious concerns in the FDA with respect to the software engineering practices employed in AECL, and the risks that these posed to the delivery of a high-quality product that was safe for the public. There was a lack of software engineering and testing documentation for the software development, and the testing of the software was inadequate. The FDA directed AECL to do extensive testing on the system each time a small software change was made to ensure the safety of the software. The main reasons for the Therac-25 disaster include:

- Initial failure to believe end users,
- Overconfidence of engineers in its correctness,
- Poor software design and development,
- Software errors,
- Poor resolution of software defects,
- Inadequate testing.

The Therac-25 disaster led to the deaths of three people and serious injury to three others. Software engineering practices were immature in the 1980s, but this is no excuse for what happened. It is basic common sense that a proper investigation should have been done after the first accident, and that all existing machines should have been judged unsafe until proved otherwise. That is, all Therac-25 machines should have been removed from operational use until the cause of the problem had been correctly identified, and appropriate solutions implemented to prevent a reoccurrence.

3.2.2 Space Shuttle Challenger Disaster

The Space Shuttle Challenger disaster is an important case study on engineering safety and workplace ethics. The disaster occurred in January 1986, when the space shuttle broke apart 73 s into its flight, and all the seven members of the crew were killed. The Rogers Commission was formed to investigate the accident, and it found that the Challenger disaster was caused by a failure in the O-Rings sealing a joint on the right solid rocket booster. The report also criticized the decision-making process that led to the launch stating that it was deeply flawed, with conflicts between engineering data and management judgements (Fig. 3.2).

Robert Boisjoly, an engineer at Morton Thiokel launched strong objections to the launch, as he was aware of the risks of erosion and failure when the 0-Rings of the Solid Rocket Booster (SRB) are exposed to low temperatures. He argued that the shuttle launch should not take place on the planned date due to the predicted temperatures.

Both the NASA project team and the management team at Morton Thiokel had the opportunity to prevent the challenger disaster by postponing the launch. During the conference call on the evening prior to the launch the entire Morton Thiokel team recommended a postponement of the launch, as they recommended a minimum launch temperature of 52 °F. Temperatures were forecast to drop to 30 °F

Fig. 3.2 Space challenger disaster

overnight which was likely to compromise the safety of the launch. They had expected NASA to rubber stamp the decision, but they were wrong, and NASA stated that the Morton Thiokel briefing was based on emotion rather than factual data. NASA requested Morton Thiokel to review their data again to determine if the data showed that it was unsafe to proceed, and the conference call was re-scheduled to later in the evening.

For a launch to take place all sub-contractors must sign-off on going ahead, and NASA seems to have encouraged (perhaps pressurized) Morton Thiokel to recommend the launch unless they could prove that it was unsafe to do so. The conference call had been delayed allowing Morton Thiokel management to consider all of the data, and the result of the Morton Thiokel management meeting (which excluded participation from Boisjoly) was to proceed with the launch. Morton Thiokel stated that its data was inconclusive at the conference call with NASA, and all sub-contractors agreed to proceed with the launch. Boisjoly later called the Morton Thiokel decision to go ahead to be unethical.

Separatism is the idea that scientists and engineers provide the technical input and advice to management concerning a particular engineering situation, and management decide how best to proceed. That is, managers act as the decision maker taking all inputs into account to make a value judgement on the best way to proceed. This approach generally works fine in engineering, but problems arise when managers are trying to balance conflicting values such as achieving a strict delivery constraint and the safety of an operation, and where management believes (or encourages their subordinates to support their belief) that there is a small but manageable risk. It is essential to have openness and transparency in decision-making, where decisions are made on the objective facts and data, and risks are kept to an absolute minimum and are manageable.

The *precautionary principle* was discussed in Chap. 2 and requires that a particular course of action be demonstrated to be safe prior to being conducted. This was the normal *modus operandi* of NASA, but NASA changed the burden of proof the night before the launch to demand that Morton Thiokel prove to NASA management that it was unsafe to proceed with launch. However, once Morton Thiokel gave their approval and ignored the input of Robert Boisjoly, it could be argued that Boisjoly had a moral responsibility to be a whistle blower given the likelihood that safety would be compromised due to the forecasted low temperatures for the launch. Boisjoly may have taken the position that he had advised management of the dangers with launch (following the principle of separatism), and that it was the responsibility of management to act by postponing the launch.

3.3 Ethical Project Management

Software projects have a history of being delivered late or over budget, and software project management is concerned with the effective management of software projects to ensure the successful delivery of a high-quality product, on time and on budget, to the customer. *A project is a temporary group activity designed to accomplish a specific goal such as the delivery of a product to a customer. It has a clearly defined beginning and end in time.*

Project management involves good project planning and estimation; the management of resources; the management of issues and change requests that arise during the project; managing quality; managing risks; managing the budget; monitoring progress; taking appropriate action when progress deviates from expectations; communicating progress to the various stakeholders; and delivering a high-quality product to the customer.

Project managers are professionals, and they must always behave professionally and ethically during the project. The *Project Management Institute* (PMI) has defined a code of ethics and professional behaviour for project management, which defines the expectations of the behaviour of project management professionals. These core values include:

- Professional responsibility,
- Respect,
- Fairness,
- Honesty.

Project management professionals have a *responsibility* for the decisions that they make (or fail to make), and the actions that they take (or fail to take). They should accept only those assignments for which they have the required competence, and commitments made should be fulfilled. Errors or omissions should be corrected promptly, and any proprietary information provided should be protected. Further, any unethical or illegal conduct should be reported to management, and project management professions should be aware of regulations and laws that govern their work.

Project managers have a duty to show *respect* to others including sensitivity of behaviour in working with others from different cultural backgrounds This involves always behaving professionally, listening to others' point of view, and seeking to understand them, and working through conflicts and disagreements with others.

Project managers have a duty to be *fair* in decision making with decisions made objectively and impartially, and they refrain from participating in decision-making where there is a potential conflict of interest. Further, favouritism and discrimination are not allowed.

Finally, it is the duty of project managers to act in a truthful and *honest* manner in their communication and conduct, and not to engage in or condone behaviour that attempts to deceive others (e.g., making misleading or false statements).

The project manager is accountable for the success of the project, and larger projects have more opportunities for ethics being compromised than smaller projects. Project managers endeavour to balance budget, schedule, effort, and quality, which may potentially lead to ethical dilemmas when the project manager is tempted to cut corners to enable the project to be delivered on time and on budget.

This could potentially result in quality being compromised, health and safety being compromised, privacy being compromised, and so on.

The selection of a subcontractor could pose a conflict of interest to the project manager, where the project manager knows one of the candidate subcontractors from a previous working relationship or family relationships. It is therefore important that in such a situation that the project manager excludes herself from the supplier selection to ensure that there is no conflict of interest.

Project management involves ethical decision-making, and good project governance is a good enabler of ethical project management. It enables the key project stakeholders to be kept informed of the key project status and the key decisions being made regularly during the project.

3.4   Ethical Software Design and Development

Ethical software design and development is concerned with ethical issues that may arise during technology development, such as questions as to how the technology will be used, and whether it could lead to harm to individuals and society. The design of a technology determines how it will be used, and this means that there needs to be an ethical dimension to the design process, where ethical values are considered as well as the desired functionality.

David Lean[1] directed the movie "*The Bridge on the River Kwai*" in 1957, and the film was based on the historical construction of the Thailand-Burma railway that took place during the Japanese occupation of Burma in the Second World War. British prisoners of war are ordered to construct the bridge, and initially the British and their leader, Colonel Nicholson, resisted participation in its construction. However, Colonel Nicholson later becomes obsessed with designing and building a proper bridge that will last well beyond the war, and that will be a tribute to the skill and ingenuity of British engineers (Fig. 3.3).

They build a solid bridge over the river and on the day that it is due to open with the first train due to pass over Nicholson finally realizes the gravity of what he has done (i.e., collaborating with the enemy and contributing to their plans for further aggression). He blows up the bridge sending the train into the river. That is, the purpose of the technology (i.e., the completed bridge) needed to be considered, as a completed bridge would cause harm to others in that it would have facilitated an expansion of Japanese aggression to other countries. Further, it was unethical for Nicholson to collaborate with his enemy who wished to harm him and his country, and his collaboration conflicted with his duties to the British army.

Software design is the process where certain functions are translated into a blueprint for a system that can fulfil these functions. There are often several design choices for a particular technology, and different designs may vary in the extent to

---

[1] David Lean was an influential film director who directed well-known movies such as Lawrence of Arabia, Doctor Zhivago and Ryan's Daughter.

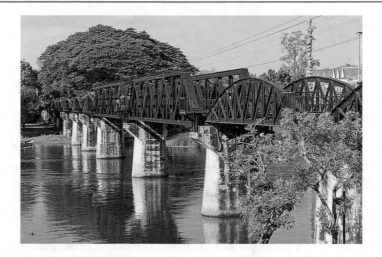

Fig. 3.3 Bridge over the River Kwaii in Kanchanburi, Thailand

which they deal with individual ethical values. The goal is to choose the design that best meets the most important ethical values and technology considerations, and this means that responsible choices must be made in the selection of the most appropriate design. Software design is a systematic process that uses technical and scientific knowledge, and there may need for trade-offs with conflicting ethical values in the different designs. It involves activities such as:

- Problem analysis,
- Requirements analysis and definition (may include prototyping),
- Architectural Design (may include design options and decision),
- Low Level Design,
- Implementation,
- Testing,
- Maintenance.

Value centred design is an approach to design that involves taking human values into account during the design process and solving value conflicts through engineering design and technological innovation. It involves investigating and determining the values that are relevant to the project and understanding conflicts to make trade-offs. There is a need to analyse designs to determine the extent to which they meet individual values, and to develop innovative designs to meet particularly relevant moral values. Valued centred design involves:

- Reasoning/clarifying values underlying conflicting design requirements,
- Social cost benefit analysis (including monetary costs for safety),
- Evaluation criteria (including value criteria, weightings may be employed),
- Thresholds for what is acceptable for each criterion,

- Evaluation of options,
- Selected option.

There may be conflicts between ethical values when choosing between two or more design options, and where the different designs score well on different criteria. This is where designers are unable to do justice to all ethical values simultaneously, and often the resolution of these moral dilemmas require a trade off or balancing between competing values. A trade off decision is where a choice needs to be made between at least two options, in which at least two moral values are relevant as choice criteria, and so finding the right balance in the trade off decisions may be a challenge (Fig. 3.4).

Software designers have a responsibility to create ethical designs that satisfy the requirements, and to ensure that their designs are robust and protect the safety of the public. Ethics is an important design concern that should be considered, and. this will determine how well the product fits within the ethical boundaries. There may be several ethical values that may be relevant, including safety, accessibility, usability, accessibility, sustainability, privacy, security, honesty, fairness, and loyalty. The evaluation of each design option should rate the extent to which the relevant moral values are addressed by that option as well as the technical criteria.

Data management is an important part of ethical software engineering, where personal data ownership as well as data rights, access rights, privacy and security rights need to be considered and protected. Software designers need to follow best practice in privacy and security principles in collecting, processing, and protecting data. An ethical system needs to be accessible, and its design should consider its accessibility for different categories of users, such as those with visual or hearing impairments, or those with different levels of language ability or education.

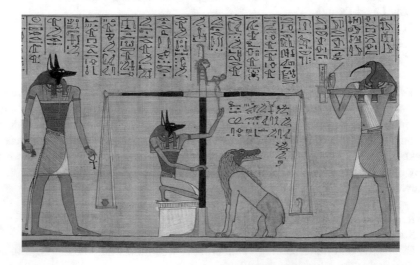

Fig. 3.4 Balancing an ethical life against a feather in Egyptian religion

The ethical design of a software system should give an open and accurate account of the system and should satisfy all relevant legal and regulatory requirements. We discuss the Volkswagen diesel gate emissions scandal in the next section, where the unethical conduct of the company and its management involved tasking software designers to develop a "*defeat device*" to cheat the emissions tests.

Ethical software designers need to be conscious of the algorithms that they create to ensure that they are unbiased, and do not discriminate against minority groups in society. This is especially important in machine learning algorithms based on pattern matching that are employed in the AI field, where *biased algorithms* may lead to discrimination such as in controversies including the Amazon hiring algorithm which discriminated against females, and predictive policing algorithm which led to racial profiling and discrimination against minorities.

Software designers should consider the ultimate purpose of the project including its benefits to society as well as harm of the technology. We discussed the purpose of the bridge over the river Kwai and argued that its design led to harm for society. Social media and various other apps are deliberately designed to be *addictive* to their users, where the software captures the attention of the human at a primal level, and the company reaps financial gain from the addiction of the users. Humans have become addicted to their smartphones, and check their phone hundreds of times a day, and their addiction has been caused by addictive software design. This poses questions on the ethics of this addictive design, and whether the consequences of design as well as the end product should be considered in ethical decision making.

The system needs to be designed for security, as it is difficult to add security after the system has been implemented. Security engineering is concerned with the development of systems that can prevent malicious attacks and recover from them. Software developers need to be aware of the threats facing a system and develop solutions to manage them. Security loopholes may be introduced in the development of the system, and so care needs to be taken to prevent these as well as preventing hackers from exploiting security vulnerabilities.

There is a need to conduct a risk assessment of the security threats facing a system early in the software development process, and this will lead to several security requirements for the system. That is, the requirements of the system should specify security and privacy requirements, and the software design and development must implement them to ensure that security and privacy are not breached. Security testing (including penetration testing) is carried out to identify any flaws in the security mechanisms of the computer system, and to verify that the security requirements such as confidentiality, availability, integrity, etc., are satisfied. However, the successful completion of security testing does not guarantee that there are no security vulnerabilities in the system. Hackers will still attempt to steal confidential data and to disrupt the services being offered by a system.

3.4.1   Volkswagen Emissions Scandal

The Volkswagen *Diesel gate* scandal arose as a result of the German company deliberately programming its turbocharged direct injection (TDI) diesel engines to activate their emissions controls only during laboratory emissions tests. This meant that the vehicles NO_x emissions passed the US regulatory requirements during laboratory tests, whereas the actual emissions were over 40 times higher in real-world driving (Fig. 3.5).

Volkswagen deployed this software in over 11 million vehicles worldwide including roughly half a million vehicles in the United States from 2009 to 2015. It became evident in 2014 that there were discrepancies in emissions between European and US models, and regulators in several countries launched an investigation into Volkswagen. Several senior executives resigned or were suspended, and Volkswagen spent billions in recalling the affected vehicles and rectifying the issues with the emissions.

Volkswagen pleaded guilty to criminal charges in 2017, and they admitted to developing a "defeat device" to enable diesel models to pass US emission tests and deliberately concealing its use. Volkswagen was fined \$2.8 billion for rigging the vehicles to cheat on the emission tests. The scandal had cost Volkswagen \$33 billion in fines, penalties, financial settlements, and buyback costs by mid-2020. Martin Winterkorn resigned his position of the CEO of Volkswagen in 2015, and he was charged with fraud and conspiracy in the United States in 2018.

The scandal highlighted how software-controlled machinery is prone to cheating, and it has opened a debate on whether there is a need for a mechanism to independently verify software that is employed to satisfy legal or regulatory requirements. That is, should all such software code be published for scrutiny by independent regulators and/or independently certified?

Fig. 3.5 Volkswagen Beetle Type 82E

The Volkswagen scandal is deeply concerning as it demonstrates the failure of corporate business ethics to act as a barrier to the pursuit of business self-interest. Volkswagen is a prestigious German company, and it is extraordinary that the professionalism that Germany is renowned for could be tarnished in this way. Unfortunately, sometimes the code of ethics of an organization are just window dressing for the public, rather than being embraced and engrained in the day-to-day work practices of corporate life. Why did engineers fail to consider their ethical responsibilities? Why did they fail to question the implementation of this device? Why were there no whistle blowers to speak out against these unethical practices? Was there a lack of moral courage among the engineers? Were there appropriate structures in place for whistle blowers to discuss ethical concerns? Volkswagen's actions were illegal and deeply unethical, and its good name has been tarnished.

A corporate environment is generally focused on the business and product implementation rather than on critical reflection on the wider implications of the technology. Engineers are often busy with their lives outside the office while trying to build a career within the office and speaking out may not be viewed as career advancing. Further, a hierarchical work environment does not actively encourage speaking out on issues outside of product development, with corporate enterprises often command driven operations, with power assigned within the hierarchy, and subordinates may fear the consequences of speaking out.

Engineers are often focused on getting the software to perform correctly to meet its specification, and so often may not consider the wide societal impacts of the technology. However, it is in the interest of both corporations and their employees to consider the bigger picture, and to actively consider ethical issues in the design process. Otherwise, they could well pay the price for their inaction later with significant damage to the reputation of the corporation and financial loss.

3.5   Ethical Software Testing

Software testers are professionals and need to always behave ethically during testing. The ISTQB Code of Ethics for test professionals is based on the IEEE and ACM code of ethics and it states that:

- Certified software testers shall act consistently in the public interest.
- They act in the best interests of their client and employer.
- They ensure that their deliverables meet the highest professional standards.
- They maintain independence and integrity in professional judgements.
- They shall promote an ethical approach to the management of software testing.
- They shall advance the integrity and reputation of the profession.
- They shall be supportive of colleagues and cooperate with software developers.
- They shall participate in lifelong learning and promote ethics in their profession.

Comprehensive testing reduces the risk of serious quality problems with the software, but it is impossible to test everything due to time constraints. This means that the testers need to focus their testing on the areas of greatest risk with the software, and on the parts of the system that the users are most likely to be using. It is essential that the testers have the appropriate expertise, that the right test environment is set up, that they have prepared test plans and test specification to test the software, and that they have all the required tools in place.

Ethical issues may arise during testing if the project is behind schedule, and when there is pressure applied to the test team to stay with the original project delivery schedule. It may be that the available time for testing is insufficient to verify the correctness of the software, or the limited time could lead to testers missing serious defects. This could lead to the quality of the released software being compromised, and the test manager needs to resist any pressure that poses risks to quality and needs to raise concerns at senior level where appropriate.

It is essential that the customer be informed of all quality problems with the software to ensure that they can manage any associated risks. The final test report should summarize the testing that has been done, the results of the testing, the open problems, the problem arrival rate, and known risks with the software. The final test report generally includes a recommendation from the test manager to release the software, and such a recommendation should be based on the key facts with a clear statement that all risks can be managed.

There may be conflicts when the project manager wishes to release the software on schedule, and where the test manager has concerns or believes that it is unsafe to do so based on the key testing status and risks. It is essential in such situations that the decision made is based on the facts and risks, and objective data should support the decision that is made.

3.6   Review Questions

1. What is ethical software engineering?
2. Explain how the Therac-25 disaster occurred.
3. Explain how the challenger disaster occurred.
4. What is ethical software design?
5. What is value centred design?
6. What is ethical software testing?
7. What is ethical project management?
8. Explain the concept of separatism?
9. What are the ethical considerations in the development of safety critical systems?

3.7 Summary

Ethical software engineering is concerned with ethical issues that may arise during software development, such as questions as to how the technology will be used, and whether it could lead to harm to individuals and society.

Ethics and professional responsibility apply to many areas in software engineering. There is a need for ethical project management where project managers have a *responsibility* for the decisions that they make (or fail to make), and the actions that they take (or fail to take). Further, they should be aware of regulations and laws that govern their work.

There is an ethical dimension to the design process, where ethical values need to be considered as well as the desired functionality. Ethical issues may arise during testing if the project is behind schedule, and when there is pressure applied to the test team to stay with the original project delivery schedule.

The space shuttle challenger disaster in the mid-1980s is an important case study in on engineering safety and workplace ethics. The disaster was caused by a failure in the O-Rings sealing, and the decision making that led to the launch was deeply flawed.

The Volkwagen dieselgate emissions scandal involved the German company deliberately programming a "defeat device" to enable diesel models to pass US emission tests and concealing its use.

Software Project Management

4

Abstract

This chapter provides an introduction to project management for traditional software engineering, and we discuss project estimation, project planning and scheduling, project monitoring and control, risk management, managing communication and change, and managing project quality.

Keywords

Business case · Estimation · Scheduling · Risk management · Project board and project governance · People management · Project reports · Project metrics · Remote project management · Outsourcing · Quality management · Prince 2 · PMP and PMBOK

4.1 Introduction

Software projects have a history of being delivered late or over budget, and software project management is concerned with the effective management of software projects to ensure the successful delivery of a high-quality product, on time and on budget, to the customer. *A project is a temporary group activity designed to accomplish a specific goal such as the delivery of a product to a customer. It has a clearly defined beginning and end in time.*

Project management involves good project planning and estimation; the management of resources; the management of issues and change requests that arise during the project; managing quality; managing risks; managing the budget; monitoring progress; taking appropriate action when progress deviates from expectations; communicating progress to the various stakeholders; and delivering a high-quality product to the customer. It involves:

© Springer Nature Switzerland AG 2022
G. O'Regan, *Concise Guide to Software Engineering*,
Undergraduate Topics in Computer Science,
https://doi.org/10.1007/978-3-031-07816-3_4

- Defining the business case for the project,
- Defining the scope of the project and what it is to achieve,
- Estimation of the cost, effort, and schedule,
- Determining the start and end dates for the project,
- Determining the resources required,
- Assigning resources to the various tasks and activities,
- Determining the project lifecycle and phases of the project,
- Staffing the project,
- Preparing the project plan,
- Scheduling the various tasks and activities in the schedule,
- Preparing the initial project schedule and key milestones,
- Obtaining approval for the project plan and schedule,
- Identifying and managing risks,
- Monitoring progress, budget, schedule, effort, risks, issues, change requests and quality,
- Taking corrective action,
- Re-planning and re-scheduling,
- Communicating progress to affected stakeholders,
- Preparing status reports and presentations.

The scope of the project needs to be determined, and the estimated effort for the various tasks and activities established. The project plan and schedule will then be developed and approved by the stakeholders, and these are maintained during the project. The project plan will contain or reference several other plans such as the project quality plan; the communication plan; the configuration management plan; and the test plan.

Project estimation and scheduling are difficult as software projects are often breaking new ground and differ from previous projects. That is, historical estimates may often not be a good basis for estimation for the current project. Often, unanticipated problems may arise for technically advanced projects, and the estimates may be overly optimistic.

Gantt charts are generally employed for project scheduling, and these show the work breakdown for the project as well as task dependencies and allocation of staff to the various tasks.

The effective management of risk during a project is essential to project success. Risks arise due to uncertainty and the risk management cycle involves[1] risk identification; risk analysis and evaluation; identifying responses to risks; selecting and planning a response to the risk; and risk monitoring.

Once the risks have been identified they are logged (e.g., in the Risk Log). The likelihood of each risk arising, and its impact is then determined. The risk is assigned an owner and an appropriate response to the risk determined.

---

[1] These are the risk management activities in the Prince 2 methodology.

Once the planning is complete the project execution commences, and the focus moves to monitoring progress, managing risks and issues, re-planning as appropriate, providing regular progress reports to the project board, and so on.

Two popular project management methodologies are the *Prince* 2 methodology, which was developed in the U.K., and *Project Management Professional (PMP)* and its associated project management body of knowledge (PMBOK) from the *Project Management Institute* (PMI) in the United States.

4.2 Project Start Up and Initiation

There are many ways in which a project may arise, but it is always essential that there is a clear rationale (*business case*) for the project. A telecoms company may wish to develop a new version of its software with attractive features to gain market share. An internal IT department may receive a request from its business users to alter its business software to satisfy new legal or regulatory requirements. A software development company may be contacted by a business to develop a bespoke solution to meet its needs, and so on.

All parties must be clear on what the project is to achieve, and how it will be achieved. It is fundamental that there is a *business case* for the project (this is the reason for the project), as it clearly does not make sense for the organization to spend a large amount of money without a sound rationale for the project. In other words, the project must make business sense (e.g., it may have a financial return on the investment or it may be to satisfy some business or regulatory requirement).

At the project start up the initial scope and costing for the project are determined, and the feasibility of the project is determined.[2] The project is authorized,[3] and a project board is set up for project governance. The project board verifies that there is a sound business case for the project, and a *project manager* is appointed to manage the project.

The *project board* (or steering group) includes the key stakeholders and is accountable for the success of the project. The project manager provides regular status reports to the project board during the project, and the project board is consulted when key project decisions need to be made.

The project manager is responsible for the day-to-day management of the project, and good planning is essential to its success. The approach to the project is decided,[4] and the project manager *kicks off the project* and mobilizes the project team. The detailed requirements and estimates for the project are determined, the schedule of activities and tasks established, and resources are assigned for the

---

[2] This refers to whether the project is technically and financially feasible.

[3] Organizations have limited resources, and as many projects may be proposed it will not be possible to authorize every project, and so several projects with weak business cases may be rejected.

[4] For example, it may be decided to outsource the development to a third-party provider, purchase an off-the-shelf solution, or develop the solution internally.

various tasks and activities.[5] The project manager prepares the project plan, which is subject to the approval of the key stakeholders. The initial risks are identified and managed, and a risk log (or repository) is set up for the project. Once the planning is complete project execution commences.

4.3 Estimation

Estimation is an important part of project management, and the accurate estimates of effort, cost and schedule are essential to delivering a project the on time and on budget, and with the right quality.[6] Estimation is employed in the planning process to determine the resources and effort required, and it feeds into the scheduling of the project. The problems with over or under-estimation of projects are well known, and good estimates allow:

- Accurate calculation of the project cost and its feasibility,
- Accurate scheduling of the project,
- Measurement of progress and costs against the estimates,
- Determining the resources required for the project.

Poor estimation leads to:

- Projects being over or under-estimated,
- Projects being over or under-resourced (impacting staff morale),
- Negative impression of the project manager.

Consequently, estimation needs to be rigorous, and there are several well-known techniques available (e.g., work-breakdown structures, function points, and so on). Estimation applies to both the early and later parts of the project, with the later phases of the project refining the initial estimates, as a more detailed understanding of the project activities is then available. The new estimates are used to re-schedule and to predict the eventual effort, delivery date and cost of the project. The following are guidelines for estimation:

- Sufficient time needs to be allowed to do estimation,
- Estimates are produced for each phase of software development,
- The initial estimates are high-level,
- The estimates for the next phase should be solid whereas estimates for the later phases may be high-level,
- The estimates should be conservative rather than optimistic,

---

[5] The project scheduling is usually done with the Microsoft Project tool.
[6] The consequences of underestimating a project include the project being delivered late, with the project team working late nights and weekends to recover the schedule, quality being compromised with steps in the process omitted, and so on.

- Estimates will usually include contingency,
- Estimates should be reviewed to ensure their adequacy,
- Estimates from independent experts may be useful,
- It may be useful to prepare estimates using various methods and to compare.

Project metrics may be employed to measure the accuracy of the estimates. These metrics are reported during the project and include:

- Effort Estimation Accuracy,
- Budget Estimation Accuracy,
- Schedule Estimation Accuracy.

Next, we discuss various estimation techniques including the work-breakdown structure, the analogy method, and the Delphi method.

4.3.1   Estimation Techniques

Estimates need to be produced consistently, and it would be inappropriate to have an estimation procedure such as "*Go ask Fred*",[7] as this clearly relies on an individual and is not a repeatable process. The estimates may be based on a work-breakdown structure, function points, or another appropriate methodology. There are several approaches to project estimation (Table 4.1) including.

4.3.2   Work Breakdown Structure

This is a popular approach to project estimation (*it is also known as decomposition*) and involves the following:

- Identify the project deliverables to be produced during the project,
- Estimate the size of each deliverable (in pages or LOC),
- Estimate the effort (number of days) required to complete the deliverable based on its complexity and size, and experience of team,
- Estimate the cost of the completed deliverable,
- The estimate for the project is the sum of the individual estimates.

The approach often uses productivity data that is available from previously completed projects. The effort required for a complex deliverable is higher than that of a simple deliverable (where both are of the same size). The project planning section in the project plan (or a separate estimation plan) will include the lifecycle phases, and the deliverables/tasks to be carried out in each phase. It may include a table along the following lines (Table 4.2).

---

[7] Unless "Go Ask Fred" is the name of the estimation methodology, or the estimation tool employed.

Table 4.1 Estimation techniques

Technique	Description
Work breakdown structure	Identify the project deliverables to be produced during the project. Estimate the size of each deliverable (in pages or LOC). Estimate the effort (number of days) required to complete the deliverable based on its size and complexity. Estimate the cost of the completed deliverable
Analogy method	This involves comparing the proposed project to a previously completed project (that is like the proposed project). The historical data and metrics for schedule, effort and budget estimation accuracy are considered, as well as similarities and differences between the projects to provide effort, schedule, and budget estimates
Expert judgement	This involves consultation with experienced personnel to derive the estimate. The expert(s) can factor in differences between past project experiences, knowledge of existing systems as well as the specific requirements of the project
Delphi method	The *Delphi Method* is a consensus method used to produce accurate schedules and estimates. It was developed by the Rand Corporation and improved by Barry Boehm and others. It provides extra confidence in the project estimates by using experts independent of the project manager or third-party supplier
Cost predictor models	These include various cost prediction models such as *Cocomo* and Slim. The Costar tool supports Cocomo, and the Qsm tool supports Slim
Function points	*Function Points* were developed by Allan Albrecht at IBM in the late 1970s and involve analysing each functional requirement and assigning a number of function points based on its size and complexity. This total number of function points is a measure of the estimate for the project

Table 4.2 Example work-breakdown structure

Lifecycle phase	Project deliverable or task description	Est. size	Est. effort	Est. cost
Planning and requirements	Project plan	40	10 days	$5000
	Project schedule	20	5 days	$2500
	Business requirements	20	10 days	$5000
	Test plan	15	5 days	$2500
	Issue/Risk log	3	2 days	$1000
	Lessons learned log	1	1 day	$500
Design	System requirements	15	5 days	$2500
	Technical/DB design	30	10 days	$5000
Coding	Source code	5000 (LOC)	10 days	$5000
	Unit tests/results	200	2 days	$1000
Testing	ST specs	30	10 days	$5000
	System testing		10 days	$5000
	UAT specs	30	10 days	$5000
	UAT testing		10 days	$5000

(continued)

Table 4.2 (continued)

Lifecycle phase	Project deliverable or task description	Est. size	Est. effort	Est. cost
Deployment	Release notes/Procedures	20	5 days	$2500
	User manuals	50	10 days	$5000
	Support procedures	15	10 days	$5000
	Training plan	25	5 days	$2500
Project closure	End project report	10	2 days	$1000
	Lessons learned report	5	2 days	$1000
Contingency	10%		13.4	$6700
Total			147.4	$73,700

4.4   Project Planning and Scheduling

A well-managed project has an increased chance of success, and good planning is
an essential part of project management. There is the well-known adage that states,
"*Fail to plan, plan to fail*".[8] The project manager and the relevant stakeholders will
consider the appropriate approach for the project and determine whether a solution
should be purchased off the shelf, whether to outsource the software development to
a third party supplier, or whether to develop the solution internally. A simple
process map for project planning is presented in Fig. 4.1.

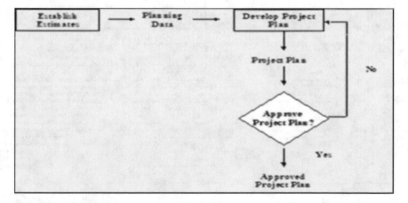

Fig. 4.1 Simple process map for project planning

---

[8] This quotation is adapted from Benjamin Franklin (an inventor and signatory to the American
declaration of independence).

Estimation is a key part of project planning, and the effort estimates are used for scheduling of the tasks and activities in a project-scheduling tool such as *Microsoft Project* (Fig. 4.2).

The schedule will detail the phases in the project, the key project milestones, the activities and tasks to be performed in each phase as well as their associated timescales, and the resources required to carry out each task. The project manager will update the project schedule regularly during the project.

Projects vary in size and complexity and the formality of the software development process employed needs to reflect this. The project plan defines how the project will be carried out, and it generally includes sections such as:

- Business Case,
- Project Scope,
- Project Goals and Objectives,
- Key Milestones,
- Project Planning and Estimates,
- Key Stakeholders,

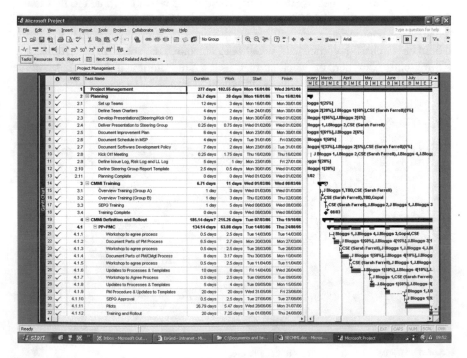

Fig. 4.2 Sample microsoft project schedule

- Project Team and Responsibilities,
- Knowledge and Skills Required,
- Communication Planning,
- Financial Planning,
- Quality and Test Planning,
- Configuration Management.

Communication planning describes how communication will be carried out during the project, and it includes the various project meetings and reports that will be produced; financial planning is concerned with budget planning for the project; quality and test planning is concerned with the planning required to ensure that a high-quality product is delivered; and configuration management is concerned with identifying the configuration items to be controlled, and systematically controlling changes to them throughout the lifecycle. It ensures that all deliverables are kept consistent following approved changes.

The project plan is a key project document, and it needs to be approved by all stakeholders. The project manager needs to ensure that the project plan, schedule, and technical work products are kept consistent with the requirements. Another words, if there are changes to the requirements then the project plan and schedule will need to be updated accordingly.

Checklists are useful in verifying that the tasks have been completed. The sample project management checklist below (Table 4.3) verifies that project planning has been appropriately performed and that controls are in place.

Table 4.3 Sample project management checklist

No.	Item to check
1.	Is the project plan complete and approved by the stakeholders?
2.	Does the project have a sound business case?
3.	Are the Risk Log, Issue Log and Lessons Learned Log set up?
4.	Are the responses to the risks and issues appropriate?
5.	Is the Microsoft Schedule available for the project?
6.	Is the project schedule up to date?
7.	Is the project appropriately resourced?
8.	Are estimates available for the project? Are they realistic?
9.	Has quality planning been completed for the project?
10.	Has the change control mechanism been set up for the project?
11.	Are all deliverables under configuration management control?
12.	Has project communication been appropriately planned?
13.	Is the project directory set up for the project?
14.	Are the key milestones defined in the project plan?

4.5   Risk Management

Risks arise due to uncertainty, and *risk management is concerned with managing uncertainty*, and especially the management of any undesired events. Risks need to be identified, analysed, and controlled in order for the project to be successful, and risk management activities take place throughout the project lifecycle.

Once the initial set of risks to the project has been identified, they are analysed to determine their *likelihood of occurrence* and their *impact* (e.g., on cost, schedule, or quality). These two parameters determine the *risk category*, and the most serious risk category refers to a risk with a high probability of occurrence and a high impact on occurrence.

Countermeasures are defined to reduce the likelihood of occurrence and impact of the risks, and contingency plans are prepared to deal with the situation of the risk actually occurring. Additional risks may arise during the project, and the project manager needs to be proactive in their identification and management.

Risks need to be reviewed regularly especially following changes to the project. These could be changes to the business case or the business requirements, loss of key personnel, and so on. Events that occur may affect existing risks (including the probability of their occurrence and their impact) and may lead to new risks. Countermeasures need to be kept up to date during the project. Risks are reported regularly throughout the project.

The risk management cycle is concerned with identifying and managing risks throughout the project lifecycle. It involves identifying risks; determining their probability of occurrence and impact should they occur; identifying responses to the risks; and monitoring and reporting. Table 4.4 describes these activities in greater detail:

Table 4.4 Risk management activities

Activity	Description
Risk management strategy	This defines how the risks will be identified, monitored, reviewed, and reported during the project, as well as the frequency of monitoring and reporting
Risk identification	This involves identifying the risks to the project and recording them in a risk repository (e.g., Risk Log). It continues throughout the project lifecycle. Prince 2 classifies risks into: • *Business* (e.g., collapse of subcontractors) • *Legal and Regulatory* • *Organzational* (e.g., skilled resources/management) • *Technical* (e.g., scope creep, architecture, design) • *Environmental* (e.g., flooding or fires)
Evaluating the risks	This involves assessing the likelihood of occurrence of a particular risk and its impact (on cost, schedule, etc.) should it materialise. These two parameters result in the risk category

(continued)

Table 4.4   (continued)

Activity	Description
Identifying risk responses	The project manager (and stakeholders) will determine the appropriate response to a risk such as reducing the probability of its occurrence, or its impact should it occur. These include: • *Prevention* aims to prevent it from occurring • *Reduction* aims to reduce the probability of occurrence or impact should it occur • *Transfer* aims to transfer the risk to a 3rd party • *Acceptance* is when nothing can be done about it • *Contingency* are actions that are carried out should the risk materialze
Risk monitoring and reporting	This involves monitoring existing risks to verify that the actions taken to manage the risks are effective, as well as identifying new risks. This provides an early warning that an identified risk is going to materialize, and *a risk that materializes is a new project issue* that needs to be dealt with
Lessons learned	This is concerned with determining the effectiveness of risk management during the project, and to learn any lessons for future projects

The project manager will maintain a risk repository (this may be a tool or a risk log) to record details of each risk, including its type and description; its likelihood and its impact (yielding the risk category); as well as the response to the risk.

4.6   People Management in Projects

People management is an integral part of project management, and the success of a project is dependent on a functioning high-performance team. This helps in getting the best performance from the team as well as improving the overall quality of the project. This means that the project manager needs to be a strong people manager in addition to her being a competent project management professional. The project manager inspires and motivates the project team, and the team may be virtual and consist of hybrid and remote teams. It is essential that team building activities take place and that team members are given orientation on the overall purpose of the project, and their role and responsibilities. If the project team is in the same physical location, then social team building activities may take place, but this is more difficult to do for remote or hybrid teams.

It takes time for the project team to perform as a team and the project manager needs to devote time to getting to know each team member, understanding them and their skill set, planning improvements to their skill set, explaining their role and responsibilities in the project, as well as getting commitment from the team member. Good people management skills help in building a good rapport with all team members and in having a positive work environment with committed team members working in harmony together to complete the project activities. A good work environment helps in improving productivity, as team members are working in harmony together to achieve the project goals. The project team development phases often include:

- Forming,
- Storming,
- Norming,
- Performing.

The project manager needs to be active in motivating team members and addressing natural drops in project commitment levels that may arise during the project. It is essential that team members feel a part of the project and that they feel that their contribution is important and recognized, as this will help in maintaining their commitment to the project. Conflicts may arise between team members during a project, and the project manager needs to play a role in resolving such situations. The project manager needs to manage people issues such as:

- Communication issues,
- Clash of personalities,
- Unrealistic expectations,
- Workplace culture.

The project manager must be proactive in monitoring completion of the deliverables of team members, ensuring that the project is kept on schedule, and giving feedback on performance to team members.

4.7 Quality Management in Projects

There are various definitions of "quality" such as Juran's definition that quality is "*fitness for purpose*", and Crosby definition of quality as "*conformance to the requirements*". The Crosby definition is useful when asking whether we are building it right, whereas the Juran definition is useful when asking whether we are building the right system. Crosby's definition is useful in requirements verification, where software inspections and testing verify that the requirements have been correctly implemented. Juran's definition is useful in requirements validation.

It is a fundamental premise in the quality field that it is more cost effective to build quality into the product, rather than adding it later during the testing phase. Therefore, quality needs to be considered at every step during the project, and every deliverable needs to be reviewed to ensure its fitness for purpose. The review may be like a *software inspection*, a *structured walkthrough* or another appropriate methodology.

The project plan will include a section on quality planning for the project (this may be a reference to a separate plan). The quality plan will define how the project plans to deliver a high-quality project, as well as the quality controls and quality assurance activities that will take place during project execution. The quality planning for the project needs to ensure that the customer's quality expectations will be achieved.

The project manager has overall responsibility for project quality, and the quality department (if one exists) will assign a quality engineer to the project, and the quality engineer will promote quality and its importance to the project team, as well as facilitating quality improvement. The project manager needs to ensure that sound software engineering processes are employed, as well as ensuring that the defined standards and templates are followed.

It is an accepted principle in the quality field that good processes and conformance to them is essential for the delivery of a high-quality product. The quality engineer will conduct process audits to ensure that the processes and standards are followed consistently during the project. An audit report is published, and any audit actions are tracked to closure.

Software Testing is conducted to verify that the software correctly implements the requirements, and a separate project test plan will define the various types of testing to be performed during the project. These will typically include unit, integration, system, performance and acceptance testing, and the results from the various test activities enables the fitness for purpose of the software to be determined, as well as judging whether it is ready to be released or not.

The project manager will report the various project metrics (including the quality metrics) in the regular project status reports, and the quality metrics provide an objective indication of the quality of the product at that moment in time.

The cost of poor quality may be determined at the end of the project, and this may require a time recording system for the various project activities. The effort involved in detecting and correcting defects may be recorded, and a COPQ chart like Fig. 10.28 presented.

Poor quality may arise due to several reasons. For example, it may be caused by inadequate reviews or testing of the software; inadequate skills or experience of the project team; or poorly defined or understood requirements.

The project manager will conduct a lessons-learned meeting at the end of the project to identify and record all the lessons learned from the project. These are then published as a lessons-learned report and shared with relevant stakeholders as part of continuous improvement.

4.8   Project Monitoring and Control

Project monitoring and control is concerned with monitoring project execution and taking corrective action when project performance deviates from expectations. The progress of the project should be monitored against the plan, and corrective actions taken as appropriate. The key project parameters such as budget, effort, and schedule as well as risks and issues are monitored, and the status of the project communicated regularly to the affected stakeholders.

The project manager will conduct progress and milestone reviews to determine the actual progress, with new issues identified and monitored. The appropriate corrective actions are identified are tracked to closure. The focus of project monitoring and control is:

- Monitor the project plan and schedule and keep on track,
- Monitor the key project parameters,
- Conduct progress and milestone reviews to determine the actual status,
- Re-plan as appropriate,
- Monitor risks and take appropriate action,
- Analyse issues and change requests and take appropriate action,
- Track corrective action to closure,
- Monitor resources and manage any resource issues,
- Report the project status to management and project board.

A sample process map for project monitoring and control is presented in Fig. 4.3. The project manager will monitor progress, risks, and issues during the project, and take appropriate corrective action. The status of the project will be reported in the regular status reports sent to management and the project board, with the status reviewed with management regularly during the project.

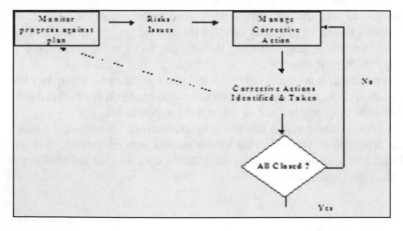

Fig. 4.3 Simple process map for project monitoring and control

Table 4.5 Activities in managing issues and change requests

Activity	Description of issue/Change request
Log issue or change request	The project manager logs the issue or change request. It is assigned a unique reference number and priority (severity) and categorized into an issue (problem) or change request
Assess impact	This involves analysis to determine the impacts such as technical, cost, schedule, and quality. The risks need to be identified
Decision on implementation	A decision is made on how to deal with the issue or change request. The CCB is often involved in the decision to authorize a change request
Implement solution	The affected project documents and software modules are identified and modified accordingly
Verify solution	Testing (Unit, System and UAT) is employed to verify the correctness of the solution
Close issue/CR	The issue or change request is closed

4.9   Managing Issues and Change Requests

The management of issues and change requests is a normal part of project management. An issue can arise at any time during the project (e.g., a supplier to the project may go out of business, an employee may resign, specialized hardware for testing may not arrive in time, and so on), and an issue refers to a problem that has occurred which may have a negative impact on the project. The severity of the issue is an indication of its impact on the project, and the project manager needs to manage it appropriately.

A *change request* is a stakeholder request for a change to the scope of the project, and it may arise at any time during the project. The impacts of the change request (e.g., technical, cost and schedule) need to be carefully considered, as a change introduces new risks to the project that may adversely affect cost, schedule, and quality. It is therefore essential to fully understand the impacts to make an informed decision on whether to authorize or reject the change request. The project manager may directly approve small change requests, with the impacts of a larger change request considered by the project *change control board* (CCB).

The activities involved in managing issues and change requests are summarized in Table 4.5.

4.10   Remote Project Management

Remote project management is concerned with managing remote and hybrid teams to ensure that the project objectives are achieved. Traditional project management involve teams based in the same physical location, whereas often today teams may operate in hybrid mode with some employees working in the office and other employees and teams working remotely in different physical locations. This means that today remote employees play important roles in the success of projects, and remote project management has become more important in managing hybrid and remote teams. A *hybrid team* is a flexible work structure with some employees working remotely and others working from the office.

The management of remote teams requires modern communication including video conferencing, shared files, and documents, as well as team communication and messaging apps. It is more challenging to build a team culture with remote teams, and while creating the team is the easy part the team building is more difficult. This is since it is much more difficult to build up a team bond and trust among team members who are not in the same physical location. The project manager will stay engaged with the team throughout the project with virtual meetings, and remote project management is like traditional project management except that the project is executed remotely. It is a flexible methodology that can support various approaches such as traditional software engineering and Agile.

The first step in assembling a remote team is to determine the remote structure that is required, and then to find the people with the appropriate technical and soft skills that are required to carry out the project. The project manager needs to communicate clear expectations to the team members at project initiation, including the process to be followed, work hours, project goals, their responsibilities, the tools that will be employed for collaboration, and so on. The project manager will keep the team engaged through regular virtual team meetings, and the team members will check in daily with the project manager to advise on progress made and this could take the form of a virtual stand-up meeting.

4.11   Outsourcing

Outsourcing is a common business practice where a company contracts out business functions such as manufacturing, software development, and call centres to third party providers. The outsourcing of a business function to a distant country is termed *offshoring*, whereas outsourcing may also be done domestically, and *nearshoring* is where the outsourcing is to a nearby country. The main benefits are outsourcing include:

- Cost savings due to reduction in business expenses,
- Availability of expertise not available in house,
- Staff augmentation of skilled personnel (usually offshore based) to supplement in-house staff for specific projects,
- Allows company to focus on core business activities,
- Makes business more flexible,
- Increased efficiencies.

Outsourcing involves handing control of various business functions over to a third party, and this leads to business risks such as the quality of the service may be below expectations, or the third party may go out of business, or that there may be risks to confidentiality and security. There are several disadvantages associated with outsourcing such as:

- Managing the day-to-day relationship with offshore team,
- Differences in times zones,
- Risks to quality, confidentiality, and security,
- Differences in culture and language.

Many large projects involve total or partial outsourcing of the software development, and it is therefore essential to select a supplier that can deliver high-quality and reliable software on time and on budget. We discuss the selection and management of a supplier in more detail in Chap. 11.

4.12 Project Board and Governance

The *project board*[9] (or steering group) is responsible for directing the project, and it is directly accountable for the success of the project. It consists of senior managers and staff in the organization who have the authority to make resources available, to remove roadblocks, and to get things done.

It is consulted whenever key project decisions need to be made, and it plays a key role in project governance. The project board ensures that there is a clear business case for the project, and that the capital funding for the project is adequate and well spent. The project board may cancel the project at any stage during project execution should there cease to be a business case or should project spending exceed tolerance and go out of control.[10]

The project manager reports to the project board and sends regular status reports to highlight progress made as well as key project risks and issues. The project board meets at an appropriate frequency during the project (with extra sessions held should serious project issues arise) (Fig. 4.4)

There are several roles on the project board (an individual could perform more than one role) and their responsibilities include (Table 4.6).

---

[9] The project board in the Prince 2 methodology includes roles such as the project executive, senior supplier, senior user, project assurance, and the project manager. These roles have distinct responsibilities.

[10] The project plan will usually specify a *tolerance level* for schedule and spending, where the project may spend (perhaps less than 10%) more than the allocated capital for the project before seeking authorization for further capital funding for the project.

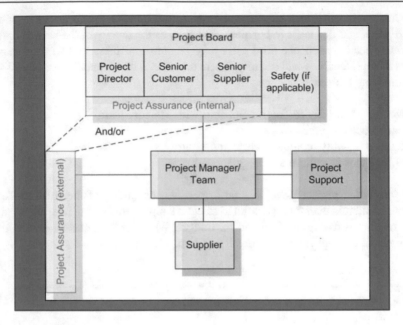

Fig. 4.4 Prince 2 project board

Table 4.6 Project board roles and responsibilities

Role	Responsibility
Project director	Ultimately responsible for the project. Provides overall guidance to the project
Senior customer	Represents the interests of users
Senior supplier	Represents the resources responsible for implementation of project (e.g., IS manager)
Project manager	Link between project board and project team
Project assurance	Internal role (optional) that provides an independent (of project manager) objective view of the project
Safety (optional)	Ensure adherence to health and safety standards

4.13   Project Reporting

The frequency of project reporting is defined in the project plan (or the communications plan). The project report advises management and the key stakeholders of the status of the project, and includes key project information such as:

- Completed Deliverables (during period),
- New risks and issues,
- Schedule, Effort and Budget Status (e.g., RAG metrics[11]),
- Quality and Test Status,
- Key Risks and Issues,
- Milestone Status,
- Deliverables planned (next period).

The project manager discusses the project report with management and the project board and presents the status of the project as well as the key risks and issues. The project manager will present a recovery plan (exception report) to deal with the situation where the project has fallen significantly outside the defined project tolerance (i.e., it is significantly behind schedule or over budget).

The key risks and issues will be discussed, and the project manager will explain how the key issues are being dealt with, and how the key risks will be managed. The new risks and issues will also be discussed, and the project board will carefully consider how the project manager plans to deal with these and will provide appropriate support.

The project board will carefully consider the status of the project as well as the input from the project manager before deciding on the appropriate course of action (which could include the immediate termination of the project if there is no longer a business case for it).

4.14   Project Closure

A project is a temporary activity, and once the project goals have been achieved and the product handed over to the customer and support group, it is ready to be closed. The project manager will prepare an end of project report detailing the extent to which the project achieved its targeted objectives. The report will include a summary of key project metrics including key quality metrics and the budget and timeliness metrics.

The success of the project is judged on the extent to which the defined objectives have been achieved, and on the extent to which the project has delivered the agreed functionality on schedule, on budget and with the right quality. This is often referred to as the project management triangle (Fig. 4.5).

The project manager presents the end project report to the project board, including any factors (e.g., change requests) that may have affected the timely delivery of the project or the allocated budget. The project is then officially closed.

The project manager then schedules a meeting with the team review the lessons learned from the project. The team records the lessons learned during the project (typically in a lessons-learned log), and the key lessons learned are summarized in

---

[11] Often, a colour coding mechanism is employed with a red flag indicating a serious issue; amber highlighting a potentially serious issue; and green indicating that everything is ok.

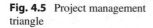
Fig. 4.5 Project management triangle

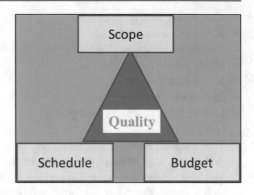

the lessons-learned report. Any actions identified are assigned to individuals and followed through to closure, and the lessons-learned report is made available to other projects (with the goal of learning from experience). The project team is disbanded, and the project team members are assigned to other duties.

4.15 Prince 2 Methodology

Prince 2 (*Projects in controlled environments*) is a popular project management methodology that is widely used in the U.K. and Europe. It is a structured, process driven approach to project management, with processes for project start up, initiating a project, controlling a stage, managing stage boundaries, closing a project, managing product delivery, planning, and directing a project (Fig. 4.6). It has procedures to coordinate people and activities in a project, as well as procedures to monitor and control project activities.

These key processes are summarized in Table 4.7, and more detailed information on Prince 2 is in [1].

4.16 Project Manager Professional

Project Manager Professional (PMP) is an internationally recognized project management qualification offered by the Project Management Institute (PMI). It involves an exam based on PMI's project management body of knowledge (PMBOK).

The project management body of knowledge is a body of knowledge for project management, and the PMBOK guide is a subset of the project management body of knowledge. It was first published by the PMI in 1996, and the 6th edition provides support for Agile [2].

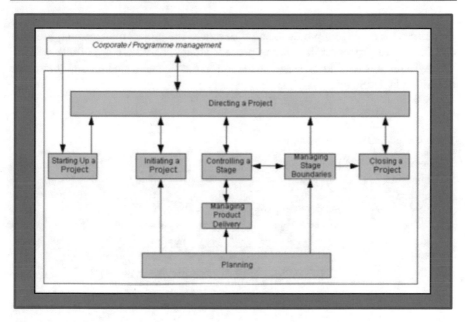

Fig. 4.6 Prince 2 processes

Table 4.7 Key processes in Prince 2

Process	Description
Start-up	Project Manager and project board appointed, project approach and project brief defined
Initiating	Project and quality plan complete, business case and risks refined, project files set up, and project authorized
Controlling a stage	Stage plan prepared, quality and risks/issues managed, progress reviewed and reported
Managing stage Boundary	Stage status reviewed and next stage planned, actual products produced vs. original stage plan compared, stage or exception report produced
Closing a project	Orderly closure of project with project board, end project report and lessons learned report
Managing product delivery	Covers product creation by the team or a 3rd party supplier. Ensure that the planned deliverables meet quality criteria
Planning	Prince 2 employs product-based planning which involves identifying the products required, and the activities and resources to provide them
Directing a project	The project board consists of senior management, and it controls the project. It has the authority to authorize and define what is required from the project, commitment of resources and funds, and management direction

It is process based with the work performed as processes, and it provides guidelines for managing projects, and it describes the project management lifecycle and its related processes. It has five process groups, and these are (Table 4.8).

PMBOK has ten knowledge areas on project management, and these are described in Table 4.9.

Table 4.8 PMBOK process groups

Process	Description
Initiating	Define a new project and obtain authorization to start the project
Planning	This involves establishing the scope of the project and defining the plan to achieve the project's objectives
Executing	This involves executing the activities defined in the project plan
Monitoring and Control	This involves tracking progress and performance of the project and taking corrective action where appropriate
Closing a project	These processes perform an orderly closure of the project

Table 4.9 PMBOK knowledge areas

Knowledge area	Description
Project integration management	The processes to identify and coordinate the various processes and project management activities
Project scope management	The processes to ensure that the project includes all the work required to complete the project (and only that)
Project schedule management	The processes to manage the timely completion of the project
Project cost management	The processes involved in planning, estimating, budgeting, and controlling costs so that the project can be completed within the approved budget
Project quality management	The processes and activities of the organization that determine the quality policies, objectives, and responsibilities so that the project satisfies the quality expectations
Project resource management	The processes to organize, manage, and lead the project team
Project communications management	The processes involved in determining the information needs of those involved in the project and fulfilling them
Project risk management	The processes involved in analysing, response planning, and controlling risk in a project
Project procurement management	The processes concerned with the purchase of products or services external to the project team
Project stakeholder management	This involves identifying all stakeholders affected by the project and analysing/managing their expectations

4.17 Project Management Office

A project management office (PMO) is a group or department within a company that defines and maintains standards for project management in the organization. The PMO will aim to standardize and enhance project management within the organization so that the projects being carried out have a defined and repeatable process. The PMO will act a centre of expertise on project management within the organization, and it will be consulted by projects for guidance and documentation on project management. It defines the project management metrics to be used and reported by the projects.

The PMO standardizes the project management methodology in the organization, and the project management practices may be based on industrial best practice such as Prince 2 or PMP. The PMO identify the tools required to support the process, and it provides training on project management throughout the organization. It may also monitor and report on active projects and portfolios in the organization and may have responsibility for reporting progress to senior management for strategic decisions on whether specific projects should continue or be terminated.

The Project Management Office provides several functions such as project governance, transparency, and reusability (Table 4.10).

4.18 Program Management

Program management is the process of managing a group of related projects in a coordinated manner to obtain benefits not available from managing them individually. It is often used in managing very large projects such as business transformation, which often involves fundamental changes in the way that business is conducted. A program is a set of related projects and program management

Table 4.10 Functions of project management office

Function	Description
Project governance	This is a project oversight function to ensure that the right decisions are made by the right people based on the right information
Transparency	This ensures that all relevant information that is required for decision-making is available and accurate
Reusability	The PMO will maintain a repository of best practice from previous successful projects such as lessons learned and a collection of templates to allow project management tasks to be consistently performed
Delivery support	The PMO provides support to the projects during project delivery by streamlining projects, and offering training, mentoring and quality assurance
Traceability	This involves managing documentation, project history and organization knowledge

coordinates their planning and execution. A project manager is responsible for the planning and execution of a single project, and for ensuring that their project is successfully delivered on time and budget, whereas the program manager is responsible for the success of the entire program.

Program management provides an environment where the projects may be run successfully, and it provides a layer above the management of projects. The program manager has oversight of the importance and status of all the projects in the program and supports project-level activity to ensure that the program goals are achieved.

The program manager is responsible for the program and does not micro-manage projects, as this is a project manager's responsibility. The program manager needs to coordinate and prioritize the resources across the projects, and needs to deal with issues, roadblocks, links, and interdependencies between the projects, as well as managing the overall risks and cost of the program.

4.19 Project Portfolio Management

A portfolio is a collection of projects and programs that will deliver business benefit or operational efficiencies in an organization. Project portfolio management (PPM) is focused on doing the right projects at the right time, and so it is the process of selecting the right projects and programs to do, the right time to do them, and managing them effectively.

PPM differs from program and project management that are focused on execution and delivery (i.e., doing the projects and programs right), whereas PPM focuses on ensuring that it does the right projects that deliver business value. Organizations have limited resources and it is not possible to do all projects, and so only the best projects that deliver real business benefit should be done. This means that rigorous project selection should be employed to ensure that only those projects that are aligned to the organization's strategic direction and deliver the greatest business benefit should be selected.

PPM ensures that project execution is aligned with the organization strategy with each selected project playing a role in carrying out its strategy. This ensures that the benefits provided from the execution of the projects provide the greatest financial return on the investment made. It ensures that the portfolio is balanced with pet projects that have a limited business return avoided, and it avoids a focus on short-term results.

PPM must ensure that there is a balance between the implementation of change initiatives and maintaining business as usual.

4.20   Project Management in the Agile World

Scrum is a framework for managing an Agile software development project. It is not a prescriptive methodology as such, and it relies on a self-organizing, cross-functional team to take the feature from idea to implementation. The cross-team includes the *product owner* who represents the interest of the users; the *scrum master* who is the coach for the team, and helps the team to understand the Scrum process and to perform at the highest level, as well as performing some light project management activities such as project tracking; and the *team* itself who decide on which person should work on which tasks and so on.

The Scrum methodology breaks the software development for the project into a series of sprints, where each sprint is of fixed time duration of 2–4 weeks. There is a planning meeting at the start of the sprint where the team members determine the number of items/tasks that they can commit to, and then create a sprint backlog (*to do list*) of the tasks to be performed during the sprint. The Scrum team takes a small set of features from idea to coded and tested functionality that is integrated into the evolving product.

The team attends a daily stand-up meeting (usually of 15 min duration) where the progress of the previous day is discussed, as well as any obstacles to progress. The new functionality is demonstrated to the product owner and any other relevant stakeholders at the end of the sprint, and this may result in changes to the delivered functionality or the addition of new items to the product backlog. There is a sprint retrospective meeting to reflect on the sprint and to identify improvement opportunities.

The main deliverable produced using the Scrum framework is the *product itself*, and Scrum expects to build a properly tested product increment (in a shippable state) at the end of each sprint. The *product backlog* is another deliverable, and it is maintained and prioritized by the product owner. There is also the *sprint backlog* which is the list of the functionality to be implemented in the sprint.

The Scrum Master is the expert on the Agile process and acts as a coach to the team thereby helping the team to achieve a high level of performance. The role differs from that of a project manager, as the Scrum Master does not assign tasks to individuals or provide day-to-day direction to the team. However, the scrum master typically performs some light project management tasks.

Many of the traditional project manager responsibilities such as task assignment and day-to-day project decisions revert to the team, and the responsibility for the scope and schedule trade-off goes to the product owner. The product owner creates and communicates a solid vision of the product and shares the vision through the product backlog. Larger Agile projects (team size > 20) will often have a dedicated project manager role.

4.21   Review Questions

1. What is a project? What is project management?
2. Describe various approaches to estimation.
3. What activities take place at project start-up and initiation?
4. What skills are required to be a good project manager?
5. What is the purpose of the project board and explain project governance.
6. What is the purpose of risk management? How are risks managed?
7. Describe the main activities in project management.
8. What is the difference between a risk and an issue?
9. What is the purpose of project reporting?
10. How is quality managed in a project?

4.22   Summary

Project management is concerned with the effective management of projects, and the goal is to deliver a high-quality product, on time and on budget, to the customer. It involves good project planning and estimation; managing resources; managing changes and issues that arise; managing quality; managing risks; managing the budget; monitoring progress and taking corrective action; communicating progress; and delivering a high-quality product to the customer.

The scope of the project needs to be determined, and estimates established. The project plan is developed and approved by the stakeholders, and it will contain or reference several other plans. It needs to be maintained during the project. Project estimation and scheduling are difficult as often software projects are quite different from previous projects. Gantt charts are often employed for project scheduling, and these show the work breakdown for the project, as well as task dependencies and the assignment of staff to the various tasks.

The effective management of risk during a project is essential to project success. Risks arise due to uncertainty and the risk management cycle involves risk identification; risk analysis and evaluation; identifying responses to risks; selecting and planning a response to the risk; and risk monitoring.

Once the planning is complete the project execution commences, and the focus moves to monitoring progress, re-planning as appropriate, managing risks and issues, re-planning as appropriate, providing regular progress reports to the project board, and so on. Finally, there is an orderly close of the project.

References

1. *Managing Successful Projects with PRINCE 2* (Office of Government Commerce, 2004)
2. *A Guide to the Project Management Body of Knowledge. PMBOK Guide*, 6th edn. (Project Management Institute, 2017)

Requirements Engineering

5

Abstract

This chapter discusses requirements engineering and discusses activities such as requirements gathering, requirements elicitation, requirements analysis, requirements management, and requirements verification and validation.

Keywords

User requirements · System requirements · Functional and non-functional requirements · Requirements elicitation · Requirements analysis · Requirements verification and validation · Requirements management · Requirements traceability

5.1 Introduction

The user requirements specify what the customer wants and define *what* the software system is required to do, as distinct from *how* this is to be done. The requirements are the foundation for the system, and if they are incorrect then irrespective of the best software development processes in the world, the implemented system will be incorrect. The process of determining the requirements, analysing, and validating them and managing them throughout the project lifecycle is termed *requirements engineering*.

Often, the initial requirements for a project arise due to a particular problem that the business or customer needs to solve. This leads to a project to implement an appropriate solution, and the first step is to determine the scope of work and the actual requirements for the project, and whether the project is feasible from the cost, time, and technical considerations.

© Springer Nature Switzerland AG 2022
G. O'Regan, *Concise Guide to Software Engineering*,
Undergraduate Topics in Computer Science,
https://doi.org/10.1007/978-3-031-07816-3_5

The *user requirements* are determined from discussions with the customer to determine their actual needs, and they are then refined into the *system requirements*, which state the *functional* and *non-functional* requirements of the system.

The requirements must be precise and unambiguous to ensure that all stakeholders are clear on what is (and what is not) to be delivered, and prototyping may be employed to clarify the requirements and to assist in their definition.

Requirements verification is concerned with ensuring that the requirements are properly implemented (i.e., *building it right*). Another words, it is concerned with ensuring that the requirements are properly addressed in the design and implementation, and a traceability matrix and testing are often employed as part of the verification activities.

Requirements validation (i.e., *building the right system*) is concerned with ensuring that the right requirements are defined, and that they are precise, complete, consistent, realizable and reflect the actual needs of the customer. The validation of the requirements is done by the stakeholders, and it involves several reviews of the requirements (and prototype), reviews of the design, and user acceptance testing.

The Agile software development methodology (discussed in more detail in Chap. 14) has become very popular, and its lightweight approach is to be contrasted with the traditional waterfall model. It argues that requirements change so quickly that a requirements document is unnecessary, since such a document would be out of date as soon as it was written.

This chapter will focus on requirements engineering as it is in traditional software engineering, and the reader may consult Chap. 14 and the various texts on Agile to understand its approach to requirements engineering.

5.2 Requirements Process

The process of determining the requirements for a proposed system involves discussions with the relevant stakeholders to determine their needs, and to explicitly define what functionality the system should provide, as well as any hardware and performance constraints.

The specification of the requirements needs to be precise and unambiguous to ensure that all parties involved share a common understanding of the system, and fully agree on what is to be developed and tested. A feasibility study may be needed to demonstrate that the requirements are feasible and may be implemented within the defined schedule and cost constraints.

The requirements are the foundation for the system, and project planning is based on the defined requirements. It is therefore essential that the requirements are *complete* (all services required by the user are defined), *consistent* (requirements should not contradict one another) and *unambiguous* (the requirements are clear and definite in meaning). Table 5.1 presents characteristics of good requirements.

Table 5.1 Characteristics of good requirements

No.	Characteristics of good requirements
1.	Each requirement is clear and unambiguous
2.	Each requirement has a priority to indicate its importance
3.	Each requirement may be implemented
4.	Each requirement is testable
5.	Each requirement is necessary
6.	Any conflicts between the requirements are resolved
7.	Each requirement is broken down as fully as possible
8.	Each requirement is consistent with the project's objectives
9.	Each requirement is stated as a stakeholder need (i.e., premature design/solution or implementation information is not included)
10.	The user (business) requirements are traceable (in both directions) throughout the development cycle
11.	The requirements are complete and consistent

Prototyping may be employed to assist in the definition and validation of the requirements, and a suitable prototype will include key parts of the system. It allows users to give early feedback on the proposed system, and on the extent to which it meets their needs. Prototyping is useful in clarifying the requirements and helps to reduce the risk of implementing the incorrect solution.

The implications of the proposed set of requirements needs to be understood, as the choice of a particular requirement may affect the choice of another requirement. For example, in the telecommunications domain, two features may work correctly in isolation, but when present together they interact in an undesirable way. Therefore, feature interactions need to be identified and investigated at the requirements phase to determine how interactions should be resolved.

In situations where an inadequate requirements process is employed, then there may be serious problems in the project. This may be manifested by requirements that are poorly defined or controlled, or requirements that are incomplete, inadequately documented, or un-testable. In other cases, there may be major scope creep with requirements accepted from any source.

Changes to the requirements may lead to a high-level of re-work, or cause major delays to the project schedule, or major increases in project cost. In other cases, where poor requirements management practices are employed the changes to the requirements may not be reflected in the project plan, and the deliverables may be inconsistent with the requirements. Table 5.2 presents symptoms of a poor requirements process.

The following activities are involved in the requirements process, and they are discussed in more detail in the following sections:

- Requirements elicitation and specification
- Requirements analysis
- Requirements verification and validation

Table 5.2   Symptoms of poor requirements process

No.	Symptom
1.	High-level of requirements creep during the project
2.	Requirements changing regularly during the project
3.	Missing requirements
4.	Changes to the requirements are not controlled
5.	Requirements accepted from any source
6.	High-level of rework during the project
7.	Design, Implementation and Test products inconsistently interpret the requirements
8.	Deliverables are inconsistent with the requirements
9.	Un-testable requirements
10.	Inability to demonstrate that the implementation satisfies the requirements

- Requirements traceability
- Requirements management.

We distinguish between the user (or business) requirements and the system requirements. The *user requirements* are the high-level requirements for the system (they tend to be high-level statements in a natural language with diagrams and tables), whereas the *system requirements* are a more detailed description of what the system is to do. The user requirements are more abstract than the system requirements, and a user requirement is typically expanded into several system requirements. The system requirements provide more detailed information on the system to be implemented, and it details the functionality to be provided and any operational constraints.

The system requirements include the functional and non-functional requirements. A *functional requirement* is a statement about the functionality of the system: i.e., a description of the behaviour of the system and how it should respond to inputs. A *non-functional requirement* is a constraint on the functionality of the system (e.g., a timing, performance, reliability, availability, portability, usability, safety, security, dependability, or a hardware constraint).

It is essential that the functional and non-functional requirements are stated precisely, and the *non-functional requirements are often quantitatively specified* so that it may be objectively determined (by testing) whether they are satisfied or not. Further, it is essential that the non-functional requirements are satisfied, as otherwise the delivered system may be unusable or unacceptable to the client. The non-functional requirements often affect the overall architecture of the system, rather than the individual components of the system.

Next, we discuss the process of determining the requirements for the system and specifying them in a requirements document.

5.2.1 Requirements Elicitation and Specification

Requirements elicitation is the process of determining the requirements for the proposed system, and it involves discussions with the relevant stakeholders to determine their needs, and to explicitly define what functionality the system should provide, as well as any operational and performance constraints. The process of eliciting the requirements from the stakeholders is difficult as

- Stakeholders often do not know what they want from the system.
- Stakeholders often do not know what is or what is not technically feasible and may have unrealistic expectations.
- Stakeholders express the requirements in the language of their domain, which may differ from the language of the business analysts.
- Different stakeholders may want different things from the system resulting in conflicts that need to be resolved.

The project manager/business analyst and the relevant stakeholders will conduct a brainstorming session to define the high-level requirements for the proposed system (or modification to an existing system). The requirements gathering may involve interviews with the stakeholders to allow them to talk about how they currently perform their work, and to determine their requirements for the proposed system. It may also include observation session where the business analyst observes the users to see how the work is currently performed (Fig. 5.1).

Further requirements workshops will review and analyse the draft user and system requirements documents and identify all other relevant information for the proposed system. There will typically be two requirements documents produced, and these are the *user* (sometimes called business) *requirements specification* (URS or BRS) and the *system requirements specification* (SRS). These two documents could be combined into one document.

The user requirements document is usually written in a natural language such as English (it may include diagrams and tables), and it describes the external behaviour of the system, and specifies the functional and non-functional requirements in non-technical language. The systems requirements document will be an expanded version of the user requirements, and it provides the detail as to how the user requirements will be provided in the system. It is a detailed specification of the entire system, with the aim of describing the external behaviour of the system and excluding (as far as possible) design information.[1] The system requirements specification may be written in:

---

[1] It is desirable that the user or system requirements describe what is to be provided rather than how it is to be provided. That is, in theory, design or implementation information should be excluded in the specification. However, in practice it is sometimes difficult to exclude all design information (e.g., consider the case where a system needs to work with an existing system).

Fig. 5.1 Requirements process

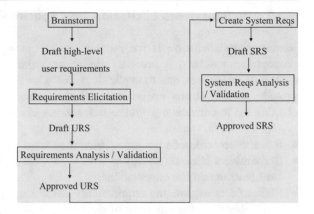

- A natural language
- A graphical language
- Formal specification language.

The system specification is generally written in a natural language such as *"English"* (with diagrams and tables included). Natural language is inherently ambiguous, and therefore care is required to ensure that the definition is precise and unambiguous, and the specification needs to be carefully reviewed to ensure that any ambiguities are identified and removed.

The specification may be written in a graphical specification language such as UML, which is often employed in defining the functional requirements of a system using use case diagrams, state diagrams and sequence diagrams. Finally, extra precision is needed for the specification of the requirements in the safety critical and security critical fields, and a formal mathematical specification language (such as VDM or Z) is often used in these domains.

Prototyping may be employed, and it helps in identifying gaps and misunderstandings in the definition of the requirements. The prototype is an early working version of the system, and it is used to give the users a flavour of what the working system will look like, and its evaluation by the stakeholders helps in clarifying the requirements. The prototype may be thrown away at the end of prototyping, or it may be re-used in the development of the system. Prototyping involves:

- Define prototype objectives
- Decide which functional requirements will be prototyped
- Develop the prototype
- Evaluate the prototype.

The project manager (or a business analyst) will facilitate the requirements workshops, and the initial workshop is an interview and brainstorming session[2]

---

[2] It may involve getting end users to talk about how they currently do a certain task and brainstorming on better ways in which the proposed system can do the same task.

focused on *requirements discovery*. This involves identifying and gathering the requirements from the various stakeholders, analysing, and prioritizing them, resolving conflicts between them, and consolidating them into a coherent set of user requirements.

This leads to the first draft of the user requirements, which is prepared by the project manager/business analyst, and the draft document is circulated to the stakeholders for review and comments. Further requirements workshops are then held to discuss and analyse the current draft of the user requirements, to ensure that they meet the needs of the stakeholders, as well as identifying new requirements and resolving any conflicts.[3] This process continues until all stakeholders agree with the user requirements and are prepared to approve them. In some cases, the user requirements may already be defined and documented by the customer.

The project manager/business analyst may employ a checklist as an aid to determine that the requirements process has been followed, and to verify that the user requirements have been fully specified, and that every requirement specified is necessary. The final version of the user requirements document is circulated to all participants for their final review and approval.

Once the user requirements have been approved by all stakeholders the work on the *system requirements* commences, and the business analyst expands the user requirements into more specific and detailed system requirements. Several workshops/reviews of the system requirement specification take place with the stakeholders, with the goal of ensuring that the system requirements are valid with respect to the user requirements, and that they meet stakeholders' needs and are fit for purpose. Finally, the stakeholders approve the system requirements specification.

Scenarios are useful in adding detail to the requirements, with each scenario covering a small number of possible interactions with the system. Use cases are often used to identify the actors involved in the interactions, and they provide a useful way to elicit the requirements from the stakeholders who interact directly with the system.

The ambiguity of natural language has led to interest in more precise notations to express requirements unambiguously. We mentioned the graphical unified modelling language (UML) [1], which has become popular in recent years. Its use case diagram is often used for requirements elicitation, with the use cases (Fig 18.2) describing the functional requirements of the system graphically. The use cases describe the scenarios (or sequences of actions) in the system from the user's viewpoint (actor). It shows how the actor interacts with the system, where an actor represents the set of roles that a user can play, and the actor may be human or an automated system. Use cases diagrams and various UML diagrams are discussed in Chap. 18.

Formal specification notations such as Z or VDM that are often employed in the safety critical or security critical fields. The advantage of these mathematical languages is that they are precise and amenable to proof, and mathematical analysis

---

[3] Conflicts are inevitable as stakeholders will have different needs, and so discussion and negotiation are required to resolve these conflicts and achieve consensus.

may be employed in a sense to debug[4] the requirements. This provides increased confidence in the correctness and validity of the requirements. However, these notations are perceived as being difficult to use by industrialists, and they are not widely employed in mainstream software engineering. Formal methods are discussed in more detail in Chap. 16.

5.2.2   Requirements Analysis

The requirements analysis activities are conducted as part of requirements elicitation, and the requirements are analysed to ensure that they are those that are required; that they are precisely and unambiguously stated; that they are complete and consistent; that they are categorized and prioritized; and that any conflicts between them are identified and resolved. There may be an initial feasibility study prior to the commencement of the project to ensure that the proposed system is technically feasible, and achievable within the defined budget and time constraints.

The resolution of any conflicts is through discussion and negotiations with the stakeholders. The requirements are generally prioritized to define the importance of each requirement, and several development models (e.g., the Rational Unified Process) implement the most important requirements first. Requirements analysis is an iterative process with feedback going back to the stakeholders in the requirements elicitation process.

The requirements workshops will verify that the system requirements are valid with respect to the user requirements, and technical workshops will need to be conducted to determine the appropriate approach to their implementation.

5.2.3   Requirements Verification and Validation

The difference between requirements validation and verification is illustrated by the phrase "*Building the right thing*" versus "*building it right*". In other words, *validation* is concerned with ensuring that the correct requirements are being implemented, whereas *verification* is concerned with ensuring that the defined requirements are being implemented correctly.

The stakeholders *validate* the requirements to ensure that they are the right set of requirements, and that their implementation will result in a system that is fit for purpose. It is essential to validate the requirements, as the cost of correction of a requirements defect increases the later that the defect is discovered. Therefore, it is essential to identify such defects as early as possible, as otherwise there may be major cost and time involved in its correction, especially if the defect is discovered late in the software development lifecycle.

---

[4] Essentially, the mathematical language provides the facility to prove that certain properties are true of the specification, and that certain undesirable properties are false in the specification.

The validation activities may involve checks that the requirements are complete, consistent, feasible, testable, and are fit for purpose. The validation may involve prototyping, several reviews (and updates) of the requirements (and prototype) by the stakeholders, until all stakeholders are ready to approve the requirements of the system.

The validation of the requirements will ensure that the requirements are complete and consistent, as well as reflecting the needs of the customer. The final validation step is the user acceptance testing, and this is performed by the customer to confirm that the completed system is fit for purpose and satisfies customer expectations. The lifecycle model employed determines the verification and validation activities to be conducted during the project, with models such as joint application development (JAD) and Agile involving a high-level of customer involvement throughout the lifecycle.

Requirements verification is concerned with ensuring that the system as built (from design, to implementation, to testing and deployment) properly implements the defined requirements. A traceability matrix (Table 5.4) shows how the requirements are implemented and tested, and it may be employed as part of requirements verification.

It shows how the user requirements have been addressed in the system requirements, and how they have been implemented in the design of the system, as well as showing how the test cases have verified that the implementation has implemented the requirements correctly.

5.2.4   Requirements Management

Requirements management is concerned with managing changes to the requirements, and in ensuring that the project maintains an up to date approved set of requirements throughout the project lifecycle. It is essential that the project deliverables are kept consistent with the latest version of the requirements, and that when the requirements document changes then all other project deliverables such as the design document, software modules and test specifications are kept consistent with the new version of the requirements.

It is an important area to get right as all project activities are planned from the approved set of requirements. Requirements management is concerned with managing changes to the requirements of the project, and in identifying inconsistencies between the requirements and the project plans and work products. Its focus is on the *activities for managing changes to the requirements*, as distinct from the activities in gathering and defining the requirements.

It is important that changes to the requirements are controlled, and that the impacts of the changes are fully understood prior to authorization. Once the system requirements have been approved, any proposed changes to the requirements are subject to formal change control. The project will set up a group that is responsible for authorizing changes to the requirements (usually called the *change control*

Table 5.3 Managing change requests

Activity	Change Request
Log change request	The change request is logged, and a unique reference number and priority assigned
Assess impact	The cost, schedule, technical and quality impacts are determined, and the risks identified
Decision	The CCB authorzes or rejects the change request
Implement solution	The affected project documents and software modules are identified and modified accordingly
Verify solution	Testing (Unit, System and UAT) are employed to verify the correctness of the solution
Close CR	The change request is closed

board (CCB)). The CCB is responsible for analysing requests to change the requirements, and it makes an informed decision on whether to accept or reject the change request based on its impacts and risks.

The need to change the requirements may be due to business or regulatory changes, or to a customer need becoming apparent at a late stage of the project when the project is nearing completion. A request to change the requirements is termed a *change request* (CR), and this is a stakeholder request for a change to the scope of the project, and it may arise at any time during the project. The impacts of the change request (e.g., technical, risks, cost, budget, and schedule) need to be carefully considered, as a change introduces new risks to the project, and may adversely affect cost, schedule, and quality.

Therefore, it is essential that the impacts of the change request be fully considered prior to its authorization. The change request is considered by the CCB, and an informed decision is made to authorize or reject the request. The activities involved in managing change requests are summarized in Table 5.3.

Following the approval of a change request the affected documents such as the system requirements, the design, and software modules are modified accordingly. This is done to ensure that all the project deliverables are kept consistent with the latest version of the requirements. Testing is carried out to verify that the changes have been implemented correctly.

5.2.5 Requirements Traceability

The objective of requirement traceability is to verify that all the defined requirements for the project have been implemented and tested. One way to do this is to consider each requirement number and to go through every part of the design document to find where the requirement is being implemented in the design, and similarly to go through the test documents and find any reference to the requirement number to show where it is being tested. This would demonstrate that the particular requirement number has been implemented and tested.

Table 5.4 Sample trace matrix	Requirement No.	Sections in design	Test cases in test plan
	Rl.l	D1.4, D1.5, D3.2	T1.2, T1.7
	R1.2	D1.8, D8.3	T1.4
	R1.3	D2.2	T1.3
	R1.50	D20.1, D30.4	T20.1, T24.2

A more effective mechanism to do this is to employ a traceability matrix, which may be employed to map the user requirements to the system requirements; the system requirements to the design; the design to the unit test cases; the system test cases; and the UAT test cases. That is, traceability is defined through the project lifecycle, and the matrix provides a crisp summary of how the requirements have been implemented and tested.

The traceability of the requirements is *bi-directional*, and the traceability matrix may be maintained as a separate document, or as part of the requirements document. The basic idea is that a mapping between the requirement numbers and sections of the design or test plan is defined, and this provides confidence that all the requirements have been implemented and tested.

Requirements will usually be numbered, and a single requirement number may map on to several sections of the design or to several test cases, i.e., the mapping is often *one to many*. The traceability matrix (Table 5.4) provides the mapping between individual requirement numbers, and the sections in the design or test plan corresponding to the requirement number.

It is essential to keep the traceability matrix up to date during the project, and especially after changes to the requirements. The traceability matrix is useful as a tool whenever there are changes to the requirements as it allows the impacts of the change on the other requirements (and other project deliverables) to be easily determined.

5.3 System Modelling

A model is an abstraction (simplification) of the physical world, and it acts as a representation of reality. The aim of the model is to capture the essential details of the real world, and as it is a simplification of the reality it does not include all aspects of the physical world. However, it is important that all the key aspects to be studied are included in the model, and to determine the adequacy of the model as a representation of the real world.

A model is considered suitable if its properties closely match those of the system being modelled. It is common to employ models in engineering: for example, in civil engineering it is normal to develop models of bridges and traffic flow prior to constructing a bridge. These models help in understanding the anticipated stresses on the bridge and play an important role in the design of a bridge that is safe to use. It is important that the models are an adequate representation of the reality, as otherwise there is the potential for serious consequences. For example, the model of the Tacoma Narrows Bridge did not include aerodynamic forces, and this proved to be a major factor in its subsequent collapse [2].

A good model will allow predictions of future behaviour to be made, and the adequacy of the model is determined from model exploration. This involves asking questions and determining the extent to which the model provides accurate answers to the questions. Inadequate models are replaced over time with better models that provide a better explanation of the reality. For example, the Ptolemaic cosmological model was replaced by the Copernican model, and Newtonian mechanics was replaced the theory of relativity when dealing with velocities that are close to the speed of light [3].

The adequacy of the model will determine its acceptability as a representation of the physical world. Models that are ineffective will be replaced with models that offer a better explanation of the manifested physical behaviour.

The principle of Occam's Razor[5] ('*principle of parsimony*') is a key principle employed in modelling [4]. It states that the number of entities employed to explain the reality should be kept to a minimum, with every entity used required for the explanation. Another words, the simplest model should be chosen with the least number of assumptions, and all superfluous concepts that are not required to explain the phenomena should be removed. This results in a crisp and simpler model.

System modelling is an abstraction of the existing and proposed system, and it helps in clarifying what the existing system does, and in communicating and clarifying requirements of the proposed system. The model is a simplification of the system, and it may be explored to identify strengths and weaknesses in the existing system. This leads to requirements for the new system.

Models of the new system may be used to communicate the proposed requirements to the other stakeholders, and more than one model (e.g., using several UML diagrams) may be employed to represent the system from several different viewpoints (e.g., environment, behaviour, structural, or behaviour). The use of the graphical UML diagrams to represent the software system is a useful type of system modelling.

Another important approach (used mainly in the safety and security critical field) is the use of mathematical models that provide abstract mathematical models of the proposed software system.

Model-driven engineering is concerned with the generation of the programs from the models, and the Rational/IBM tools allow programs to be generated from the UML diagrams.

---

[5] This principle is named after the medieval philosopher, William of Ockham.

5.4   Requirements Definition in the Agile World

Every aspect of Agile development such as requirements and design is continuously revisited during the development, and the direction of the project is regularly evaluated. Agile has a strong collaborative style of working, and ongoing changes to requirements are considered normal in the agile world. It argues that it is more realistic to change requirements regularly throughout the project, rather than attempting to define all the requirements at the start of the project (as in the waterfall methodology).

Agile includes controls to manage changes to the requirements, and good communication and early regular feedback is an essential part of the process. A user story may be a new feature or a modification to an existing feature. The feature is reduced to the minimum scope that can deliver business value, and a feature may give rise to several stories. Stories often build upon other stories and the entire software development lifecycle is employed for the implementation of each story. Stories are either done or not done (i.e., there is no such thing as 50% done), and the story is complete only when it passes its acceptance tests. Stories are prioritized based on several factors including the business value of story, mitigation of risk and dependencies on other stories.

The *product backlog* is maintained and prioritized by the product owner. It is a complete list of the functionality (user stories) to be added to the product. Once the iteration is complete the latest product increment is demonstrated to a review audience including the product owner. This is to receive feedback and to identify new requirements. The team also conducts a retrospective meeting to identify what went well and what went poorly during the iteration, as part of continuous improvement for future iterations.

5.5   Review Questions

1. What is the difference between a functional and non-functional requirement?
2. What is the difference between requirements verification and validation?
3. What is requirements engineering? How are requirements elicited from the customer?
4. Explain the difference between a user requirement and a system requirement?
5. How are changes to the requirements managed? Why is it important to keep project deliverables consistent with the requirements?
6. What is the purpose of requirements traceability?

7. Explain the advantages and disadvantages of specifying the system requirements in a natural language. Describe other approaches.
8. Explain the purpose of a model and how models may be used in requirements engineering.

5.6   Summary

The user requirements specify what the customer wants and define what the software system is required to do, as distinct from how this is to be done. The requirements are the foundation for the system, and so if they are incorrect then the implemented system will be incorrect. The process of determining the requirements, analysing and validating them and managing them throughout the project lifecycle is termed requirements engineering.

The user requirements are determined from discussions with the customer to determine their actual needs, and they are then refined into the system requirements, which state the functional and non-functional requirements of the system. The requirements must be precise and unambiguous to ensure that all stakeholders are clear on what is (and what is not) to be delivered.

Prototyping may be employed to assist in the definition of the requirements. Requirements verification is concerned with ensuring that the requirements are properly implemented, and it is concerned with ensuring that the requirements are properly addressed in the design and implementation. A traceability matrix and testing are often employed as part of the verification activities.

Requirements validation is concerned with ensuring that the right requirements are defined, and that they are complete, consistent, and reflect the actual needs of the customer. The validation of the requirements is done by the stakeholders, and it involves several reviews of the requirements (and prototype), reviews of the design, and user acceptance testing.

Requirements management is concerned with managing changes to the requirements, and in ensuring that the project maintains an up to date approved set of requirements throughout the project lifecycle. It ensures that the project deliverables are kept consistent with the latest version of the requirements, and when the requirements document changes then all other project deliverables need to be kept consistent with the new version of the requirements.

The objective of requirement traceability is to verify that all the defined requirements for the project have been implemented and tested. The traceability matrix provides a crisp summary of how the requirements have been implemented and tested, and it provides a bi-directional mapping of the requirements to the design and test cases.

References

1. I.J.G. Booch, J. Rumbaugh, *The Unified Software Modelling Language User Guide* (Addison-Wesley, 1999)
2. G. O'Regan, *A Practical Approach to Software Quality* (Springer Verlag, New York, 2002)
3. T. Kuhn, *The Structure of Scientific Revolutions* (University of Chicago Press, 1970)
4. M.M. An Airchinnigh, *Conceptual Models and Computing*. PhD Thesis. Department of Computer Science, University of Dublin, Trinity College, Dublin, 1990

Software Design and Development

6

Abstract

This chapter discusses design and development, and software design is the blueprint of the solution to be developed. It is concerned with the high-level architecture of the system, as well as the detailed design that describes the algorithms and functionality of the individual programs. The detailed design is then implemented in a programming language such as C++ or Java. We discuss software development topics such as software reuse, customized-off-the-shelf software (COTS), and open-source software development.

Keywords

Architectural design · Detailed design · Function-oriented design · Object-oriented design · Object-oriented development · User-interface design · Open-source development · Customized off the shelf software (COTS) · Software reuse · Software maintenance and evolution

6.1 Introduction

The user requirements specify what the customer wants and define *what* the software system is required to do, as distinct from *how* this is to be done. The user requirements are determined from discussions with the stakeholders to determine their actual needs, and they are then refined into the system requirements, which state the functional and non-functional requirements of the system.

The software design of the system is a blueprint of the solution of the system to be developed. It is concerned with the high-level architecture of the system, as well as the detailed design that describes the algorithms and functionality of the

© Springer Nature Switzerland AG 2022
G. O'Regan, *Concise Guide to Software Engineering*,
Undergraduate Topics in Computer Science,
https://doi.org/10.1007/978-3-031-07816-3_6

individual programs. The detailed design is then implemented in a programming language such as C++ or Java.

Software design is a creative process that is concerned with how the system will be organized and implemented. It consists of the high-level system architecture and the low-level detailed design. The system architecture may include hardware such as personal computers and servers, as well as the definition of the subsystems with the various software modules and their interfaces. The choice of the architecture of the system is a key design decision, as it affects the performance and maintainability of the system.

The architecture is often modelled with block diagrams that give a high-level picture of the system structure, where each diagram represents a sub-system (or component) with arrows indicating the flow of data or control. The architecture facilitates discussion of the system design, as well as recording the design decisions. Architecture in the small is concerned with the architecture of individual programs, whereas architecture in the large is concerned with the architecture of large complex systems that may include other systems.

The system architecture is analogous to the architecture of a building, and it describes how the system is organized as a set of communicating structures (or sub-systems). It presents the high-level design of the system, and there may be several views of the architecture (e.g., Kruchten's 4+1 model), which describe the system from different viewpoints (e.g., end-users and managers). The views (e.g., logical, development, process and physical) may be presented using various UML diagrams (e.g., class, activity, and state diagrams).

The choice of the architectural design will determine the extent to which key non-functional requirements such as performance, reliability and availability are satisfied. Further, the architecture of the system is costly and difficult to modify, and so it is essential that the right architecture be chosen first time (issues such as scalability may also need to be considered). Detailed (Low-level) design is concerned with the specification of the design of the modules or individual programs.

The software development is concerned with the actual implementation of the design, and it is implemented is in some programming language such as C++ or Java. The software may be developed internally, or it may be outsourced to another company; existing open-source software may be employed or modified accordingly; or a solution may be purchased off-the-shelf (COTS). It is essential that the design is valid with respect to the requirements, and that the implemented system is valid with respect to the design.

6.2   Architecture Design

The design of the system consists of engineering activities to describe the *architecture model or structure of the system* that will satisfy the functional and non-functional requirements, as well as the *design of the individual programs* to describe the algorithms and functionality required to implement the system requirements.

The design is concerned with how the system will be organized, and the architecture design is often presented as a set of interacting components. The design activities include architecture design, interface design, component design, algorithm design, and data structure design. There are often several possible design solutions for a particular system, and the designer will need to choose the most appropriate design of the system.

The architectural model of the system is an abstract visual representation of the structure of the system, and it is often presented as a set of boxes or block diagrams. It shows the major components of the system (i.e., the subsystems) and their interactions, and each box represents a component with the architecture showing all of the components and their connections. A box within a box represents a sub-component, and arrows are used to represent the flow of data between the components. This abstract description of the system provides a high-level view of the system and is an effective way to facilitate discussion about the system design with the relevant stakeholders.

There is often a need to present multiple views of the system architecture such as how the system is decomposed into modules, how the run-time processes interact, how the hardware is distributed across the processors in the system. These views may include Krutchen's 4+1 model (Table 6.1) [1].

The process view may be described by data-flow diagrams (part of the SSADM method), which show the flow of data through a system. UML is a popular design method that gives several views of the architecture of the system.

The interface design defines the interfaces between the system components, and this allows a component to be used without knowing how it is implemented. Once the interface designs have been specified the components may be designed and developed concurrently. The component design defines how each component will operate, and the database design defines the data structures that are required. It is essential to validate the design with respect to the system requirements, and to ensure that the architecture will satisfy the functional and non-functional requirements.

Table. 6.1 Views of system architecture

View	Description
Logical	This view shows the key abstractions in the system as objects or object classes
Process view	This view shows how the system is composed of interacting processes at run-time
Development view	This view shows how the software is decomposed into modules/components for development
Physical view	This view shows the system hardware and how the software components are distributed across the processors in the system

Fig. 6.1 C.A.R Hoare.
(Public domain)

Architectural design patterns are popular and date back to the mid-1990s. These act as a reusable solution that may be used in many situations. There are many examples of *design patterns* such as the client server pattern which includes servers and clients with services delivered from the servers.

The views of C.A.R. Hoare (Fig. 6.1) on software design are interesting. He states that there are two ways of constructing a software design.

> One way is to make it so simple that there are obviously no deficiencies.
> The other way is to make it so complex that there are no obvious deficiencies.

He argues that the first method is far more difficult to achieve, and that it requires skill and insight. The starting point in design is always the problem domain, and it is essential that the problem to be solved be understood from several different viewpoints. Several potential solutions may then be identified, and each potential solution is evaluated. This leads to the chosen solution that may, for example, be the simplest and least costly.

Design is an iterative process, and the goal is to describe the system architecture that will satisfy the functional and non-functional requirements. It involves describing the system at several different levels of abstraction, with the designer starting off with an informal picture of the design that is then refined by adding more information.

Parnas's ideas on architecture and design have been quite influential, and he recognized that the structure of a software system matters and getting the structure right is important. His 1972 paper *"On the criteria to be used in decomposing systems into modules"* [2] is a classic in software engineering. He introduced the revolutionary *information hiding* principle, which allows software to be *designed in a way to deal with change* (Fig. 6.2).

A module is characterized by its knowledge of a design decision (*secret*) that it hides from all other modules. Every information-hiding module has an *interface* that provides the only means to access the services provided by the modules. *The interface hides the module's implementation.* Information hiding is a fundamental

Fig. 6.2 David Parnas

principle that is used in object-oriented programming, and Parnas argues in his 1972 paper that:

> It is almost always incorrect to begin the decomposition of a system into modules on the basis of a flowchart. We propose instead that one begins with a list of difficult design decisions or design decisions which are likely to change. Each module is then designed to hide such a decision from the others

The design may be specified in various ways such as graphical notations that display the relationships between the various components making up the design. The notation may include block diagrams, flow charts, or various UML diagrams such as sequence diagrams, state charts, and so on.

The design of programs may employ pseudo code to specify the algorithms, as well as the data structures that are the basis for implementation. Natural language is often used to express information that cannot be expressed formally, but it is essential that the natural language description is precise and unambiguous. The design activities include:

- Architecture design of system (with all sub-systems)
- Abstract specification of each sub-system
- Interface design (for each subsystem)
- Component design
- Data structure design
- Algorithm design.

The quality of the software architecture directly impacts the robustness, performance, and maintainability of the system. The software architecture needs to manage the inherent complexity of the system, and it must be sufficiently robust to ensure that the system performance is within the bounds specified in the non-functional requirements, with safety, security, availability, and maintainability requirements properly addressed.

There is a need to understand the relationship between the software to be designed and its external environment. This may involve using UML to develop models such as a system context model that shows the other systems in its environment, and an interaction model that shows the interaction between the system and its environment.

6.3 Low-Level Design and Development

The design of the system consists of engineering activities to describe the components of the system, as well as the algorithms and functions required to implement the system requirements. Design and development are concerned with developing an executable software system.

Function-oriented design involves starting with a high-level view of the system and refining it into a more detailed design. The system state is centralized and shared between the functions operating on that state. Functional design has been overtaken by object-oriented design, and so it is mainly of historic interest today.

Object-oriented design (OOD) is popular, and it is based on the concept of information hiding developed by Parnas. The system is viewed as a collection of *objects* rather than functions, with each object managing its own state information. The system state is decentralized, and an object is a member of an object class. The definition of a *class* includes *attributes* and *operations* on class members, and these may be inherited from super classes. Objects communicate by exchanging *messages*, and messages are the only way to access an object. The internal details of the object are kept private.

Software design and development are closely linked, and often proceed in parallel. Software design is the creative process that identifies the software components and their relationships, whereas software development is concerned with the implementation of the design in some programming language. The choice of language reflects the problem domain, and it may be an object-oriented language such as C++ or Java, or a procedural language such as C or FORTRAN. It is important that the software code is subject to a peer review to ensure that it is of high quality, and that it is a valid implementation of the requirements and design. The coding standards for the language need to be followed, as this helps with the maintainability of the code.

Software reuse has become important during software development. Its advantages are that it improves software productivity, and potentially provides higher quality software. Customized off-the-shelf software (COTS) provides specific functionality that may be purchased and tailored for use in the software development. It may be possible to buy the entire system off-the-shelf, and so one of the earliest design decisions is whether *to buy* or *build* the application.

Open-source software development has become popular, and the idea is that the source code is not proprietary but is freely available (under an open-source license) for software developers to use and modify as they wish. It offers a way to speed up software development, as well as potentially providing a high-quality cost-effective solution.

6.3.1 Function-Oriented Design

Function-oriented design is one of the older design methodologies, and it involves starting with a high-level view of the system and refining it into a more detailed design. The system is a set of modules with clearly defined behaviour, and which interact with each other in a defined manner to produce some system behaviour.

Function-oriented design views the software design as a set of functions that share state, and the functions transform the inputs to the desired outputs. The system state is centralized and shared between the functions operating on the state, and at the end of the phase all the major modules (as well as their interactions) and all the main data structures of the system have been defined.

The system design (top level design) first determines which modules are needed for the system, and the low-level design expands on the system design and is focused on the internal design and specification of the modules. The detailed design is concerned with how the modules are interconnected and implemented.

The functional design is a refinement of the architectural design in that the architectural design has identified the key components, and the functional design then in a sense then determines the module structure for each component (the modules created need to be consistent with the architecture). Functional design is mainly of historic interest, as it has been overtaken by object-oriented design.

6.3.2 Object-Oriented Design

Object-oriented design (OOD) is a design method that models the system as a set of cooperating objects (rather than as a set of functions), and where the individual objects are viewed as instances of a class. Object-oriented design is concerned with the object-oriented decomposition of the system, and it involves defining the required objects and their interactions to solve the problem. The system state is decentralized with each object managing its own state information. The objects have a collection of attributes that define their state, and operations that act on the state. The data in the object is hidden, and the only access to the data is with the operations.

The difference between a class and an object may be seen from the example that walls and windows are classes, whereas individual doors and windows are objects. A class is a set of objects (rather than an individual object), and all members of the class share the same attributes, operations, and relationships. A class may represent a software thing or a hardware thing.

A class may inherit its behaviour from one or more super-classes, with the class definition setting out the differences between the class and its super-classes. The communication between objects is done by exchanging messages (in practice, an object calls a procedure associated with another object).

An object is a "black box" that sends and receives *messages*. A black box consists of *code* (computer instructions) and *data* (information which these instructions operate on). The traditional way of programming kept code and data separate. For example, functions and data structures in the C programming language are not connected. However, in the object-oriented world code and data are merged into a single indivisible thing called an *object*.

The reason that an object is called a black box is that the user of an object never needs to look inside the box, since all communication to it is done via messages. Messages define the *interface* to the object. Everything an object can do is represented by its message interface. Therefore, there is no need to know anything about what is in the black box (or object) to use it. The access to an object is only through its messages, while keeping the internal details private. This is called *information hiding* and is due to work by Parnas in the early 1970s.

The main features of the object-oriented paradigm are described in Table 6.2.

The architectural design shows the major components of the system and their interactions. The UML diagrams help in identifying the objects and operations in the system, and the various UML models (e.g., sequence diagrams and state diagrams) show the relationships between the objects. UML may be used to develop an

Table 6.2 Object-oriented paradigm

Feature	Description
Class	A class defines the abstract characteristics of a thing, including its attributes (or properties), and its behaviours (or methods). The members of a class are termed objects
Object	An object is a particular instance of a class with its own set of attributes. The set of values of the attributes of a particular object is called its state
Method	The methods associated with a class represent the behaviours of the objects in the class
Message passing	Message passing is the process by which an object sends data to another object or asks the other object to invoke a method
Inheritance	A class may have sub-classes (or children classes) that are more specialized versions of the class. A subclass inherits the attributes and methods of the parent class. This allows the programmer to create new classes from existing classes. The derived classes inherit the methods and data structures of the parent class
Encapsulation (Information Hiding)	One fundamental principle of the object-oriented world is encapsulation (or information hiding). The internals of an object are kept private to the object and may not be accessed from outside the object. That is, encapsulation hides the details of how a particular class works, and it requires a clearly specified interface around the services provided
Abstraction	Abstraction simplifies complexity by modelling classes and removing all un-necessary detail. All essential detail is represented, and non-essential information is ignored
Polymorphism	Polymorphism is behaviour that varies depending on the class in which the behaviour is invoked. Two or more classes may react differently to the same message. The same name is given to methods in different subclasses: i.e., one interface, and multiple methods

interaction model that shows the interaction between the system and its environment. The various UML diagrams are described in more detail in Chap. 18.

Design patterns (best practice of solutions to common problems that may be reused) are often employed in object-oriented design.

6.3.3   User-Interface Design

User interface design is concerned with the design of the user interface for machines and software. The user interface is the boundary between the user and the system, and the usability of the system (as well as the user experience) will be determined by the quality of the user interface design. The user interface needs to consider the knowledge and experience of the user, and the user interactions with the system should be as simple and efficient as possible.

User interface design requires a good understanding of user needs, as well as how the user will interact with the system. It may involve prototyping of the interface, and usability testing of the prototypes to judge its fitness for use. There are usability standards (e.g., ISO 9241 and ISO 16982:2002) that provide guidance on usability.

Today's graphical user interfaces (GUI) have become ubiquitous for applications on personal computers, and a GUI is characterized by:

- Multiple windows on the screen
- Use of icon to represent information
- Command selection via menus
- Use of a mouse.

The advantages of GUIs are that they are easy to learn and use, with users with limited computing experience able to learn the user interface quite quickly.

6.3.4   Open-Source Development

Open-source development is a modern approach to software development in which the source code is published, and thousands of volunteer software developers from around the world participate in developing and improving the software. The idea is that the source code is not proprietary, and that it is freely available for software developers to use and modify as they wish. One useful benefit is that it may potentially speed up development time thereby shortening time to market.

The roots of open-source development are in the Free Software Foundation (FSF). This is a non-profit organization founded by Richard Stallman [3] to promote the free software movement, and it has developed a legal framework for the free software movement.

The Linux operating system is a well-known open-source product, and other products include mySQL, Firefox and Apache HTTP server. The quality of software produced by the open-source movement is generally good, and defects are generally identified and fixed faster than with proprietary software development.

A company needs to decide whether the product to be developed should use an open-source approach, as well as determining the risks and benefits associated with this approach. It is essential that there are no security or quality risks associated with the software. The type of open-source license required needs to be identified and obtained.

6.3.5 Customized-off-the-Shelf Software

Customized-off-the-shelf software (COTS) is software (or a system) that is ready made, and may be purchased off-the-shelf, and adapted to the user's requirements. A COTS product typically needs to be configured for the specific use required, and the tailoring is within the parameters of the commercial software, and so custom development is usually not required.

The use of COTS components may shorten the time to market and help to reduce software development costs, as the components may be purchased from a third-party vendor rather than developed internally. Further, there is greater confidence in the quality and reliability of the COTS software (compared to custom built software), as its reliability has already been shown through its use with other organizations.

The disadvantages of COTS are that it could lead to dependency on a particular vendor, or the risk that the COTS product could become obsolete with the vendor no longer supporting it. Further, there may also be security risks if the COTS software contains security vulnerabilities (this is even more serious if the COTS software is integrated with other software products to create larger systems). For this reason, the product development strategy needs to be clearly thought through, with all risks carefully considered.

6.3.6 Software Reuse

Software reuse is the systematic reuse of existing software technology to build software. It involves the reuse of software deliverables produced during the software development lifecycle (e.g., designs, code, and test suites), and its successful implementation may shorten the time to market, as well as reducing software costs and improving software quality and productivity.

The successful introduction of reuse in an organization requires an infrastructure to support reuse. It is a lot more than creating a repository of software assets, where software engineers add software items to the depository, with the hope that other software engineers will use the contents of the repository.[1]

---

[1] I recall Parnas making a joke many years ago that we have developed all this reusable software that nobody reuses.

The reuse process involves activities to manage the reuse infrastructure and establishing the reuse goals and the roles involved. It includes activities to create reusable assets which involves understanding the domain in which the software will be used, and designing the software for use in multiple products, as well as identifying, collecting, and representing the required software assets.

Finally, it involves activities to classify and retrieve the assets in the reuse library, and activities to search and retrieve the required software assets from the library.

6.3.7   Design Patterns

A design pattern is a design problem that has been solved by others in the past and its solution may be reused to speed up the software development process. It is an abstract description of best practice that has worked successfully in different systems and environments, and it acts as a reusable solution that may be used in many situations. It is more a description or template on how to solve the problem within a particular context, rather than a finished solution. There are many examples of design patterns (e.g., the client server pattern includes servers and clients with services delivered from the servers).

6.3.8   Object-Oriented Programming

Object-oriented programming has become popular in large-scale software development, and it became the dominant paradigm in programming from the early 1990s. Its proponents argue that it is easier to learn, and simpler to develop and maintain such programs, and its growth in popularity was helped by the rise in popularity of Graphical User Interfaces (GUI), which are well suited to object-oriented programming. The C++ programming language has become popular, and it is an object-oriented extension of the C programming language.

The traditional view of programming is that a program is a collection of functions, or a list of instructions to be performed on the computer. *Object-oriented programming* is a paradigm shift in programming, where a computer program is viewed as a collection of objects that act on each other. Each object may send and receive messages and process data. That is, each object may be viewed as an independent entity or actor with a distinct role or responsibility.

The origins of object-oriented programming go back to the invention of Simula 67 at the Norwegian Computing Research Centre[2] in the late 1960s. It introduced the notion of a class and instances of a class.[3] Simula 67 influenced later languages such as the Smalltalk object-oriented language developed at Xerox PARC in the mid-1970s.

---

[2] The inventors of Simula-67 were Ole-Johan Dahl and Kristen Nygaard.

[3] Dahl and Nygaard were working on ship simulations and were attempting to address the huge number of combinations of different attributes from different types of ships. Their insight was to group the different types of ships into different classes of objects, with each class of objects being responsible for defining its own data and behaviour.

Xerox introduced the term '*Object-oriented programming*' for the use of objects and messages as the basis for computation. Most modern programming languages support object-oriented programming, and object-oriented features have been added to many existing languages such as BASIC, FORTRAN and Ada.

C++ and Java

Bjarne Stroustrup developed the C++ programming language in 1983 as an object-oriented extension of the C programming language. It was designed to use the power of object-oriented programming, and to maintain the speed and portability of C. It provides a significant extension of C's capabilities, but it does not force the programmer to use the object-oriented features of the language.

A key difference between C++ and C is the concept of a class. A *class* is an extension to the C concept of a structure. The main difference is that while a C data structure can hold only data, a C++ class may hold both data and functions. An *object* is an instantiation of a class: i.e., the class is essentially the type, whereas the object is essentially a variable of that type. Classes are defined in C++ by using the keyword class.

Java is an object-oriented programming language developed by James Gosling and others at Sun Microsystems in the early 1990s. C and C++ influenced the syntax of the language, and the language was designed with portability in mind. The objective is for a program to be written once and executed anywhere. Platform independence is achieved by compiling the Java code into Java bytecode, which are simplified machine instructions specific to the Java platform.

This code is then run on a Java Virtual Machine (JVM) that interprets and executes the Java bytecode. The JVM is specific to the native code on the host hardware. The problem with interpreting bytecode is that it is slow compared to traditional compilation. However, Java has a few techniques to address this including just in time compilation and dynamic recompilation. Java also provides automatic garbage collection. This is a very useful feature as it protects programmers who forget to deallocate memory (thereby causing memory leaks).

The reader is referred to [4] for a more detailed explanation of the design and development activities.

6.4 Software Maintenance and Evolution

Software maintenance is the process of changing a system after it has been delivered to the customer, and it involves correcting any defects that are present in the software and enhancing the system to meet the evolving needs of the customer. The defects may be due to coding, design, or requirements errors, with coding defects the cheapest to fix and requirements defects the most expensive to correct. The resolution to the defects involves identifying the affected software components and modifying them and verifying that the solution is correct and that no new problems have been introduced.

Software systems often have a long lifetime (e.g., some systems have a lifetime of 20–30 years), and so the software needs to be continuously enhanced over its lifetime to meet the evolving needs of the customer. Software evolution is concerned with the continued development and maintenance of the software after its initial release, with new releases of the software prepared each year. Each new release includes new functionality and corrections to the known defects.

6.5   Software Design and Development in the Agile World

Pair programming is an agile technique where two programmers work together at one computer. The author of the code is termed the *driver*, and the other programmer is termed the *observer* (or *navigator*) and is responsible for reviewing each line of written code. The observer also considers the strategic direction of the coding and proposes improvement suggestions and potential problems that may need to be ad-dressed. The driver can focus on the implementation of the current task and use the observer as a safety net. The two programmers switch roles regularly during the development of the new functionality.

Pair programming requires more programming effort to develop code compared to programmers working individually. However, the resulting code is of higher quality, with fewer defects and a reduction in the cost of maintenance. Further, pair programming enables a better design solution to be created as more design alternatives are considered.

This is since two programmers are bringing different experiences to the problem, and they may have different ways of solving the problem. This leads them to explore a larger number of ways of solving the problem than an individual programmer. Finally, pair programming is good for knowledge sharing and learning, and it allows knowledge to be shared on programming practice and design and al-lows knowledge about the system to be shared throughout the team.

Refactoring is employed in Agile as a design and coding practice. The objective is to change how the software is written without changing what it does. Re-factoring is a tool for evolutionary design where the design is regularly evaluated, and improvements are implemented as they are identified. It helps in improving the maintainability and readability of the code and in reducing complexity. The auto-mated test suite is essential in demonstrating that the integrity of the software is maintained following refactoring.

Continuous integration allows the system to be built with every change. Early and regular integration allows early feedback to be provided, and it also al-lows all the automated tests to be run thereby identifying problems earlier.

6.6   Review Questions

1. What is the difference between requirements and design?
2. Explain the difference between architectural design and detailed design.
3. Explain the difference between functional oriented design and object-oriented design.
4. What are the advantages and disadvantages of COTS software?
5. What is object-oriented programming?
6. What is software reuse and how is it accomplished?
7. Explain the differences between COTS, software reuse, and open source software.
8. Explain the difference between software maintenance and evolution.

6.7   Summary

The success of business is highly influenced by software, and companies may develop their own software internally, or they may acquire software solutions off-the-shelf or from bespoke software development.

The user requirements specify what the customer wants and define *what* the software system is required to do, as distinct from *how* this is to be done. The requirements are the foundation for the system, and it is essential that they are correct and reflect the needs of the customer.

The software design of the system is a blueprint of the system to be developed. It is concerned with the high-level architecture of the system, as well as the detailed design that describes the algorithms and functionality of the individual programs. Software design is a creative process that is concerned with how the system will be organized and implemented.

The system architecture may include hardware such as computers and servers, as well as the definition of the subsystems with the various software modules and their interfaces. The choice of the architecture of the system is a key design decision, as it affects the performance and maintainability of the system.

The detailed software design of the system is concerned with activities to describe the algorithms and functions required to implement the system requirements. It may include hardware as well as the various software modules and their interfaces. Design and development are concerned with developing an executable software system.

The software development is concerned with the actual implementation of the design in some programming language such as C++ or Java. The software may be developed internally, or it may be outsourced to another company, or a solution may be purchased off-the-shelf. It is essential that the design is valid with respect to the requirements, and that the implemented system is valid with respect to the design.

References

1. P. Kruchten, Architectural blueprints—The "4+1" view model of software architecture. IEEE Softw. **12**(6), 42–50 (1995)
2. D. Parnas, On the criteria to be used in decomposing systems into modules. Commun. ACM **15** (12) (1972)
3. G. O'Regan, *Giants of Computing* (Springer, 2013)
4. I. Sommerville, *Software Engineering*, 9th edn. (Pearson, 2011)

Software Inspections

7

Abstract

This chapter discusses software inspections, which play an important role in building quality into a product. The well-known Fagan inspection process that was developed at IBM in the 1970s is discussed, as well as lighter review and walkthrough methodologies.

Keywords

Informal review · Structured walkthrough · Fagan inspection · Gilb inspections · Economic benefits of inspections · Inspection guides · Entry and exit criteria · Automated software inspections

7.1 Introduction

The objective of software inspections is to build quality into the software product, rather than adding quality later. There is clear evidence that the cost of correction of a defect increases the later that it is detected, and it is therefore more cost effective to build quality in rather than adding it later in the development cycle. Software inspections are an effective way of doing this.

There are several approaches to software inspections, and these vary in the formality of the process. An informal review consists of a walkthrough of the document or code by an individual other than the author. The meeting usually takes place at the author's desk (or in a meeting room), and the reviewer and author discuss the document or code informally.

There are formal software inspection methodologies such as the well-known *Fagan inspection* methodology [1] and the Gilb methodology [2]. These methodologies include pre-inspection activity, an inspection meeting, and post-inspection

© Springer Nature Switzerland AG 2022   117
G. O'Regan, *Concise Guide to Software Engineering*,
Undergraduate Topics in Computer Science,
https://doi.org/10.1007/978-3-031-07816-3_7

activity. Several inspection roles are typically employed, including an *author* role, an *inspector* role, a *tester* role, and a *moderator* role.

The Fagan inspection methodology was developed by Michael Fagan (Fig. 7.1) at IBM in the mid-1970s, and Tom Gilb developed Gilb's approach in the early 1990s. The formality of the software inspection methodology employed is influenced by the impacts of software failure on the customer's business, as a failure may have a major negative impact on the customer. For example, an incorrect one-line change to telecommunications software could lead to failure resulting in a major telecommunications outage, and significant disruption to customers.

Further, there may be financial impacts, as the service level agreement details the service level that will be provided, and the compensation given for service disruption. Consequently, a telecommunications company needs to ensure that its software is fit for purpose, and a formal software inspection process tends to be employed to ensure that quality is built in. This means that requirement documents, high-level and detailed design documents, and software code are all inspected, and generally inspections are explicitly planned in the project schedule.

Another words, an organization needs to define an inspection process that is appropriate to its business, and it may adopt a rigorous approach such as the Fagan or Gilb methodology, or a less formal process where the impact of failure is less severe. It may not be possible to have all the participants present in a room, and participation by conference call or video link may need to be employed. A formal process may not suit some organizations, and a structured walkthrough may be the adopted approach.

Software inspections play an important role in building quality into the software, and in ensuring that the quality of the delivered product is good. The quality of the delivered software product is only as good as the quality at the end each phase, and therefore a phase should be exited only when the desired quality has been achieved.

The effectiveness of an inspection is influenced by the expertise of the inspectors, adequate preparation, the speed of the inspection, and compliance to the inspection process. The inspection methodology provides guidelines on the inspection and preparation rates for an inspection, and guidelines on the entry and exit criteria for an inspection.

Fig. 7.1 Michael Fagan

There are typically at least two roles in the inspection methodology. These include the *author* role and the *inspector* role. The *moderator, tester*, and the *reader* roles may also be present in the methodology.

The next section describes the benefits of software inspections, and this is followed by a discussion of a simple review methodology where the reviewers send comments directly to the author. Then, a structured walkthrough and a semi-formal review process are described, and finally the Fagan inspection process is described in detail.

7.2 Economic Benefits of Software Inspections

There is clear evidence that a software inspection program provides a return on investment, and has tangible benefits in terms of quality, productivity, time to market, and customer satisfaction. For example, IBM Houston employed software inspections for the Space Shuttle missions: 85% of the defects were found by inspections and 15% were found by testing. There were no defects found on the space missions, and about 2 million lines of computer software were inspected. IBM, North Harbour in the UK quoted a 9% increase in productivity with 93% of defects found by software inspections.

Software inspections are useful for educating new employees on the product, and on the standards and procedures used in the organization. They ensure that knowledge is shared among the employees, rather than understood by just one individual. Inspections improve software productivity, as less time is spent in correcting defective software.

The cost of correction of a defect increases the later that it is identified in the lifecycle. Boehm [3] states that the *cost of correction of a requirements defect identified in the field is over 40 times more expensive than if it were detected at the requirements phase*, and so it is most economical to detect and fix the defect in phase. The cost of correction of a requirements defect identified at the customer site includes the cost of correcting the requirements, the cost of design, coding, unit testing, system testing, and regression testing. It may be necessary to send an engineer on site to fix the problem, and there may be hidden costs in the negative perception of the company with a subsequent loss of sales.

There is a powerful argument to identify defects as early as possible, and software inspections are a cost-effective way of doing this. There are various estimates of the *cost of poor quality* (COPQ) in an organization (Fig. 10.28), and some estimates suggest that it could be as high as 20–40% of sales. The exact calculation may be determined by a time sheet accountancy system, which details the cost of internal and external failure, and the cost of appraisal and prevention.

The return on investment from the introduction of software inspections may be calculated, and the evidence is that it leads to reductions in the cost of poor quality. Inspections provide a cost-effective way of improving quality and productivity.

Table 7.1 Informal review

Step	Description
1.	The author circulates the deliverable (either physically or electronically) to the review audience
2.	The author advises the review audience of the due date for comments
3.	The due date for comments is typically one week or longer
4.	The author checks that all comments have been received by the due date
5.	The author contacts any reviewers who have not provided feedback, and requests comments
6.	The author analyses all comments received and implements the appropriate changes
7.	The deliverable is circulated to the review audience for sign-off
8.	The reviewers sign off (with any final comments) indicating that the document has been correctly amended by the author
9.	The author/project leader stores the comments received

7.3   Informal Reviews

This type of review involves reviewers sending comments directly to the author (e.g., email or written), and there is no actual review meeting. It is not as effective as the Fagan inspection process, but it helps in identifying some defects in the work products.

The author is responsible for making sure that the review happens, and advises the participants that comments are due by a certain date. The author analyses the comments received, makes the required changes, and circulates the document for approval. The activities are described in Table 7.1.

Comment:

The informal review process may help to improve quality in an organization. It is dependent on the participants adequately reviewing the deliverable and sending comments to the author. The author can only request the reviewer to send comments. There is no independent monitoring of the author to ensure that the review happens and is effective, and that comments are requested, received, and implemented.

7.4   Structured Walkthrough

A structured walkthrough is a peer review in which the author of a deliverable (e.g., a project document or actual code) brings one or more reviewers through the deliverable. The objective is to get feedback from the reviewers on the quality of the document or code, and to familiarize the review audience with the author's work. The walkthrough includes several roles namely the *review leader* (usually the author), the *author*, the *scribe* (may be the author) and the *review audience* (Table 7.2).

Table 7.2 Structured walkthroughs

Step	Description
1.	The author circulates the deliverable (either physically or electronically) to the review audience
2.	The author schedules a meeting with the reviewers
3.	The reviewers familiarize themselves with the deliverable
4.	The review leader (usually the author) chairs the meeting
5.	The author brings the review audience through the deliverable, explaining what each section is aiming to achieve, and requesting comments from them as to its correctness
6.	The scribe (usually the author) records errors, decisions, and any action items
7.	A meeting outcome is agreed, and the author addresses all agreed items. If the meeting outcome is that a second review should be held then go to step 1
8.	The deliverable is circulated to reviewers for signoff and the reviewers sign off (with any final comments) indicating that the deliverable has been correctly amended by the author
9.	The author/project leader stores the comments and sign-offs

7.5 Semi-formal Review Meeting

A semi-formal review (a simplified version of the Fagan inspection) is a moderated review meeting chaired by the review leader. The author selects the reviewers and appoints a review leader (who may be the author). The review leader chairs the meeting and verifies that the follow-up activity has been completed. The author distributes the deliverable to be reviewed and provides a brief overview as appropriate. The material in this section is adapted from O'Hara [4].

The review leader schedules the review meeting with the reviewers (with possible participation via a conference call). The review leader chairs the meeting and is responsible for keeping the meeting focused and running smoothly, resolving any conflicts, recording actions, and completing the review form.

The review leader checks that all participants, including conference call participants are present, and that all have done adequate preparation. Each reviewer is invited to give general comments, as this will determine whether the deliverable is ready to be reviewed, and whether the review should take place. Participants who are unable to attend are required to send their comments to the review leader prior to the review, and the review leader will present these comments at the meeting.

The material is typically reviewed page per page for a document review, and each reviewer is invited to comment on the current page. Code reviews may focus on coding standards, or on both coding standards and on finding defects in the software code. The issues noted during the review are recorded, and these may include items requiring further investigation.

The review outcome is decided at the end of the review (i.e., whether the deliverable needs a second review). The author then carries out the necessary corrections and investigation, and the review leader verifies that the follow up activities have been completed. The document is then circulated to the review audience for sign-off.

Comment:

The semi-formal review process works well for an organization when the review leader is not the author. This ensures that the review is conducted effectively, and that the follow up activity takes place. It may work with the author acting as review leader provided the author has received the right training on software inspections and follows the review process.

The process for semi-formal reviews is summarized in Table 7.3. Figure 7.2 presents a template to record the issues identified during the review.

Table 7.3 Activities for semi-formal review meeting

Phase	Review task	Roles
Planning	Ensure document/code is ready to be reviewed Appoint *review leader* (may be author) Select reviewers with appropriate knowledge/experience and assign roles	Author Leader
Distribution	Distribute document/code and other material to reviewers (at least 3 days before the meeting) Schedule the meeting	Author Leader
Optional meeting	Give overview of deliverable to be reviewed Allow reviewers to ask any questions	Author Reviewers
Preparation	Read through document/code, marking up issues/questions Mark minor issues on their copy of the document/code	Reviewers
Review meeting	Review Leaders chairs the meeting Explains purpose of the review and how it will proceed Set time limit for meeting Keep review meeting focused and moving Review document page by page Code reviews may focus on standards/defects Resolve any conflicts or defer as investigates Note comments/shortcomings on review form **Raise issues**—(*Do not fix them*) Present comments/suggestions/questions Pass review documents/code with marked up minor issues directly to the author Respond to any questions or issues raised Propose outcome of review meeting Complete review summary form/return to Author Keep a record of the review form	Leader Reviewers
Post review	Investigate and resolve any issues/shortcomings identified at review Verify that the author has made the required corrections	Author Leader

Date _____ Deliverable _____ Version No. _____ #Reviews _____
Author _____Review Leader _____
Reviewers_____
Page/Line No.   Description   Action

Unresolved Issued / Investigates
Issue   **Reason unresolved**   **Verified.**

Review Outcome (Tick)
No changes required □   Verification by Review Leader only □   Full review required □
Review incomplete □

Review Summary (Optional)
#Major Defects_____ # Minor Defects _____ Estimated Rework time _____
Hours Preparation _____ #Hours Review _____ Amount Reviewed _____

Fig. 7.2 Template for semi-formal review

7.6   Fagan Inspections

The Fagan methodology (Table 7.4) is a well-known software inspection methodology. It is a seven-step process that includes planning, overview, preparation, an inspection meeting, process improvement, re-work, and follow-up activities. Its objectives are to identify and remove errors in the work products, and to identify any systemic defects in the processes used to create the work products.

The Fagan inspection process stipulates that requirement documents, design documents, source code and test plans all be formally inspected by experts independent of the author, and the inspection is conducted from different viewpoints such as requirements, design, test, etc.

Table 7.4 Overview Fagan inspection process

Activity	Role/Responsibility	Objective
Planning	Moderator	Identify inspectors and roles Verify material is ready for inspection Distribute inspection material Book a room for the inspection
Overview (Optional)	Author	Brief participants on material Give background information
Preparation	Inspectors	Prepare for the meeting and role Checklist may be employed Read through the deliverable and mark up issues/questions
Inspection meeting	Moderator/Inspectors	The moderator will cancel the inspection if inadequate preparation is done Time limit set for inspection Moderator keeps meeting focused The inspectors perform their roles Emphasis on finding defects not solutions Defects are recorded and classified Author responds to any questions The duration of the meeting.is recorded An inspection outcome is agreed
Process improvement	Inspectors	Continuous improvement of development and inspection process The causes of major defects are recorded Root cause analysis to identify any systemic defect with development or inspection process Recommendations are made to the process improvement team
Rework	Author	The author corrects the defects and carries out any necessary investigations
Follow up	Moderator/Author	The moderator verifies that the author has resolved the defects and investigations

There are various roles defined in the inspection process, including the moderator, who chairs the inspection; the reader, who paraphrases the deliverable; the author, who is the creator of the deliverable; and the tester, who is concerned with the testing viewpoint. The inspection process will also consider whether the design is correct with respect to the requirements, and whether the source code is correct with respect to the design.

The goal is to identify as many defects as possible, and to confirm the correctness of a particular deliverable. Inspection data are recorded and may be used to determine the effectiveness of the organization in detecting and preventing defects.

The moderator records the defects identified during the inspection, and the defects are classified according to their type and severity. The defect data may be entered into an inspection database to enable analysis to be performed, and metrics to be generated. The severity of the defect is recorded, and the major defects are classified (e.g., according to the Fagan defect classification or some other scheme such as the *orthogonal defect classification* (ODC)).

The next section describes the Fagan inspection guidelines, which include recommendations on the time to spend on the various inspection activities. An organization may need to tailor the Fagan inspection process to suit its needs, and the tailored guidelines need evidence to confirm that they are effective.

7.6.1 Fagan Inspection Guidelines

The Fagan inspection guidelines are based on studies by Michael Fagan, and they provide recommendations on the time to spend on the various inspection activities. It is important that sufficient time is spent on the various inspection activities, and that the speed of the inspection is appropriate. We present the strict Fagan guidelines as defined by the Fagan methodology (Table 7.5), and more relaxed guidelines that have been shown to be effective in the telecommunications field (Table 7.6).

The effort involved in adherence to the strict Fagan guidelines is substantial, and this led to the development of tailored guidelines. The tailoring of any methodology

Table 7.5 Strict Fagan inspection guidelines

Activity	Area	Amount/Hr	Max/Hr
Preparation time	Requirements	4 pages	6 pages
	Design	4 pages	6 pages
	Code	100 LOC	125 LOC
	Test plans	4 pages	6 pages
Inspection time	Requirements	4 pages	6 pages
	Design	4 pages	6 pages
	Code	100 LOC	125 LOC
	Test plans	4 pages	6 pages

Table 7.6 Tailored (Relaxed) Fagan inspection guidelines

Activity	Area	Amount/Hr	Max/Hr
Preparation time	Requirements	10–15 pages	30 pages
	Design	10–15 pages	30 pages
	Code	300 LOC	500 LOC
	Test Plans	10–15 pages	30 pages
Inspection time	Requirements	10–15 pages	30 pages
	Design	10–15 pages	30 pages
	Code	300 LOC	500 LOC
	Test Plans	10–15 pages	30 pages

requires care, and the effectiveness of the tailored process needs to be demonstrated by empirical evidence. (e.g., as a pilot prior to its deployment as well as quantitative data to show that the inspection is effective, and results in a low number of escaped customer defects).

It is important to comply with the guidelines once they are deployed in the organization, and trained moderators and inspectors will ensure awareness and compliance. Audits may be employed to verify compliance.

The tailored guidelines are presented in Table 7.6.

7.6.2 Inspectors and Roles

There are four inspector roles identified in a Fagan Inspection and these include (Table 7.7).

7.6.3 Inspection Entry Criteria

There are explicit entry and exit criteria defined for the various types of inspections. These criteria need to be satisfied to ensure that the inspection is effective. The entry criteria (Table 7.8) for the various inspections are:

Table 7.7 Inspector roles

Role	Responsibilities
Moderator	Manages the inspection process and ensures compliance to the process Plans the inspection and chairs the meeting Keeps the meeting focused and resolves any conflicts Keeps to the inspection guidelines Verifies that the deliverables are ready to be inspected Verifies that the inspectors have done adequate preparation Records the defects on the inspection sheet Verifies that the agreed follow-up work has been completed Skilled in the inspection process and appropriately trained Skilful, diplomatic, and occasionally forceful
Reader	Paraphrases the deliverable and gives an independent view of it Actively participates in the inspection
Author	Creator of the work product being inspected Has an interest in finding all defects present in the deliverable Ensures that the work product is ready to be inspected Gives an overview to inspectors (if required) Participates actively during inspection and answers all questions Resolves all identified defects and carries out any required investigation
Tester	Role is focused on how the product would be tested Role often employed in requirements inspection / test plan inspection The tester participates actively in the inspection

Table 7.8 Fagan entry criteria

Inspection type	Entry criteria	Roles
Requirements	Inspector(s) with sufficient expertise available Preparation done by inspectors Correct requirements template used	Moderator/Inspectors
Design inspection	Requirements inspected and signed off Correct design template used to produce design Inspector(s) have sufficient domain knowledge Preparation done by inspectors	Moderator/Inspectors
Code inspection	Requirements/Design inspected and signed off Overview provided Preparation done by inspectors Code Listing available Clean compile of source code Coding standards satisfied Inspector(s) have sufficient domain knowledge	Moderator/Inspectors
Test plan inspection	Requirements/Design inspected and signed off Preparation done by inspectors Inspector(s) have sufficient domain knowledge Correct Test Plan template employed	Moderator/Inspectors

7.6.4 Preparation

Preparation is a key part of the inspection process, as the inspection will be ineffective if the inspectors are insufficiently prepared. The moderator is required to cancel the inspection if any of the inspectors has been unable to do appropriate preparation.

7.6.5 The Inspection Meeting

The inspection meeting (Table 7.9) consists of a formal meeting between the author and at least one inspector. It is concerned with finding defects in the deliverable and verifying the correctness of the inspected material. The effectiveness of the inspection is influenced by

- The expertise and experience of the inspector(s),
- Preparation done by inspector(s),
- The speed of the inspection.

These factors are quite clear since an inexperienced inspector will lack the appropriate domain knowledge to understand the material in depth. Second, an inspector who has inadequately prepared will be unable to make a substantial contribution during the inspection. Third, the inspection is ineffective if it tries to cover too much material in a short space of time. The moderator will complete the inspection form (Fig. 7.3) to record the results from the inspection.

Table 7.9 Inspection meeting

Inspection type	Purpose	Procedure
Requirements	Find requirements defects Confirm requirements correct	Inspectors review each page of requirements and raise questions or concerns. Defects recorded by Moderator
Design	Find defects in design Confirm correct (with respect to requirements)	Inspectors review each page of design (compare to requirements) and raise questions or concerns. Defects recorded by Moderator
Code	Find defects in the code Confirm correct (with respect to design/reqs)	Inspectors review the code and compare to requirements/design and raise questions or concerns. Defects recorded by Moderator
Test	Find defects in test cases/test plan Confirm test cases can verify design/requirements	Inspectors review each page of test plan/specification, compare to requirements/design and raise questions or concerns. Defects recorded by moderator

Inspection Type _____   Deliverable _____   Project _____
Date _____   Amount Inspected _____   Version No. ____
Author_____   Moderator_____   No. of Reviews _____
Inspectors _____
#Hours Preparation _____ # Hours Inspection _____ #Hours Rework _____
Summary of Findings: # Majors _____ # Minors _____ # PIs _____ # INVs ____
 ODC Summary (Majors): #CHK __ #ASS___ #ALG___ #TIM___ # INT__ #FUN____ # DOC___ # BLD___

No.   Page/Line No.   Severity   Type   Description

Top 3 Root Causes of Major Defects / Process Improvement Actions
1.
2.
3.

Review Outcome
No changes ☐   Verification by Moderator ☐   Full Review ☐ Review Incomplete ☐
Defects per KLOC _____   Defects per page _____   Verification of Rework _____
Date Verified _____   Inspection Data in Database ____

Fig. 7.3 Template for Fagan inspection

The final part of the inspection is concerned with process improvement. The inspector(s) and author examine the major defects, identify the root causes of the defect, and determine corrective action to address any systemic defects in the software process. The moderator is responsible for completing the inspection summary form and the defect log form, and for entering the inspection data into the inspection database. The moderator will give any process improvement suggestions directly to the process improvement team.

7.6.6   Inspection Exit Criteria

The exit criteria (Table 7.10) for the various inspections are:

7.6.7   Issue Severity

The severity of an issue identified in the Fagan inspection may be classified as major, minor, a process improvement item, or an item requiring further investigation. It is classified as *major* if its non-detection would lead to a defect report being raised later in the development cycle, whereas a defect report would generally not be raised for a *minor* issue. An issue classified as an investigate item requires further study, and an issue classified as process improvement is used to improve the software development process (Table 7.11).

7.6.8   Defect Type

There are several defect-type classification schemes employed in software inspections. These include the Fagan inspection defect classification (Table 7.12) and the Orthogonal Defect Classification scheme (Table 7.13).

Table 7.10   Fagan exit criteria

Inspection type	Exit criteria
Requirements	Requirements satisfy the customer's needs All requirements defects are corrected
Design	Design satisfies the requirements All identified defects are corrected Design satisfies the design standards
Code	Code satisfies the design and requirements Code satisfies coding standards and compiles cleanly All identified defects corrected
Test	Test plan sufficient to test the requirements/design Test plan follows test standards All identified defects corrected

Table 7.11 Issue severity

Issue severity	Definition
Major (M)	A defect in the work product that would lead to a customer reported problem if undetected
Minor (m)	A minor issue in the work product
Process Improvement (PI)	A process improvement suggestion based on analysis of major defects
Investigate (INV)	An item to be investigated

Table 7.12 Classification of defects in Fagan inspections

Code inspection	Type	Design inspections	Type	Requirements inspections	Type
Logic (code)	LO	Usability	UY	Product objectives	PO
Design	DE	Requirements	RQ	Documentation	DS
Requirements	RQ	Logic	LO	Hardware interface	HI
Maintainable interface	MN IF	Systems interface	IS	Competition analysis	CO
Data usage	DA	Portability	PY	Function	FU
Performance	PE	Reliability	RY	Software Interface	SI
Standards	ST	Maintainability	MN	Performance	PE
Code	CC	Error handling	EH	Reliability	RL
Comments		Other	OT	Spelling	GS

Table 7.13 Classification of ODC defect types

Defect type	Code	Definition
Checking	CHK	Omission or incorrect validation of parameters or data in conditional statements
Assignment	ASN	Value incorrectly assigned or not assigned at all
Algorithm	ALG	Efficiency or correctness issue in algorithm
Timing	TIM	Timing/serialization error between modules, shared resources
Interface	INT	Interface error (error in communications between modules, operating system, etc.)
Function	FUN	Omission of significant functionality
Documentation	DOC	Error in user guides, installation guides or code comments
Build/Merge	BLD	Error in build process/library system or version control
Miscellaneous	MIS	None of the above

The Orthogonal Defect Classification (ODC) scheme was developed at IBM [5], and a defect is classified according to three (orthogonal) viewpoints. Thee *defect trigger* is the catalyst that led the defect to manifest itself; the *defect type* indicates the change required for correction; and the *defect impact* indicates the impact of the defect at the phase in which it was identified. The ODC classification yields a rich pool of information about the defect, but effort is required to record this information. The defect type classification is described in Table 7.13.

The defect impact provides a mechanism to relate the impact of the software defect to customer satisfaction. The impact of a defect identified pre-release is viewed as the impact of it being detected by an end-user, and for a customer-reported defect its impact is the actual information reported by the customer.

The inspection data is typically recorded in an inspection database, which allows analysis to be performed on the most common types of defects, and the preparation of action plans to minimize reoccurrence (Fig. 7.4). The frequency of defects per category is identified, and causal analysis is employed to identify preventive actions. Often, the most problematic areas are targeted first (as identified in a pareto chart), and an investigation into the category is conducted. The action plans will identify actions to be carried out to improve the existing processes.

The ODC classification scheme may be used to give early warning on the quality and reliability of the software, as its use leads to an expected profile of defects for the various lifecycle phases. The actual profile may then be compared to the expected profile, and the presence of significant differences between these may indicate risks to quality.

For example, if the actual defect profile at the system test phase resembles the defect profile of the unit-testing phase, then it is likely that there are quality problems. This is clear since the unit-testing phase is expected to yield a certain

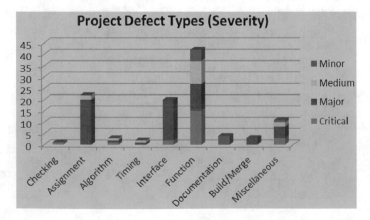

Fig. 7.4 Sample-defect types in a project (ODC)

pool of defects, with system testing receiving higher-quality software with the defects found during unit testing corrected. Consequently, ODC may be applied to make a judgement of product quality and performance (Fig. 7.3).

The inspection data will enable the *phase containment effectiveness* (PCE) metric to be determined (Fig. 10.19) and to determine if the software is ready for release to the customer.

7.7   Automated Software Inspections

Static code analysis is the analysis of software code without executing the code, and is usually performed with automated tools. The sophistication of the tool determines the actual analysis done, with some tools analysing individual statements or declarations, whereas others may analyse the whole source code. The objective of the analysis is to highlight potential coding errors early in the software development lifecycle.

These automated software inspection tools provide quality assessment reports on the extent to which the coding standards are satisfied. Many integrated development environments (IDEs) provide basic functionality for automated code reviews. These include Microsoft Visual Studio and Eclipse.

The LDRA Testbed Tool automatically determines the complexity of the source code, and it provides metrics that give an indication of the maintainability of the code. A useful feature of the LDRA tool is that it gives a visual picture of system complexity, and it has a re-factoring tool to assist with reducing complexity. It automatically generates code assessment reports listing all the files examined, and provides metrics on the clarity, maintainability, and testability of the code.

Compliance to coding standards is important in producing readable code and in preventing error prone coding styles. There are tools available to check conformance to coding standards including the LDRA TB vision tool, which has reporting capabilities to show code quality as well as fault detection and avoidance measures. It includes functionality to allow users to view the results presented intuitively in various graphs and reports. A selection of LDRA tools is presented in Chap. 21.

7.8   Review Questions

1. What are software inspections?
2. Explain the difference between informal reviews, structured walkthroughs, semi-formal reviews and formal inspections.
3. What are the benefits of software inspections?
4. Describe the seven steps in the Fagan Inspection process.
5. What is the purpose of entry and exit criteria in software inspections?

6. What factors influence the effectiveness of a software inspection?
7. Describe the roles involved in a Fagan inspection.
8. Describe the benefits of automated inspections.

7.9 Summary

The objective of software inspections is to build quality into the software product, and there is clear evidence that the cost of correction of a defect increases the later in the software development cycle in which it is detected. Consequently, there is an economic argument to employing software inspections, as it is more cost effective to build quality in rather than adding it later in the development cycle.

There are several approaches to software inspections, and these vary in the level of formality employed. A simple approach consists of a walkthrough of the document or code by an individual other than the author. The meeting is informal and usually takes place at the author's desk or in a meeting room, and the reviewer and author discuss the document or code informally.

There are formal software inspection methodologies such as the well-known *Fagan inspection* methodology. This approach includes pre-inspection activity, an inspection meeting, and post-inspection activity. Several inspection roles are typically employed, including an *author* role, an *inspector* role, a *tester* role, and a *moderator* role.

An organization will need to devise an inspection process that is suitable for its needs. The level of formality is influenced by its business, its culture, and the potential impact of a software defect on its customers. It may not be possible to have all the participants present in a room, and participation by conference call may be employed.

Software inspections play an important role in building quality into each phase, and in ensuring that the quality of the delivered product is good. The quality of the delivered software product is only as good as the quality at the end each phase, and therefore a phase should be exited only when the desired quality has been achieved.

The effectiveness of an inspection is influenced by the expertise of the inspectors, adequate preparation, and speed of the inspection, and compliance to the inspection process. The inspection methodology provides guidelines on the inspection and preparation rates for an inspection, and guidelines on the entry and exit criteria for an inspection.

References

1. M. Fagan, Design and code inspections to reduce errors in software development. IBM Syst. J. **15**(3) (1976)
2. T. Gilb, D. Graham, *Software Inspections* (Addison Wesley, 1994)
3. B. Boehm, *Software Engineering Economics* (Prentice Hall, New Jersey, 1981)
4. F. O'Hara, *Peer Reviews—The Key to Cost Effective Quality* (European SEPG, Amsterdam, 1998)
5. I. Bhandari, A case study of software process improvement during development. IEEE Trans. Softw. Eng. **19**(12) (1993)

Software Testing

8

Abstract

This chapter is concerned with software testing and discusses the various types of testing that may be carried out during the project. We discuss test planning, test case definition, test environment set-up, test execution, test tracking, test metrics, test reporting, and testing in an e-commerce environment.

Keywords

Tool planning · Test case design · Unit testing · System testing · Performance testing · E-commerce testing · Acceptance Testing · White box testing · Black box testing · Test tools · Test Environment · Test Reporting

8.1 Introduction

Testing plays a key role in verifying the correctness of software and confirming that the requirements have been correctly implemented. It is a constructive and destructive activity in that while on the one hand it aims to verify the correctness of the software, on the other hand it aims to find as many defects as possible in the software. The majority of defects (e.g., 80%) may be detected by software inspections in a mature software organization, with the remainder detected by the various types of testing carried out during the project.

Software testing provides confidence that the product is ready for release to potential customers, and the recommendation of the testing department is crucial in the decision as to whether the software product should be released or not. The test manager highlights any risks associated with the product, and these are considered prior to its release. The test manager and test department can be influential in an organization by providing strategic advice on product quality, and in encouraging

© Springer Nature Switzerland AG 2022
G. O'Regan, *Concise Guide to Software Engineering*,
Undergraduate Topics in Computer Science,
https://doi.org/10.1007/978-3-031-07816-3_8

organization change to improve the quality of the software product using best practice in software engineering.

The testers need a detailed understanding of the software requirements to enable them to develop appropriate test cases to verify the correctness of the software. Test planning commences at the early stages of the project, and testers play a role in building quality into the software product as well as verifying its correctness. The testers generally participate in the review of the requirements, and the testing viewpoint is important during the review to ensure that the requirements are correct and are testable.

The test plan for the project is documented (this could be part of the project plan or a separate document), and it includes the personnel involved, the resources and effort required, the definition of the testing environment to enable effective testing to take place, any special hardware and test tools required, and the planned schedule. There is a separate test specification plan for the various types of testing, and it records the test cases, including the purpose of the test case, the inputs and expected outputs, and the test procedure for the test case.

Various types of testing are performed during the project, including unit, integration, system, regression, performance, and user acceptance testing. The software developers perform the unit testing, and the objective is to verify the correctness of a module. This type of testing is termed "*white box*" testing and is based on knowledge of the internals of the software module. White box testing typically involves checking that every path in a module has been tested, and it involves defining and executing test cases to ensure code and branch coverage. The objective of "*black box*" testing is to verify the functionality of a module (or feature or the complete system itself), and knowledge of the internals of the software module is not required.

Test reporting is an important part of the project, and it ensures that all project participants understand the current quality of the software, as well as understanding what needs to be done to ensure that the product achieves the required quality criteria. The test status is reported regularly during the project, and once the tester discovers a defect, a problem report is opened, and the problem is analysed and corrected by the software developers. The problem may indicate a genuine defect, a misunderstanding by the tester, or a request for an enhancement.

An *independent test group* is generally more effective than a test group that is directly reporting to the development manager. The independence of the test group helps to ensure that quality is not compromised when the project is under pressure to make its committed delivery dates. A good test group will play a proactive role in quality improvement, and this may involve participation in the analysis of the defects identified during testing phase at the end of the project, with the goal of prevention or minimization of the reoccurrence of the defects.

Real world issues such as the late delivery of the software from the developers often complicate the software testing. Software development is challenging and deadline-driven and missed developer deadlines may lead to compression of the testing schedule, as the project manager may wish to stay with the original schedule. There are risks associated with shortening the test cycle, as the testers may be unable to complete the planned test activities. This means that insufficient data is available to make an informed judgement as to whether the software is ready for release, leading to risks that a defect-laden product may be shipped to the customer.

Test departments may be understaffed, as management may consider additional testers to be expensive and may wish to minimize costs. The test manager needs to be assertive in presenting the test status of the project, stating the known quality and risks, and the recommendation of the test manager needs to be carefully considered by the project manager and other stakeholders.

8.2   Test Process

The quality of the testing is dependent on the maturity of the test process, and a good test process will include test planning, test case analysis and design, test execution and test reporting. A simplified test process is sketched in Fig. 8.1, and the test process will include:

- Test planning and risk management.
- Dedicated test environment and test tools.
- Test case definition.
- Test automation.
- Test execution.
- Formality in handover to test department.
- Test result analysis.
- Test reporting.
- Measurements of test effectiveness.
- Lessons learned and test process improvement.

Test planning consists of a documented plan defining the scope of testing and the various types of testing to be performed, the definition of the test environment, the required hardware or software for the test environment, the estimation of effort and resources for the various activities, risk management, the deliverables to be produced, the key test milestones, and the test schedule.

The test plan is reviewed to ensure its fitness for purpose, and to obtain commitment to the plan, as well as ensuring that all involved understand and agree to their responsibilities. The test plan may be revised in a controlled manner during the project. It is described in more detail in Sect. 7.3.

The test environment varies according to the type of business and project requirements. Large organizations may employ dedicated test laboratories, whereas a single workstation may be sufficient in a small organization. A dedicated test environment may require significant capital investment, but it will pay for itself in reducing the cost of poor quality, by identifying defects, and verifying that the software is fit for purpose.

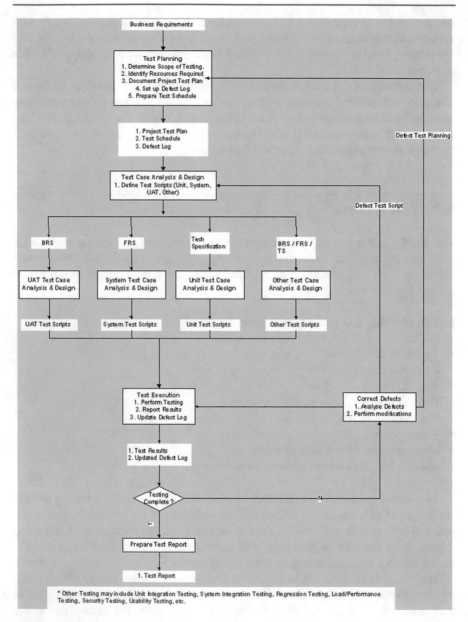

Fig. 8.1 Simplified test process

The test environment includes the hardware and software needed to verify the correctness of the software. It is defined early in the project so that any required hardware or software may be ordered in time. It may include simulation tools, automated regression, and performance test tools, as well as tools for defect reporting and tracking.

The software developers produce a software build under configuration management control, and the build is verified for integrity to ensure that testing may commence. There is generally a formal or informal handover of the software to the test department, and a formal handover includes criteria that must be satisfied for the handover to take place. The test department must be ready for testing with the test cases and test environment prepared.

The various types of testing employed to verify the correctness of the software are described in Table 8.1. They may include.

The effectiveness of the testing is dependent on the definition of good test cases, which need to be complete in the sense that their successful execution will provide confidence in the correctness of the software. Hence, the test cases must relate or cover the software requirements, and we discussed the concept of a traceability

Table 8.1 Types of testing

Test type	Description
Unit testing	This testing is performed by the software developers, and it verifies the correctness of the software modules
Component testing	This testing is used to verify the correctness of software components, to ensure that the component is correct and may be reused
System testing	This testing is (usually) carried out by an independent test group to verify the correctness of the complete system
Performance testing	This testing is (usually) carried out by an independent test group to ensure that the performance of the system is within the defined parameters. It may require tools to simulate clients and heavy loads, and precise measurements of performance are made
Load/stress testing	This testing is used to verify that the system performance is within the defined limits for heavy system loads over long or short periods of time
Browser compatibility	This testing is specific to web-based applications and verifies that the web site functions correctly with the supported browsers
Usability testing	This testing verifies that the software is easy to use, and that the look and feel of the application is good
Security testing	This testing verifies that the confidentiality, integrity, and availability requirements are satisfied
Regression testing	This testing verifies that the core functionality is preserved following changes or corrections to the software. Test automation may be employed to increase its productivity and efficiency
Test simulation	This testing simulates part of the system where the real system currently does not exist, or where the real live situation is hard to replicate
Acceptance testing	This testing carried out by the customer to verify that the software matches the customer's expectations prior to acceptance

matrix (that maps the requirements to the design and test cases) in Chap. 5 (Table 5.4). The traceability matrix provides confidence that each requirement has a corresponding test case for verification. The test cases will be of the form:

- Purpose of the test case.
- Set-up required to execute the test case.
- Inputs to the test case.
- The test procedure.
- Expected outputs or results.

The test execution will follow the procedure defined in the test cases, and the tester will compare the actual results obtained with the expected results. The test completion status will be passed, failed, or blocked (if unable to run at this time). The test results summary will indicate which test cases could be executed, which passed, which failed and which test cases could not be executed.

The tester documents the test results including detailed information on the passed and failed tests. This will assist the software developers in identifying the precise causes of failure and the appropriate corrective actions. The developers and tester will agree to open a defect report in the defect tracking system to track the successful correction of the defect.

The test status (Fig. 8.2) consists of the number of tests planned, the number of test cases run, the number that have passed, and the number of failed and blocked tests. The test status is reported regularly to management during the testing cycle. The test status and test results are analysed, and extra resources provided where necessary to ensure that the product is of high quality with all defects corrected prior to the acceptance of the product.

Test tools and test automation are used to support the test process, and lead to improvements in quality, reduced cycle time, and productivity. Tool selection needs to be performed in a controlled manner, and it is best to identify the requirements for the tool first, and then to examine a selection of tools to determine which best meets the requirements. Tools may be applied to test management and reporting, test results management, defect management, and to the various types of testing.

Fig. 8.2 Sample test status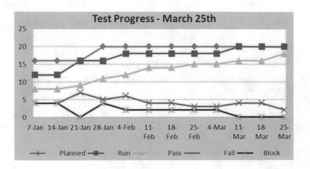

A good test process will maintain measurements to determine its effectiveness, and an end of testing review is conducted at the end of testing to identify any lessons that need to be learned for continual improvement. The test metrics employed will answer questions such as:

- What is the current quality of the software?
- How stable is the product?
- Is the product ready to be released at this time?
- What are the key risks and are they all managed?
- How good was the quality of the software that was handed over?
- How does the product quality compare to other products?
- How effective was the testing performed on the software?
- How many open problems are there and how serious are they?
- How much testing remains to be done?

8.3 Test Planning

Testing is a sub-project of a project and needs to be managed as such, and so good project planning and monitoring and control is required. The IEEE 829 standard includes a template for test planning, and test planning involves defining the scope of the testing to be performed; defining the test environment; estimating the effort required to define the test cases and to perform the testing; identifying the resources needed (including people, hardware, software, and tools); assigning the resources to the tasks; defining the schedule; and identifying any risks to the testing and managing them.

The monitoring and control of the testing involves tracking progress and taking corrective action; re-planning as appropriate where the scope of the testing has changed; providing test reports to give visibility of the test status to the project team (including the number of tests planned, executed, passed, blocked and failed); re-testing corrections to the failed or blocked test cases; taking corrective action to ensure quality and schedule are achieved; managing risks; and providing a final test report with a recommendation to go to acceptance testing. Test management involves:

- Identify the scope of testing to be done.
- Determine types of testing to be performed.
- Estimates of time, resources, people, hardware, software and tools.
- Determine how test progress and results will be communicated.
- Define how test defects will be logged and reported.
- Provide resources needed.
- Definition of test environment.
- Assignment of people to tasks.
- Define the schedule.

Table 8.2 Simple test schedule

Activity	Resource name (s)	Start date	End/re-plan date	Comments
Review requirements	Test Team	15.02.2017	16.02.2017	Complete
Project test plan and review	J.DiNatale	15.02.2017	28.02.2017	Complete
System test plan/review	P.Cuitino	01.03.2017	22.03.2017	Complete
Performance test plan/review	L.Padilla	15.03.2017	31.03.2017	Complete
Regression plan/review	P.Cuitino	01.03.2017	15.03.2017	Complete
Set up test environment	P.Cuitino	15.03.2017	31.03.2017	Complete
System testing	P.Cuitino	01.04.2017	31.05.2017	In progress
Performance testing	L.Padilla	15.04.2017	07.05.2017	In progress
Regression testing	L.Padilla	07.05.2017	31.05.2017	In progress
Test reporting	J.DiNatale	01.04.2017	31.05.2017	In progress

- Identify and manage risks.
- Track progress and take corrective action.
- Provide regular test status of passed, blocked, failed tests.
- Re-plan if scope of the project changes.
- Conduct post-mortem to learn any lessons.

Table 8.2 presents a simple test schedule for a small project, and the test manager will often employ Microsoft Project (or a similar scheduling tool) for planning and tracking of larger projects (e.g., Fig. 4.2). The activities in the test schedule are tracked and updated accordingly to record the tasks that have been completed, and dates are re-scheduled as appropriate. Testing is a key sub-project of the main project, and the project manager will track the key test milestones and will maintain close contact with the test manager.

It is prudent to consider risk management early in test planning, and to identify risks that could potentially arise during the testing, and to estimate the probability of occurrence of the risk and its impact should it occur, and to identify (as far as is practical) actions to mitigate the risk or a contingency plan to address the risk if it materializes.

8.4   Test Case Design and Definition

Several types of testing that may be performed during the project were described in Table 8.1, and there is often a separate test plan for Unit, System and UAT testing. The unit tests are based on the software design; the system tests are based on the system requirements, and the UAT tests are based on the business (or user) requirements.

Each of these test plans contains test scripts (e.g., the Unit Test Plan contains the Unit Test scripts and so on), and the test scripts are traceable to the design (for the Unit Tests), and for the system requirements (for the System Test scripts). The unit tests are more focused on white box testing whereas the system test and UAT tests are focused on black box testing.

Each test script contains the objective of the test script and the procedure by which the test is carried out. Each test script includes:

- Test Case ID
- Test Type (e.g., Unit, System, UAT)
- Objective/Description
- Test Script Steps
- Expected Results
- Actual Results
- Tested By

Regression testing involves carrying out a subset of the defined tests to verify that the core functionality of the software remains in place following changes to the system.

8.5 Test Execution

The software developers will carry out the unit and integration testing as part of the normal software development activities. The developers will correct any identified defects, and the development continues until all unit and integration tests pass, and the software is fit to be released to the test group.

The test group will usually be *independent* (i.e., it has an independent reporting channel), and it will usually perform the system testing, performance testing, usability testing, and so on. There is usually a formal handover from development to the test group prior to the commencement of testing, and the handover criteria needs to be satisfied for the software to be accepted for testing by the test group.

The handover criteria will generally require that all unit and integration tests have been run and passed, that all known risks have been identified, that the test environment is ready for independent testing, and that the system, performance and all other relevant test scripts are available, and that all required resources required for testing are available.

Test execution then commences, and the testers run the system tests and other tests, log any defects in the defect-tracking tool, and communicate progress to the test manager. The test status is communicated to the project team, and the developers correct the identified defects, and produce new releases. The test group retests the failed and blocked tests and performs regression testing to ensure that the core functionality remains in place. This continues until the quality goals for the project have been achieved.

8.6   Test Reporting and Project Sign-Off

The test manager will report progress regularly during the project. The report provides the status of testing for the project and includes:

- Quality Status (including tests run, passed, and blocked).
- Risks and issues.
- Status of Test Schedule.
- Deliverables planned (next period).

The test manager discusses the test status with management and highlights the key risks and issues to be dealt with. The test manager may require management support to deal with these.

The test status is important in judging whether the software is ready to be released to the customer. Various quality metrics may be employed to measure the quality of the software, and the key risks and issues are considered. The test manager will make a recommendation to release or not based on the actual test status. One useful metric (one of many) is the cumulative arrival rate (Fig. 8.3) that gives an indication of the stability of the product.

The slope of the curve is initially steep as testing commences and defects are detected. As testing continues and defects are corrected and retested, the slope of the curve levels off, and over time the indications are that the software has stabilized, and is potentially ready to be released to the customer.

However, it is important not to rush to conclusions based on an individual measurement. For example, the above chart could possibly indicate that testing halted on May 13th with no testing since then, and that would explain why the defect arrival rate per week is zero. Careful investigation and analysis must be done before the interpretation of a measurement is made, and usually several measurements rather than one are employed to make a sound decision.

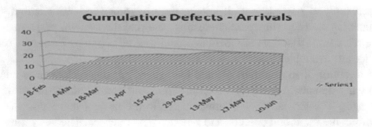

Fig. 8.3 Cumulative defects

8.7   Testing and Quality Improvement

Testing is an essential part of the software development process, and the recommendation of the test manager is carefully considered in the decision to release the software product. Decision-making is based on objective facts, and measurements are employed to assess the quality of the software. The open-problem status (Figs. 10.16 and 10.17), the problem arrival rate (Fig. 10.18) and the cumulative problem arrival rate (Fig. 8.3) give an indication of the quality and stability of the software and may be used in conjunction with other measures to decide on whether it is appropriate to release the software, or whether further testing should be performed.

Test defects are valuable in the sense that they provide the organization the opportunity to improve its software development process to prevent the defects from reoccurring in the future. A mature development organization will perform internal reviews of requirements, design, and code prior to testing. The effectiveness of the internal review process and the test process may be seen in the phase containment metric (PCE), which is discussed in Chap. 10.

Figure 10.19 indicates that the project had a phase containment effectiveness of approximately 54%. That is, the developers identified 54% of the defects, the system-testing phase identified approximately 23% of the defects, acceptance testing identified approximately 14% of the defects, and the customer identified approximately 9% of the defects. Many organizations set goals with respect to the phase containment effectiveness of their software. For example, a mature organization might aim for their software development department to have a phase containment effectiveness goal of 80%. This means that 80% of the defects should be found by software inspections.

The improvement trends in phase containment effectiveness may be tracked over time. There is no point in setting a goal for a particular group or area unless there is a clear mechanism to achieve the goal. Thus, to achieve a goal of 80% phase containment effectiveness the organization will need to implement a formal software inspection methodology as described in Chap. 6. Training on inspections will be required, and the effectiveness of software inspections monitored and improved.

A mature organization will aim to have 0% of defects reported by the customer, and this goal requires improvements in its software inspection methodology and its software testing methodology. Measurements provide a way to verify that the improvements have been successful. Each defect is potentially valuable as it, in effect, enables the organization to identify weaknesses in the software process and to target improvements.

Escaped customer defects offer an opportunity to improve the testing process, as it indicates a weakness in the test process. The defects are categorized, causal analysis is performed, and corrective actions are identified to improve the testing process. This helps to prevent a reoccurrence of the defects. Thus, software testing plays an important role in quality improvement.

8.8   Traceability of Requirements

The objective of requirements traceability (as discussed in Chap. 5) is to verify that all the requirements have been implemented and tested. One way to do this would be to examine each requirement number and to go through every part of the design document to find any reference to the requirement number, and similarly to go through the test plan and find any reference to the requirement number. This would demonstrate that the requirement number has been implemented and tested.

A more effective mechanism to do this is with a traceability matrix (Table 5.4). This may be a separate document or part of the test documents. The idea is that a mapping between the requirement numbers and the associated test cases is defined, and this provides confidence that all the requirements have been implemented and tested.

A requirement number may map on to several test cases, i.e., the mapping may be one to many with several test cases employed to verify the correctness of a particular requirement. Traceability provides confidence that each requirement number has been implemented in the software design and tested via the test plan.

8.9   Test Tools

Test tools are employed to support the test process, and are used to enhance quality, reduce cycle time, and increase productivity. Tool selection needs to be planned, and the evaluation and selection of a particular tool involves defining the requirements for the proposed tool and identifying candidate tools to evaluate against the requirements. Each tool is then evaluated to yield an evaluation profile, and the results are analysed to enable an informed decision to be made. Tools to support the various software engineering activities (including testing) are described in Chap. 21.

There are various tools to support testing such as test planning and management tools; defect tracking tools; regression test automation tools; performance tools; and so on. There are tools available from various vendors such as Compuware, Software Research, Inc., HP, LDRA, McCabe and Associates, and IBM Rational.

Test Management Tools

There are various test management tools available (e.g., the Quality Center tool from HP), and the main features of such a tool are:

- Management of entire testing process.
- Test planning.
- Support for building and recording test scripts.
- Test status and reporting.
- Graphs for presentation.

- Defect control system.
- Support for many testers.
- Support for large volume of test data.
- Audit trail proof that testing has been done.
- Test automation.
- Support for various types of testing.

The Quality Center™ tool standardizes and manages the entire test and quality process, and it is a web-based system for automated software quality management and testing. It employs dashboard technology to give visibility into the process.

It provides a consistent repeatable process for gathering requirements; planning and scheduling tests; analysing results; and managing defects. It supports a high-level of collaboration and communication between the stakeholders. It allows the business analysts to define the application requirements and testing objectives. The test managers and testers may then design test plans, test cases and automated scripts. The testers then run the manual and automated tests, report results and log the defects.

The developers review and correct the logged defects. Project and test managers can create status reports and manage test resources. Test and product managers decide objectively whether the application is ready to be released.

Miscellaneous Testing Tools

There is a wide collection of test tools to support activities such as static testing, unit testing, system testing, performance testing, and regression testing.

Code coverage tools are useful for unit testing, and, for example, the LDRA Testbed can analyse source files to report on areas of code that were not executed at run time, thereby facilitating the identification of missing test data. Code coverage tools are useful in identifying the sources of errors, as they will typically show the code areas that were executed through textual or graphic reports.

Regression testing involves re-running existing test cases to verify that the software remains correct following the changes made. It is often automated with capture and playback tools, and the Winrunner tool[1] that was developed by Mercury (now part of HP) captures, verifies, and replays user interactions, and allows regression testing to be automated. Effort is required to set up the tests for automation, but the payback is improvements in quality and productivity.

The purpose of performance testing is to verify that system performance is within the defined limits, and it requires measures on the server side, network side, and client side disc. It includes load testing and stress testing tools. Mercury's LoadRunner (now called HP Loadrunner) tool allows the software application to be tested with hundreds or thousands of concurrent users to determine its performance under heavy loads. It allows the scalability of the software system to be tested, to determine if can support the predicted growth.

---

[1] The Winrunner tool has been replaced by HP Unified Functional Testing Software.

The decision on whether to automate and what to automate often involves a test process improvement team. It tends to be difficult for a small organization to make a major investment in test tools (especially if the projects are small). However, larger organizations will require a more sophisticated testing process to ensure that high-quality software is consistently produced.

8.10   E-Commerce Testing

There has been an explosive growth in electronic commerce, and web site quality and performance is a key concern. A web site is a software application and so standard software engineering principles are employed to verify the quality of a web site. E-commerce applications are characterized by:

- Distributed system with millions of servers and billions of participants.
- High availability requirements (24 * 7 * 365).
- Look and feel of the web site is highly important.
- Browsers may be unknown.
- Performance may be un-predictable.
- Users may be unknown.
- Security threats may be from anywhere.
- Often rapid application development is required.
- Design a little, implement a little, and test a little.
- Rapidly changing technologies.

The standard waterfall lifecycle model is rarely employed for the front end of a web application, and instead RAD/JAD/Agile models are employed. The use of lightweight development methodologies does not mean that anything goes in software development, and similar project documentation should be produced (except that the chronological sequence of delivery of the documentation is more flexible). Joint application development allows early user feedback to be received on the look and feel and correctness of the application, and the method of design a little, implement a little, and test a little is valid for web development. The various types of web testing include:

- Static testing.
- Unit testing.
- Functional Testing.
- Browser compatibility testing.
- Usability testing.
- Security testing.
- Load/performance/stress testing.
- Availability testing.
- Post deployment testing.

Static testing generally involves inspections and reviews of documentation. The purpose of static testing of web sites is to check the content of the web pages for accuracy, consistency, correctness, and usability, and to identify any syntax errors or anomalies in the HTML. There are tools available (e.g., NetMechanic) for statically checking the HTML for syntax correctness.

The purpose of unit testing is to verify that the content of the web pages corresponds to the design, that the content is correct, that all the links are valid, and that the web navigation operates correctly.

The purpose of functional testing is to verify that the functional requirements are satisfied. It may be quite complex as e-commerce applications may involve product catalogue searches, order processing, credit checking and payment processing, and the application may liaise with legacy systems. Also, testing of cookies, whether enabled or disabled, needs to be considered.

The purpose of browser compatibility testing is to verify that the web browsers that are to be supported are supported. The purpose of usability testing is to verify that the look and feel of the application is good, and that web performance (loading web pages, graphics, etc.) is good. There are automated browsing tools which go through all the links on a page, attempt to load each link, and produce a report including the timing for loading an object or page. Usability needs to be considered early in design and is important in GUI applications.

The purpose of security testing is to ensure that the web site is secure. The purpose of load, performance and stress testing is to ensure that the performance of the system is within the defined parameters.

The purpose of post-deployment testing is to ensure that web site performance remains good, and this may be done as part of a service level agreement (SLA). The SLA generally includes a penalty clause if the availability of the system or its performance falls outside the defined parameters. Consequently, it is important to identify performance and availability issues early before they become a problem. Post-deployment testing includes monitoring of web site availability, performance, and security, and taking corrective action. E-commerce sites operate 24 h a day for 365 days a year, and major financial loss is incurred in the case of a major outage.

8.11 Testing in the Agile World

Test-driven development (TDD) was developed by Kent Beck and others as part of extreme programming, and it is employed in Agile software development. It ensures that test cases are written early with the software code written to pass the test cases. It is a paradigm shift from traditional software engineering, where unit tests are written and executed after the code has been written.

The set of test cases is derived from the requirements, and the software is then written to pass the test cases. Another words, the test-driven development of a new feature begins with writing a suite of test cases based on the requirements for the feature, and the code for the feature is then written to pass the test cases.

Initially all tests fail as no code has been written, and so the first step is to write some code that enables the new test cases to pass. This new code may be imperfect (it will be improved later), but this is initially acceptable as the only purpose is to pass the new test cases. The next step is to ensure that the new feature works with the existing features, and this involves executing all new and existing test cases.

This may involve modification of the source code to enable all the tests to pass, and to ensure that all features work correctly together. The final step is refactoring the code, and this involves cleaning up and restructuring the code. The test cases are re-run during the refactoring to ensure that the functionality is not altered in any way. The process repeats with the addition of each new feature. Agile software development is described in more detail in Chap. 14.

8.12 Review Questions

1. Describe the main activities in test planning.
2. What does the test environment consist of? When should it be set up?
3. Explain the traceability of the requirements to the test cases?
4. Describe the various types of testing that may be performed.
5. Investigate available test tools to support testing? What areas of testing do they support and what are their benefits?
6. Describe an effective way to evaluate and select a test tool.
7. What are the characteristics of e-commerce testing that make it unique from other domains.
8. Discuss test reporting and the influence of the test manager in project sign-off.
9. Explain test driven development.

8.13 Summary

This chapter discussed software testing and how testing may be used to verify that the software is of a high quality and fit to be released to potential customers. Testing is both a constructive and destructive activity, in that while on the one hand it aims to verify the correctness of the software, on the other hand it aims to find as many defects as possible.

Various test activities were discussed including test planning, setting up the test environment, test case definition, test execution, defect reporting, and test management and reporting.

We discussed black and white box testing, unit and integration testing, system testing, performance testing, security and usability testing. Testing in an e-commerce environment was considered.

Test reporting enables all project participants to understand the current quality of the software, and to understand what needs to be done to ensure that the product meets the required quality criteria.

Various tools to support the testing process were discussed, and a methodology to assist in the selection and evaluation of tools is essential. Metrics are useful in providing visibility into test progress and into the quality of the software. The role of testing in promoting quality improvement was discussed.

Testing is often complicated by the late delivery of the software from the developers, and this may lead to the compression of the testing schedule. The recommendation of the test manager on whether to release the product needs to be carefully considered.

Ethics and Privacy

9

Abstract

This chapter discusses ethics and privacy where professional ethics are a code of conduct that governs how members of a profession deal with each other and with third parties. It expresses ideals of human behaviour, and the fundamental values of the organization, and is an indication of its professionalism. Privacy is defined as "the right to be left alone", and specifies there should be no intrusion upon seclusion, and no public disclosure of private facts or false information.

Keywords

Business ethics · Computer ethics · Privacy and the law · GDPR · Security · AI · Internet of things · Social media

9.1 Introduction

Ethics is a practical branch of philosophy that deals with moral questions such as the nature of what is right or wrong, as well as how a person should behave in a particular situation in a complex world. Ethics explore what actions are right or wrong within a specific context or within a certain society and seek to find satisfactory answers to moral questions. It is a search for moral principles to guide the behaviour of individuals or groups, and ethical issues occur when a conflict arises between an individual's moral compass, and the values or moral principles held by the society that the individual belongs to. The origin of the word "ethics" is from the Greek word ἠθικός, which means habit or custom.

There are various schools of ethics such as the *relativist* position (as defined by Protagoras), which argues that each person decides on what is right or wrong for them; *cultural relativism* argues that the particular society determines what is right

© Springer Nature Switzerland AG 2022
G. O'Regan, *Concise Guide to Software Engineering*,
Undergraduate Topics in Computer Science,
https://doi.org/10.1007/978-3-031-07816-3_9

or wrong based upon its cultural values; *deontological ethics* (as defined by Kant) argues that there are moral laws to guide people in deciding what is right or wrong; and *utilitarianism* which argues that an action is right if its overall effect is to produce more happiness than unhappiness in society.

Professional ethics are a code of conduct that governs how members of a profession deal with each other and with third parties. A professional code of ethics expresses ideals of human behaviour, and it defines the fundamental principles of the organization, and is an indication of its professionalism. Several organizations such as the Association Computing Machinery (ACM), the Institute of Electrical and Electronic Engineers (IEEE) and the British Computer Society (BCS) have developed a code of conduct for their members, and violations of the code by members are taken seriously and are subject to investigations and disciplinary procedures (see Chap. 2).

Business ethics define the core values of the business and are used to guide employee behaviour. Should an employee accept gifts from a supplier to a company as this could lead to a conflict of interest? A company may face ethical questions on the use of technology. For example, should the use of a new technology be restricted because people can use it for illegal or harmful actions as well as beneficial ones? How can we balance the rights of a business to sell products that benefit society and the rights of citizens to be protected from harm from any unintended consequences of the technology?

Consider mobile phone technology, which has transformed communication between people, and thus is highly beneficial to society. What about mobile phones with cameras? On the one hand, they provide useful functionality in combining a phone and a camera. On the other hand, they may be employed to take indiscreet photos without permission of others, which may then be placed on inappropriate sites. In other words, how can citizens be protected from inappropriate use of such technology?

Professional responsibility in the computing and software engineering fields refer to the responsibility of computer professionals to carry out their work professionally to the highest standards, and to use sound judgement in the exercise of their duties. Engineers are accountable to themselves and others for their actions, and they must be willing to accept professional responsibility when performance does not meet professional standards.

Professional engineers have a duty to their clients to ensure that they are solving the real problem of the client. They need to precisely state the problem before working on its solution. Engineers need to be honest about current capabilities when asked to work on problems that have no appropriate technical solution, rather than accepting a contract for something that cannot be done. That is, engineers have a professional responsibility and are required to behave ethically with their clients. The membership of the professional engineering body requires the member to adhere to the code of ethics of the profession.

9.2 Business Ethics

Business ethics (also called corporate ethics) is concerned with ethical principles and moral problems that arise in a business environment (Fig. 9.1). They refer to the core principles and values of the organization and apply throughout the organization. They guide individual employees in carrying out their roles, and ethical issues include the rights and duties of a company, its employees, customers, and suppliers.

Many corporation and professional organizations have a written *"code of ethics"* that defines the professional standards expected of all employees in the company. Unfortunately, sometimes the code of ethics of an organization are window dressing, where they give the impression that these are the core values of the organization, whereas in reality they have not been properly implemented on the ground or are not being followed rigorously by employees in their day-to-day work practices and are not ingrained in the organization culture.

All employees are expected to adhere to the core values in the code whenever they represent the company. The human resource function in a company plays an important role in promoting ethics, and in putting internal HR policies in place relating to the ethical conduct of the employees, as well as addressing discrimination, sexual harassment and ensuring that employees are treated appropriately (including cultural sensitivities in a multi-cultural business environment). HR has a responsibility to provide training and awareness to staff on its core values.

Fig. 9.1 Corrupt legislation. 1896. Public domain

Companies are expected to behave ethically and not to exploit its workers. There was a case of employee exploitation at the Foxconn plant (an Apple supplier of the *i*Phone) in Shenzhen in China in 2006, where conditions at the plant were so dreadful (long hours, low pay, unreasonable workload, and crammed accommodation) that several employees committed suicide. The scandal raised questions on the extent to which a large corporation such as Apple should protect the safety and health of the factory workers of its suppliers. Further, given the profits that Apple makes from the *i*Phone, is it ethical for Apple to allow such workers to be exploited?

Today, the area of *corporate social responsibility* (CSR) has become applicable to the corporate world, and it requires the corporation to be an ethical and responsible citizen in the communities in which it operates (even at a cost to its profits). It is therefore reasonable to expect a responsible corporation to pay its fair share of tax, and to refrain from using tax loopholes to avoid paying billions in taxes on international sales. Today, environment ethics has become topical, and it is concerned with the responsibility of business in protecting the environment in which it operates. It is reasonable to expect a responsible corporation to make protection of the environment and sustainability part of its business practices, even if this has an impact on its profitability.

Unethical business practices refer to those business actions that don't meet the standard of acceptable business operations, and they give the company a bad reputation. It may be that the entire business culture is corrupt, or it may be result of the unethical actions of an employee. It is important that such practices be exposed, and this may place an employee in an ethical dilemma (i.e., the loyalty of the employee to the employer versus doing the right thing such as becoming a *whistle-blower* and exposing the unethical or unsafe business practices). There are dangers that a whistle-blower could suffer career suicide following her exposure of unethical practices, and organizations need to create an effective structure or mechanism, where employees can raise serious ethical issues so that these may be resolved without fear of negative consequences to their career.

Some accepted business practices in the workplace might cause ethical concerns. For example, in many companies it is normal for the employer to monitor email and Internet use to ensure that employees do not abuse it, and so there may be grounds for privacy concerns. On the one hand, the employer is paying the employee's salary, and has a reasonable expectation that the employee does not abuse email and the Internet. On the other hand, the employee has reasonable rights of privacy provided that the computer resources are not abused.

The nature of privacy is relevant in the business models of several technology companies. For example, Google specializes in Internet based services and products, and its many products include Google Search (the world's largest search engine); Gmail for email; and Google Maps (a web mapping application that offers satellite images and street views). Google's products gather a lot of personal data, and create revealing profiles of the users, which can then be used for commercial purposes.

A Google search leaves traces on both the computer and in records kept by Google, which has raised privacy concerns as such information may be obtained by a forensic examination of the computer, or in records obtained from Google or the Internet Service Providers (ISP). Gmail automatically scans the contents of emails to add context sensitive advertisements to them and to filter spam, which raises privacy concerns, as it means that all emails sent or received are scanned and read by some computer. Google has argued that the automated scanning of emails is done to enhance the user experience, as it provides customized search results, tailored advertisements, and the prevention of spam and viruses. Google maps provides location information which may be used for targeted advertisements, and smartphones with Google maps may be used for the surveillance of users by tracking the places that they visit as well as the times and duration that they visit.

9.3   What is Computer Ethics?

Computer ethics is a set of principles that guide the behaviour of individuals when using computer resources. Several ethical issues that may arise include intellectual property rights, privacy concerns, as well as the impacts of computer technology on wider society.

The Computer Ethics Institute (CEI) is an American organization that examines ethical issues that arise in the information technology field. It published the *ten commandments on computer ethics* (Table 9.1) in the early 1990s [1], which attempted to outline principles and standards of behaviour to guide people in the ethical use of computers.

Table 9.1 Ten commandments on computer ethics

No.	Description
1	Thou shalt not use a computer to harm other people
2	Thou shalt not interfere with other people's computer work
3	Thou shalt not snoop around in other people's computer files
4	Thou shalt not use a computer to steal
5	Thou shalt not use a computer to bear false witness
6	Thou shalt not copy or use proprietary software for which you have not paid
7	Thou shalt not use other people's computer resources without authorization or proper compensation
8	Thou shalt not appropriate other people's intellectual output
9	Thou shalt think about the social consequences of the program you are writing or the system you are designing
10	Thou shalt always use a computer in ways that ensure consideration and respect for your fellow humans

The first commandment says that it is unethical to use a computer to harm another user (e.g., destroy their files or steal their personal data), or to write a program that on execution does so. That is, activities such as spamming, malware, spyware, phishing, ransomware, and cyberbullying are unethical. The second commandment is related and may be interpreted that malicious software and viruses that disrupt the functioning of computer systems are unethical. The third commandment says that it is unethical (with some exceptions such as dealing with cybercrime and international terrorism) to read another person's emails, files, and personal data, as this is an invasion of their privacy.

The fourth commandment argues that the theft or leaking of confidential electronic personal information is unethical (computer technology has made it easier to commit fraud from the theft of personal information). The fifth commandment states that it is unethical to spread false or incorrect information (e.g., fake news or misinformation spread via email or social media). The sixth commandment states that it is unethical to obtain illegal copies of copyrighted software, as software is considered an artistic or literary work that is subject to copyright or license. All copies should be obtained legally.

The seventh commandment states that it is unethical to break into a computer system with another user's id and password (without their permission), or to gain unauthorized access to the data on another computer by hacking into the computer system. The eight commandment states that it is unethical to claim ownership of an intellectual creation that does not belong to you (e.g., to claim ownership of a program that was written by another, or to use an invention that is protected by a patent without proper authorization).

The ninth commandment states that it is important for companies and individuals to think about the social impacts of the software that is being created, and to create software only if it is beneficial to society (i.e., it is unethical to create malicious software or addictive software). That is, individual and companies need to consider the common good as well as profitability. The tenth commandment states that communication over computers and the Internet should be courteous and users should show courtesy and respect for others (e.g., there should be no use of abusive language or spreading of false information).

9.3.1 Ethical Problems in Computing

The ten commandments of computer ethics outline various principles to guide ethical behaviour in the information technology field. The computing field has introduced a unique set of ethical problems such as the unauthorized use of computer resources, the problem of hacking and theft of personal data, the problem of computer viruses, the professional responsibility of computer professionals in their work, the protection of personal data and privacy, and computer crime. Some ethical problems that arise in the computing field are summarized in Table 9.2.

Table 9.2 Some ethical problems in computing

Type	Description
Privacy	The use of computer technology raises concerns on data protection and privacy, as sensitive data may be compromised
Computer Crime	This may involve the theft of funds using a computer, or the theft of confidential information through unauthorized access of computer resources
Viruses	A virus is malicious code that an individual places on a network, and it is designed to spread and infect other machines. The virus may have destructive behaviour such as destroying data
Hacking	This is where a hacker who uses his (or her) computer skills to gain unauthorized access to computer files or networks (to cause damage or steal confidential information)
Cyberbullying	This is where an individual is bullied by others online, and it may lead to deep emotional distress to the individual
Professional responsibility	The development of a software product is a professional activity, and software engineers have a professional responsibility to ensure that the software product adheres to the highest possible standards. Software engineers must be accountable for their decisions and must ensure that the software is safe to use
Fake news	This refers to the systematic spreading of false or misleading information in traditional media or social media

9.3.2 The Ethical Software Engineer

Software engineers have a professional responsibility to create ethical designs that satisfy the requirements, and to ensure that their designs are robust and protect the safety of the public. Software designers need to follow best practice in privacy and security in collecting, processing, and protecting data. The ethical design of a software system should give an open and accurate account of the system and should satisfy all relevant legal and regulatory requirements.

Ethical software designers need to be conscious of the algorithms that they create to ensure that they are unbiased, and do not discriminate against minority groups in society. This is especially important in machine learning algorithms based on pattern matching that are employed in the AI field, where *biased algorithms* may lead to discrimination against minorities.

Software engineers should consider the ultimate purpose of the project including its benefits to society as well as harm of the technology. Social media and various other apps are deliberately designed to be *addictive* to their users, where the software captures the attention of the human at a primal level, and the company reaps financial gain from the addiction of the users. This poses questions on the ethics of this addictive design, and whether the consequences of design as well as the product should be considered in ethical decision making.

The system needs to be designed for security, as it is difficult to add security after the system has been implemented. Security engineering is concerned with the development of systems that can prevent malicious attacks and recover from them. Software developers need to be aware of the threats facing a system and develop solutions to manage them. Security loopholes may be introduced in the development of the system, and so care needs to be taken to prevent these as well as preventing hackers from exploiting security vulnerabilities.

Software testers need to always behave ethically during the development and testing of the software. The ISTQB Code of Ethics for test professionals is based on the IEEE and ACM code of ethics, and it states that software testers should act in the public interest and in the best interest of their client and employer. They ensure that their deliverables meet the highest standards, and they are independent in their professional judgements. They are required to be ethical and to be supportive of their colleagues, and to work closely with software developers. Software testers need to keep their knowledge up to date with lifelong learning.

Ethical issues may arise during testing if the project is behind schedule, and when there is pressure applied to the test team to stay with the original project delivery schedule. This could lead to the quality of the released software being compromised, and the test manager needs to resist any pressure that poses risks to quality.

9.3.3   Ethics in Data Science

Information is power in the digital age, and the collection, processing and use of information needs to be regulated. Data science is a multi-disciplinary field that extracts knowledge from data sets that consist of structured and unstructured data, and large data sets (*big data*[1]) may be analysed to extract useful information. The field has great power to harm and to help, and data scientists have a responsibility to use this power wisely. Data science may be regarded as a branch of statistics as it uses many concepts from the field, and it is essential that both the data and models are valid to prevent errors occurring during data analysis.

Personal data is collected about individuals from their use of computer resources such as their use of email, their Google searches, their Internet, and Social media use to build up revealing profiles of the user that may be targeted to advertisers. Modern technology has allowed governments to conduct mass surveillance on its citizens, with face recognition software allowing citizens to be recognized at demonstrations or other mass assemblies.

Further, smartphones provide location data that allows the location of the user to be tracked. It is important that such technologies are regulated and not abused by the state. Privacy has become more important in the information age, and it is the way in which we separate ourselves from other people and is the right to be left alone. The European GDPR law has become an important protector of privacy and personal data, and both European and other countries have adapted it.

---

[1] Big data involves combining data from lots of sources such as bar codes, cctv, shopping data, drivers license, and so on.

Companies collect lots of personal data about individuals, and so the question is how should a company respond to a request for personal information on users? Does it have a policy to deal with that situation? What happens to the personal data that a bankrupt company has gathered? Is the personal data part of the assets of the bankrupt company and sold on with the remainder of the company? How does this affect privacy agreements and compliance to them or does the agreement cease on termination of business activities?

The consequence of an error in data collection or processing could result in harm to an individual, and so the data collection and processing needs to be accurate. Decisions may be made based on public and private data, and often individuals are unaware as to what data was collected about them, whether the data is accurate, and whether it is possible to correct errors in the data.

Further, the conclusions from the analysis may be invalid due to errors in incorrect or biased algorithms, and so a reasonable question is how to keep algorithmically driven systems from harming people? Data scientists have a responsibility to ensure that the algorithm is fit for purpose and uses the right training data, and as far as practical to detect and eliminate unintentional discrimination in algorithms against individuals or groups.

That is, problems may arise when the algorithm uses criteria tuned to fit the majority, as this may be unfair to minorities. Another words, the results are correct, but presented in an over simplistic manner. This could involve presenting the correct aggregate outcome but ignoring the differences within the population, and so leading to the suppression of diversity, and discriminating against the minority group. Another example is where the data may be correct but presented in a misleading way (e.g., the scales of the axis may be used to present the results visually in an exaggerated way).

The ownership of personal data is important, for example, if I take a picture of another individual does the picture belong to me (as owner of the camera and the collector of the data)? Or does it belong to the individual who is the subject of the image? Most reasonable people would say that the image is my property, and if so what responsibilities or obligations do I have (if any) to the other individual?

That is, although I may technically be the owner of the image, the fact that it contains the personal data (or image) of another should indicate that I have an ethical responsibility or obligation to ensure that the image (or personal data) is not misused in any way to harm that individual. Further, if I misuse the image in any way then I may be open to a lawsuit from the individual.

Ethical rules are shared values that are followed voluntarily to make the world a better place, whereas legal rules are used to enforce social values. Often, the benefits of following the rules outweigh the costs of following them. For example, following the defined rules of the road leads to safe and predictable travel, whereas the cost of obeying the rules is that an individual must drive under the speed limit on the correct side of the road.

There has been a phenomenal growth in the use of digital data in information technology, with vast amounts of data collected, processed, and used, and so the ethics of data science has become important. There are social consequences to the use of data, and the ethics of data science aims to investigate what is fair and ethical in data science, and what should or should not be done with data.

A fundamental principle of ethics in data science refers to *informed consent*, and this has its origins in the ethics of medical experiments on individuals. The concept of informed consent in medical ethics is where the individual is informed about the experiment and gives their *consent voluntarily*. The individual has the right to withdraw consent at any time during the experiment. Such experiments are generally conducted to benefit society, and often there is a board that approves the study and oversees it to ensure that all participants have given their informed consent and attempts to balance the benefits to society with any potential harm to individuals. Once individuals have given their informed consent data may be collected about them.

The principle of informed consent is part of information technology, in the sense that individuals accept the terms and conditions before they may use software applications, and these terms state that data may be collected, processed, and shared. However, it is important to note that generally users do not give informed consent in the sense of medical experiments, as the details of the data collection and processing is hidden in the small print of the terms and condition, and this is generally a long and largely unreadable document. Further, the consent is not given voluntarily, in the sense that if a user wishes to use the software, then he or she has no choice but to click acceptance of the terms and conditions of use for the site. Otherwise, they are unable to access the site, and so for many software applications (apps) consent is essentially coerced rather than freely given.

There was some early research done on user behaviour by Facebook in 2012, where they conducted an experiment to determine if they could influence the mood of users by posing happy or sad stories to their news feed. The experiment was done without the consent of the users, and while the study indicated that happy or sad stories did influence the user's mood and postings, it led to controversy and major dissatisfaction with Facebook when users became aware that they were the *subject of a psychological experiment without their consent*.

The dating site OKCupid uses an algorithm to find compatibility matches for its users based on their profiles, and two people are assigned a match rating based on the extent to which the algorithm judges them to be compatible. OKCupid also conducted psychological experiments on its users without their knowledge, with the first experiment being a "love is blind" day where all images were removed from the site, and so compatibilities were determined without the use of images.

Another experiment was controversial and unethical, as the site lied to the users on their match ratings (e.g., two people with a compatibility rating of 90% were given a rating of 30%, and vice versa). The site was trying to determine the extent that two people would get along irrespective of the rating that they were given, and it showed that two people talked more when falsely told that the algorithm matched them, and vice versa. The controversy arose once users became aware of the deception by the company, and it provides a case study on the *socially unacceptable manipulation of user data* by an Internet company.

Data collection is not a new phenomenon as devices such as cameras and telephones have been around for some time. People have reasonable expectations on privacy, and do not expect their phone calls to be monitored and eavesdropped by others, or they do not expect to be recorded in a changing room or in their home. Individuals will wish to avoid the harm that could occur due to data about them being collected, processed, and shared. The question is whether reasonable rules can be defined and agreed, and whether trade-offs may be made to balance the conflicting rights and to protect the individual as far as is possible.

The consequence of an error in the data analysis or with the analysis method could result in harm to the individual. There are many sources of error such as the sample chosen, which may not be representative of the entire population. Other problems arise with knowledge acquisition by machine learning, where the learning algorithm has used incomplete training data for pattern (or other knowledge) recognition. Training data may also be incomplete if the future population differs from the past population.

The data collection needs to decide on the data and attributes to be collected, and often the attributes chosen are limited to what is available, and the data scientist will also need to decide what to do with missing attributes. Often errors arise in data processing tasks such as analysing text information or recognizing faces from photos. There may be human errors in the data (e.g., spelling errors or where the data field was misunderstood), and errors may lead to poor results and possible harm to the user. The problem with such errors is that often decisions are made based on public and private data, and often individuals are unaware as to what data was collected and whether there is a method to correct it.

Even with perfect data the conclusions from the analysis may be invalid due to errors in the model, and there are many ways in which the model may be incorrect. Many machine-learning algorithms just estimate parameters to fit a pre-determined model, without knowing whether the model is appropriate or not (e.g., the model may be attempting to fit a linear model to a non-linear reality). This becomes problematic when estimating (or extrapolating) values outside of the given data unless there is confidence in the correctness of the model.

Further, care is required before assigning results to an individual from an analysis of group data, as there may be other explanations (e.g., Simpson's paradox in probability/statistics is where a trend that appears in several groups of data disappears or reverses when these groups are combined). It is important to think about the population that you are studying, and to make sure that you are collecting data on the right population, and whether to segment it into population groups, as well as how best to do the segmentation.

It may seem reasonable to assume that data-driven analysis is fair and neutral, but unfortunately the problem is that humans may unintentionally introduce bias, as they set the boundary conditions. The bias may be through their choice of the model, the use of training data that may not be representative of the population, or the past population may not be representative of the future population, and so on. This may potentially lead to algorithmic decisions that are unfair (e.g., the Amazon hiring algorithm discriminated against female applicants, and so the question is how to be confident that the algorithms are fair and unbiased. Data scientists have a responsibility to ensure that the algorithm is fit for purpose and uses the right training data, and as far as practical to detect and eliminate unintentional discrimination (individual or target group).

Another problem that may arise is data that is correct but presented in a misleading way. One simple way to do this is to manipulate the scales of the axis to present the results visually in an exaggerated way. Another example is where the results are correct, but presented in an over simplistic manner (e.g., there may be two or more groups in the population with distinct behaviour where one group is the dominant), where the correct aggregate outcome is presented but this is misleading due to the differences within the population, and by suppressing diversity there may be discrimination against the minority group. In other words, the algorithm may use criteria tuned to fit the majority and may be unfair to minorities.

Exploration is the first phase in data analysis, and a hypothesis may be devised to fit the observed data (this is the opposite of traditional approaches where the starting point is the hypothesis, and the data is used to confirm or reject the hypothesis based on the data from the control and target groups, and so this approach needs to be used carefully to ensure the validity of the results).

9.4 Privacy

Privacy is a fundamental concept in modern society, and it has become an important area in the computing field. In Greek mythology there was a giant called Argus Panoptes, who was an all-seeing giant with one hundred eyes looking in every direction, and he would always have some eyes open even when asleep. That is, he was always watching and monitoring the world around him, and so was the perfect guardian. He was later slain by Hermes (the messenger of the gods).

Jeremy Bentham designed a circular prison in the eighteenth century termed the Panopticon, where a single guard in the centre of the complex could observe all the prisoners. His idea was that although individual prisoners did not know if they were being watched or not at a given time instant (as this depended on the direction that the guard was facing), that they would behave as if they were being watched, and so they would behave all the time (Fig. 9.2).

The modern version of the Panopticon is a set of security cameras that is watching people, or websites that are monitoring the behaviour of individuals who are visiting the site, or the entire Internet, which is working out everything that we are doing by watching us. The question is whether we as individuals should be concerned about this, and whether it matters if we as individuals are doing nothing wrong. Some have argued that everyone would be completely honest due to zero privacy, and where everyone could know what everyone else is doing. Others respond by saying that privacy is a basic human right, and that it is needed for freedoms to be exercised in society.

Fig. 9.2 Bentham's panopticon prison

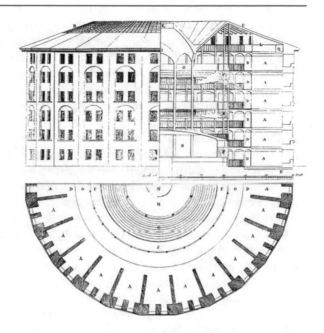

The "*Right to have privacy*" was an influential legal article written by Louis Brandeis and Samuel Warren and published in the Harvard Law Review in 1890 [2]. The article advocates for *privacy* as "*the right to be left alone*". William Prosser wrote an article in the Californian Law Review in 1960 in which he outlined four types of privacy torts [3]:

- Intrusion upon seclusion
- Public disclosure of private facts
- Publishing objectionable, false information
- Misappropriation of name or likeness.

There has traditionally been a difference between rural and urban living, where in a small-town people know everything about every other person in the town, and there is essentially very little privacy from all the gossip (*pueblo pequeño infierno grande*). In a larger city, people are anonymous, and nobody knows or cares about what others are doing, and so there is a greater sense of privacy. Further, an individual living in a small town has a choice of moving to a new town for a fresh start or waiting in the town for the community to forget a particular event, whereas in a large city this problem is a lot less relevant due to the anonymous nature of city living.

There are some parallels of the Internet being like the small village, except that the relationship is asymmetric. Another words, in a small town everyone knows as much about another as vice versa (i.e., it is a symmetric relationship), whereas the relationship is asymmetric for the Internet. This makes it a very unequal relationship, with one party gathering lots of information and building up a profile about all other parties and using that information for commercial purposes. The other parties are not actively gathering information and have a very limited picture of what is going on with all the data that is gathered.

Further, while events and information may be forgotten in a village over time this does not happen with the Internet: i.e., it is very difficult to forget things on the Internet with web pages surviving forever in some archive even if taken down. Another issue is that once a page is put up many copies of it are made, and even if page is taken down there may still be many copies remaining elsewhere, and so there is no way of really deleting something once it has been published on the web. This could create major problems for individuals who pose indiscreet content online, as that content may be there in perpetuity.

People need an understanding of how their personal information and data is collected, shared, and used across the many computer platforms that they use, and the extent to which they have control over their personal information. New technology has led to major changes in the way in which privacy is experienced by society, and so it is important to understand the nature of privacy, and to consider the problems and risks that exist, as well as privacy laws and rules that are available to protect individuals from its abuse. The main sources of personal data that are collected include (Table 9.3).

These sources of information can collect vast amounts of data, and the collected data may potentially result in harm to an individual. The collected data is commercially valuable, especially when data about individuals are linked from several

Table 9.3 Sources of information

Source	Answers
Data collected by merchants and service providers	This includes personal data entered for the purchase of products and services such as name, address, date of birth, products and services purchased, etc.
Activity tracking	This involves monitoring the user's activity on the site (or app), and recording the user's searches, and the products browsed and purchased It may involve recording the user's interests, their activities, and their interactions and communications with others on the site
Search Profile	The history of a person's searches over a period of time on a search engine such as Google reveals information about the individual and their interests
Sensors from devices	There are many sensors in the world around us such as personal devices as part of the Internet of Things that may record information such as health data or what the individual is eating Third party devices such as security cameras may be conducting public or private surveillance GPS technology on smart phones may be tracking the user's location

sources. *Data brokers* are companies that aggregate and link information from multiple sources to create more complete and valuable information products (i.e., profiles of individuals) that may then be sold on to interested parties. Meta data (i.e., data about the data such as the time of a phone call or who the call is made to) also provides useful information that may be collected and shared.

For example, suppose that the probability of an individual buying a pair of hiking boots is very low (say 1 in 5000 probability). Next, that individual starts scanning a website (say Amazon) for boots then that individual is now viewed as being more likely to buy a pair of hiking boots (say a 1 in 100 probability). This large increase in probability will mean that the individual is now of interest to advertisers and sellers, and various targeted (popup) advertisements will appear advertising different hiking boots to the individual. This may become quite tedious and annoying to the user, who may have been just browsing, and is now subject to an invasion of advertisements, but many apps are free and often the source of their revenue is from advertisements, and so they gather data about the user that is then sold on to advertisers.

De-identification is the removal of identifiable information from data and includes the removal of fields (or attributes) such as name, address, and phone number so that no personally identifiable attributes remain in the dataset. This means that the identity of the person is not immediately identifiable, and so it provides some safeguards to the individual. However, it is possible that the individual's identity may be determined from the other retained fields, and this means that care must be taken if public records are to be released. That is, it may still be possible even if de-identification has taken place to identify individuals. Anonymity is limited or virtually impossible given the extent of public and private information that is available about individuals, and facial recognition technology allows the rapid identification of individuals from the images of their faces.

Privacy is important, and individuals should be able to express themselves without worrying about who may be watching. Individuals naturally desire rights such as the right to be left alone, for secret or intimate information to be kept secure from others, and for *control over personal information* where individuals can decide what information will be shared, when it will be shared, and how it will be communicated and shared with others (Fig. 9.3).

That is, users should be in control of how their data is used, and most user agreements are "all-or-nothing" in the sense that a user must give up control of their data to use the application, and so essentially the user has no control. That is, a user must click acceptance of the terms and conditions to use the services of a web application. Clearly, users would be happier and feel that they are in control if they were offered graduated choices by the vendor, to allow them to make trade-offs, and to choose a level of privacy that they are comfortable with.

Privacy has become quite topical with recent developments in the information age, and especially with the rise of social media, the Internet of Things and Artificial Intelligence. However, privacy concerns are not a new phenomenon, and they initially grew out of the development of early technologies such as the first cameras, microphones and telephones, where indiscreet or unauthorized images or recordings

Fig. 9.3 Cardinals eavesdropping in the Vatican

could be made leading to concerns of an invasion of privacy by a prying media or others.

The early concerns over privacy were often with maintaining the security and confidentiality of a message, and so this led to some people and groups to communicate with each other using ciphers. For example, Julius Caesar communicated important messages using an alphabetic cipher during his campaign in Gaul in the first century B.C., and the emperor Augustus used a similar approach for communication. Further, some of the leaders during the American War of Independence used codes and pseudonyms to protect their identity during sensitive communication.

Societies vary in terms of their political systems, with democracies offering a peaceful way of replacing an unpopular government, whereas totalitarian states are often ruthless in their control of the population. Some autocratic societies run by dictators employ a culture of surveillance on the population, and this may include identifying individuals who pose a potential threat to the regime and removing such individuals from society either by imprisonment or political assassination. Often, these societies are characterized by mass surveillance of individuals, police searches and seizure of private property, police brutality, and so on. In democratic societies there are usually laws to protect the citizen against unreasonable police searches and behaviour.

The importance of privacy in the information technology field became apparent in the early 1970s with the introduction of databases. These could hold private information about individuals, and there was a need for a set of rules to protect how information should be collected and used. This led to the development of a set of fair information processing principles (FIPPs) that was concerned with the way that data is used, collected and privacy. This was developed by the US Secretary's Advisory Committee on Automated Personal Data Systems, and published in their 1973 report on Records, Computers, and the Rights of Citizens [4]. This led to the Privacy Act in 1974, and this act remains the basis on which data collection is governed in the United States. The report outlined several principles such as:

- Transparency of collection and storage of information,
- Accessibility of personal information,
- Purpose limitations (consent),
- Correction of personal data,
- Personal data safeguards and accountability.

That is, the organization that is collecting personal data must be doing so openly (i.e., it is not secretly or covertly collecting data), and an individual must be able to access any data that the organization has about her. There must be a way for an individual to prevent information that was gathered for one purpose to be used for another purpose without their consent. Further, there must be a way for an individual to correct or amend information about him. Finally, any organization that is creating, maintaining, or disseminating personal must ensure the reliability of the data for the identified use, and take reasonable precautions to prevent against any misuse of the data.

Computing technology has evolved in a major way from the mainframes and databases of the early 1970s, and today modern society has embraced a plethora of leading-edge technologies such as smart phones, social media, the Internet of Things, and Artificial Intelligence. It is reasonable to ask what privacy means in the modern digital world and whether there is privacy anymore? Users of social media share large parts of their lives with a massive on-line audience as well as with large corporations, and social media companies gather lots of data about its users that may be used to determine patterns, and to generate profiles that may be targeted to advertisers. So much data is being collected about individuals, and the question is where does it go? Who controls it? Are companies adequately managing risks of data breaches? What happens when data privacy is breached or data is not secured properly? Is there transparency? Is user data encrypted? Is confidentiality and authenticity maintained?

The *Internet of Things* (IoT) is not a single technology as such, and instead it is a collection of devices, sensors and services that capture data to monitor and control the world around them. It refers to interconnected technology that is now an integral part of modern society, where computation and data communication are embedded in the environment. It allows everyday devices to connect to other devices or people over the Internet, and this may include smart phone to smart phone communication, vehicle to vehicle communication, connected cameras, GPS tracking, the smart grid, and so on. It allows a vast amount of data to be gathered and transmitted to and processed by companies. It means that information processing is now an integral part of people's lives, and IoT connects many devices to the Internet.

The level of interconnectivity and data gathered with IoT means that security and privacy have become important concerns, and it is essential to control both the devices and the data. For example, control could be lost if someone hacks into the smart phone, as the smart phone often links to bank accounts, email accounts and even household appliances. A lot of user data is potentially gathered painting a profile of individual users through their online activities as well as their searches, and the data gathered is used to improve the user experience, and the profile of users may be sold on to advertisers. Data should only be gathered with user consent, and there are risks of hacking or eavesdropping.

There has been a major growth in AI technology in recent years, and AI has been applied to self-driving cars, facial recognition, machine translation and so on. Facial recognition technology may be used to unlock phones to authenticate identity, and it has also been applied to read facial expression during job interviews, as well as following the movement of individuals.

A vehicle may contain several on-board computers for processing various vehicle controls as well as for entertainment systems. Vehicles that connect to the Internet are potentially at risk of being hacked, where a hacker may potentially commandeer vehicle controls such as steering and the brakes.

It is often unclear who is collecting personal information, the type of information that they are collecting, what is being done with the data, and who the data is being shared with. Information privacy refers to control over information and is a value that in a sense protects from certain kinds of harm. For example, if others have information about a particular individual, they may be able to use it against the individual. For example, if the individual has been the victim of phishing or identity theft where their personal financial information such as credit cards are stolen, then the perpetrators have power over the individual since they have personal and sensitive information about the individual.

9.4.1   Social Media

Social media involves the use of computer technology for the creation and exchange of user-generated content. These web-based technologies allow users to discuss and modify the created content, and it has led to major changes in communication between individuals, communities, and organizations (Fig. 9.4).

Social media is designed to have the individual share as much information as possible, and to continue to do so while they are on the site, and with every disclosure (or post) the individual reveals a little bit more about himself or herself. It is very easy to post photos and information on social media sites such as Facebook or Twitter, and social media is designed in such a way that it is addictive and poses risks to the privacy of an individual.

There is a danger that both social media companies and other users could harm the individual's privacy. The harm from other users may arise when a piece of the user's information is shared with the wrong audience, and this later leads to problems for the user. There are two distinct audiences for the individual's

Fig. 9.4 Young peoples on smart phones and social media. Public domain

information namely other users and the platform itself. The social media platform maintains a vast quantity of electronic information consisting of immense databases, which can collect a vast amount of data on the individual and other users.

There is a power imbalance between the platform and the user, with the platform designed to have the individual share as much as possible, and people may potentially pose risks in social interaction. An individual's information may be viewed by friends, family, employer, work colleagues and nameless others, and so everyone in the individual's network as well as others could be an unwanted audience.

Users often may not realize the full extent of their audience when they post, and the people who are authorized in an individual's network may not be the desired recipients of certain posts (disclosures). It is difficult to delete online messages, and destructive posts may last long after an incident. Therefore, it is very much in the interests of users to keep their Social Media posts discreet, as both friends and outsiders of their social media network pose risks to their privacy.

Another words, it is difficult for an individual to protect herself from the risks of social media, and there are several threats such as:

- Manufactured disclosures
- Extracting consent
- Overexposure
- Faithless friends
- Online harassment

Manufactured disclosures refer to how a social media site gets people to disclose more and more information, and this is similar in a way to surveillance. Traditional surveillance involves watching people to learn something about them, whereas modern surveillance as in social media has less to do with this, and it generally involves getting people to disclose something more about themselves and so in effect to learn something new about the person.

Extracting consent refers to how a social media site obtains consent from its users on the various practices employed on the site. A user must click acceptance of the associated terms and conditions to use the site, and often this involves accepting invasive practices described in a long, dense, and largely unreadable terms of use document. The social media site may also request access to the camera, location, and address book of the individual. Often, users just accept the terms and conditions and permission requests because they are so worn down with so many requests from different apps, and they have no choice but to accept the terms of use and invasive practices so that they may use the site.

Social media sites constantly introduce new features to make user data more visible, more searchable, and more complete to others and may result in *over exposure* of their information. *Faithless friends* refer to when information that has been shared in the individual's network is shared more widely by one of the "friends" of the individual. This may lead to embarrassment or harm to the individual. Finally, *online harassment* is where repeated insults or bullying of an individual takes place online, which may even include threats of violence, posting of indiscreet images or even revenge porn.

9.4.1.1 Data Analytics for Social Media

Data analytics provides a quantitative insight into human behaviour on a social media website and is a way to understand users and how to communicate with them better. It enables the business to understand its audience better, to improve the user experience, and to create content that will be of interest to them. Data analytics consist of a collection of data that says something about the social media conversation, and it involves the collection, monitoring, analysis, summarization, and a graph to visualize insight into the behaviour of users.

Another words, *data analytics* involves learning to read a social media community through data, and the interpretations of the quantifiable data (or metrics) gives information on the activities, events, and conversations. This includes what users like when they are online, but other important information such as their opinions and emotions need to be gathered through *social listening*. Social listening involves monitoring keywords and mentions in social media conversations in the target audience and industry, to understand and analyse what the audience is saying about the business and allows the business to engage with its audience.

Social media companies use data analytics to gain an insight into customers, and elementary data such as the number of likes, the number of followers, the number of times a video is played on YouTube, and so on are gathered to obtain a quantified understanding of a conversation. This data is valuable in judging the effectiveness of a social media campaign, where the focus is to determine how effective the campaign has been in meeting its goals. The goals may be to increase the number of users or to build a brand, and data analytics combined with social listening help in understanding how people are interacting, as well as what they are interacting about and how successful the interactions has been.

Facebook and Twitter maintain a comprehensive set of measurements for data analytics, with Facebook maintaining several metrics such as the number of page views and the number of likes and reach of posts (i.e., the number of people who saw posts at least once). Twitter includes a dashboard view to summarize how successful tweet activity has been, as well as the interests and locations of the user's followers. Social listening considers user opinions, emotions, views, evaluations, and attitude, and social media data contains rich collection of human emotions.

The design of a social media campaign is often an iterative process, with the first step being to determine the objective of the campaign and designing the campaign to meet the requirements. The effectiveness of a campaign is judged by a combination of social media analytics and social listening, with the campaign refined appropriately to meet its goals and the cycle repeating. The key performance indicators (KPI) may include increased followers/subscribers or an increase in the content shared, and so on.

9.4.2   Internet of Things

The Internet of Things is a collection of devices, sensors and services that capture data to monitor and control the world around them, and these include cars, clothing, fridges, fitness monitors, and many of the things that are in a person's day to day life have potential as an internet device. An individual may be continuously connected to multiple home devices with sensors (e.g., microphones and cameras), and connection and access to these devices increases the risk to data security (Fig. 9.5).

The fact that there are many devices with sensors connected to the Internet means that there are, in effect, more eyes watching the individual and gathering data about her, and there are also more points of failure. This means that IoT poses increased risks to the safety of individuals than when using basic computers, and the risks include:

- Security risks,
- Privacy risks.

Fig. 9.5 Fitbit Surge. Smart-watch activity tracker. Creative commons

The fact that these devices consist of both hardware and software means that there are now two points of failure: i.e., hardware failure and software failure. Hardware is generally more reliable than software, and hardware failures tend to be because of components wearing out over time. Software failures are often due to design issues, and software often requires regular updates to correct problems or to deal with security vulnerabilities. The fact that these devices are connected to the Internet means that software upgrades are possible but being connected to the Internet means that the device may be targeted by hackers in a similar way to which a computer is hacked.

Further, these Internet devices contain sensors that gather a lot of personal data about the individual, and they collect, use, and share this data, and so the IoT devices pose similar data security risks as laptops or smart phones. Many IoT devices are inexpensive and have serious security vulnerabilities, with some Internet devices failing to encrypt data when transmitting data or images to the cloud. This means that that an eavesdropper could intercept this Internet traffic, and cause harm to the individual.

IoT has serious implications for privacy in that the IoT devices can produce granular personal data such as when the individual is at home, what the individual eats, and so on. They gather a lot of personal data the individual, and the data may be shared with other devices or platforms thereby posing risks to the privacy of the individual.

9.4.3 AI and Facial Recognition

There has been a major growth in the AI field in recent years, and facial recognition is a new AI technology that offers the ability to unlock phones to authenticate identity, and so it may be used to protect the individual. Facial recognition has advanced in sophistication to allow individuals to be recognized at demonstrations and street protests, and this means that some authoritarian governments could potentially use facial recognition technology as a tool for authoritarian control. That is, surveillance combined with facial recognition could be oppressive to individuals and society and lead to a totalitarian state.

A society that adopts a paradigm of constant surveillance, where individuals are living in a world with technology monitoring their activities, learning to recognize patterns, and drawing inferences is moving towards totalitarianism. Facial recognition is a potentially dangerous technology that may challenge civil liberties, and it could severely impact marginalized groups in society.

- Faces are hard to hide,
- Faces are central to identity,
- Existing face and name databases,
- Facial recognition is widespread.

   Facial recognition is a biometric technology that analyses visual data from social media and other sources, and they can detect facial features and to essentially reduce each face to a mathematical equation using factors such as the distance between the individual's eyes, the width of the nose, and so on, and the patterns in the visual data are compared to patterns in facial recognition databases to confirm identity.

   Some companies have applied facial recognition technology to read facial expression during job interviews, and this provides a mechanism for the company to obtain data that they may not otherwise receive. Deep fakes are an AI technology that allows convincing images and videos to be created of individuals doing things that they never did or said, and this disruptive technology has been applied to misrepresent individuals in a variety of ways. An individual may be seen to make false or even preposterous claims, and this is achieved from content taken from social media and other media that is then manipulated and edited in various ways to achieve the desire effect. This technology could potentially show an individual committing a crime or present the individual in a very negative way. The technology has at this time mainly been applied to humour as in political satire, but as the technology improves it may become difficult to distinguish the real from the fake with serious consequences for society.

9.4.4   Privacy and the Law

Data collection laws focus on how data is collected, used, and shared, and data protection includes the right to information self-determination. The web is full of privacy policies that specify what type of personal data will be collected, how it will be processed and used, how it is shared, and what can be done about it. Further, individuals may take a lawsuit against another for a tort, for example, when someone pries or stalks them, or publishes a defamatory article, or violates their privacy. There are three main areas that impact upon an individual's privacy namely:

- The Media,
- Surveillance,
- Personal Data.

   Media laws protect an individual against intrusion, where another party may be held liable for the invasion of the individual's privacy (e.g., phone tapping, snooping, examining a person's bank account, and so on). The tort of the public disclosure of private facts is part of the legal system in many states, and its goal is to prevent the public disclosure of private facts concerning the private life of an individual, where the matter is not of legitimate concern to the public. That is, others are prevented from widely spreading private facts such as the individual's face or identity for their own benefit, and there are slander and libel laws to protect an individual's good name and reputation, and to prevent defamation of character.

There are laws and rights to regulate surveillance with search warrants required in most countries to search the home of a private individual, as well as the right to · seize personal property. Warrants are generally required to obtain personal electronic records held by telecommunication companies (e.g., the calls made and received as well as meta data such as geo-location data), and warrants may be required to obtain records held by Internet technology companies (e.g., emails, web sites visited, searches, and other electronic messages).

Countries vary in their laws for the protection of security and privacy, but many countries recognize that the security and privacy commitments made by a company in their policies should be fully implemented. Further, companies should be held accountable for any security breaches that occur that lead to data security or privacy being compromised, and the company may be liable for any losses suffered by individuals resulting from the breach.

Further, people must not be misled about the functionality of a website or mobile app that places their security or privacy at risk, and users must give their consent to any changes to the privacy policy that would allow for the collection of additional personal data, and users must be informed about the extensiveness of tracking and data collection. The collection and use of personal information of Facebook[2] users by Cambridge Analytica was a factor in the victory of Donald Trump over Hilary Clinton in the 2016 presidential election in the United States.

9.4.5   EU GDPR Privacy Law

Europe has been active in the development of data protection regulation, and the European General Data Protection Regulation (EU GDPR 2016/679) is a comprehensive data protection framework that became operational in 2018. The importance of both privacy and data protection has been recognized in Europe, and these are regarded as fundamental human rights in the EU. The goal is to give individuals control over their personal data, and it has had a huge impact on privacy laws of other countries around the world, with other countries using it to develop similar laws (e.g., Japan and the state of California in the US). GDPR also addresses the transfer of personal data outside of the EU, and it prohibits the transfer of personal data outside of the EU to countries that do not provide an equivalent or adequate data protection framework as GDPR (Fig. 9.6).

GDPR consists of a data governance framework that attempts to place privacy on a par with other laws. It creates protections that follow the data, and it places responsibilities on companies in managing privacy and information. GDPR applies whenever personal data is processed, and it starts from the presumption that the processing of the personal data is illegitimate. This means that companies carry the burden of legitimizing their actions, and they must be able to show that they have a legitimate basis for processing data. That is, they must be able to show that they

---

[2] Facebook was fined $5 billion in 2019 for deceptive and unfair trade practices related to Facebook's user interface.

Fig. 9.6 EU GDPR
2016/679

have the consent of the data subject, or that the processing is necessary because of
the contract that exists between them and the data subject, or where they have a
legitimate interest, and where the interest of the data controller prevails over that of
the data subject. The company must be able to demonstrate adherence to the fair
information practice below:

- Standards for data quality
- Standards for transparency
- Special protections for sensitive data
- Standards of enforcement.

This means that data must be obtained legitimately and is used in the manner of
the purpose for which it was acquired, and there must be openness and transparency
so that individuals will know how their data will be used. There should be special
protections for sensitive data with the ability to opt in for consent (e.g., race, sexual
orientation, political beliefs), and there must be standards for enforcement to ensure
compliance to the standards. The *Data Privacy Impact Assessment* (DPIA) is
mentioned in GDPR, and it is needed if the processing of personal information is
likely to result in a high risk to the rights and freedoms of individuals. This
assessment helps to ensure that companies are complying with privacy requirements.

The standard for informed consent is very high which means that it is freely given
and informed. GDPR also gives very strong data subject rights, including the right to
access data, data portability, the right to rectify data, the right to erase data, the right
to object to processing, and the right to restrict processing. These rights provide a
powerful tool for data subjects to exercise control over their personal information.

9.5   Review Questions

1. What is data science?
2. What is the role of the data scientist?
3. What is privacy? Why is it important?

4. What are the main sources of personal data collected on line?
5. What are the main risks to an individual using social media?
6. What are the main risks to an individual using a fitness device (as part of the Internet of Things)?
7. What are the main risks with AI facial recognition technology?
8. Explain the importance of the EU GDPR law.
9. What is a digital privacy impact assessment?

9.6   Summary

Ethics is a practical branch of philosophy that deals with moral questions such as the nature of what is right or wrong, as well as how a person should behave in a particular situation in a complex world. Computer ethics is a set of principles that guide the behaviour of individuals when using computer resources. Business ethics (also called corporate ethics) is concerned with ethical principles and moral problems that arise in a business environment. Ethics guide individual employees in carrying out their roles, and ethical issues include the rights and duties of a company, its employees, customers, and suppliers. Several ethical issues that may arise include intellectual property rights, privacy concerns, as well as the impacts of computer technology on wider society.

Companies collect lots of personal data about individuals from their use of computer resources such as email, search engines, their Internet and Social media use, and the data is processed to build up revealing profiles of the user that may be targeted to advertisers. Modern technology allows mass surveillance to be conducted by governments on its citizens, with face recognition software allowing citizens to be recognized at demonstrations or other mass assemblies.

Privacy is important in the information age, and it is the way in which we separate ourselves from other people and is the right to be left alone. The European GDPR law has become an important protector of privacy and personal data, and both European and other countries have adapted it.

References

1. R.C. Barquin, In Pursuit of a 'ten commandments' for computer ethics. Computer Ethics Institute (1992)
2. L. Brandeis, S. Warren, BrW:90 the right to have privacy. Harvard Law Rev., (1890)
3. W. Prosser, Privacy. Californian Law Rev., (1960)
4. Records, Computers and the Rights of Citizens, US Secretary's Advisory Committee on Automated Personal Data Systems (1973). https://aspe.hhs.gov/report/records-computers-and-rights-citizens

Software Metrics and Problem Solving

10

Abstract

This chapter is concerned with metrics and problem solving, and this includes a discussion of the balanced score card which assists in identifying appropriate metrics for the organization. The Goal, Question, Metrics (GQM) approach is discussed, and this allows metrics related to the organization goals to be defined. A selection of sample metrics for an organization is presented, and problem-solving tools such as fishbone diagrams, pareto charts, trend charts are discussed.

Key words

Measurement · Goal, question, metric · Balanced scorecard · Problem solving · Data gathering · Fishbone diagram · Histogram · Pareto chart · Trend graph · Scatter graph · Statistical process control

10.1 Introduction

Measurement is an essential part of mathematics and the physical sciences, and it has been successfully applied to the software engineering field. The purpose of a measurement program is to establish and use quantitative measurements to manage the software development processes and software quality in an organization; to assist the organization in understanding its current software engineering capability; and to provide an objective indication that software process improvements have been successful.

Measurements provide visibility into the various functional areas in the organization, and the quantitative data allow trends to be seen over time. The analysis of the measurements allows action plans to be produced for continuous improvement. Measurements may be employed to track the quality, timeliness, cost, schedule, and

effort of software projects. The term "*metric*" and "*measurement*" are used inter-
changeably in this book. The formal definition of measurement given by Fenton [1] is:

> Measurement is the process by which numbers or symbols are assigned to attributes or
> entities in the real world in such a way as to describe them according to clearly defined rules.

Measurement plays a key role in the physical sciences and everyday life: for
example, calculating the distance to the planets and stars; determining the mass of
objects; computing the speed of mechanical vehicles; calculating the electric current
flowing through a wire; computing the rate of inflation; estimating the unemploy-
ment rate, and so on. Measurement provides a more precise understanding of the
entity under study.

Often several measurements are used to provide a detailed understanding of the
entity under study. For example, the cockpit of an aeroplane contains measurements
of altitude, speed, temperature, fuel, latitude, longitude, and various devices
essential to modern navigation and flight, and clearly an airline offering to fly
passengers using just the altitude measurement would not be taken seriously.

Metrics play a key role in problem solving, and various problem-solving techniques will be discussed later in this chapter. Measurement data are essential in
quantifying how serious a particular problem is, and they provide a precise quantitative measure of the extent of the problem. For example, a telecommunications
outage is measured as the elapsed time between the down time and the subsequent
up time, and the longer the outage lasts the more serious it is. It is essential to
minimize outages and their impact should one occur, and measurement data are
invaluable in proving an objective account of the extent of the problem. Measurement data may be used to perform analysis on the root cause of a particular
problem, e.g., of a telecommunications outage, and to verify that the actions taken
to correct the problem have been effective.

Metrics provide an internal view of the quality of the software product, but care is
needed before deducing the behaviour that a product will exhibit externally from the
various internal measurements of the product. A *leading measure* is a software
measure that usually precedes the attribute that is under examination; for example,
the arrival rate of software problems is a leading indicator of the maintenance effort.
Leading measures provide an indication of the likely behaviour of the product in the
field and need to be examined closely. A *lagging indicator* is a software measure that
is likely to follow the attribute being studied; for example, escaped customer defects
are an indicator of the quality and reliability of the software. It is important to learn
from lagging indicators even if the data can have little impact on the current project.

10.2 The Goal Question Metric Paradigm

Many software metrics programs have failed because they had poorly defined, or
non-existent goals and objectives, with the metrics defined unrelated to the
achievement of the business goals. The *Goal Question Metric* (GQM) paradigm
was developed by Victor Basili and others of the University of Maryland [2]. It is a

rigorous goal-oriented approach to measurement, in which goals, questions, and measurements are closely integrated.

The business goals are first defined, and then questions that relate to the achievement of the goal are identified. For each question a metric that gives an objective answer to the question is defined. The statement of the business goal is precise, and it is related to individuals or groups. The GQM approach is a simple one, and managers and engineers proceed according to the following three stages:

- Set goals specific to needs in terms of purpose, perspective and environment.
- Refine the goals into quantifiable questions.
- Deduce the metrics and data to be collected (and the means for collecting them) to answer the questions.

GQM has been applied to several domains, and so we consider an example from the software field. Consider the goal of determining the effectiveness of a new programming language L. There are several valid questions that may be asked at this stage, including who are the programmers that use L?, and what is their level of experience? What is the quality of software code produced with language L? What is the productivity of language L? This leads naturally to the quality and productivity metrics as detailed in Fig. 10.1.

Goal
The focus on improvements should be closely related to the business goals, and the first step is to identify the key goals that are essential for business success (or to the success of an improvement program). The business goals are related to the strategic direction of the organization and the problems that it is currently facing. There is little sense in directing improvement activities to areas that do not require improvement, or for which there is no business need to improve, or from which there will be a minimal return to the organization.

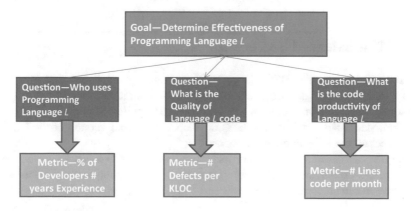

Fig. 10.1   GQM example

Question

These are the key questions that determine the extent to which the goal is being satisfied, and for each business goal the set of pertinent questions need to be identified. The information that is required to determine the status of the goal is determined, and this naturally leads to the set of questions that must be answered to provide this information. Each question is analysed to determine the best approach to obtain an objective answer, and to define the metrics that are needed, and the data that needs to be gathered to answer the question objectively.

Metrics

These are measurements that give a quantitative answer to the particular question, and they are closely related to the achievement of the goals. They provide an objective picture of the extent to which the goal is currently satisfied. Measurement improves the understanding of a specific process or product, and the GQM approach leads to measurements that are closely related to the goal, *rather than measurement for the sake of measurement*.

GQM helps to ensure that the defined measurements will be relevant and used by the organizations to understand its current performance, and to improve and satisfy the business goals more effectively. Successful improvement is impossible without clear improvement goals that are related to the business goals. GQM is a rigorous approach to software measurement, and the measures may be from various viewpoints, e.g., manager viewpoint, project team viewpoint, etc. The idea is always first to identify the goals, and once the goals have been decided common-sense questions and measurement are employed.

There are two key approaches to software process improvement: i.e., *top-down*, or *bottom-up* improvement. Top-down approaches are based on process improvement models and appraisals: e.g., models such as the CMMI, ISO 15504, and ISO 9000, whereas GQM is a bottom-up approach to software process improvement and is focused on improvements related to certain specific goals. The top down and bottom-up approaches are often combined in practice.

10.3   The Balanced Scorecard

The balanced scorecard (BSC) (Fig. 10.2) is a management tool that is used to clarify and translate the organization vision and strategy into action. It was developed by Kaplan and Norton [3], and has been applied to many organizations. The European Software Institute (ESI) developed a tailored version of the BSC for the IT sector (the IT Balanced Scorecard).

The BSC assists in selecting appropriate measurements to indicate the success or failure of the organization's strategy. There are four perspectives in the scorecard: *customer, financial, internal process*, and *learning and growth*. Each perspective

Fig. 10.2 The balanced scorecard

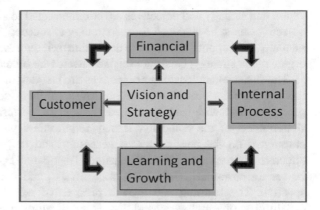

Fig. 10.3 Balanced score card and implementing strategy

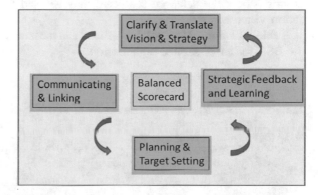

includes objectives to be accomplished for the strategy to succeed, measures to indicate the extent to which the objectives are being met, targets to be achieved in the perspective, and initiatives to achieve the targets. The balanced scorecard includes financial and non-financial measures.

The BSC is useful in selecting the key processes that the organization should focus its process improvement efforts on to achieve its strategy (Fig. 10.3). Traditional improvement is based on improving quality; reducing costs; and improving productivity, whereas the balanced scorecard takes the future needs of the organization into account and identifies the processes that the organization needs to excel at in future to achieve its strategy. This results in focused process improvement, and the intention is to yield the greatest business benefit from the improvement program.

The starting point is for the organization to define its *vision* and *strategy* for the future. This often involves strategy meetings with the senior management to clarify the vision, and to achieve consensus on the strategic direction for the organization among the senior management team. The vision and strategy are then translated into *objectives* for the organization or business unit. The next step is communication, and the vision and strategy and objectives are communicated to all employees. These critical objectives must be achieved for the strategy to succeed, and so all employees (with management support) will need to determine their own local objectives to support the organization strategy. Goals are set and rewards are linked to performance measures.

The financial and customer objectives are first determined from the strategy, and the key business processes to be improved are then identified. These are the key processes that will lead to a breakthrough in performance for customers and shareholders of the company. It may require new processes with re-training of employees on the new processes necessary, and the balanced scorecard is very effective in driving organization change. The financial objectives require targets to be set for customer, internal business process, and the learning and growth perspective. The learning and growth perspective will examine competencies and capabilities of employees and the level of employee satisfaction. Figure 10.3 describes how the balanced scorecard may be used for implementing the organization vision and strategy.

Table 10.1 presents sample objectives and measures for the four perspectives in the BSC for an IT service organization.

Table 10.1 BSC objectives and measures for IT service organization

Financial	Customer
Cost of provision of services	Quality service
Cost of hardware/software	Reliability of solution
Increase revenue	Rapid response time
Reduce costs	Accurate information
Timeliness of solution	Timeliness of solution
99.999% network availability	99.999% network availability
24 × 7 customer support	24 × 7 customer support
Internal business process	**Learning and growth**
Requirements definition	Expertise of staff
Software design	Software development capability
Implementation	Project management
Testing	Customer support
Maintenance	Staff development career structure
Customer support	Objectives for staff
Security/proprietary information	Employee satisfaction
Disaster prevention and recovery	Leadership

10.4 Metrics for an Organization

The objective of this section is to present a set of metrics to provide visibility into various areas in the organization, and to show how metrics can facilitate improvement. The metrics presented may be applied or tailored to individual organizations, and the objective is to show how metrics may be employed for effective management. Many organizations have monthly quality or operation reviews in which the presentation of metrics plays an important part.

We present sample metrics for the various functional areas in a software development organization, including human resources, customer satisfaction, supplier quality, internal audit, project management, requirements and development, testing, and process improvement. These metrics are typically presented at a monthly management review, and performance trends observed. The main output from a management review is a series of improvement actions.

10.4.1 Customer Satisfaction Metrics

Figure 10.4 shows the customer survey arrival rate per customer per month, and it indicates that there is a customer satisfaction process in place in the organization, that the customers are surveyed, and the extent to which they are surveyed. It does not provide any information as to whether the customers are satisfied, whether any follow-up activity from the survey is required, or whether the frequency of surveys is sufficient (or excessive) for the organization.

Figure 10.5 gives the customer satisfaction measurements in several categories including quality, the ability of the company to meet the committed dates and to deliver the agreed content, the ease of use of the software, the expertise of the staff and the value for money. Figure 10.5 is interpreted as follows:

8–10	Exceeds expectations
7	Meets expectations
5–6	Fair
0–4	Below expectations

Fig. 10.4 Customer survey arrivals

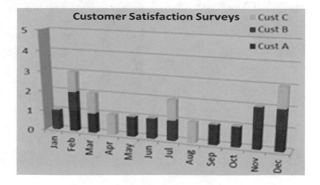

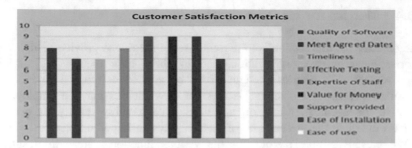

Fig. 10.5 Customer satisfaction measurements

Another words, a m score of 8 for quality indicates that the customers consider the software to be of high quality, and a score of 9 for value for money indicates that the customer considers the solution to be excellent value. It is fundamental that the customer feedback is analysed (with follow up meetings held with the customer where appropriate). There may be a need to produce an action plan to deal with customer issues, and to communicate the plan to the customer, and to execute the action plan in a timely manner.

10.4.2   Process Improvement Metrics

The objective of process improvement metrics is to provide visibility into the process improvement program in the organization. Figure 10.6 shows the arrival rate of improvement suggestions from the software community. The chart indicates that initially the arrival rate is high and the closure rate low, which is consistent with the commencement of a process improvement program. The closure rate then improves which indicates that the improvement team is active and acting upon the improvement suggestions. The closure rate is low during July and August, which may be explained by the traditional holiday period.

Fig. 10.6 Process
improvement measurements

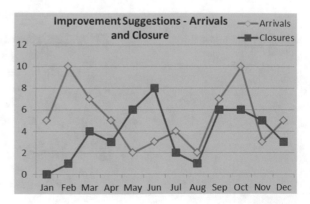

Fig. 10.7 Status of process improvement suggestions

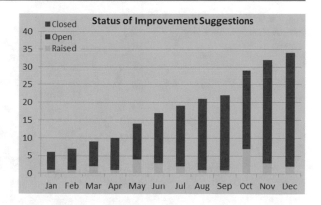

Fig. 10.8 Age of open process improvement suggestions

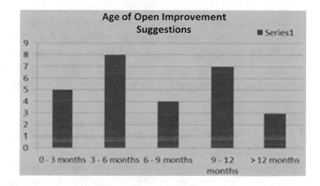

The chart does not indicate the effectiveness of the process improvement suggestions and the overall impact the suggestion has on quality, cycle time, or productivity. There are no measurements of the cost of performing improvements, and this is important for a cost benefit analysis of the benefits of the improvements obtained versus the cost of the improvements.

Figure 10.7 provides visibility into the status of the improvement suggestions, and the number of raised, open, and closed suggestions per month. The chart indicates that gradual progress has been made in the improvement program with a gradual increase in the number of suggestions that are closed.

Figure 10.8 provides visibility into the age of the improvement suggestions, and this is a measure of the productivity of the improvement team and its ability to do its assigned work.

Figure 10.9 gives an indication of the productivity of the improvement program, and it shows how often the team meets to discuss the improvement suggestions and to act upon them. This chart is slightly naive as it just tracks the number of improvement meetings that have taken place during the year, and it has no information on the actual productivity of the meeting. The chart could be considered with Figs. 10.6, 10.7, and 10.8, to get more accurate information on the productivity of the team.

Fig. 10.9 Process
improvement productivity

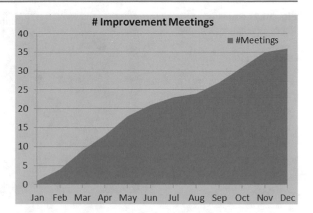

There will usually be other charts associated with an improvement program, for example, a metric to indicate the status of the CMMI program is provided in Fig. 10.26. Similarly, a measure of the status of an ISO 9000 implementation could be derived from the number of actions which are required to implement ISO 9000, the number implemented, and the number outstanding.

10.4.3   Human Resources and Training Metrics

These metrics give visibility into the human resources and training areas of a company. They provide visibility into the current headcount (Fig. 10.10) of the organization per calendar month and the turnover of staff in the organization (Fig. 10.11). The human resources department will typically maintain measurements of the number of job openings to be filled per month, the arrival rate of resumes per month, the average number of interviews to fill one position, the percentage of employees that have received their annual appraisal, etc.

The key goals of the HR department are defined and the questions and metrics are associated with the key goals. For example, one of the key goals of the HR department is to attract and retain the best employees, and this breaks down into the two obvious sub-goals of attracting the best employees and retaining them. The

Fig. 10.10 Employee
headcount in current year

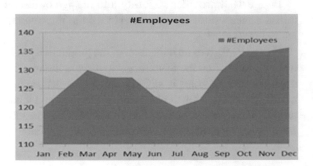

Fig. 10.11 Employee turnover in current year

next chart gives visibility into the turnover of staff during the calendar year. It indicates the effectiveness of staff retention in the organization.

10.4.4 Project Management Metrics

The goal of project management is to deliver a high-quality product that is fit for purpose on time and on budget. The project management metrics provide visibility into the effectiveness of the project manager in delivering the project on time, on budget, and with the right quality.

The timeliness metric provides visibility into the extent to which the project has been delivered on time (Fig. 10.12), and the number of months over or under schedule per project in the organization is shown. The schedule timeliness metric is a lagging measure, as it indicates that the project has been delivered within schedule or not after the event.

The on-time delivery of a project requires that the various milestones in the project be carefully tracked, and corrective actions taken to address slippage in milestones during the project.

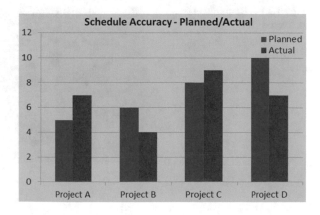

Fig. 10.12 Schedule timeliness metric

Fig. 10.13 Effort timeliness metric

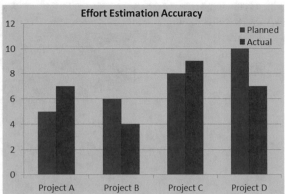

The second metric provides visibility into the effort estimation accuracy of a project (Fig. 10.13). Effort estimation is a key component in calculating the cost of a project, and in preparing the schedule, and its accuracy is essential. We mentioned the Standish Research data on projects in an earlier chapter, and this report showed that accurate effort and schedule estimation is difficult.

The effort estimation chart is like the schedule estimation chart, except that the schedule metric is referring to time as recorded in elapsed calendar months, whereas the effort estimation chart refers to the planned number of person months required to carry out the work, and the actual number of person months that it took. Projects need an effective estimation methodology for successful estimation, and the project manager will use metrics to determine how accurate the estimation has actually been.

The next metric is related to the commitments that are made to the customer with respect to the content of a particular release, and it indicates the effectiveness of the projects in delivering the agreed requirements to the customer (Fig. 10.14). This chart could be adapted to include enhancements or fixes promised to a customer for a particular release of a software product.

Fig. 10.14 Requirements delivered

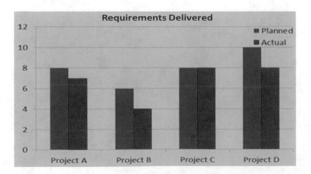

10.4.5 Development Quality Metrics

These metrics give visibility into the development and testing of the software product, and we presented a sample of testing metrics in Chap. 8. Figure 10.15 gives an indication of the quality of the software produced, and the quality of the definition of the initial requirements. It shows the total number of defects, and the total number of change requests raised during the project, as well as details on their severities. The presence of many change requests suggests that the initial definition of the requirement was incomplete, and that there is considerable room for improvement in the requirements elicitation process.

Figure 10.16 gives the status of open issues with the project, which gives an indication of the current quality of the project, and the effort required to achieve the desired quality in the software. This chart is not used in isolation, as the project manager will need to know the arrival rate of problems to determine the stability of the software product.

Fig. 10.15 Total number of issues in project

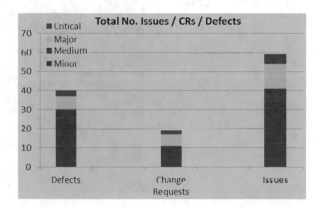

Fig. 10.16 Open issues in project

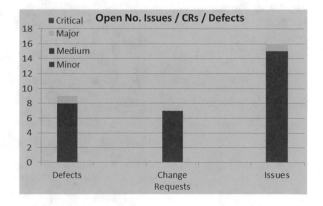

The organization may decide to release a software product with open problems provided that the associated risks with the known problems can be managed. It is important to perform a risk assessment to ensure that these may be managed, and the known problems (and workarounds) should be documented in the release notes for the product.

The project manager will need to know the age of the open problems to determine the effectiveness of the project team in resolving problems in a timely manner. Figure 10.17 presents the age of the open defects, and it highlights the fact that there is one major problem that has been open for over one year. The project manager needs to prevent this situation from arising, as critical and major problems need to be swiftly resolved.

The problem arrival rate enables the project manager to judge the stability of the software, and this (with other metrics) helps in judging whether the software is fit for purpose and ready for release to potential customers. Figure 10.18 presents a

Fig. 10.17 Age of open defects in project

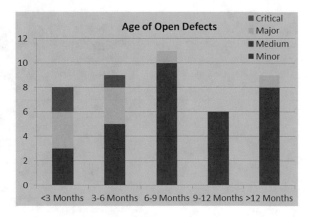

Fig. 10.18 Problem arrivals per month

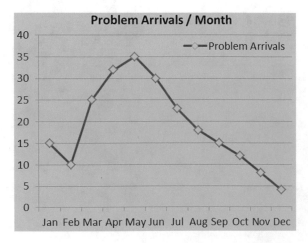

Fig. 10.19 Phase
containment effectiveness

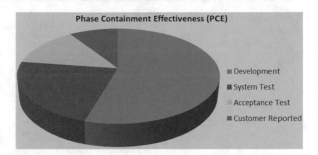

sample problem arrival chart, and the chart indicates positive trends with the arrival
rate of problems falling to very low levels.

The project manager will need to do analysis to determine if there are other
causes that could contribute to the fall in the arrival rate; for example, it may be the
case that testing was completed in September, which would mean, in effect, that no
testing has been performed since then, with an inevitable fall in the number of
problems reported. The important point is not to jump to a conclusion based on a
particular chart, as the circumstances behind the chart must be fully known and
taken into account in order to draw valid conclusions.

Figure 10.19 measures the effectiveness of the project in identifying defects in
the development phase, and the effectiveness of the test groups in detecting defects
that are present in the software. The development portion typically includes defects
reported on inspection forms and in unit testing.

The various types of testing (e.g., unit, system, performance, usability, acceptance) were discussed in Chap. 8. Figure 10.19 indicates that the project had a
phase containment effectiveness of approximately 54%. That is, the developers
identified 54% of the defects, the system-testing phase identified approximately
23% of the defects, acceptance testing identified approximately 14% of the defects,
and the customer identified approximately 9% of the defects. The objective is that
the number of defects reported at acceptance test and after the product is officially
released to customer should be minimal.

10.4.6 Quality Audit Metrics

These metrics provide visibility into the audit program, and include metrics for the
number of audits planned and performed (Fig. 10.20), and the status of the audit
actions (Fig. 10.21). Figure 10.20 presents visibility into the number of audits
carried out in the organization, and the number of audits that remain to be done.

It shows that the organization has an audit program and gives information on the
number of audits performed during a particular period. The chart does not give a
breakdown into the type of audits performed, e.g., supplier audits, project audits,
and audits of departments in the organization, but it could be adapted to provide this
information.

Fig. 10.20 Annual audit
schedule

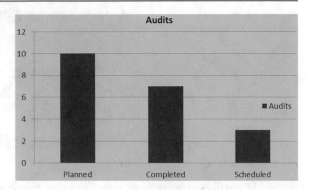

Figure 10.21 chart gives an indication of the status of the various audits performed. An auditor performs an audit, and the results are documented in an audit report, and the associated audit actions need to be completed by the affected individuals and groups. Figure 10.21 presents the status of the audit actions assigned to the affected groups.

Figure 10.22 gives visibility into the type of actions raised during the audit of a particular area. They could potentially include entry and exit criteria, planning issues, configuration management issues, issues with compliance to the lifecycle or

Fig. 10.21 Status of audit
actions

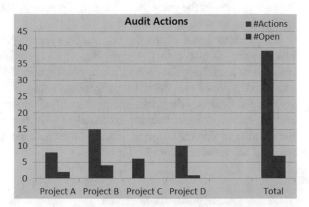

Fig. 10.22 Audit action
types

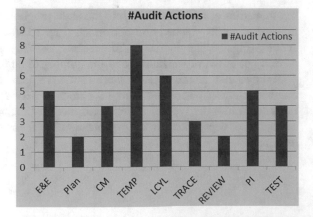

templates, traceability to the requirements, issues with the review of various deliverables, issues with testing, or process improvement suggestions.

10.4.7 Customer Care Metrics

The goals of the customer care group in an organization are to respond efficiently and effectively to customer problems, to ensure that their customers receive the highest standards of service from the company, and to ensure that its products function reliably at the customer's site. The organization will need to know its efficiency in resolving customer queries, the number of customer queries, the availability of its software systems at the customer site, and the age of open queries. A customer query may result in a defect report in the case of a problem with the software.

Figure 10.23 presents the arrival and closure rate of customer queries (it could be developed further to include a severity attribute for the query). Quantitative goals are generally set for the resolution of queries (especially in the case of service level agreements). A chart for the age of open queries (like Fig. 10.17) is often maintained. The organization will need to know the status of the backlog of open queries per month, and a simple trend graph would provide this. Figure 10.23 shows that the arrival rate of queries in the early part of the year exceeds the closure rate of queries per month. This indicates an increasing backlog that needs to be addressed.

The customer care department responds to any outages and ensures that the outage time is kept to a minimum. Many companies set ambitious goals for network availability; e.g., the *"five nines initiative"* has the objective of developing systems which are available 99.999% of the time, i.e., approximately five minutes of down time per year. The calculation of availability is from the formula:

$$\text{Availability} = \frac{\text{MTBF}}{\text{MTBF} + \text{MTTR}}$$

where the mean time between failure (MTBF) is the average length of time between outages.

$$\text{MTBF} = \frac{\text{Sample Interval Time}}{\#\text{Outages}}$$

The formula for MTBF above is for a single system only, and the formula is adjusted when there are multiple systems.

$$\text{MTBF} = \frac{\text{Sample Interval Time}}{\#\text{ Outages}} * \#\text{ Systems}$$

The mean time to repair (MTTR) is the average length of time that it takes to correct the outage, i.e., the average duration of the outages that have occurred, and it is calculated from the following formula:

$$\text{MTTR} = \frac{\text{Total Outage Time}}{\#\text{Outages}}$$

Figure 10.24 presents outage information on the customers impacted by the outage during the month, and the extent of the impact on the customer.

An effective customer care department will ensure that a post-mortem of an outage is performed to ensure that lessons are learned to prevent a reoccurrence. This causal analysis details the root causes of the outage, and corrective actions are implemented to prevent a reoccurrence. Metrics to record the amount of system availability and outage time per month will typically be maintained by the customer care group in the form of a trend graph.

Figure 10.25 provides visibility on the availability of the system at the customer sites, and many organizations are designing systems to be available 99.999% of the time. System availability and software reliability are discussed in more detail in Chap. 15.

Fig. 10.23 Customer queries (arrivals/closures)

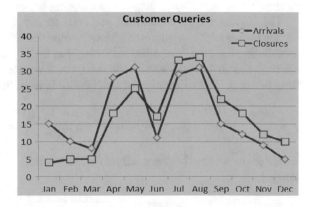

Fig. 10.24 Outage time per customer

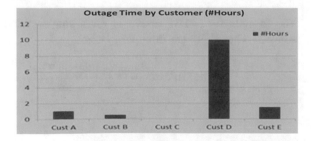

Fig. 10.25 Availability of
system per month

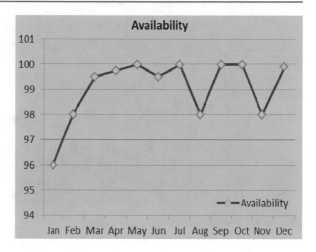

10.4.8   Miscellaneous Metrics

Metrics may be applied to many other areas in the organization. This section
includes metrics on the CMMI maturity of an organization (where an organization
is implementing the CMMI), configuration management, and the cost of poor
quality. Figure 10.26 given visibility into the time to create a software release from
the configuration management system.

The internal CMMI maturity of the organization is given by Fig. 10.27, and this
chart is an indication of its readiness for a formal CMMI assessment. A numeric
score of 1–10 is used to rate each process area, and a score of 7 or above indicates
that the process area is satisfied.

Crosby argued that the most meaningful measurement of quality is the cost of
poor quality [4], and that the emphasis on the improvement activities in the organization should therefore be to reduce the *cost of poor quality* (COPQ). The cost of
quality includes the cost of external and internal failure, the cost of providing an
infrastructure to prevent the occurrence of problems, and the cost of the infrastructure to verify the correctness of the product.

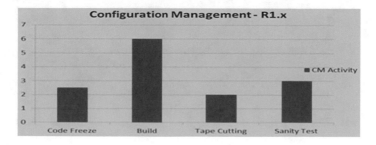

Fig. 10.26 Configuration management

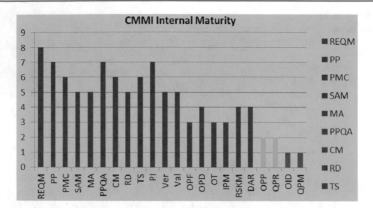

Fig. 10.27 CMMI maturity in current year

The cost of quality was divided into four subcategories (Table 10.2) by Feigenbaum in the 1950s and evolved further by James Harrington of IBM.

The cost of quality graph (Fig. 10.28) will initially show high external and internal costs and low prevention costs, and the total quality costs will be high. However, as an effective quality system is put in place and becomes fully operational, there will be a noticeable decrease in the external and internal cost of quality, and a gradual increase in the cost of prevention and appraisal.

The total cost of quality will substantially decrease, as the cost of provision of the quality system is substantially below the cost of internal and external failure. The COPQ curve will indicate where the organization is in relation to the cost of poor quality, and the organization will need to execute its improvement plan to put an effective quality management system in place to minimize the cost of poor quality.

Table 10.2 Cost of quality categories

Type of cost	Description
Cost external	This includes the cost of external failure and includes engineering repair, warranties, and a customer support function
Cost internal	This includes the internal failure cost and includes the cost of reworking and re-testing of any defects found internally
Cost prevention	This includes the cost of maintaining a quality system to prevent the occurrence of problems, and includes the cost of software quality assurance, the cost of training, etc.
Cost appraisal	This includes the cost of verifying the conformance of a product to the requirements and includes the cost of provision of software inspections and testing processes

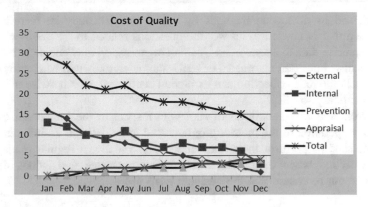

Fig. 10.28 Cost of poor quality (COPQ)

10.5 Implementing a Metrics Program

The metrics discussed in this chapter may be adapted and tailored to meet the needs of organizations. The metrics are only as good as the underlying data, and good data gathering is essential. The following are typical steps in the implementation of a metrics program (Table 10.3).

The business goals are the starting point in the implementation of a metrics program, as there is no sense in measurement for the sake of measurement, and so metrics must be closely related to the business goals. The next step is to identify the relevant questions to determine the extent to which the business goal is being satisfied, and to define metrics that provide an objective answer to the questions.

The organization defines its business goals, and each department develops specific goals to meet the organization's goals. Measurement will indicate the extent to which specific goals are being achieved, and good data gathering, and recording are essential. First, the organization will need to determine which data need to be

Table 10.3 Implementing metrics

Implementing metrics in organization
Define the business goals
Determine the pertinent questions
Define the metrics
Identify tools to (semi-) automate metrics
Determine data that needs to be gathered
Identify and provide needed resources
Gather data and prepare metrics
Communicate the metrics/review monthly
Provide training

gathered, and to determine methods by which the data may be recorded. The information that is needed to answer the questions related to the goals will determine the precise data to be recorded. A small organization may decide to record the data manually, but often automated or semi-automated tools will be employed. It is essential that the data collection and extraction is efficient, as otherwise the metrics program is likely to fail.

The roles and responsibilities of staff with respect to the implementation and day-to-day operation of the metrics program need to be defined. Training is needed to enable staff to perform their roles effectively. Finally, a regular management review is needed, where the metrics and trends are presented, and actions identified and carried out to ensure that the business goals are achieved.

10.5.1   Data Gathering for Metrics

Metrics are only as good as the underlying data, and so data gathering is a key activity in a metrics program. The data to be recorded will be closely related to the questions, and the data are used to give an objective answer to the questions. The business goals are often expressed quantitatively for extra precision, and Table 10.4 presents an example of how the questions related to a particular goal are identified.

Table 10.5 is designed to determine the effectiveness of the software development process, and to enable the above questions to be answered. It includes a column for inspection data that records the number of *defects* recorded at the

Table 10.4   Goals and questions

Goal	Reduce escaped defects from each lifecycle phases by 10%
Questions	How many defects are identified within each lifecycle phase?
	How many defects are identified after each lifecycle phase is exited?
	What % of defects escaped from each lifecycle phase?

Table 10.5   Phase containment effectiveness

Phase of origin								
Phase	Inspect defects	Reqs	Design	Code	Accept test	In-phase defects	Other defects	% PCE
Reqs	4		1	1		4	6	40%
Design	3					3	4	42%
Code	20					20	15	57%
Unit test		2	2	10				
System test		2	2	5				
Accept test								

various inspections. The *defects* include the phase where the defect originated; for example, a defect identified in the coding phase may have originated in the requirements or design phase. This data is typically maintained in a spreadsheet, e.g., Excel (or a dedicated tool), and it needs to be kept up to date. It enables the phase containment effectiveness (PCE) to be calculated for the various phases.

We will distinguish between a defect that is detected *in-phase* versus a defect that is detected *out-of-phase*. An in-phase defect is a problem that is detected in the phase in which it is created (e.g., usually by a software inspection). An out-of-phase defect is detected in a later phase (e.g., a problem with the requirements may be discovered in the design phase, which is a later phase from the phrase in which it was created).

The effectiveness of the requirements phase in Table 10.5 is judged by its success in identifying defects as early as possible, as the cost of correction of a requirements defect increases the later in the cycle that it is identified. The requirements PCE is calculated to be 40%, i.e., the total number of requirements defects identified in phase divided by the total number of requirements defects identified. There were four defects identified at the inspection of the requirements, and six defects were identified outside of the requirements phase: one in the design phase, one in the coding phase, two in the unit testing phase, and two at the system testing phase: i.e., 4/10 = 40%. Similarly, the code PCE is calculated to be 57%.

The overall PCE for the project is calculated to be the total number of defects detected in phase in the project divided by the total number of defects, i.e., 27/52 = 52%. Table 10.4 is a summary of the collected data, and its construction consists of:

- Maintain inspection data of requirements, design, and code inspections.
- Identify defects in each phase and determine their phase of origin.
- Record the number of defects in each phase per phase of origin.

The staff who perform inspections need to record the problems identified, whether it is a defect, and its phase of origin. Staff will need to be appropriately trained to do this consistently.

The above is just one example of data gathering, and in practice the organization will need to collect various data to enable it to give an objective answer to the extent that the goal is being satisfied.

10.6 Problem-Solving Techniques

Problem solving is a key part of quality improvement, and a *quality circle* (or problem-solving team) is a group of employees who do similar work and volunteer to come together on company time to identify and analyse work-related problems. Quality circles were first proposed by Ishikawa in Japan in the 1960s.

Various tools that assist problem solving include *process mapping*, *trend charts*, *bar charts*, *scatter diagrams*, *fishbone diagrams*, *histograms*, *control charts,* and *pareto charts* [5]. These provide visibility into the problem and help to quantify the extent of the problem. The main features of a problem-solving team include:

- Group of employees who do similar work.
- Voluntarily meet regularly on company time.
- Supervisor as leader.
- Identify and analyse work-related problems.
- Recommend solutions to management.
- Implement solution where possible.

The facilitator of the quality circle coordinates the activities, ensures that the team leaders and teams members receive sufficient training, and obtains specialist help where required. The facilitator has the following responsibilities:

- Focal point of quality circle activities.
- Train circle leaders/members.
- Coordinate activities of all the circle groups.
- Assist in inter-circle investigations.
- Obtain specialist help when required.

The circle leaders receive training in problem-solving techniques and are responsible for training the team members. The leader needs to keep the meeting focused and requires skills in team building. The steps in problem solving include:

- Select the problem.
- State and restate the problem.
- Collect the facts.
- Brainstorm.
- Choose course of action.
- Present to management.
- Measurement of success.

The benefits of a successful problem-solving culture in the organization include:

- Savings of time and money.
- Increased productivity.
- Reduced defects.
- Fire prevention culture.

Various problem-solving tools are discussed in the following sections.

10.6.1 Fishbone Diagram

This well-known problem-solving tool consists of a cause-and-effect diagram that is in the shape of the backbone of a fish. The objective is to identify the various causes of some problem, and then these causes are broken down into several sub-causes. The various causes and sub-causes are analysed to determine the root cause of the problem, and actions to address the root cause are then defined to prevent a reoccurrence of the manifested effect. There are various categories of causes, and these may include people, methods and tools, and training.

The great advantage of the fishbone diagram is that it offers a crisp mechanism to summarize the collective knowledge that a team has about a particular problem, as it focuses on the causes of the problem, and facilitates the detailed exploration of the causes.

The construction of a fishbone diagram involves a clear statement of the particular effect, and the effect is placed at the right-hand side of the diagram. The major categories of cause are drawn on the backbone of the fishbone diagram; brainstorming is used to identify causes; and these are then placed in the appropriate category. For each cause identified the various sub-causes may be identified by asking the question *"Why does this happen?"* This leads to a more detailed understanding of the causes and sub-causes of a particular problem.

Example 10.1 An organization wishes to determine the causes of a high number of reported defects from the customer. There are various categories that may be employed such as people, training, methods, tools, and environment. In practice, the fishbone diagram in Fig. 10.29 would be more detailed than that presented, as sub-causes would also be identified by a detailed examination of the identified causes. The root cause(s) are determined from detailed analysis.

This example suggests that the organization has significant work to do in several areas, and that an improvement program is required. The improvements needed include the implementation of a software development process and a software test

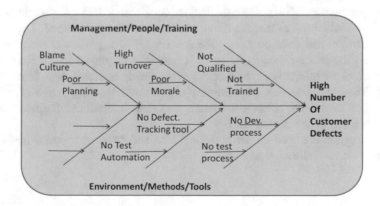

Fig. 10.29 Fishbone cause-and-effect diagram

process; the provision of training to enable staff to do their jobs more effectively; and the implementation of better management practices to motivate staff and to provide a supportive environment for software development.

The causes identified may be symptoms rather than actual root causes: for example, high staff turnover may be the result of poor morale and a "blame culture", rather than a cause in itself of poor-quality software. The fishbone diagram gives a better understanding of the possible causes of the high number of customer reported defects. A small subset of these causes is then identified as the root cause (s) of the problem following further discussion and analysis.

The root causes are then addressed by appropriate corrective actions (e.g., an appropriate software development process and test process are defined and providing training to all development staff on the new processes). The management attitude and organization culture will need to be corrected to enable a supportive software development environment to be put in place.

10.6.2 Histograms

A histogram is a way of representing data in bar chart format, and it shows the relative frequency of various data values or ranges of data values. It is typically employed when there are many data values, and it gives a very crisp picture of the spread of the data values, and the centring and variance from the mean.

The histogram has an associated shape, e.g., it may be a *normal distribution*, a *bimodal* or *multi-modal distribution*, or be positively or negatively skewed. The variation and centring refer to the spread of data, and the relation of the centre of the histogram to the customer requirements. The spread of the data is important as it indicates whether the process is too variable, or whether it is performing within the requirements. The histogram is termed process centred if its centre coincides with the customer requirements; otherwise, the process is too high or too low. A histogram enables predictions of future performance to be made if the future will resemble the past.

The construction of a histogram first requires that a frequency table be constructed, and this requires that the range of data values be determined. The data are divided into several data buckets, where a bucket is a particular range of data values, and the relative frequency of each bucket is displayed in bar format. The number of class intervals or buckets is determined, and the class intervals are defined. The class intervals are mutually disjoint and span the range of the data values. Each data value belongs to exactly one class interval and the frequency of each class interval is determined.

The histogram is a well-known statistical tool, and its construction is made more concrete with the following example.

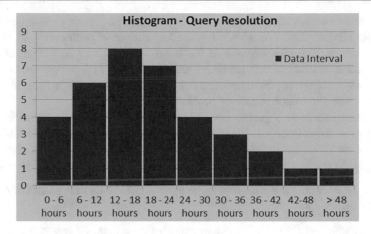

Fig. 10.30 Histogram

Example 10.2 An organization wishes to characterize the behaviour of the process for the resolution of customer queries to achieve its customer satisfaction goal.

Goal
Resolve all customer queries within 24 h.

Question
How effective is the current customer query resolution process?
What action is required (if any) to achieve this goal?

The data class size chosen for the histogram below is six hours, and the data class sizes are of the same in standard histograms (they may be of unequal size for non-standard histograms). The sample mean is 19 h for this example. The histogram shown (Fig. 10.30) is based on query resolution data from 36 samples. The organization goal of customer resolution of all queries within 24 hours is not met, and the goal is satisfied in (25/36 = 70% for this sample).

Further analysis is needed to determine the reasons why 30% of the goals are outside the target 24-hour target. It may prove to be impossible to meet the goal for all queries, and the organization may need to refine the goal to state that instead all critical and major queries will be resolved within 24 h.

10.6.3   Pareto Chart

The objective of a pareto chart is to identify and focus on the resolution of problems that have the greatest impact (as *often 20% of the causes are responsible for 80% of the problems*). The problems are classified into various categories, and the frequency of each category of problem is determined. The pareto chart is displayed in a descending sequence of frequency, with the most significant cause presented first, and the least significant cause presented last.

The pareto chart is a key problem-solving tool, and a properly constructed chart will enable the organization to resolve the key causes of problems, and to verify their resolution. The effectiveness of the improvements may be judged at a later stage from the analysis of new problems and the creation of a new pareto chart. The results should show tangible improvements, with less problems arising in the category that was the major source of problems.

The construction of a pareto chart requires the organization to decide on the problem to be investigated; to identify the causes of the problem via brainstorming; to analyse the historical or real time data; to compute the frequency of each cause; and finally, to display the frequency in descending order for each cause category.

Example 10.3 An organization wishes to understand the various causes of outages, and to minimize their occurrence.

The pareto chart (Fig. 10.31) below includes data from an analysis of outages, where each outage is classified into a particular cause. The six causal categories identified are: hardware, software, operator error, power failure, an act of nature, and unknown. The three main causes of outages are hardware, software, and operator error, and analysis is needed to identify appropriate actions to address these. The hardware category may indicate that there are problems with the reliability of the system hardware, and that existing hardware systems may need improvement or replacement. There may be a need to address availability and reliability concerns with more robust hardware solutions.

The software category may be due to the release of poor-quality software, or to usability issues in the software, and this requires further investigation. Finally, operator issues may be due to lack of knowledge or inadequate training of the operators. An improvement plan needs to be prepared and implemented, and its effectiveness will be judged by a reduction in outages, and reductions of problems in the targeted category.

Fig. 10.31 Pareto chart outages

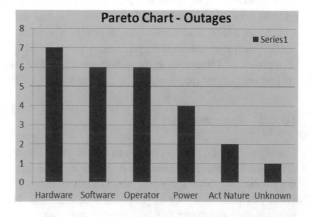

10.6.4 Trend Graphs

A trend graph monitors the performance of a variable over time, and it allows trends in performance to be identified, as well as allowing predictions of future trends to be made (if the future resembles the past). Its construction involves deciding on the variable to measure, and to gather the data points to plot the data.

Example 10.4 An organization plans to deploy an enhanced estimation process and wishes to determine if estimation is actually improving with the new process.

The estimation accuracy determines the extent to which the actual effort differs from the estimated effort. A reading of 25% indicates that the project effort was 25% more than estimated, whereas a reading of −10% indicates that the actual effort was 10% less than estimated.

The trend chart (Fig. 10.32) indicates that initially that estimation accuracy is very poor, but then there is a gradual improvement coinciding with the implementation of the new estimation process.

It is important to analyse the performance trends in the chart. For example, the estimation accuracy for August (17% in the chart) needs to be investigated to determine the reasons why it occurred. It could potentially indicate that a project is using the old estimation process, or that a new project manager received no training on the new process). A trend graph is useful for noting positive or negative trends in performance, with negative trends analysed and actions identified to correct performance.

10.6.5 Scatter Graphs

The scatter diagram is used to determine whether there is a relationship or correlation between two variables, and where there is to measure the relationship between them. The results may be a positive correlation, negative correlation, or no correlation. Correlation has a precise statistical definition, and it provides a precise

Fig. 10.32 Trend chart estimation accuracy

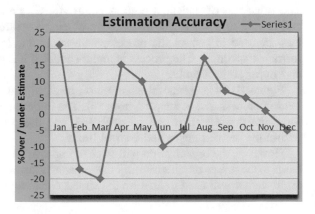

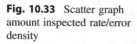

Fig. 10.33 Scatter graph
amount inspected rate/error
density

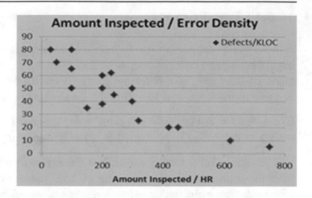

mathematical understanding of the extent to which the two variables are related or unrelated.

The scatter graph provides a graphical way to determine the extent that two variables are related, and it is often used to determine whether there is a connection between an identified causes and the effect. The construction of a scatter diagram requires the collection of paired samples of data, and the drawing of one variable as the *x*-axis, and the other as the *y*-axis. The data are then plotted and interpreted.

Example 10.5 An organization wishes to determine if there is a relationship between the inspection rate and the density of defects identified.

The scatter graph (Fig. 10.33) provides evidence for the hypothesis that there is a relationship between the lines of code inspected, and the error density recorded (per KLOC). The graph suggests that the density of defects identified during inspections is low if the speed of inspection is high, and the density is high if the speed of inspection is below 300 lines of code per hour. A regression line may be drawn through the data that indicates a linear relationship.

10.6.6 Metrics and Statistical Process Control

The principles of statistical process control (SPC) are important in the monitoring and control of a process. It involves developing a control chart, which is a tool that may be used to control the process, with upper and lower limits for process performance specified. The process is under control if it is performing within the lower and upper control limits.

Figure 10.34 presents an example on breakthrough in performance of an estimation process and is adapted from [6]. The initial upper and lower control limits for estimation accuracy are set at ±40%, and the performance of the process is within the defined upper and control limits.

However, the organization will wish to improve its estimation accuracy, and this leads to the organization's revising the upper and lower control limits to ±25%. The organization will need to analyse the slippage data to determine the reasons for the

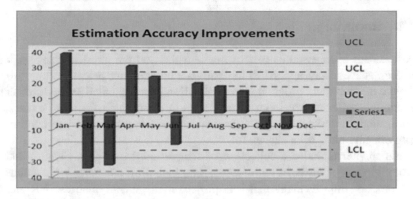

Fig. 10.34 Estimation accuracy and control charts

wide variance in the estimation, and part of the solution will be the use of enhanced estimation methods in the organization. In this chart, the organization succeeds in performing within the revised control limit of ±25%, and the limit is revised again to ±15%.

This requires further analysis to determine the causes for slippage and further improvement actions are needed to ensure that the organization performs within the ±15% control limit.

10.7   Review Questions

1. Describe the Goal, Question, Metric model.
2. Explain how the Balanced Scorecard may be used in the implementation of organization strategy.
3. Describe various problem-solving techniques.
4. What is a fishbone diagram?
5. What is a histogram and describe its applications?
6. What is a scatter graph?
7. What is a pareto chart? Describe its applications.
8. Discuss how a metrics program may be implemented.
9. What is statistical process control?

10.8 Summary

Measurement is an essential part of mathematics and the physical sciences, and it has been successfully applied to the software engineering field. The purpose of a software measurement program is to establish and use quantitative measurements to manage the software development processes in the organization, and to assist the organization in understanding its current software capability and to confirm that improvements have been successful.

This chapter included a collection of sample metrics to give visibility into the various functional areas in the organization, including customer satisfaction metrics, process improvement metrics, project management metrics, HR metrics, development and quality metrics, and customer care metrics.

The balanced scorecard assists the organization in selecting appropriate measurements to indicate the success or failure of the organization's strategy. Each of the four scorecard perspectives includes objectives that need to be achieved for the strategy to succeed, and measurements indicate the extent to which the objectives are being met.

The Goal, Question, Metric paradigm is a rigorous, goal-oriented approach to measurement in which goals, questions, and measurements are closely integrated. The business goals are first defined, and then questions that relate to the achievement of the goal are identified, and for each question a metric that gives an objective answer to the question is defined.

Metrics play a key role in problem solving, and various problem-solving techniques were discussed. These include histograms, pareto charts, trend charts and scatter graphs. The measurement data are used to assist the analysis and to determine the root cause of a particular problem, and to verify that the actions taken to correct the problem have been effective. Trends may be seen over time, and the analysis of the trends allows action plans to be prepared for continuous improvement.

Metrics may be employed to track the quality, timeliness, cost, schedule, and effort of software projects. They provide an internal view of the quality of the software product, but care is needed before deducing the behaviour that a product will exhibit externally.

References

1. N. Fenton, *Software Metrics: A Rigorous Approach* (Thompson Computer Press, 1995)
2. V. Basili, H. Rombach, The TAME project. Towards improvement-oriented software environments. IEEE Trans. Softw. Eng. **14**(6) (1988)
3. R.S. Kaplan, D.P. Norton, *The Balanced Scorecard, Translating Strategy into Action* (Harvard Business School Press, 1996)
4. P. Crosby, *Quality Is Free, The Art of Making Quality Certain* (McGraw Hill, 1979)
5. M. Brassard, D. Ritter, *The Memory Jogger. A Pocket Guide of Tools for Continuous Improvement and Effective Planning* (Goal/QPC. Methuen, MA, 1994)
6. G. Keeni et al., The evolution of quality processes at Tate Consulting Services. IEEE Softw. **17** (4) (2000)

Supplier Selection and Management 11

Abstract

This chapter is concerned with the selection and management of a software supplier. It discusses how candidate suppliers may be identified, formally evaluated against defined selection criteria, and how the appropriate supplier is selected. We discuss how the selected supplier is managed during the project.

Keywords

Request for proposal · Supplier evaluation · Formal agreement · Statement of work · Managing supplier · Service level agreement · Escrow · Breach of contract · Acceptance of software

11.1 Introduction

Outsourcing is a common business practice where a company contracts out business functions such as manufacturing, software development, and call centres to third party providers. The outsourcing of a business function to a distant country is termed *offshoring*, whereas outsourcing may also be done domestically, and *nearshoring* is where the outsourcing is to a nearby country. The main benefits are outsourcing include:

- Cost savings due to reduction in business expenses.
- Availability of expertise not available in house.
- Allows company to focus on core business activities.
- Increased efficiencies.

Outsourcing involves handing control of various business functions over to a third party, and this leads to business risks such as the quality of the service may be below expectations, or the third party may go out of business, or that there may be risks to confidentiality and security. Outsourcing involves managing the day-to-day relationship with the offshore/onshore team in possibly different time zones, and there may be differences in language and culture.

Many large projects involve total or partial outsourcing of the software development, and it is therefore essential to select a supplier that can deliver high-quality and reliable software on time and on budget. Supplier selection and management is concerned with the selection and management of a third-party software supplier. Many large projects involve total or partial outsourcing of the software development, and it is therefore essential to select a supplier that can deliver high-quality and reliable software on time and on budget.

This means that the process for the selection of the supplier needs to be rigorous, and that the capability of the supplier is clearly understood, and the associated risks are known prior to selection. The selection is based on objective criteria such as cost, the approach, the ability of the supplier to deliver the required solution, the supplier capability, and while cost is an important criterion, it is just one among several other important factors.

Once the selection of the supplier is finalized a legal agreement is drawn up between the contractor and supplier, which states the terms and condition of the contract, as well as the statement of work. The statement of work details the work to be carried out, the deliverables to be produced, when they will be produced, the personnel involved their roles and responsibilities, any training to be provided, and the standards to be followed.

The supplier then commences the defined work and is appropriately managed for the duration of the contract. This will involve regular progress reviews, and acceptance testing is carried out prior to accepting the software from the supplier. The following activities are generally employed for supplier selection and management (Table 11.1).

Remote project management is concerned with managing remote and hybrid teams to ensure that the project objectives are achieved. Traditional project management involve teams based in the same physical location, whereas often today teams may operate in hybrid mode with some employees working in the office and other employees and teams working remotely in different physical locations. This means that remote employees often play important roles in the success of projects, and remote project management has become more important in managing hybrid and remote teams.

The management of remote teams requires modern communication including video conferencing, shared files, and documents, as well as team communication and messaging apps. The creation of the team is the easy part as it is more challenging to build a team culture with remote teams. The project manager will stay engaged with the team throughout the project with virtual meetings, and remote

Table 11.1 Supplier selection and management

Activity	Description
Planning and requirements	This involves defining the approach to the procurement. It involves • Defining the procurement requirements • Forming the evaluation team to rate each supplier against objective criteria
Identify suppliers	This involves identifying suppliers and may involve research, recommendations from colleagues or previous working relationships. Usually, three to five potential suppliers will be identified
Prepare and issue RFP	This involves the preparation and issuing of the request for proposal (RFP) to potential suppliers. The RFP may include the evaluation criteria and a preliminary legal agreement
Evaluate proposals	The received proposals are evaluated, and a short-list produced. The short-listed suppliers are invited to make a presentation of their proposed solution
Select supplier	Each supplier makes a presentation followed by a Q&A session. The evaluation criteria are completed for each supplier and reference sites checked (as appropriate). The decision on the preferred supplier is made
Define supplier agreement	A formal agreement is made with the preferred supplier. This may include • Negotiations with the supplier/involvement with legal department • Agreement may vary (statement of work, service level agreement, Escrow, etc.) • Formal agreement signed by both parties • Unsuccessful parties informed • Purchase order raised
Managing the supplier	This is concerned with monitoring progress, project risks, milestones and issues, and taking action when progress deviates from expectations
Acceptance	This is concerned with the acceptance of the software and involves acceptance testing to ensure that the supplied software is fit for purpose
Rollout	This is concerned with the deployment of the software and support/maintenance activities

project management is like traditional project management except that the project is executed remotely. It is a flexible methodology that can support various approaches such as traditional software engineering and Agile.

The project manager needs to determine the remote structure that is required, and then to find the people with the appropriate skills to carry out the project. The project expectations need to be communicated clearly to the team members at project initiation, including the process to be followed, work hours, project goals, their responsibilities, the tools that will be employed for collaboration, and so on. Regular virtual team meetings will be conducted by the project manager, and the team members will check in daily with the project manager to advise on progress made.

11.2 Planning and Requirements

The potential acquisition of software arises as part of a make-or-buy analysis at project initiation. The decision is whether the project team should (or has the competence to) develop a particular software system (or component of it), or whether there is a need to outsource (or purchase off-the-shelf) the required software. The supplied software may be the complete solution to the project's requirements, or it may need to be integrated with other software produced for the project. The following tasks are involved:

- The requirements are defined (these may be a subset of the overall business requirements).
- The solution may be available as an off-the-shelf software package (with configuration needed to meet the requirements).
- The solution may be to outsource all or part of the software development.
- The solution may be a combination of the above.

Once the decision has been made to outsource or purchase an off-the-shelf solution an evaluation team is formed to identify potential suppliers, and evaluation criteria is defined to enable each supplier's solution to be objectively rated.

A plan will be prepared by the project manager detailing the approach to the procurement, defining how the evaluation will be conducted, defining the members of the evaluation team and their roles and responsibilities, and preparing a schedule of the procurement activities to be carried out.

The remainder of this chapter is focused on the selection of a supplier for the outsourcing of all (or part) of the software development, but it could be easily adapted to deal with the selection of an off-the-shelf software package.

11.3 Identifying Suppliers

A list of potential suppliers may be determined in various ways including:

- Previous working relationship with suppliers.
- Research via the Internet/Gartner.
- Recommendations from colleagues or another company.
- Advertisements/other.

A previous working relationship with a supplier provides useful information on the capability of the supplier, and whether it would be a suitable candidate for the work to be done. Further, a supplier that is ISO 9001 certified for quality and ISO 27001 certified for Information Security has independent indications of reasonable capability. Companies will often maintain a list of preferred suppliers, and these are the suppliers that have worked previously with the company, and whose capability is known. The risks associated with a supplier on the preferred supplier list are known and are generally less than those of an unknown supplier. If the experience of working with the supplier is poor, then the supplier may be removed from the preferred supplier list.

There may be additional requirements for public procurement to ensure fairness in the procurement process, and often-public contracts need to be more widely advertised to allow all interested parties the opportunity to make a proposal to provide the product or service.

The list of candidate suppliers may potentially be quite large, and so short listing may be employed to reduce the list to a more manageable size of around five candidate suppliers.

11.4   Prepare and Issue RFP

The Request for Proposal (RFP) is prepared and issued to potential suppliers, and the suppliers are required to complete a proposal detailing the solution that they will provide, as well as the associated costs, by the closing date. The proposal will need to detail the specifics of the supplier's solution, and it needs to show how the supplier plans to implement the requirements.

The RFP details the requirements for the software and must contain sufficient information to allow the candidate supplier to provide a complete and accurate response. The completed proposal will include technical and financial information, which allows a rigorous evaluation of each received proposal to be carried out.

The RFP may include the criteria defined to evaluate the supplier, and often weightings are employed to reflect the importance of individual criteria. The evaluation criteria may include several categories such as:

- Functional (related to business requirements).
- Technology (related to the technologies/non-functional requirements).
- Supplier capability and maturity.
- Delivery approach.
- Overall Cost.

Once the proposals have been received further short listing may take place to limit the formal evaluation to around 3–5 suppliers.

11.5   Evaluate Proposals and Select Supplier

The evaluation team will evaluate all received proposals using an evaluation spreadsheet (or similar mechanism), and the results of the evaluation yield a short list of around three suppliers. The short-listed suppliers are then invited to make a presentation to the evaluation team, and this allows the team to question each supplier in detail to gain a better understanding of the solution that they are offering, and any risks associated with the supplier and their proposed solution.

Following the presentations and Q&A sessions the evaluation team will follow up with checks on reference sites for each supplier. The evaluation spread sheet is updated with all the information gained from the presentations, the reference site checks, and the risks associated with individual suppliers.

Finally, an evaluation report is prepared to give a summary of the evaluation, and this includes the recommendation of the preferred supplier. The project board then makes a decision to accept the recommendation; select an alternate supplier; or restart the procurement process.

11.6 Formal Agreement

The preferred supplier is informed on the outcome of the evaluation, and negotiations on a formal legal agreement commences. The agreement will need to be signed by both parties, and may (depending on the type of agreement) include (Fig. 11.1):

- Legal Contract.
- Statement of Work.
- Implementation Plan.
- Training Plan.
- User Guides and Manuals.
- Customer Support to be Provided.
- Service Level Agreement.
- Escrow Agreement.
- Warranty Period.

Fig. 11.1 Legal contract

The *statement of work* (SOW) is employed in bespoke software development, and it details the work to be carried out, the activities involved, the deliverables to be produced, the personnel involved and their roles and responsibilities.

A *service level agreement* (SLA) is an agreement between the customer and service provider which specifies the service that the customer will receive as well as the response time to customer issues and problems. It will also detail the penalties should the service performance fall below the defined levels.

An *Escrow agreement* is an agreement made between two parties where an independent trusted third-party acts as an intermediary between both parties. The intermediary receives money from one party and sends it to the other party when contractual obligations are satisfied. Under an Escrow agreement the trusted third party may also hold documents and source code.

11.7 Managing the Supplier

The activities involved in the management of the supplier are like the standard project management activities discussed in Chap. 4. The supplier may be based in a different physical location (possibly in another country or it may consist of hybrid teams), and so regular communication is essential for the duration of the contract. The project manager is responsible for managing the supplier and will typically communicate with the supplier daily. The supplier will send regular status reports detailing progress made as well as any risks and issues. The activities involved include:

- Monitoring progress.
- Managing schedule, effort, and budget.
- Managing risks and issues.
- Managing changes to the scope of the project.
- Obtaining weekly progress reports from the supplier.
- Managing project milestones.
- Managing quality.
- Reviewing the supplier's work.
- Performing audits of the project.
- Monitoring test results and correction of defects.
- Acceptance testing of the delivered software.

The project manager will maintain daily/weekly contact with the supplier, and will monitor progress, milestones, risks, and issues. The risks associated with the supplier include the supplier delivering late or delivering poor quality, and all risks need to be managed.

11.8   Acceptance of Software

Acceptance testing is carried out to ensure that the software developed by the supplier is fit for purpose. The supplied software may just be a part of the overall system, and it may need to be integrated with other software. The acceptance testing involves:

- Preparation of acceptance test cases (this is the acceptance criteria).
- Planning and scheduling of acceptance testing.
- Setting up the Test Environment.
- Execution of test cases (UAT testing) to verify acceptance criteria is satisfied.
- Test Reporting.
- Communication of defects to supplier.
- Correction of the defects by supplier.
- Re-testing and Acceptance of software.

The project manager will communicate any defects with the software to the supplier, and the supplier makes the required corrections and modifications to the software. Re-testing then takes place and once all acceptance tests have successfully passed the software is accepted.

11.9   Rollout and Customer Support

This activity is concerned with the rollout of the software at the customer site, and the handover to the support and maintenance team. It involves:

- Deployment of the software at customer site.
- Provision of training to staff.
- Handover to the Support and Maintenance Team.
- On-going customer support.
- On-going maintenance.

11.10   Ethical Software Outsourcing

Software outsourcing is a way for a business to hire a third-party subcontractor to develop all or part of a software development project, rather than carrying out the project in-house. It has become popular for western companies to outsource software developments to countries in Asia and Eastern Europe, with India now a major player for software outsourcing, and Poland and the Ukraine[1] have also become popular.

---

[1] This was before Putin's Russia invaded Ukraine in 2022.

There are various motivations for outsourcing such as the desire to reduce the cost of software development, or it may be that the company may wish to focus on its core business and to outsource non-core activities, or it may that the company lacks the expertise or capacity to implement the project internally. There are various models of outsourcing including where a company may partner with a third party supplier as a way to obtain extra IT resources for a company project, or it might outsource all or parts of the project to a third party supplier under the company's supervision, or it may outsource with the subcontractor having full responsibility for the work from the start to the end with minimal supervision.

The costs of outsourcing may be significantly cheaper than developing the software internally, but there are risks that it could be work out more expensive where there are delays or significant rework due to poor quality. There are risks of disruption of business activities depending on the political climate of the country where the subcontractor is based. Further, there may be risks of pandemics, natural disasters, or the subcontractor becoming bankrupt. It is essential that contractors are qualified for the work that they are to perform, and all associated risks must be managed.

The area of corporate social responsibility (CSR) has become important in recent years, and companies have a responsibility to be good corporate citizens and to consider wider society in their actions and their impact on the world. That is, corporations are expected to behave ethically, and to be conscious of their carbon footprint and the sustainability of their business in the countries in which they are operating (even at the expense of profits).

There are several ethical issues with outsourcing such as the fact that outsourcing may lead to loss of jobs in the home country of the company when it decides to outsource its software development to a cheaper country. It would seem reasonable to expect an ethical corporation to protect jobs in the countries where it is operating.

Ethical corporations have a responsibility to ensure that there are reasonable work practices in place at the subcontractor company, and that workers receive a fair salary, have reasonable conditions of employment, and are not exploited by the subcontractor. Globalization and the outsourcing of manufacturing operations led to many sweatshops in Asia, and there is the infamous case of Foxconn, an Apple supplier of the *iPhone* based in Shenzhen in China. Several Foxconn employees committed suicide due to their working conditions and their exploitation by the company, and this raised important questions on the responsibilities of Apple for the welfare of the employees of one of its key suppliers. It is reasonable to expect a company as profitable as Apple to ensure that the staff of its suppliers are not exploited.

Advanced economies have many laws and regulations to protect the environment, and the health and safety of employees. However, the laws and regulations in Asia or wherever the subcontractor is based may not be as stringent. An ethical corporate citizen has responsibilities to the environment, and it is not sufficient for the corporation to say that it is complying fully with the laws of every country it is operating, where these laws are not fit for purpose. The corporation has ethical responsibilities for the health and safety of the subcontractor staff that are working on their projects.

There may be significant cultural differences between the country where the country where the corporation is based and the country where the subcontractor is based, and potentially very different values between both countries. There may be problems with the political system in the country where the subcontractor is based, where an authoritarian government may maintain a strong control over the state and its citizens. There may be problems with corruption, where bribes are paid to officials and others to get things done, and to remove roadblocks. There may be unethical practices over price fixing, and there may be cultural differences in the understanding of the importance and protection of proprietary information, intellectual property, and compliance to security and privacy standards. It is important to be explicit in the software outsourcing so that there is no room for misunderstanding.

An ethical corporation will wish to seek the cheapest offering, but it is also important to consider the ethical implications of outsourcing. An ethical corporation will need to check ethical behaviour of the subcontractor on a regular basis including salary and working conditions, and one way to do this is to perform audits of suppliers. Audits provide visibility into the technical software development work being done to verify its compliance to standards and all appropriate laws and regulations, and special ethical audits could be conducted to provide insight into any work practices that could create ethical difficulties.

It is generally inappropriate to award the contract to a subcontractor just on price alone, and while price is an important criterion it is just one among many criteria, and ethical criteria should also be considered. It is best to build a stable relationship with suppliers, where there is a deep understanding of each supplier and any associated risks.

11.11   Legal Breach of Contact

The legal agreement between the company and the subcontractor specifies the terms to be satisfied and the obligations on both parties for the duration of the contract. These include the deliverables to be produced, the timelines, the responsibilities of both parties, and the financial payments to be made at agreed milestones. A contract is legally binding on both parties with both having defined obligations and should one party fail to deliver according to the terms of the agreement then they are in breach of the contract.[2]

---

[2] It is also possible that two parties make a verbal contract that is legally enforceable.

A *material breach* is where one party does not fulfil their obligations under the contract or delivers a significantly different result from that defined in the contract. An *anticipatory breach* is where one party has indicated that they will not be fulfilling their obligations under the contract, and while an actual breach has not yet occurred there is an intention to be in breach of the contract. Both parties will generally discuss and attempt to resolve any such breaches, and it is generally easy to resolve *minor breaches*. However, if both parties are unable to resolve their dispute over a material breach in the contract, then one party may decide to sue the other party for being in breach of contract. However, legal disputes tend to be expensive and time consuming, and it is often more economical and in the best interest of both parties to come to a resolution of their dispute without the involvement of their lawyers.

The plaintiff will bring the lawsuit to court claiming a material breach in the contract, and the plaintiff will need to show that there was a legally binding contract between the two parties, that the plaintiff fulfilled all of his obligations under the contract (unless there was a legitimate reason not to), that the defendant failed to honour the terms of the legal agreement, and that the defendant's actions led to loss being suffered by the plaintiff. That is, the breach of contract claim involves proving that:

- Existence of contract.
- Plaintiff honoured contract.
- Defendant did not fulfil conditions of contract.
- Plaintiff suffered loss or damages.

The court will need to decide if there was a material breach of the contract and will consider the arguments made by the plaintiff and the defendant. The defence may argue that misunderstandings, misinterpretations, and errors in the terms of the contract agreed by both the plaintiff and defendant led to the breach of contract, and the judge will need to weigh up and consider all of the evidence and issue a judgement. The judgement is based on the facts of the case and the details of the contract, and it may be in favour of the defendant or the plaintiff depending on the circumstances of the case. For example, if the judge decides in favour of the plaintiff the remedy may be restitution and could potentially include:

- Award of financial compensation for the breach of contract.
- Punitive damages to punish the wrongdoer.

There are many possible breaches that could occur such as (Table 11.2).

Table. 11.2 Possible breaches of contract

Breach	Description
Missing deliverables	This is where the supplier has failed to deliver one or more deliverables, or where they have been delivered late
Deliverables not fit for purpose	This is where one or more deliverables do not satisfy the requirements, or they may fail to adhere to the defined standards or be unusable
Missing personnel	This is where the agreed human resources for the contract have not been provided
Unskilled resources	This is where the resources provided lack the skills and experience to perform their roles effectively
Inadequate development environment	This is where the software engineering environment provided is not fit for purpose for developing and testing the software
Intellectual property not protected	This is where the intellectual property (e.g., patents and copyright) has not been properly protected
Proprietary information not protected	This is where the confidentiality of proprietary information provided to the subcontractor has not been protected
Quality problems	This is where there are serious quality problems in testing or with the software produced, and where the software does not perform correctly under real world conditions
Inadequate support (SLA)	This is where the support provided has been below the level agreed between the parties. It may be that the resolution of problems has not achieved the targets in the service level agreement
Bankrupt supplier	This is where the supplier has become bankrupt and is unable to fulfil their obligations

11.12   Review Questions

1. What are the main activities in supplier selection and management?
2. What factors would lead an organization to seek a supplier rather than developing a software solution in-house?
3. What are the benefits of out-sourcing?
4. Describe how a supplier should be selected.
5. Describe how a supplier should be managed.
6. What is a service level agreement?
7. Describe the purpose of a statement of work?
8. What is an Escrow agreement?
9. What is ethical outsourcing?
10. What is a breach of contract and how should it be managed?

11.13 Summary

Supplier selection and management is concerned with the selection and management of a third-party software supplier. Many large projects often involve total or partial outsourcing of the software development, and it is therefore essential to select a supplier who can deliver high-quality and reliable software on time and on budget.

The process for the selection of the supplier needs to be rigorous, and the capability of the supplier including the associated risks needs to be clearly understood. The selection is based on objective criteria, and the evaluation team will rate each supplier against the criteria and recommend their preferred supplier.

Once the selection is finalized a legal agreement is drawn up (which usually includes the terms and condition of the contract as well as a statement of work). The supplier then commences the defined work and is appropriately managed for the duration of the contract.

The project manager is responsible for managing the supplier, and this involves communicating with the supplier daily and managing issues and risks. The software is subject to acceptance testing before it is accepted from the supplier.

Configuration Management

12

Abstract

This chapter discusses configuration management and discusses the fundamental concept of a baseline. Configuration management is concerned with identifying those deliverables that must be subject to change control and controlling changes to them.

Keywords

Configuration management system · Configuration items · Baseline · File naming conventions · Version control · Change control · Change control board · Configuration management audits

12.1 Introduction

Software configuration management (SCM) is concerned with tracking and controlling changes to the software and project deliverables, and it provides full traceability of the changes made during the project. It provides a record of what has been changed, as well as who changed it. SCM involves identifying the configuration items of the system; controlling changes to them; and maintaining integrity and traceability.

The origins of software configuration management go back to the early days of computing when the principles of configuration management used in the hardware design and development field were applied to software development in the 1950s. It has evolved over time to a set of procedures and tools to manage changes to the software.

The configuration items are generally documents in the early part of the software development lifecycle, whereas the focus is on source code control management and software release management in the later parts of development. Software configuration management involves:

- Identifying what needs to be controlled,
- Ensuring those items are accurately defined and documented,
- Ensuring that changes are made in a controlled manner,
- Ensuring that the correct version of a work product is being used,
- Knowing the version and status of a configuration item at any time,
- Ensuring adherence to standards,
- Planning builds and releases.

Software configuration management allows the orderly development of software, and it ensures that only authorized changes to the software are made. It ensures that releases are planned, and that the impacts of proposed changes are considered prior to their authorization. The integrity of the system is always maintained, and the constituents of the software (including their version numbers) are known at any time.

Effective configuration management allows questions such as the following (Table 12.1) to be easily answered.

The symptoms of poor configuration management include corrected defects that suddenly begin to reappear; difficulty in or failure to locate the latest version of source code; or failure to determine the source code that corresponds to a software release.

Therefore, it is important to employ sound configuration management practices to enable high-quality software to be consistently produced. Poor configuration management practices lead to quality problems resulting in a loss of the credibility and reputation of a company. Several symptoms of poor configuration management practices are listed in Table 12.2.

Table 12.1 Features of good configuration management	Features of good configuration management
	What is the correct version of the software module to be updated?
	Where can I get a copy of R4.7 of software system X?
	What versions of the software system X are installed at the various customer sites?
	What changes have been introduced in the new release of software (version R4.8 from the previous release of R4.7)?
	What version of the design document corresponds to software system version R3.5?
	What customers use R3.5 of the software system?
	Are there undocumented or unapproved changes included in the released version of the software?

Table 12.2 Symptoms of poor configuration management

Symptoms of poor configuration management
Defects corrected suddenly begin to re-appear
Cannot find the latest version of the source code
Unable to match the source code and object code
Wrong version of software sent to the customer
Wrong code tested
Cannot replicate previously released code
Simultaneous changes to same source component by multiple developers with some changes lost

Configuration management involves identifying the configuration items to be controlled, and systematically controlling change to them, to maintain the integrity and traceability of the configuration throughout the software development lifecycle. There is a need to manage and control changes to documents and source code, including the project plan, the requirements document, design documents, code, and test plans.

A key concept in configuration management is that of a "*baseline*", which is *a set of work products that have been formally reviewed and agreed upon and serves as the foundation for future development work.*

A baseline can only be changed through formal change control procedures, which leads to a new baseline. It provides a stable basis for the continuing evolution of the configuration items, and all approved changes move forward from the current baseline leading to the creation of a new baseline. The change control board (CCB) or a similar mechanism authorizes the release of baselines, and the content of each baseline is documented. All configuration items must be approved before they are entered into the released baselines.

Therefore, it is necessary to identify the configuration items that need to be placed under formal change control, and to maintain a history of the changes made to the baseline. There are four key parts to software configuration management (Table 12.3).

A typical set of software releases (e.g., in the telecommunications domain) consists of incremental development, where the software to be released consists of several release builds with the early builds consisting of new functionality, and the later builds consisting of fix releases.

Software configuration management is planned for the project, and each project will typically have a configuration management plan which will detail the planned delivery of functionality and fix release for the project (Table 12.4).

Each of the R.1.0.0. k baselines are termed release builds, and they consist of new functionality and fixes to the identified problems. The content of each release build is known, i.e., the project team and manager will target specific functionality and fixes for each build, and the actual content of the particular release baseline is documented. Each release build can be replicated, as the version of source code to create the build is known, and the source code is under control management.

Table 12.3 Software configuration management activities

Area	Description
Configuration identification	This requires identifying the configuration items to be controlled, and implementing a sound configuration management system, including a repository where documents and source code are placed under controlled access. It includes a mechanism for releasing documents or code, a file naming convention and a version numbering system for documents and code, and baseline/release planning. The version and status of each configuration item should be known
Configuration control	This involves tracking and controlling change requests and controlling changes to the configuration items. Any changes to the work products are controlled and authorized by a change control board or similar mechanism. Problems or defects reported by the test groups or customer are analysed, and any changes made are subject to change control. The version of the work product is known, and the constituents of a particular release are known and controlled. The previous versions of releases can be recreated, as the source code constituents are fully known and available
Configuration auditing	This includes audits to verify the integrity of the baseline, and audits of the configuration management system verify that the standards and procedures are followed. The results of the audits are communicated to the affected groups, and corrective action taken to address the findings
Status accounting	This involves data collection and report generation. These reports include the software baseline status, the summary of changes to the software baseline, problem report summaries, and change request summaries

Table 12.4 Build plan for project

Release baseline	Contents	Date
R. 1.0.0.0	F_4, F_5, F_7	31.01.17
R. 1.0.0.1	F_1, F_2, F_6 + fixes	15.02.17
R. 1.0.0.2	F_3 + fixes	28.02.17
R. 1.0.0.3	F_8 + fixes (functionality freeze)	07.03.17
R. 1.0.0.4	Fixes	14.03.17
R. 1.0.0.5	Fixes	21.03.17
R. 1.0.0.6	Official release	31.03.17

There are various tools employed for software configuration management activities, and these include well-known tools such as Clearcase, PVCS, and Visual Source Safe (VSS) for source code control management. The PV tracker tool and Clearquest may be used for tracking defects and change requests. A defect-tracking tool will list all the open defects against the software, and a defect may require several change requests to correct the software (as a problem may affect different parts of the software product as well as different versions of the product, and a change request may be necessary for each part). The tool will generally link the

Table 12.5 CMMI requirements for configuration management

Specific goal	Specific practice	Description of specific practice/goal
SG 1		*Establish baselines*
	SP 1.1	Identify configuration items
	SP 1.2	Establish a configuration management system
	SP 1.3	Create or release baselines
SG 2		*Track and control changes*
	SP 2.1	Track change requests
	SP 2.2	Control configuration items
SG 3		*Establish integrity*
	SP 3.1	Establish configuration management records
	SP 3.2	Perform configuration audits

change requests to the problem report. The status of the problem report can be determined, and the targeted release build for the problem identified.

The CMMI provides guidance on practices to be implemented for sound configuration management (Table 12.5).

The CMMI requirements are concerned with establishing a configuration management system; identifying the work products that need to be subject to change control; controlling changes to these work products over time; controlling releases of work products; creating baselines; maintaining the integrity of baselines; providing accurate configuration data to stakeholders; recording and reporting the status of configuration items and change requests; and verifying the correctness and completeness of configuration items with configuration audits. We shall discuss the key parts of configuration management in the following sections.

12.2 Configuration Management System

The configuration management system enables the controlled evolution of the documents and the software modules produced during the project. It includes:

- Configuration management planning,
- A document repository with check in/check out features,
- A source code repository with check in/check out features,
- A configuration manager (may be a part time role),
- File naming convention for documents and source code,
- Project directory structure,
- Version Numbering System for documents,
- Standard templates for documents,
- Facility to create a baseline,
- A release procedure,

- A group (change control board) to approve changes to baseline,
- A change control procedure,
- Configuration management audits to verify integrity of baseline.

12.2.1   Identify Configuration Items

The configuration items are the work products to be placed under configuration management control, and they include project documents, source code and data files. They may also include compilers as well as any supporting tools employed in the project.

The project documentation will typically include project plans; the user requirements specification; the system requirements specification; the architecture and technical design documents; the test plans, etc.

The items to be placed under configuration management control are identified and documented early in the project lifecycle. Each configuration item needs to be uniquely identified and controlled. This may be done with a naming convention for the project deliverables and source code and applying it consistently. For example, a simple approach is to employ mnemonics labels and version numbers to uniquely identify project deliverables. A user requirements specification for project 005 in the Finance business area may be represented simply by:

FIN_005_URS

12.2.2   Document Control Management

The project documents are stored in a document repository using a configuration management tool such as PVCS or VSS. For consistency, a standard directory structure is often employed for projects, as this makes it easier to locate particular configuration items. A single repository may be employed for both documents and software code (or a separate repository for each).

Clearly, it is undesirable for two individuals to modify the same document at the same time, and the document repository will include *check in/check out* procedures. The document must be checked out prior to its modification, and once it is checked out, another user may not modify it until it has been checked back in. An audit trail of all modifications made to a particular document is maintained, including details of the person who made the change, the date that the change was made, and the rationale for the change.

Version Numbering of Documents
A simple version numbering system may be employed to record the versions of documents: e.g., v0.1, v0.2, v0.3 is often used for draft documents, with version v1.0 being the first approved version of the document. Each time a document is

modified its version number is incremented, and the document history records the reasons for modification.

- V0.1 Initial draft of document
- V0.x Revised draft ($x > 0$)
- V1.0 Approved baseline version
- V1.x Approved minor revision ($x > 0$)
- Vn.0 Approved major revision ($n > 1$)
- Vn.x Approved minor revision ($x > 0$, $n > 1$).

The document will provide information on whether it is a draft or approved, as well as the date of last modification, the person who made the modification, and the rationale for the modification. The configuration management system will provide records of the configuration management activities, as well as the status of the configuration items and the status of the change requests. The revision history of the configuration items will be maintained.

12.2.3   Source Code Control Management

The source code and data files are stored in a source code repository using a tool such as PVCS, VSS or Clearcase, and the repository provides an audit trail of all the changes made to the source code. An item must first be checked out for modification, the changes are made, and it is then checked back into the repository. The source code management system provides security and control of the configuration items, and the procedures include:

- Access controls,
- Checking in/out configuration items,
- Merging and Branching,
- Labels (labelling releases),
- Reporting.

The source code configuration management tool ensures the integrity of the source code and prevents more than one person from altering the software code at the same time.

12.2.4   Configuration Management Plan

A software *configuration management plan* (it may be part of the project plan or a separate plan) is prepared early in the project, and it defines the configuration management activities for the project. It will detail the items to be placed under configuration management control, the standards for naming configuration items, the version numbering system, as well as version control and release management.[1] The CM plan is placed under configuration management control.

The content of each software release is documented as well as installation and rollback instructions. The content includes the requirements and change requests implemented, as well as the defects corrected and the version of the new release. A list is maintained of the customer sites of where the release has been installed. All software releases are tested prior to their approval. The CM plan will include:

- Roles and responsibilities,
- Configuration Items,
- Naming Conventions,
- Version Control,
- Filing Structure for project.

The stakeholders and roles involved are identified and documented in the CM plan. Often, the role of a *software configuration manager* is employed, and this may be a full time or part time role.[2] The CM manager ensures that the configuration management activities are carried out correctly and will conduct and report the results of the CM audits.

12.3 Change Control

A change request (CR) database[3] is set up to record change requests made during the project. The change requests are documented and considered by the change control board (CCB). The CCB may just consist of the project manager and the system owner for small projects, or a management and technical team for larger projects.

The impacts and risks of the proposed change need to be considered, and an informed decision made on whether to reject or approve the CR. The proposed change may have technical impacts, as well as introducing new project risks, and may adversely affect the schedule and budget. It is important to keep change to a minimum at the later stages of the project to reduce risks to quality.

Figure 12.1 describes a simple process for raising a change request; performing an impact assessment; deciding on whether to approve or reject the change request; and proceeding with implementation (where applicable).

The results of the CCB review of each change request (including the rationale of the decision made) will be recorded. Change requests and problem reports for all configuration items are recorded and analysed, reviewed, approved (or rejected) and tracked to closure.

---

[1] These may be defined in a Configuration Management procedure and referenced in the CM plan.
[2] This depends on the size of the organization and projects. The project manager may perform the CM manager role for small projects.
[3] This may just be a simple Excel spread sheet or a sophisticated tool.

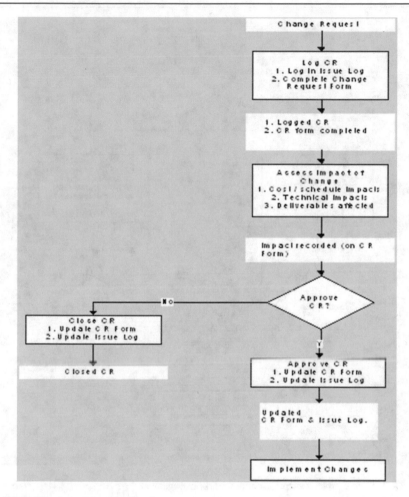

Fig. 12.1 Simple process map for change requests

A sample configuration management process map is detailed in Fig. 12.2, and it shows the process for updates to configuration information following an approved change request. The deliverable is checked out of the repository; modifications are made, and the changes approved; configuration information is updated, and the deliverable is checked back into the repository.

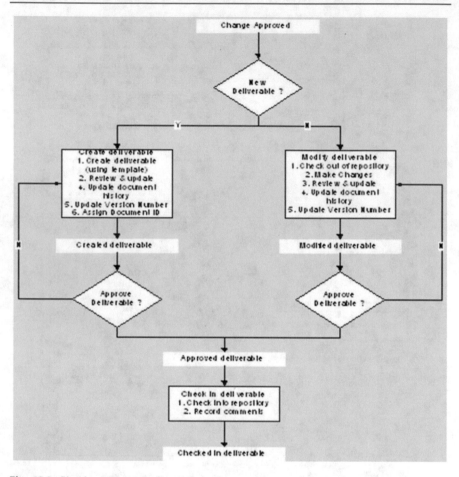

Fig. 12.2 Simple process map for configuration management

12.4   Configuration Management Audits

Configuration management audits are conducted during the project to verify that
the configuration is consistent and complete. Every project should have at least one
configuration audit, and the objective is to verify the completeness and correctness
of the configuration system for the project. The audit will check that the records
correctly identify the configuration, and that the configuration management standards and procedures have been followed. Table 12.6 presents a sample configuration management checklist.

Table 12.6 Sample configuration management audit checklist

No.	Item to check
1.	Is the directory structure set up for the project?
2.	Are the configuration items identified and listed?
3.	Have the latest versions of the templates been used?
4.	Is a unique document Id employed for each document?
5.	Is the standard version numbering system followed for the project?
6.	Are all versions of documents and software modules in the document/source code repository?
7.	Is the configuration management plan up to date?
8.	Are the roles defined in the configuration management plan performing their assigned responsibilities?
9.	Are changes to the approved documents formally controlled?
10.	Is the version number of a document incremented following an agreed change to an approved document?
11.	Is there a change control board set up to approve change requests?
12.	Is there a record of which releases are installed at the various customer sites?
13.	Are all documents/software modules produced by vendors under appropriate configuration management control?

There may also be a *librarian role* to set up the filing structure for the project, or the configuration manager may perform this role. The project manager assigns responsibilities for performing configuration management activities. All involved in the process receive appropriate training on the process.

12.5 Review Questions

1. What is software configuration management?
2. What is change control?
3. What is a baseline?
4. Explain source code control management.
5. Explain document control management.
6. What is a configuration management audit and explain how it differs from a standard audit?
7. Describe the role of the configuration manager and librarian.
8. Describe the main elements in a software configuration management system.

12.6 Summary

Software configuration management is concerned with the orderly development and evolution of the software. It is concerned with tracking and controlling changes to the software and project deliverables, and it provides full traceability of the changes made during the project.

It involves identifying the configuration items that are subject to change control, controlling changes to them, and maintaining integrity and traceability throughout the software development lifecycle. The configuration items are generally documents in the early part of the development lifecycle, whereas the focus is on source code control management and software release management in the later parts of the development lifecycle.

The company standards need to be adhered to, and the correct version of a work product should be always known. There is a need for a document and source code repository, which has access controls, checking in and checking out procedures; and labelling of releases.

A project will have a configuration management plan, and the configuration manager role is responsible for ensuring that the configuration management activities are carried out correctly.

Configuration management ensures that the impacts of proposed changes are considered prior to authorization. It ensures that releases are planned and that only authorized changes to the software are made. The integrity of the system is maintained, and the constituents of the software system and their version numbers are always known. Configuration audits will be conducted to verify that the CM activities have been carried out correctly.

Software Quality Assurance

13

Abstract

This chapter discusses software quality assurance and the importance of process quality. It is a premise in the quality field that good processes and conformance to them is essential for the delivery of high quality product, and this chapter discusses audits, and describes how they are carried out.

Keywords

Auditor · Independence of auditor · SQA team · Audit planning · Audit meeting · Audit reporting · Audit actions · Tracking actions · Audit escalation · Training

13.1 Introduction

The purpose of software quality assurance is to provide visibility to management on the processes being followed and the work products being produced in the organization. It is a systematic enquiry into the way that things are done in the organization, and involves conducting audits of projects, suppliers, and departments. It provides:

- Visibility into the extent of compliance to the defined processes and standards.
- Visibility into the processes and standards in use in the organization.
- Visibility into the effectiveness of the defined processes.
- Visibility into the fitness for use of the work products produced.

Software quality assurance involves planning and conducting audits; reporting the results to the affected groups; tracking the assigned audit actions to completion; and conducting follow up audits, as appropriate. It is generally conducted by the

Table 13.1 Auditing activities

Activity	Description
Audit planning	• Select projects/areas to be audited during period • Agree audit dates with affected groups • Agree scope of audit and advise attendees what needs to be brought to the meeting • Book room and send invitation to the attendees • Prepare/update the audit schedule
Audit meeting	• Ask attendees as to their specific role (in the project), the activities performed and determine the extent to which the process is followed • Employ an audit checklist as an aid • Review agreed documentation • Determine if processes are followed and effective
Audit reporting	• Revise notes from the audit meeting and review any appropriate additional documentation • Prepare audit report and record audit actions (Consider getting feedback on report prior to publication) • Agree closure dates of the audit actions • Circulate approved report to attendees/management
Track actions	• Track audit actions to closure • Record the audit action status • Escalation (where appropriate) to resolve open actions
Audit closure	• Once all actions are resolved the audit is closed

SQA group,[1] and this group is independent of the groups being audited. The activities involved include (Table 13.1).

All involved in the audit process need to receive appropriate training. This includes the participants in the audit who receive appropriate orientation on the purpose of audits and their role in it. The auditor needs to be trained in interview techniques, including asking open and closed questions, as well as possessing effective documentation skills in report writing, in order to record the results of the audit. The auditor needs to be able to deal with any conflicts that might arise during an audit.[2]

The flow of activities in a typical audit process is sketched in Fig. 13.1, and they are described in more detail in the following sections.

---

[1] This group may vary from a team of auditors in a large organization to a part-time role in a small organization.

[2] The auditor may face a situation where one or more individuals become defensive and will need to reassure individuals that the objective of the audit is not to find fault with individuals, rather the objective is to determine if the process is fit for purpose and to promote continuous improvement, as well as identifying any quality risks with the project. The culture of an organization has an influence on how open individuals will be during an audit (for example, individuals may be defensive if there is a blame culture in the organization rather than an emphasis on fixing the process).

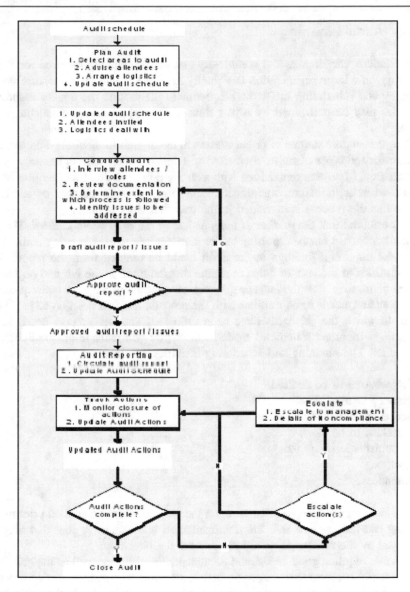

Fig. 13.1 Sample audit process

13.2   Audit Planning

Organizations vary in size and complexity and so the planning required for audits will vary. In a large organization the quality manager or auditor is responsible for planning and scheduling the audits. In a small organization the quality assurance activities may be performed by a part time auditor who plans and schedules the audits.

A representative sample of projects/areas in the organization will be audited, and the number and types of audits conducted will depend on the current maturity of the organization. Mature organizations with a strong process culture will require fewer audits, whereas immature organizations may need a larger number of audits to ensure that the process is ingrained in the way that work is done.

It is essential that the *auditor is independent of the area being audited*. That is, the auditor should not be reporting to the manager whose area is being audited, as otherwise important findings in the audit could be omitted from the report. The independence of the auditor helps to ensure that the findings are fair and objective, as the auditor may state the facts as they are without fear of negative consequences.

The auditor needs to be familiar with the process, and in a position to judge the extent to which the standards have been followed. The audit report needs to be accurate, as incorrect statements made in the report will damage the credibility of the auditor. The planning and scheduling activities will include:

- Project/Area to be audited,
- Planned Date of Audit,
- Scope of Audit,
- Checklist to be used,
- Documentation required,
- Auditor,
- Attendees.

The auditor may receive orientation on the project/area to be audited prior to the meeting and may review relevant documentation in advance. A checklist may be employed by the auditor as an aid to structure the interview.

The role requires good verbal and documentation skills, as well as the ability to deal with any conflicts that may arise during the audit. The auditor needs to be fair and objective, and audit criteria will be employed to establish the facts in a non-judgmental manner.

Software quality assurance requires that an independent group (e.g., the SQA group) be set up. This may be a part time group of one person in a small organization or a team of auditors in a large organization. The auditors must be appropriately trained to carry out their roles. The individuals being audited need to receive orientation on the purpose of audits and their role in the audit.

13.3 Audit Meeting

An audit consists of interviews and document reviews and involves a structured interview of the various team members. The goal is to give the auditor an understanding of the work done, the processes employed, and the extent to which they are followed and effective. A checklist tailored to the audit being conducted is often employed. This will assist in determining relevant facts to judge whether the process is followed and effective. Table 13.2 gives a small selection of questions that may be part of an audit checklist.

Table 13.2 Sample auditing checklist

Item to check
Project management
Has the project planning process been consistently followed?
Is the project plan complete and approved?
Are the risk log, issue log and lessons learned log set up?
Is the microsoft schedule (or equivalent) available and up to date?
Are the weekly status reports available and do they follow the template?
Configuration management
Are the appropriate people involved in defining, assessing the impact, and approving the change request?
Are the affected deliverables (with the CR) identified and updated?
Are all documents and source code in the repository?
Are checking in/checking out procedures followed?
Supplier management
Is the statement of work complete?
Have the PM skills of the supplier been considered in the evaluation?
Does the formal agreement include strict change control?
Requirements, design and testing
Are the user requirements complete and approved?
Are the system requirements complete and approved?
Is the design complete and approved?
Are the requirements traceable to the design and test deliverables?
Are the unit test scripts available with the results recorded?
Are the system test cases available with results recorded?
Are UAT test cases available with results recorded?
Deployment and support
Are the user manuals complete and available?
Are all open problems documented?

The audit is an enquiry into to the role of each attendee, the activities performed, the output produced, the standards followed, and so on. The auditor needs to be familiar with the process and in a position to judge the extent to which it has been followed.

The auditor opens the meeting with an explanation of the purpose and scope of the audit, and usually starts with one or more open questions to get the participants to describe their role. Each attendee is asked to describe their specific role, the activities performed, the deliverables produced, and the standards followed. Closed questions are employed to obtain specific information when required.

The auditor will take notes during the meeting, and these are reviewed and revised after the audit. There may be a need to review additional documentation after the meeting or to schedule follow up meetings.

13.4 Audit Reporting

Once the audit meeting and follow up activities have been completed, the auditor will need to prepare an audit report to communicate the findings from the audit. A draft audit report is prepared and circulated to the attendees, and the auditor reviews any comments received, and makes final changes to address any valid feedback.[3] The approved audit report is then circulated to the attendees and management.

The audit report will include audit actions that need to be addressed by groups and individuals, and the auditor will track these actions to completion. In rare cases the auditor may need to escalate the audit actions to management to ensure resolution.

The audit report generally includes three parts namely the overview, the detailed findings, and an action plan. This is described in Table 13.3:

Table 13.3 Sample audit report

Area	Description
Overview of audit	This gives an overview of the audit including the area audited, the date of the audit, its scope, the auditor and attendees and the number of audit actions raised
Audit findings	These will vary depending on the type of audit, but it may include findings from project management, requirements, design, coding, configuration management, testing and peer reviews, customer support, etc.
Action plan	This will include an action plan to address the findings

---

[3] It is essential that the audit report is accurate, as otherwise the auditor will lose credibility and become ineffective. Therefore, it is useful to get feedback from the attendees prior to publication of the report, to validate the findings. However, in some implementations of software quality assurance, the audit report is issued directly to the attendees without the performance of this step.

13.5   Follow Up Activity

Once the auditor has circulated the audit report to the affected groups, the focus then moves to closure of the assigned audit actions. The auditor will follow up with the affected individuals to monitor closure of the actions by the agreed date, and where appropriate a time extension may be granted. The auditor will update the status of an audit action to closed once it has been completed correctly. In rare cases the auditor may need to escalate the audit action to management for resolution. This may happen when an assigned action has not been dealt with despite one or more-time extensions. Once all audit actions have been closed the audit is closed.

13.6   Audit Escalation

In rare cases the auditor may encounter resistance from one or more individuals in completing the agreed audit actions. The auditor will remind the individual(s) of the audit process and their responsibilities in the process. In rare cases, where the individual(s) fail to address their assigned action(s) in a reasonable time frame, the auditor will escalate the non-compliance to management. The escalation may involve:

- Escalation of actions to Middle Management,
- Escalation to Senior Management.

Escalation is generally a rare occurrence, especially if good software engineering practices are embedded in the organization.

13.7   Review of Audit Activities

The results of the audit activities will be reviewed with management on a periodic basis. Audits provide important information to management on the processes being used in the organization; the extent to which they are followed; and the extent to which they are effective.

An independent audit (usually a third party or separate internal audit function) of SQA activities may be conducted to ensure that the SQA function is effective. Any non-compliance issues identified and assigned to the auditor and quality manager for resolution.

13.8   Other Audits

The audit process that we discussed has been focused on process audits conducted during a project. Other audits that may be conducted include supplier audits, where the auditor visits the supplier to determine the extent to which they are following the agreed processes and standards for the outsourced work.

The SQA team is often the point of contact to facilitate customer audits, where an audit team from the customer visits the organization to determine the extent to which they are following processes and standards.

13.9   Review Questions

1. What is the purpose of an audit?
2. What planning is done prior to the audit?
3. Explain why the auditor needs to be independent?
4. Describe the activities in the audit process.
5. What happens at an audit meeting?
6. What happens after an audit meeting?
7. How will the auditor deal with a situation where the audit actions are still open after the due date?

13.10   Summary

The purpose of software quality assurance is to provide visibility to management on the processes being followed and the work products being produced in the organization. It is a systematic enquiry into the way that things are done in the organization, and it involves conducting audits of projects, suppliers, and departments.

It provides visibility into the processes and standards in use, their effectiveness, and the extent of compliance to them. It involves planning and conducting audits; reporting the results to the affected groups; tracking the assigned audit actions to completion; and conducting follow up audits, as appropriate. It is generally conducted by the SQA group, and this group is independent of the groups being audited.

The audit planning is concerned with selecting projects/areas to be audited, determining who needs to be involved and dealing with the logistics. The audit meeting is a formal meeting with the audit participants to discuss their specific responsibilities in the project, the processes followed, and so on.

The audit report details the findings from the audit and includes audit actions that need to be resolved. Once the audit report has been published the auditor will track the assigned audit actions to completion, and once all actions have been addressed the audit may then be closed.

Agile Methodology

14

Abstract

This chapter discusses the Agile methodology which is a popular lightweight approach to software development. Agile provides opportunities to assess the direction of a project throughout the development lifecycle, and ongoing changes to requirements are considered normal in the Agile world. It has a strong collaborative style of working, and it advocates adaptive planning and evolutionary development.

Keywords

Sprints · Stand-up meeting · Scrum · Stories · Refactoring · Pair programming · Test driven development · Continuous integration

14.1 Introduction

Agile is a popular lightweight software development methodology that provides opportunities to assess the direction of a project throughout the development lifecycle. There has been a growth in interest in lightweight software development methodologies since the 1990s, and these include approaches such as rapid application development (RAD), dynamic systems development method (DSDM), and extreme programming (XP). These approaches are referred to collectively as agile methods.

Every aspect of Agile development such as requirements and design is continuously revisited during the development, and the direction of the project is regularly evaluated. Agile focuses on rapid and frequent delivery of partial solutions developed in an iterative and incremental manner. Each partial solution is evaluated by the product owner, and the feedback is used to determine the next steps for the

© Springer Nature Switzerland AG 2022
G. O'Regan, *Concise Guide to Software Engineering*,
Undergraduate Topics in Computer Science,
https://doi.org/10.1007/978-3-031-07816-3_14

project. Agile claims to be more responsive to customer needs than traditional methods such as the waterfall model, and its adherents believe that it results in:

- higher quality,
- higher productivity,
- faster time to market,
- improved customer satisfaction.

It advocates adaptive planning, evolutionary development, early development, continuous improvement, and a rapid response to change. The term '*agile*' was coined by Kent Beck and others in the Agile Manifesto in 2001 [1]. The traditional waterfall model is similar to a wide and slow-moving value stream, and halfway through the project 100% of the requirements are typically 50% done. However, 50% of the requirements are typically 100% done halfway through an agile project.

Agile has a strong collaborative style of working, and ongoing changes to requirements are considered normal in the agile world. It argues that it is more realistic to change requirements regularly throughout the project, rather than attempting to define all the requirements at the start of the project (as in the waterfall methodology). Agile includes controls to manage changes to the requirements, and good communication and early regular feedback is an essential part of the process.

A user story may be a new feature or a modification to an existing feature. The feature is reduced to the minimum scope that can deliver business value, and a feature may give rise to several stories. Stories often build upon other stories and the entire software development lifecycle is employed for the implementation of each story. Stories are either done or not done (i.e., there is no such thing as 50% done), and the story is complete only when it passes its acceptance tests.

Scrum is an Agile method for managing iterative development, and it consists of an outline planning phase for the project, followed by a set of sprint cycles (where each cycle develops an increment). *Sprint planning* is performed before the start of the iteration, and stories are assigned to the iteration to fill the available time. Each scrum sprint is of a fixed length (usually 2–4 weeks), and it develops an increment of the system.

The estimates for each story and their priority are determined, and the prioritized stories are assigned to the iteration. A short (usually 15 min) morning stand up meeting is held daily during the iteration, and it is attended by the scrum master, the project manager[1] and the project team. It discusses the progress made the previous day, problem reporting and tracking, and the work planned for the day ahead. A separate meeting is held for issues that require more detailed discussion.

Once the iteration is complete the latest product increment is demonstrated to a review audience including the product owner. This is to receive feedback and to identify new requirements. The team also conducts a retrospective meeting to

---

[1] Agile teams are self-organizing and small teams (team size < 20 people) do not usually have a project manager role, and the scrum master performs some light project management tasks.

identify what went well and what went poorly during the iteration, as part of continuous improvement for future iterations.

The planning for the next sprint then commences. The scrum master is a facilitator who arranges the daily meetings and ensures that the scrum process is followed. The role involves removing roadblocks so that the team can achieve their goals and communicating with other stakeholders. Agile employs pair programming and a collaborative style of working with the philosophy that two heads are better than one. This allows multiple perspectives in decision making which provides a broader understanding of the issues.

Software testing is very important in verifying that the software is fit for purpose, and Agile generally employs automated testing for unit, acceptance, performance, and integration testing. Agile employs *test driven development* with tests written before the code. The developers write code to make a test pass with ideally developers only coding against failing tests. This approach forces the developer to write testable code, as well as ensuring that the requirements are testable. Tests are run frequently with the goal of catching programming errors early. They are generally run on a separate build server to ensure that all the dependencies are checked. Tests are re-run before making a release.

Refactoring is employed in Agile as a design and coding practice. The objective is to change how the software is written without changing what it does. Refactoring is a tool for evolutionary design where the design is regularly evaluated, and improvements are implemented as they are identified. It helps in improving the maintainability and readability of the code and in reducing complexity. The automated test suite is essential in demonstrating that the integrity of the software is maintained following refactoring.

Continuous integration allows the system to be built with every change. Early and regular integration allows early feedback to be provided, and it also allows all the automated tests to be run thereby identifying problems earlier. The main philosophy and features of Agile are:

- Working software is more useful than presenting documents,
- Direct interaction preferred over documentation,
- Change is accepted as a normal part of life in the Agile world,
- Customer involved throughout the project,
- Demonstrate value early,
- Feedback and adaptation employed in decision making,
- Aims is to achieve a narrow fast flowing value stream,
- User Stories and sprints are employed,
- A project is divided into iterations,
- An iteration has a fixed length (i.e., Time boxing is employed),
- Entire software development lifecycle is employed for implementation of the story,
- Stories are either done are not done (no such thing as 50% done),
- Iterative and Incremental development is employed,
- Emphasis on Quality,

- Stand Up Meetings held daily,
- Rapid conversion of requirements into working functionality,
- Delivery is made as early as possible,
- Maintenance is seen as part of the development process,
- Refactoring and Evolutionary Design Employed,
- Continuous Integration is employed,
- Short Cycle Times,
- Plan regularly,
- Early decision making.

Stories are prioritized based on several factors including:

- Business Value of Story,
- Mitigation of risk,
- Dependencies on other stories.

14.2   Scrum Methodology

Scrum is a framework for managing an Agile software development project. It is not a prescriptive methodology as such, and it relies on a self-organizing, cross-functional team to take the feature from idea to implementation. The cross-functional team includes the *product owner* who represents the interest of the users and ensures that the right product is built; the *scrum master* who is the coach for the team, and helps the team to understand the Scrum process and to perform at the highest level, as well as performing some light project management activities such as project tracking; and the *team* itself who decide on which person should work on which tasks and so on.

The Scrum methodology breaks the software development for the project into a series of sprints, where each sprint is of fixed time duration of 2–4 weeks. There is a planning meeting at the start of the sprint where the team members determine the number of items/tasks that they can commit to, and then create a sprint backlog (*to do list*) of the tasks to be performed during the sprint. The Scrum team takes a small set of features from idea to coded and tested functionality that is integrated into the evolving product.

The team attends a daily stand-up meeting (usually of 15 min duration) where the progress of the previous day is discussed, as well as any obstacles to progress. The new functionality is demonstrated to the product owner and any other relevant stakeholders at the end of the sprint, and this may result in changes to the delivered functionality or the addition of new items to the product backlog. There is a sprint retrospective meeting to reflect on the sprint and to identify improvement opportunities.

The main deliverable produced using the Scrum framework is the *product itself*, and Scrum expects to build a properly tested product increment (in a shippable state) at the end of each sprint. The *product backlog* is another deliverable, and it is maintained and prioritized by the product owner. It is a complete list of the functionality (user stories) to be added to the product, and there is also the *sprint backlog* which is the list of the functionality to be implemented in the sprint. Other deliverables are the *sprint burnout* and *release burnout* charts, which show the amount of work remaining in a sprint or release and indicate the extent to which the sprint or release is on schedule.

The Scrum Master is the expert on the Agile process and acts as a coach to the team thereby helping the team to achieve a high level of performance. The role differs from that of a project manager, as the Scrum Master does not assign tasks to individuals or provide day-to-day direction to the team. However, the scrum master typically performs some light project management tasks.

Many of the traditional project manager responsibilities such as task assignment and day-to-day project decisions revert to the team, and the responsibility for the scope and schedule trade-off goes to the product owner. The product owner creates and communicates a solid vision of the product and shares the vision through the product backlog. Larger Agile projects (team size > 20) will often have a dedicated project manager role.

14.3   User Stories

A *user story* is a short simple description of a feature written from the viewpoint of the user of the system. They are often written on index cards or sticky notes and arranged on walls or tables to facilitate discussion. This approach facilitates the discussion of the functionality rather than the written text.

A user story can be written at varying levels of detail, and a large, detailed user story is known as an epic. An epic story is often too large to be implemented in one sprint, and such a story is often split into several smaller user stories.

It is the product owner's responsibility to ensure that a product backlog of user stories exist, but the product owner is not required to write all stories. In fact, anyone can write a user story, and each team member usually writes a user story during an Agile project. User stories are written throughout an Agile project, with a user story-writing workshop held at the beginning of the project. This leads to the product backlog that describes the functionality to be added during the project. Some of these will be epics, and these will need to be decomposed into smaller stories that will fit into the timeboxed sprint. New user stories may be written at any time and added to the product backlog.

There is no requirements document as such in Agile, and the product backlog (i.e., the prioritized list of the functionality of the product to be developed) is closest to the idea of a requirements document for a traditional project. However, the written part of a user story in Agile is incomplete until the discussion of that story takes place. It is often useful to think of the written part of a story as a pointer to the real requirement, such as a diagram showing a workflow or the formula for a calculation.

14.4 Estimation in Agile

Planning poker is a popular consensus-based estimation technique often used in Agile, and it is used to estimate the effort required to implement a user story. The planning session starts with the product owner reading the user story or describing a feature to the estimators.

Each estimator holds a deck of planning poker cards with values like 0, 1, 2, 3, 5, 8, 13, 20, 40 and 100, where the values represent the units in which the team estimates. The estimators discuss the feature with the product owner, and when the discussion is fully complete and all questions answered, each estimator privately selects a card to reflect his or her estimate.

All cards are then revealed and if all values are the same then that value is chosen as the estimate. Otherwise, the estimators discuss their estimates with the rationale for the highest and lowest discussed in detail. Each estimator then reselects an estimate card, and the process continues until consensus is achieved, or if consensus cannot be achieved the estimation of the item is deferred until more information is available.

The initial estimation session usually takes place after the initial product backlog is written. This session may take several days, and it is used to create the initial estimates of the size and scope of the project. Further estimation and planning sessions take place regularly during the project as user stories are added to the product backlog, and these will typically take place towards the end of the current sprint.

The advantage of the estimation process employed is that it brings multiple expert opinions from the cross-functional team together, and the experts justify their estimates in the detailed discussion. This helps to improve the estimation accuracy in the project.

14.5 Test Driven Development

Test-driven development (TDD) is a software development process often employed in Agile. It was developed by Kent Beck and others as part of extreme programming, and the developers focus on testing the requirements before writing the code. The application is written with testability in mind, and the developers must consider how to test the application in advance. Further, it ensures that test cases for every feature are written and writing tests early help in gaining a deeper understanding of the requirements.

TDD is based on the transition of the requirements into a set of test cases, and the software is then written to pass the test cases. Another words, the test-driven development of a new feature begins with writing a suite of test cases based on the requirements for the feature, and the code for the feature is written to pass the test cases. This is a paradigm shift from traditional software engineering where the unit tests are written and executed after the code is written.

The tests are written for the new feature, and initially all tests fail as no code has been written, and so the first step is to write some code that enables the new test cases to pass. This new code may be imperfect (it will be improved later), but this is acceptable at this time as the only purpose is to pass the new test cases. The next step is to ensure that the new feature works with the existing features, and this involves executing all new and existing test cases.

This may involve modification of the source code to enable all the tests to pass, and to ensure that all features work correctly together. The final step is refactoring the code, and this involves cleaning up and restructuring the code, and improving its structure and readability. The test cases are re-run during the refactoring to ensure that the functionality is not altered in any way. The process repeats with the addition of each new feature.

Continuous integration allows the system to be built with every change, and this allows early feedback to be provided. It also allows all the automated tests to be run, thereby ensuring that the new feature works with the existing functionality and identifying problems earlier.

14.6 Pair Programming

Pair programming is an agile technique where two programmers work together at one computer. The author of the code is termed the *driver*, and the other programmer is termed the *observer* (or *navigator*) and is responsible for reviewing each line of written code. The observer also considers the strategic direction of the coding and proposes improvement suggestions and potential problems that may need to be addressed. The driver can focus on the implementation of the current task and use the observer as a safety net. The two programmers switch roles regularly during the development of the new functionality.

Pair programming requires more programming effort to develop code compared to programmers working individually. However, the resulting code is of higher quality, with fewer defects and a reduction in the cost of maintenance. Further, pair programming enables a better design solution to be created as more design alternatives are considered.

This is since two programmers are bringing different experiences to the problem, and they may have different ways of solving the problem. This leads them to explore a larger number of ways of solving the problem than an individual programmer. Finally, pair programming is good for knowledge sharing and learning, and it allows knowledge to be shared on programming practice and design and allows knowledge about the system to be shared throughout the team.

14.7 Review Questions

1. What is Agile?
2. How does Agile differ from the waterfall model?
3. What is a user story?
4. Explain how estimation is done in Agile
5. What is test-driven development?
6. Describe the scrum methodology and the role of the Scrum Master
7. Explain pair programming and describe its advantages

14.8 Summary

This chapter gave a brief introduction to Agile, which is a popular lightweight software development methodology. Agile advocates adaptive planning, evolutionary development, early development, continuous improvement, and a rapid response to change. The traditional waterfall model is similar to a wide and slow-moving value stream, and halfway through the project 100% of the requirements are typically 50% done. However, 50% of the requirements are typically 100% done halfway through an agile project.

Agile has a strong collaborative style of working, and ongoing changes to requirements are considered normal in the Agile world. It includes controls to manage changes to the requirements, and good communication and early regular feedback is an essential part of the process.

A story may be a new feature or a modification to an existing feature. It is reduced to the minimum scope that can deliver business value, and a feature may give rise to several stories. Stories often build upon other stories and the entire software development lifecycle is employed for the implementation of each story. Stories are either done or not done and the story is complete only when it passes its acceptance tests.

The Scrum approach is an Agile method for managing iterative development, and it consists of an outline planning phase for the project followed by a set of sprint cycles (where each cycle develops an increment). Each scrum sprint is of a fixed length (usually 2–4 weeks), and it develops an increment of the system.

The estimates for each story and their priority are determined, and the prioritized stories are assigned to the iteration. A short (usually 15 min) morning stand up meeting is held daily during the iteration and attended by the project manager and the project team. It discusses the progress made the previous day, problem reporting and tracking, and the work planned for the day ahead.

Once the iteration is complete the latest product increment is demonstrated to a review audience including the product owner. This is to receive feedback and to identify new requirements. The team also conducts a retrospective meeting to identify what went well and what went poorly during the iteration, as part of continuous improvement for future sprints.

Reference

1. K. Beck et al., *Manifesto for Agile Software Development* (Agile Alliance, 2001). http://agilemanifesto.org/

Software Reliability and Dependability 15

Abstract

This chapter discusses software reliability and dependability, and covers topics such as software reliability and software reliability models, the Cleanroom methodology, system availability, safety and security critical systems, and dependability engineering.

Keywords

Software reliability · Software reliability models · System availability · Dependability · Computer security · Safety critical systems · Cleanroom

15.1 Introduction

This chapter introduces the important area of software reliability and dependability, and it introduces important topics in software engineering such as software reliability and availability; software reliability models; the Cleanroom methodology; dependability and its various dimensions; security engineering; and safety critical systems.

Software reliability is the probability that the program works without failure for a period of time, and it is usually expressed as the mean time to failure. It is different from hardware reliability, in that hardware is characterized by components that physically wear out, whereas software is intangible and software failures are due to design and implementation errors. Another words, software is either correct or incorrect when it is designed and developed, and it does not physically deteriorate over time.

Harlan Mills and others at IBM developed the Cleanroom approach to software development, and the process is described in [1]. It involves the application of statistical techniques to calculate a software reliability measure based on the expected usage of the software.[1] This involves executing tests chosen from the population of all possible uses of the software in accordance with the probability of its expected use. Statistical usage testing is more effective at finding defects that lead to failure than coverage testing.

Models are simplifications of the reality, and a good model allows accurate predictions of future behaviour to be made. A model is judged effective if there is good empirical evidence to support it, and a good software reliability model will have good theoretical foundations and realistic assumptions. The extent to which the software reliability model can be trusted depends on the accuracy of its predictions, and empirical data will need to be gathered to judge its accuracy.

It is essential that software that is widely used is dependable, which means that the software is available whenever required, and that it operates safely and reliably without any adverse side effects. Today, billions of computers are connected to the Internet, and this has led to a growth in attacks on computers. It is essential that computer security is carefully considered, and that developers are aware of the threats facing a system, and techniques to eliminate them. The developers need to be able to develop secure dependable systems that can deal with and recover from external attacks.

15.2 Software Reliability

The design and development of high-quality software has become increasingly important for society. The hardware field has been very successful in developing sound reliability models, which allow useful predictions of how long a hardware component (or product) will function reliably. This has led to a growing interest in the software field in the development of a sound software reliability model. An effective software reliability model would provide a sound mechanism to predict the reliability of the software prior to its deployment at the customer site, as well as confidence that the software is fit for purpose and safe to use.

Definition 15.1 (*Software Reliability*)
Software reliability is the probability that the program works without failure for a specified length of time, and it is a statement of the future behaviour of the software. It is generally expressed in terms of the *mean-time-to-failure* (MTTF) or the *mean-time-between-failure* (MTBF).

---

[1] The expected usage of the software (or operational profile) is a quantitative characterization (usually based on probability) of how the system will be used.

Statistical sampling techniques are often employed to predict the reliability of hardware, as it is not feasible to test all items in a production environment. The quality of the sample is then used to make inferences on the quality of the entire population, and this approach is effective in manufacturing environments where variations in the manufacturing process often lead to defects in the physical products.

There are similarities and differences between hardware and software reliability. A hardware failure generally arises due to a component wearing out due to its age, and often a replacement component is required. Many hardware components are expected to last for a certain period, and the variation in the failure rate of a hardware component is often due to variations in the manufacturing process, or to the operating environment of the component. Good hardware reliability predictors have been developed, and each hardware component has an expected mean time to failure. The reliability of a product may be determined from the reliability of the individual components of the hardware.

Software is an intellectual undertaking involving a team of designers and programmers. It does not physically wear out as such, and software failures manifest themselves from user inputs. Each copy of the software code is identical, and the software code is either correct or incorrect. That is, software failures are due to design and implementation errors, rather than to the software physically wearing out over time. Several software reliability models (e.g., the software reliability growth models) have been developed, but the software engineering community has not yet developed a sound software reliability predictor model that can be trusted.

The software population to be sampled consists of all possible execution paths of the software, and since this is potentially infinite it is generally not possible to perform exhaustive testing. The way in which the software is used (i.e., the inputs entered by the users) will impact upon its perceived reliability. Let I_f represent the fault set of inputs (i.e., $i_f \in I_f$ if and only if the input of i_f by the user leads to failure). The randomness of the time to software failure is due to the unpredictability in the selection of an input $i_f \in I_f$. It may be that the elements in I_f are inputs that are rarely used, and therefore the software will be perceived as being reliable.

Statistical usage testing may be used to make predictions on the future performance and reliability of the software. This requires an understanding of the expected usage profile of the system, as well as the population of all possible usages of the software. The sampling is done in accordance with the expected usage profile, and a software reliability measure calculated.

15.2.1 Software Reliability and Defects

The release of an unreliable software product may result in damage to property or injury (including loss of life) to a third party. Consequently, companies need to be confident that their software products are fit for purpose prior to their release. The project team needs to conduct extensive inspections and testing of the software, as well as considering all associated risks prior to its release.

Table 15.1 Adam's 1984 study of software failures of IBM products

	Rare					Frequent		
	1	2	3	4	5	6	7	8
MTTF (years)	5000	1580	500	158	50	15.8	5	1.58
Avg % fixes	33.4	28.2	18.7	10.6	5.2	2.5	1.0	0.4
Prob failure	0.008	0.021	0.044	0.079	0.123	0.187	0.237	0.300

Objective product quality criteria may be set (e.g., 100% of tests performed and passed) to be satisfied prior to release. This provides a degree of confidence that the software has achieved the desired quality and is safe and fit for to use at the customer site. However, these results are historical in the sense that they are a statement of past and present quality. The question is whether the past behaviour and performance provides a sound indication of future behaviour.

Software reliability models are an attempt to predict the future reliability of the software, and to assist in deciding on whether the software is ready for release. A defect does not always result in a failure, as it may occur on a rarely used execution path. Studies indicate that many observed failures arise from a small proportion of the existing defects.

Adam's 1984 case study [2] indicate that over 33% of the defects led to an observed failure with mean time to failure greater than 5000 years, whereas less than 2% of defects led to an observed failure with a mean time to failure of less than 50 years. This suggests that a small proportion of defects often lead to almost all the observed failures (Table 15.1).

The analysis shows that 61.6% of all fixes (Group 1 and 2) were for failures that will be observed less than once in 1580 years of expected use, and that these constitute only 2.9% of the failures observed by typical users. On the other hand, groups 7 and 8 constitute 53.7% of the failures observed by typical users and only 1.4% of fixes.

This case study showed that *coverage testing* is not cost effective in increasing MTTF. *Usage testing*, in contrast, would allocate 53.7% of the test effort to fixes that will occur 53.7% of the time for a typical user. Harlan Mills has argued [3] that the data in the table shows that usage testing is 21 times more effective than coverage testing.

There is a need to be careful with *reliability growth models*, as there is no tangible growth in reliability unless the corrected defects are likely to manifest themselves as a failure.[2] Many existing software reliability growth models assume that all remaining defects in the software have an equal probability of failure, and that the correction of a defect leads to an increase in software reliability. These assumptions are questionable.

---

[2] We are assuming that the defect has been corrected perfectly with no new defects introduced by the changes made.

Table 15.2 New and old version of software

Similarities and differences between new/old version
• The new version of the software is identical to the previous version except that the identified defects have been corrected
• The new version of the software is identical to the previous version, except that the identified defects have been corrected, but the developers have introduced some new defects
• No assumptions can be made about the behaviour of the new version of the software until further data is obtained

The defect count and defect density may be poor predictors of operational reliability, and an emphasis on removing many defects from the software may not be sufficient to achieve high reliability.

The correction of defects in the software leads to a newer version of the software, and reliability models assume reliability growth: i.e., the new version is more reliable than the older version as several identified defects have been corrected. However, in some sectors (such as the safety critical field) the view is that the new version of a program is a new entity, and that no inferences may be drawn until further investigation has been done. There are several ways to interpret the relationship between the new version of the software and the older version as shown by Table 15.2.

The safety critical industry (e.g., the nuclear power industry) takes the conservative viewpoint that any change to a program creates a new program. The new program is therefore required to demonstrate its reliability, and so extensive testing needs to be performed before any conclusions may be made.

15.2.2 Cleanroom Methodology

Harlan Mills and others at IBM developed the Cleanroom methodology to develop high-quality software [3]. Cleanroom helps to ensure that the software is released only when it has achieved the desired quality level, and the probability of zero-defects is very high.

The way in which the software is used will impact on its perceived quality and reliability. Failures will manifest themselves on certain input sequences only, and as users often employ different input sequences, each user may have a different perception of the reliability of the software. The knowledge of how the software will be used allows the software testing to focus on verifying the correctness of common everyday tasks carried out by users.

This means that it is important to determine the operational profile of users to enable effective software testing to be performed. The operational profile may be difficult to determine, and it could change over time, as users may change their behaviour as their needs evolve over time. The determination of the operational profile involves identifying the common operations to be performed, and the probability of each operation being performed.

Table 15.3 Cleanroom results in IBM

Project	Results
Flight control project (1987) 33 KLOC	Completed ahead of schedule Error-fix effort reduced by factor of five
Commercial product (1988)	Deployment failures of 0.1/KLOC Certification testing failures 3.4/KLOC Productivity 740 LOC/month
Satellite control (1989) 80 KLOC (Partial cleanroom)	50% improvement in quality Certification testing failures of 3.3/KLOC Productivity 780 LOC/month 80% improvement in productivity
Research project (1990) 12 KLOC	Certified to 0.9978 with 989 test cases

Cleanroom employs *statistical usage testing* rather than coverage testing, and it applies statistical quality control to certify the mean time to failure of the software. This software reliability measure is calculated by statistical techniques based on the expected usage of the software, and the statistical usage testing involves executing tests chosen from the population of all possible uses of the software in accordance with the probability of expected use.

Coverage testing involves designing tests that cover every path through the program, and this type of testing is as likely to find a rare execution failure as well as a frequent execution failure. It is highly desirable to find failures that occur on frequently used parts of the system.

The advantage of statistical usage testing (that matches the actual execution profile of the software) is that it has a better chance of finding execution failures on frequently used parts of the system. This helps to maximize the expected mean time to failure of the software.

The Cleanroom software development process and calculation of the software reliability measure is described in [1], and the Cleanroom development process enables engineers to deliver high-quality software on time and on budget. Some of the successes and benefits of the use of Cleanroom on projects at IBM are described in [3] and summarized in Table 15.3.

15.2.3 Software Reliability Models

Models are simplifications of the reality, and a good model allows accurate predictions of future behaviour to be made. It is important to determine the adequacy of the model, and this is done by model exploration, and determining the extent to which it explains the actual manifested behaviour, as well as the accuracy of its predictions.

A model is judged effective if there is good empirical evidence to support it, and more accurate models are sought to replace inadequate models. Models are often modified (or replaced) over time, as further facts and observations are identified that

Table 15.4 Characteristics of good software reliability model

Characteristics of good software reliability model
Good theoretical foundation
Realistic assumptions
Good empirical support
As simple as possible (Ockham's Razor)
Trustworthy and accurate

cannot be explained with the current model. A good software reliability model will have the following characteristics (Table 15.4).

There are several software reliability predictor models employed (Table 15.5) with varying degrees of success. Some of them just compute defect counts rather than estimating software reliability in terms of mean time to failure. They may be categorized into:

- *Size and Complexity Metrics*
  These are used to predict the number of defects that a system will reveal in operation or testing.

- *Operational Usage Profile*
  These predict failure rates based on the expected operational usage profile of the system. The number of failures encountered is determined and the software reliability predicted (e.g., Cleanroom and its prediction of the MTTF).

- *Quality of the Development Process*
  These predict failure rates based on the process maturity of the software development process in the organization (e.g., CMMI maturity).

The extent to which the software reliability model can be trusted depends on the accuracy of its predictions, and empirical data will need to be gathered to make a judgement. It may be acceptable to have a little inaccuracy during the early stages of prediction, provided the predictions of operational reliability are close to the observations. A model that gives overly optimistic results is termed 'optimistic', whereas a model that gives overly pessimistic results is termed 'pessimistic'.

The assumptions in the reliability model need to be examined to determine whether they are realistic. Several software reliability models have questionable assumptions such as:

- All defects are corrected perfectly
- Defects are independent of one another
- Failure rate decreases as defects are corrected.
- Each fault contributes the same amount to the failure rate.

Table 15.5 Software reliability models

Model	Description	Comments
Jelinski/Moranda model	The failure rate is a Poisson process[a] and is proportional to the current defect content of program. The initial defect count is N; the initial failure rate is Nφ; it decreases to $(N - 1)\varphi$ after the first fault is detected and eliminated, and so on. The constant φ is termed the proportionality constant	Assumes defects corrected perfectly and no new defects are introduced Assumes each fault contributes the same amount to failure rate
Littlewood/Verrall model	Successive execution time between failures is independent exponentially distributed random variables[b]. Software failures are the result of the particular inputs and faults introduced from the correction of defects	Does not assume perfect correction of defects
Seeding and tagging	This is analogous to estimating the fish population of a lake (Mills). A known number of defects are inserted into a software program, and the proportion of these identified during testing determined Another approach (Hyman) is to regard the defects found by one tester as tagged, and then to determine the proportion of tagged defects found by a 2nd independent tester	Estimate of the total number of defects in the software but not a not s/w reliability predictor Assumes all faults equally likely to be found and introduced faults representative of existing
Generalized Poisson model	The number of failures observed in ith time interval τ_i has a Poisson distribution with mean $\phi(N - M_{i-1}) \tau_i^\alpha$ where N is the initial number of faults; M_{i-1} is the total number of faults removed up to the end of the $(i - 1)$th time interval; and ϕ is the proportionality constant	Assumes faults removed perfectly at end of time interval

[a]The Poisson process is a widely used counting process (especially in counting the occurrence of certain events that appear to happen at a certain rate but at random). A Poisson random variable is of the form P$\{X = i\} = e^{-\lambda} \lambda^i/i!.$
[b]The exponential distribution is used to model the time between the occurrence of events in an interval of time. Its probability density function is given by $f(x) = \lambda e^{-\lambda x}$

15.3   Dependability

Software is ubiquitous and is important to all sections of society, and so it is essential that widely used software is dependable (or trustworthy). In other words, the software should be available whenever required, as well as operating properly, safely, and reliably, without any adverse side effects or security concerns. It is essential that the software used in the safety and security critical fields is dependable, as the consequence of failure (e.g., the failure of a nuclear power plant)

Table 15.6 Dimensions of dependability

Dimension	Description
Availability	The system is available for use at any time
Reliability	The system operates correctly and is trustworthy
Safety	The system operates safely and does not injure people or damage the environment
Security	The system is secure and prevents unauthorized intrusions

could be massive damage leading to loss of life or endangering the lives of the public.

Dependability engineering is concerned with techniques to improve the dependability of systems, and it involves the use of a rigorous design and development process to minimize the number of defects in the software. A dependable system is generally designed for fault tolerance, where the system can deal with (and recover from) faults that occur during software execution. Such a system needs to be secure, and able to protect itself from accidental or deliberate external attacks. Table 15.6 lists several dimensions to dependability.

Modern software systems are subject to attack by malicious software such as viruses that may change its behaviour, or corrupt data causing the system to become unreliable. Other malicious attacks include a denial-of-service attack that negatively impacts the system's availability.

The design and development of dependable software needs to include protection measures to prevent against such external attacks that compromise the availability and security of the system. Further, a dependable system needs to include recovery mechanisms to enable normal service to be restored as quickly as possible following an attack.

Dependability engineering is concerned with techniques to improve the dependability of systems, and in designing dependable systems. A dependable system will generally be developed using an explicitly defined repeatable process, and it may employ redundancy (spare capacity) and diversity (different types) to achieve reliability.

There is a trade-off between dependability and performance of the system, as dependable systems will need to carry out extra checks to monitor themselves and to check for erroneous states, and to recover from faults before failure occurs. This inevitably leads to increased costs in the design and development of dependable systems.

Software availability is the percentage of the time that the software system is running and is a measure of the uptime/downtime of the software during a particular time period. The downtime refers to a period of time when the software is unavailable for use (including planned and unplanned outages), and many companies aim to develop software that is available for use 99.999% of the time in the year (i.e., an annual downtime of less than 5 min per annum). This goal is known as *five nines*, and it is a common goal in the telecommunications sector. We discussed availability metrics in Chap. 10.

Safety-critical systems are systems where it is essential that the system is safe for the public, and that people or the environment are not harmed in the event of system failure. These include aircraft control systems and process control systems for chemical and nuclear power plants. The failure of a safety critical system could in some situations lead to loss of life or serious economic damage.

Formal methods are discussed in Chap. 16, and they provide a precise way of specifying the requirements and demonstrating (using mathematics) that key properties are satisfied in the formal specification. Further, they may be used to show that the implemented program satisfies its specification. The use of formal methods leads to increased confidence in the correctness of safety critical and security critical systems.

The security of the system refers to its ability to protect itself from accidental or deliberate external attacks, which are common today since most computers are networked and connected to the Internet. There are various security threats in any networked system including threats to the confidentiality and integrity of the system and its data, and threats to the availability of the system.

Therefore, controls are required to enhance security and to ensure that attacks are unsuccessful. Encryption is one way to reduce system vulnerability, as encrypted data is unreadable to the attacker. There may be controls that detect and repel attacks, and these controls are used monitor the system and to take action to shut down parts of the system or restrict access in the event of an attack. There may be controls that limit exposure (e.g., insurance policies and automated backup strategies) that allow recovery from the problems introduced.

It is important to have a reasonable level of security as otherwise all the other dimensions of dependability (reliability, availability, and safety) are compromised. Security loopholes may be introduced in the development of the system, and so care needs to be taken to prevent hackers from exploiting security vulnerabilities.

Risk analysis plays a key role in the specification of security and dependability requirements, and this involves identifying risks that can result in serious incidents. This leads to the generation of specific security requirements as part of the system requirements to ensure that these risks do not materialize, or if they do materialize then serious incidents will not materialize.

15.4 Computer Security

The introduction of the Internet in the early 1990s has transformed the world of computing, and it has led inexorably to more and more computers being connected to the Internet. This has subsequently led to an explosive growth in attacks on computers and systems, as hackers and malicious software seek to exploit known security vulnerabilities. It is therefore essential to develop secure systems that can deal with and recover from such external attacks.

Hackers will often attempt to steal confidential data and to disrupt the services being offered by a system. Security engineering is concerned with the development of systems that can prevent such malicious attacks and recover from them. It has become an important part of software and system engineering, and software developers need to be aware of the threats facing a system and develop solutions to eliminate them.

Hackers may probe parts of the system for weaknesses, and system vulnerabilities may lead to attackers gaining unauthorized access to the system. There is a need to conduct a risk assessment of the security threats facing a system early in the software development process, and this will lead to several security requirements for the system.

The system needs to be designed for security, as it is difficult to add security after it has been implemented. Security loopholes may be introduced in the development of the system, and so care needs to be taken to prevent these as well as preventing hackers from exploiting security vulnerabilities. Encryption is one way to reduce system vulnerability, as encrypted data is unreadable to the attacker. There may be controls that detect and repel attacks, and these controls are used monitor the system and to take action to shut down parts of the system or restrict access in the event of an attack.

The choice of architecture and how the system is organized is fundamental to the security of the system, and different types of systems will require different technical solutions to provide an acceptable level of security to its users. The following guidelines for designing secure systems are described in [4]:

- Security decisions should be based on the security policy,
- A security critical system should fail securely,
- A secure system should be designed for recoverability,
- A balance is needed between security and usability,
- A single point of failure should be avoided,
- A log of user actions should be maintained,
- Redundancy and diversity should be employed,
- Organization information in system into compartments.

It is important to have a reasonable level of security, as otherwise all the other dimensions of dependability (reliability, availability and safety) are compromised.

15.5 System Availability

System availability is the percentage of time that the software system is running without downtime, and robust systems will generally aim to achieve 5-nines availability (i.e., 99.999% availability). This is equivalent to approximately 5 min of down time (including planned/unplanned outages) per year. The availability of a system is measured by its performance when a subsystem fails, and its ability to resume service in a state close to the original state. A fault tolerant system continues to operate correctly (possibly at a reduced level) after some part of the system fails, and it aims to achieve 100% availability.

System availability and software reliability are related, with availability measuring the percentage of time that the system is operational, and reliability measuring the probability of failure free operation over a period of time. The consequence of a system failure may be to freeze or crash the system, and system availability is measured by how long it takes to recover and restart after a failure. A system may be unreliable and yet have good availability metrics (fast restart after failure), or it may be highly reliable with poor availability metrics (taking a long time to recover after a failure).

Software that satisfies strict availability constraints is usually reliable. The downtime generally includes the time needed for activities such as re-booting a machine, upgrading to a new version of software, planned and unplanned outages. It is theoretically possible for software to be highly unreliable but to be highly available. Consider, for example, software that fails consistently for 0.5 s every day. Then the total failure time is 183 s or approximately 3 min, and such a system would satisfy 5-nines availability. However, this scenario is highly unlikely for almost all systems, and the satisfaction of strict availability constraints usually means that the software is also highly reliable.

It is also theoretically possible that software that is highly reliable may satisfy poor availability metrics. Consider the upgrade of the version of software at a customer site to a new version, where the upgrade path is complex or poorly designed (e.g., taking 2 days). Then the availability measure is very poor even though the product may be highly reliable. Further, the time that system unavailability occurs is relevant, as a system that is unavailable at 03:00 in the morning may have minimal impacts on users. Consequently, care is required before drawing conclusions between software reliability and software availability metrics.

15.6   Safety Critical Systems

A safety critical system is a system whose failure could result in significant economic damage or loss of life. There are many examples of safety critical systems including aircraft flight control systems and missile system, and it is therefore essential to employ rigorous processes in their design and development Software testing alone is usually insufficient in verifying the correctness of these systems.

The safety critical industry takes the view that any change to safety critical software creates a new program. The new program is therefore required to demonstrate that it is reliable and safe to the public, and so extensive testing needs to be performed. Other techniques such as formal verification and model checking may be employed to provide an extra level of assurance in the correctness of the safety critical system.

Safety critical systems need to be dependable and available for use whenever required. Safety critical software must operate correctly and reliably without any adverse side effects. The consequence of failure (e.g., the failure of a weapons system) could be massive damage, leading to loss of life or endangering the lives of the public.

The development of a safety critical system needs to be rigorous, and subject to strict quality assurance to ensure that the system is safe to use and that the public will not be in danger. This involves rigorous design and development processes to minimize the number of defects in the software, as well as comprehensive testing to verify its correctness.

Formal methods consist of a set of mathematical techniques to rigorously state the requirements of the proposed system. They may be employed to derive a program from its mathematical specification, and they may be used to provide a rigorous proof that the implemented program satisfies its specification. Formal methods provide the facility to prove that certain properties are true of the specification, and this is valuable, especially in safety critical and security critical applications. The advantage of a mathematical specification is that it is not subject to the ambiguities inherent in a natural language description of a system, and it may be subjected to a rigorous analysis to demonstrate the presence or absence of key properties.

Safety critical systems are generally designed for fault tolerance, where the system can deal with (and recover from) faults that occur during execution. Fault tolerance is achieved by anticipating exceptional events, and in designing the system to handle them. A fault tolerant system is designed to fail safely, and programs are designed to continue working (possibly at a reduced level of performance) rather than crashing after the occurrence of an error or exception. Many fault tolerant systems mirror all operations, where each operation is performed on two or more duplicate systems, and so if one fails then the other system can take over.

15.7 Review Questions

1. Explain the difference between software reliability and system availability.
2. What is software dependability?
3. Explain the significance of Adam's 1984 study of software defects at IBM.
4. Describe the Cleanroom methodology.
5. Describe the characteristics of a good software reliability model.
6. Explain the relevance of security engineering.
7. What is a safety critical system?

15.8 Summary

This chapter introduced some important topics in software engineering including software reliability and the Cleanroom methodology; dependability; availability; security; and safety critical systems.

Software reliability is the probability that the program works without failure for a period of time, and it is usually expressed as the mean time to failure. Cleanroom involves the application of statistical techniques to calculate software reliability, and it is based on the expected usage of the software.

It is essential that software that software used in the safety and security critical fields is dependable, with the software available when required, as well as operating safely and reliably without any adverse side effects. Many of these systems are fault tolerant and are designed to deal with (and recover) from faults that occur during execution.

Such a system needs to be secure and able to protect itself from external attacks and needs to include recovery mechanisms to enable normal service to be restored as quickly as possible. Another words, it is essential that if the system fails then it fails safely.

Today, billions of computers are connected to the Internet, and this has led to a growth in attacks on computers. It is essential that developers are aware of the threats facing a system and are familiar with techniques to eliminate them.

References

1. G. O' Regan, *Mathematical Approaches to Software Quality* (Springer, London, 2006)
2. E. Adams, Optimizing preventive service of software products. IBM Res. J. **28**(1), 2–14 (1984)
3. R.H. Cobband, H.D. Mills, *Engineering Software under Statistical Quality Control* (IEEE Software 1990)
4. I. Sommerville,*Software Engineering*, 9th edn. (Pearson. 2011)

Formal Methods

16

Abstract

This chapter discusses formal methods, which consist of a set of mathematic techniques that provide an extra level of confidence in the correctness of the software. They consist of a formal specification language, and employ a collection of tools to support the syntax checking of the specification, as well as the proof of properties of the specification. They allow questions to be asked about what the system does independently of the implementation, and they may be employed to formally state the requirements of the proposed system, and to derive a program from its mathematical specification. They may be employed to provide a rigorous proof that the implemented program satisfies its specification, and they have been applied mainly to the safety critical field.

Keywords

Formal specification · Vienna development method · Z specification language · B Method · Model-oriented approach · Axiomatic approach · Process calculus · Refinement · Finite state machines · Usability of formal methods

16.1 Introduction

The term *"formal methods"* refer to various mathematical techniques used for the formal specification and development of software. They consist of a formal specification language and employ a collection of tools to support the syntax checking of the specification, as well as the proof of properties of the specification. They allow questions to be asked about what the system does independently of the implementation.

The use of mathematical notation avoids speculation about the meaning of phrases in an imprecisely worded natural language description of a system. Natural language is inherently ambiguous, whereas mathematics employs a precise rigorous notation. Spivey [1] defines formal specification as:

G. O'Regan, *Concise Guide to Software Engineering*,
Undergraduate Topics in Computer Science,
https://doi.org/10.1007/978-3-031-07816-3_16

Definition 16.1 (*Formal Specification*)
Formal specification is the use of mathematical notation to describe in a precise way the properties that an information system must have, without unduly constraining the way in which these properties are achieved.

The formal specification thus becomes the key reference point for the different parties involved in the construction of the system. It may be used as the reference point for the requirements; program implementation; testing and program documentation. It promotes a common understanding for all those concerned with the system. The term "*formal methods*" is used to describe a formal specification language and a method for the design and implementation of a computer system. Formal methods may be employed at several levels:

- Formal specification only (program developed informally),
- Formal specification, refinement, and verification (some proofs),
- Formal specification, refinement, and verification (with extensive theorem proving).

The specification is written in a mathematical language, and the implementation may be derived from the specification via stepwise refinement.[1] The refinement step makes the specification more concrete and closer to the actual implementation. There is an associated proof obligation to demonstrate that the refinement is valid, and that the concrete state preserves the properties of the abstract state. Thus, assuming that the original specification is correct and the proofs of correctness of each refinement step are valid, then there is a very high degree of confidence in the correctness of the implemented software.

Stepwise refinement is illustrated as follows: the initial specification S is the initial model M_0; it is then refined into the more concrete model M_1, and M_1 is then refined into M_2, and so on until the eventual implementation $M_n = E$ is produced.

$$S = M_0 \sqsubseteq M_1 \sqsubseteq M_2 \sqsubseteq M_3 \sqsubseteq \ldots \ldots \ldots \sqsubseteq Mn = E$$

Requirements are the foundation of the system to be built, and irrespective of the best design and development practices, the product will be incorrect if the requirements are incorrect. The objective of requirements validation is to ensure that the requirements reflect what is required by the customer (to build the right system). Formal methods may be employed to model the requirements, and the model exploration yields further desirable or undesirable properties.

---

[1] It is questionable whether stepwise refinement is cost effective in mainstream software engineering, as it involves re-writing a specification *ad nauseum*. It is time-consuming to proceed in refinement steps with significant time also required to prove that the refinement step is valid. It is more relevant to the safety–critical field. Others in the formal methods field may disagree with this position.

Formal methods provide the facility to prove that certain properties are true of the specification, and this is valuable, especially in safety critical and security critical applications. The properties are a logical consequence of the mathematical requirements, and the requirements may be amended where appropriate. Thus, formal methods may be employed in a sense to debug the requirements during requirements validation.

The use of formal methods generally leads to more robust software and to increased confidence in its correctness. Formal methods may be employed at different levels (e.g., it may just be used for specification with the program developed informally). The challenges involved in the deployment of formal methods in an organization include the education of staff in formal specification, as the use of these mathematical techniques may be a culture shock to many staff.

Formal methods have been applied to a diverse range of applications, including the safety and security critical fields to develop dependable software. The applications include the railway sector, microprocessor verification, the specification of standards, and the specification and verification of programs. Parnas and others have criticized formal methods on the following grounds (Table 16.1).

Table 16.1 Criticisms of formal methods

No	Criticism
1	Often the formal specification is as difficult to read as the program[a]
2	Many formal specifications are wrong[b]
3	Formal methods are strong on syntax but provide little assistance in deciding on what technical information should be recorded using the syntax[c]
4	Formal specifications provide a model of the proposed system. However, a precise unambiguous mathematical statement of the requirements is what is needed[d]
5	Stepwise refinement is unrealistic.[e] It is like, for example, deriving a bridge from the description of a river and the expected traffic on the bridge. There is always a need for the creative step in design
6	Much unnecessary mathematical formalisms have been developed rather than using the available classical mathematics[f]

[a] Of course, others might reply by saying that some of Parnas's tables are not exactly intuitive, and that the notation he employs in some of his tables is quite unfriendly. The usability of all the mathematical approaches needs to be enhanced if they are to be taken seriously by industrialists
[b] Obviously, the formal specification must be analysed using mathematical reasoning and tools to provide confidence in its correctness. The validation of a formal specification can be carried out using mathematical proof of key properties of the specification; software inspections; or specification animation
[c] Approaches such as VDM include a method for software development as well as the specification language
[d] Models are extremely valuable as they allow simplification of the reality. A mathematical study of the model demonstrates whether it is a suitable representation of the system. Models allow properties of the proposed requirements to be studied prior to implementation
[e] Stepwise refinement involves rewriting a specification with each refinement step producing a more concrete specification (that includes code and formal specification) until eventually the detailed code is produced. It is difficult and time consuming but, tool support may make refinement easier
[f] Approaches such as VDM or Z are useful in that they add greater rigour to the software development process. They are reasonably easy to learn, and there have been some good results obtained by their use. Classical mathematics is familiar to students and therefore it is desirable that new formalisms are introduced only where necessary

However, formal methods are potentially quite useful and reasonably easy to use. The use of a formal method such as Z or VDM forces the software engineer to be precise and helps to avoid ambiguities present in natural language. Clearly, a formal specification should be subject to peer review to provide confidence in its correctness. New formalisms need to be intuitive to be usable by practitioners, and the advantage of classical mathematics is that it is familiar to students.

16.2 Why Should We Use Formal Methods?

There is a strong motivation to use best practice in software engineering to produce software adhering to high quality standards. Quality problems with software may cause minor irritations or major damage to a customer's business including loss of life. Formal methods are a leading-edge technology that may be of benefit to companies in reducing the occurrence of defects in software products. Brown [2] argues that for the safety critical field that:

Comment 16.1 (Missile Safety) *Missile systems must be presumed dangerous until shown to be safe, and that the absence of evidence for the existence of dangerous errors does not amount to evidence for the absence of danger.*

This suggests that companies in the safety critical field will need to demonstrate that every reasonable practice was taken to prevent the occurrence of defects. One such practice is the use of formal methods, and its exclusion may need to be justified in some domains. It is quite possible that a software company may be sued for software which injures a third party, and this suggests that companies will need a rigorous quality assurance system to prevent the occurrence of defects.

There is some evidence to suggest that the use of formal methods provides savings in the cost of the project. For example, a 9% cost saving is attributed to the use of formal methods during the CICS project, and the T800 project attributed a 12-month reduction in testing time to the use of formal methods. These are discussed in more detail in chapter one of [3].

The use of formal methods is mandatory in certain circumstances. The Ministry of Defence (MOD) in the United Kingdom issued two safety–critical standards[2] in the early 1990s related to the use of formal methods in the software development lifecycle.

The first was Defence Standard 00-55, "*The Procurement of safety critical software in defense equipment*" [4] which made it mandatory to employ formal methods in the development of safety–critical software in the UK. The standard mandates the use of formal proof that the most crucial programs correctly implement their specifications.

---

[2] The U.K. Defence Standards 0055 and 0056 were later revised to be less prescriptive on the use of formal methods.

The other was Def. Stan 00-56 *"Hazard analysis and safety classification of the computer and programmable electronic system elements of defense equipment"* [5]. The objective of this standard is to provide guidance to identify which systems or parts of systems being developed are safety-critical and thereby require the use of formal methods. This proposed system is subject to an initial hazard analysis to determine whether there are safety-critical parts.

The reaction to these defence standards 00-55 and 00-56 was quite hostile initially, as most suppliers were unlikely to meet the technical and organization requirements of the standard. This is described in [6].

16.3 Applications of Formal Methods

Formal methods have been employed to verify the correctness of software in several domains such as the safety and security critical fields. This includes applications to the nuclear power industry, the aerospace industry, the security technology area, and the railroad domain. These sectors are subject to stringent regulatory controls to ensure that safety and security are properly addressed.

Several organizations have piloted formal methods in their organizations (with varying degrees of success). IBM developed the VDM specification language at its laboratory in Vienna, and it piloted the Z formal specification language on the CICS (Customer Information Control System) project at its plant in Hursley, England (with a 9% cost saving).

The mathematical techniques developed by Parnas (i.e., his requirements model and tabular expressions) have been employed to specify the requirements of the A-7 aircraft as part of a research project for the US Navy.[3] Tabular expressions were also employed for the software inspection of the automated shutdown software of the Darlington Nuclear power plant in Canada.[4] These were two successful uses of mathematical techniques in software engineering.

There are examples of the use of formal methods in the railway domain, with GEC Alsthom and RATP using B for the formal specification and verification of the computerized signalling system on the Paris Metro. Several examples dealing with the modelling and verification of a railroad gate controller and railway signalling are described in [3]. Clearly, it is essential to verify safety critical properties such as *"when the train goes through the level crossing then the gate is closed"*.

---

[3] However, the resulting software was never actually deployed on the A-7 aircraft.

[4] This was an impressive use of mathematical techniques, and it has been acknowledged that formal methods must play an important role in future developments at Darlington. However, given the time and cost involved in the software inspection of the shutdown software some managers have less enthusiasm in shifting from hardware to software controllers [7].

PVS is a mechanized environment for formal specification and verification, and it was developed at SRI in California. It includes a specification language integrated with support tools and an interactive theorem prover. The specification language is based on higher-order logic, and the theorem prover is guided by the user in conducting proof. It has been applied to the verification of hardware and software, and PVS has been used for the formal specification and partial verification of the micro-code of the AAMP5 microprocessor.

Formal methods has been applied to the specification of services [8], and a selection of applications of formal methods to industry is presented in [9].

16.4 Tools for Formal Methods

Formal methods have been criticized for the limited availability of tools to support the software engineer in writing the formal specification and in conducting proof. Many of the early tools were criticized as not being of industrial strength. However, in recent years more advanced tools have become available to support the software engineer's work in formal specification and formal proof, and this is likely to continue in the coming years.

The tools include syntax checkers that determine whether the specification is syntactically correct; specialized editors which ensure that the written specification is syntactically correct; tools to support refinement; automated code generators that generate a high-level language corresponding to the specification; theorem provers to demonstrate the correctness of refinement steps, and to identify and resolve proof obligations, as well as proving the presence or absence of key properties; and specification animation tools where the execution of the specification can be simulated.

The B-Toolkit[5] from B-Core is an integrated set of tools that supports the B-Method. It provides functionality for syntax and type checking, specification animation, proof obligation generator, an auto-prover, a proof assistant, and code generation. This, in theory, allows the complete formal development from the initial specification to the final implementation, with every proof obligation justified, leading to a provably correct program. There is also the Atelier B tool to support formal specification and development in B.

The IFAD Toolbox[6] is a support tool for the VDM-SL specification language, and it provides support for syntax and type checking, an interpreter and debugger to execute and debug the specification, and a code generator to convert from VDM-SL to C++. The Overture Integrated Development Environment (IDE) is an open-source tool for formal modelling and analysis of VDM-SL specifications.

---

[5] The source code for the B-Toolkit is now available.
[6] The IFAD Toolbox has been renamed to VDMTools as IFAD sold the VDM Tools to CSK in Japan. The CSK VDM tools are available for worldwide use.

There are various tools for model checking including Spin, Bandera, SMV, and UppAal. These tools perform a systematic check on property P in all states and are applicable if the system generates a finite behavioural model. Spin is an open-source tool, and it checks finite state systems with properties specified by linear temporal logic. It generates a counterexample trace if determines that a property is violated.

There are tools to support theorem provers, and the Boyer-Moore Theorem prover (NQTHM) was developed at the University of Texas in the late 1970s. It is far more automated than many other interactive theorem provers, but it requires detailed human guidance (with suggested lemmas) for difficult proofs. The user therefore needs to understand the proof being sought and the internals of the theorem prover. Many mathematical theorems have been proved including Gödel's incompleteness theorem.

The HOL system was developed at the University of Cambridge, and it is an environment for interactive theorem proving in a higher-order logic. It requires skilled human guidance and has been used for the verification of microprocessor design. It is one of the most widely used theorem provers.

16.5 Approaches to Formal Methods

There are two key approaches to formal methods: namely the *model-oriented approach* of VDM or Z, and the *algebraic* or *axiomatic approach* of the process calculi such as the calculus communicating systems (CCS) or communicating sequential processes (CSP).

16.5.1 Model-Oriented Approach

The model-oriented approach to specification is based on mathematical models, where a model is a simplification or abstraction of the real world that contains only the essential details. For example, the model of an aircraft will not include the colour of the aircraft, and the objective would be to model the aerodynamics of the aircraft. There are many models employed in the physical world, such as meteorological models that allow weather forecasts to be given.

The importance of models is that they serve to explain the behaviour of a particular entity and may also be used to predict future behaviour. Models may vary in their ability to explain aspects of the entity under study. One model may be good at explaining some aspects of the behaviour, whereas another model might be good at explaining other aspects. The *adequacy* of a model is a key concept in modelling, and it is determined by the effectiveness of the model in representing the underlying behaviour, and in its ability to predict future behaviour. Model exploration consists of asking questions and determining the extent to which the model can give an effective answer to the particular question. A good model is chosen as a representation of the real world and is referred to whenever there are questions in relation to the aspect of the real world.

It is fundamental to explore the model to determine its adequacy, and to determine the extent to which it explains the underlying physical behaviour and allows accurate predictions of future behaviour to be made. There may be more than one possible model of a particular entity: for example, the Ptolemaic model and the Copernican model are different models of the solar system. This leads to the question as to which is the best or most appropriate model to use, and on the criteria to use to determine which is more suitable. The ability of the model to explain the behaviour, its simplicity, and its elegance will be part of the criteria. The principle of "*Ockham's Razor*" (law of parsimony) is often used in modelling, and it suggests that the simplest model with the least number of assumptions required should be selected.

The adequacy of the model will determine its acceptability as a representation of the physical world. Models that are ineffective will be replaced with models that offer a better explanation of the manifested physical behaviour. There are many examples in science of the replacement of one theory by a newer one. For example, the Copernican model of the universe replaced the older Ptolemaic model, and Newtonian physics was replaced by Einstein's theories of relativity. The structure of the revolutions that take place in science are described in [10].

Modelling can play a key role in computer science, as computer systems tend to be highly complex, whereas a model allows simplification or an abstraction of the underlying complexity, and it enables a richer understanding of the underlying reality to be gained. We discussed system modelling in Chap. 5, and it provides an abstraction of the existing and proposed system, and it helps in clarifying what the existing system does, and in communicating and clarifying the requirements of the proposed system.

The model-oriented approach to software development involves defining an abstract model of the proposed software system, and the model is then explored to determine its suitability as a representation of the system. This takes the form of model interrogation, i.e., asking questions, and determining the extent to which the model can answer the questions. The modelling in formal methods is typically performed via elementary discrete mathematics, including set theory, sequences, functions, and relations.

Various models have been applied to assist with the complexities in software development. These include the Capability Maturity Model (CMM), which is employed as a framework to enhance the capability of the organization in software development; UML, which has various graphical diagrams that are employed to model the requirements and design; and mathematical models that are employed for formal specification.

VDM and Z are model-oriented approaches to formal methods. VDM arose from work done at the IBM laboratory in Vienna in formalizing the semantics for the PL/1 compiler in the early 1970s, and it was later applied to the specification of software systems. The origin of the Z specification language is in work done at Oxford University in the early 1980s.

16.5.2 Axiomatic Approach

The axiomatic approach focuses on the properties that the proposed system is to satisfy, and there is no intention to produce an abstract model of the system. The required properties and behaviour of the system are stated in mathematical notation. The difference between the axiomatic specification and a model-based approach may be seen in the example of a stack.

The stack includes operators for pushing an element onto the stack and popping an element from the stack. The properties of *pop* and *push* are explicitly defined in the axiomatic approach. The model-oriented approach constructs an explicit model of the stack, and the operations are defined in terms of the effect that they have on the model. The axiomatic specification of the *pop* operation on a stack is given by properties, for example, *pop(push(s, x)) = s*.

Comment 16.2 (Axiomatic Approach) *The property-oriented approach has the advantage that the implementer is not constrained to a particular choice of implementation, and the only constraint is that the implementation must satisfy the stipulated properties.*

The emphasis is on specifying the required properties of the system, and implementation issues are avoided. The properties are typically stated using mathematical logic (or higher-order logics). Mechanized theorem-proving techniques may be employed to prove results.

One potential problem with the axiomatic approach is that the properties specified may not be realized in any implementation. Thus, whenever a "formal axiomatic theory" is developed a corresponding "model" of the theory must be identified, to ensure that the properties may be realized in practice. That is, when proposing a system that is to satisfy some set of properties, there is a need to prove that there is at least one system that will satisfy the set of properties.

16.6 Proof and Formal Methods

A mathematical proof typically includes natural language and mathematical symbols, and often many of the tedious details of the proof are omitted. The proof may employ a "*divide and conquer*" technique, i.e., breaking the conjecture down into sub-goals and then attempting to prove each of the sub-goals.

Many proofs in formal methods are concerned with crosschecking the details of the specification, or in checking the validity of the refinement steps, or checking that certain properties are satisfied by the specification. There are often many tedious lemmas to be proved, and theorem provers[7] are essential in dealing with these. Machine proof is explicit and reliance on some brilliant insight is avoided.

---

[7] Many existing theorem provers are difficult to use and are for specialist use only. There is a need to improve the usability of theorem provers.

Proofs by hand are notorious for containing errors or jumps in reasoning, while machine proofs are explicit but are often extremely lengthy and unreadable. The infamous machine proof of the correctness of the VIPER microprocessor[8] consisted of several million formulae [6].

A formal mathematical proof consists of a sequence of formulae, where each element is either an axiom or derived from a previous element in the series by applying a fixed set of mechanical rules.

The application of formal methods in an industrial environment requires the use of machine-assisted proof, since thousands of proof obligations arise from a formal specification, and theorem provers are essential in resolving these efficiently. Automated theorem proving is difficult, as often mathematicians prove a theorem with an initial intuitive feeling that the theorem is true. Human intervention to provide guidance or intuition improves the effectiveness of the theorem prover.

The proof of various properties about a program increases confidence in its correctness. However, an absolute proof of correctness[9] is unlikely except for the most trivial of programs. A program may consist of legacy software that is assumed to work; a compiler that is assumed to work correctly creates it. Theorem provers are programs that are assumed to function correctly. The best that formal methods can claim is increased confidence in correctness of the software, rather than an absolute proof of correctness.

16.7 The Future of Formal Methods

The debate concerning the level of use of mathematics in software engineering is still ongoing. Many practitioners are against the use of mathematics and avoid its use. They tend to employ methodologies such as software inspections and testing (or more recently the Agile approach has become popular) to improve confidence in the correctness of the software. They argue that in the current competitive industrial environment, where time to market is a key driver, that the use of such formal mathematical techniques would seriously impact the market opportunity. Industrialists often need to balance conflicting needs such as quality, cost, and delivering on time head of competitors. They argue that the commercial realities require methodologies and techniques that allow them to achieve their business goals effectively.

---

[8] This verification was controversial with RSRE and Charter overselling VIPER as a chip design that conforms to its formal specification.

[9] This position is controversial with others arguing that if correctness is defined mathematically then the mathematical definition (i.e., formal specification) is a theorem, and the task is to prove that the program satisfies the theorem. They argue that the proofs for non-trivial programs exist, and that the reason why there are not many examples of such proofs is due to a lack of mathematical specifications.

The other camp argues that the use of mathematics is essential in the delivery of high-quality and reliable software, and that if a company does not place sufficient emphasis on quality, then it will pay the price in terms of poor quality and the loss of its reputation in the marketplace.

It is generally accepted that mathematics and formal methods must play a role in the safety critical and security critical fields. Apart from that the extent of the use of mathematics is a hotly disputed topic. The pace of change in the world is extraordinary, and companies face significant competitive forces in a global marketplace. It is unrealistic to expect companies to deploy formal methods unless they have clear evidence that it will support them in delivering commercial products to the marketplace ahead of their competition, at the right price and with the right quality. Formal methods need to prove that it can do this if it wishes to be taken seriously in mainstream software engineering. The issue of technology transfer of formal methods to industry is discussed in [11].

16.8 The Vienna Development Method

VDM dates from work done by the IBM research laboratory in Vienna. This group was specifying the semantics of the PL/1 programming language using an operational semantic approach. That is, the semantics of the language were defined in terms of a hypothetical machine which interprets the programs of that language [12, 13]. Later work led to the Vienna Development Method (VDM) with its specification language, Meta IV. This was used to give the denotational semantics of programming languages, i.e., a mathematical object (set, function, etc.) is associated with each phrase of the language [13]. The mathematical object is termed the *denotation* of the phrase.

VDM is a *model-oriented approach* and this means that an explicit model of the state of an abstract machine is given, and operations are defined in terms of the state. Operations may act on the system state, taking inputs, and producing outputs as well as a new system state. Operations are defined in a precondition and post-condition style. Each operation has an associated proof obligation to ensure that if the precondition is true, then the operation preserves the system invariant. The initial state itself is, of course, required to satisfy the system invariant.

VDM uses keywords to distinguish different parts of the specification, e.g., preconditions, post-conditions, as introduced by the keywords *pre* and *post* respectively. In keeping with the philosophy that formal methods specify *what* a system does as distinct from *how*, VDM employs post-conditions to stipulate the effect of the operation on the state. The previous state is then distinguished by employing *hooked variables*, e.g., $v\urcorner$, and the post-condition specifies the new state which is defined by a logical predicate relating the pre-state to the post-state.

VDM is more than its specification language VDM-SL, and is, in fact, a software development method, with rules to verify the steps of development. The rules enable the executable specification, i.e., the detailed code, to be obtained from the initial specification via refinement steps. Thus, we have a sequence $S = S_0, S_1, ...,$ $S_n = E$ of specifications, where S is the initial specification, and E is the final (executable) specification.

Retrieval functions enable a return from a more concrete specification to the more abstract specification. The initial specification consists of an initial state, a system state, and a set of operations. The system state is a particular domain, where a domain is built out of primitive domains such as the set of natural numbers, integers, etc., or constructed from primitive domains using domain constructors such as Cartesian product, disjoint union, etc. A domain-invariant predicate may further constrain the domain, and a *type* in VDM reflects a domain obtained in this way. Thus, a type in VDM is more specific than the signature of the type, and thus represents values in the domain defined by the signature, which satisfy the domain invariant. Another words, VDM types may not be "statically type checked".

VDM specifications are structured into modules, with a module containing the module name, parameters, types, operations, etc. Partial functions occur frequently in computer science as many functions, may be undefined, or fail to terminate for some arguments in their domain. VDM addresses partial functions by employing non-standard logical operators, namely the logic of partial functions (LPFs), which is discussed in [14].

VDM has been used in industrial projects, and its tool support includes the IFAD Toolbox.[10] VDM is described in more detail in [11]. There are several variants of VDM, including VDM[++], the object-oriented extension of VDM, and the Irish school of the VDM, which is discussed in the next section.

16.9 VDM*, the Irish School of VDM

The Irish School of VDM is a variant of standard VDM, and is characterized by its constructive approach, classical mathematical style, and its terse notation [15]. This method aims to combine the *what* and *how* of formal methods in that its terse specification style stipulates in concise form *what* the system should do; further-more, the fact that its specifications are constructive (or functional) means that the *how* is included with the *what*.

However, it is important to qualify this by stating that the how as presented by VDM* is not directly executable, as several of its mathematical data types have no corresponding structure in high-level or functional programming languages. Thus, a conversion or reification of the specification into a functional or high-level language must take place to ensure a successful execution. Further, the fact that a specification is constructive is no guarantee that it is a good implementation strategy, if the construction itself is naive.

---

[10] The VDM Tools are now available from the CSK Group in Japan.

The Irish school follows a similar development methodology to standard VDM, and it is a model-oriented approach. The initial specification is presented, with the initial state and operations defined. The operations are presented with preconditions; however, no post-condition is necessary as the operation is "functionally" (i.e., explicitly) constructed.

There are proof obligations to demonstrate that the operations preserve the invariant. That is, if the precondition for the operation is true, and the operation is performed, then the system invariant remains true after the operation. The philosophy is to exhibit existence *constructively* rather than providing a theoretical proof of existence that demonstrates the existence of a solution without presenting an algorithm to construct the solution.

The school avoids the existential quantifier of predicate calculus, and reliance on logic in proof is kept to a minimum, with emphasis instead placed on equational reasoning. Structures with nice algebraic properties are sought, and one nice algebraic structure employed is the monoid, which has closure, associative, and a unit element. The concept of isomorphism is powerful, reflecting that the two structures are essentially identical, and thus we may choose to work with either, depending on which is more convenient for the task in hand.

The school has been influenced by the work of Polya and Lakatos. The former [16] advocated a style of problem solving characterized by first considering an easier sub-problem and considering several examples. This generally leads to a clearer insight into solving the main problem. Lakatos's approach to mathematical discovery [17] is characterized by heuristic methods. A primitive conjecture is proposed and if global counterexamples to the statement of the conjecture are discovered, then the corresponding *hidden lemma* for which this global counterexample is a local counter example is identified and added to the statement of the primitive conjecture. The process repeats, until no more global counterexamples are found. A sceptical view of absolute truth or certainty is inherent in this.

Partial functions are the norm in VDM$^{\clubsuit}$, and as in standard VDM, the problem is that functions may be undefined, or fail to terminate for several of the arguments in their domain. The logic of partial functions (LPFs) is avoided, and instead care is taken with recursive definitions to ensure termination is achieved for each argument. Academic and industrial projects have been conducted using the method of the Irish school, but tool support is limited.

16.10   The Z Specification Language

Z is a formal specification language founded on Zermelo set theory, and it was developed by Abrial at Oxford University in the early 1980s. It is used for the formal specification of software and is a model-oriented approach. An explicit model of the state of an abstract machine is given, and the operations are defined in terms of the effect on the state. It includes a mathematical notation that is like VDM and the visually striking schema calculus. The latter consists essentially of boxes (or schemas), and these are used to describe operations and states. The schema calculus enables schemas to be used as building blocks and combined with other schemas. The Z specification language was published as an ISO standard (ISO/IEC 13,568:2002) in 2002.

The schema calculus is a powerful means of decomposing a specification into smaller pieces or schemas. This helps to make Z specification highly readable, as each individual schema is small and self-contained. Exception handling is done by defining schemas for the exception cases, and these are then combined with the original operation schema. Mathematical data types are used to model the data in a system and these data types obey mathematical laws. These laws enable simplification of expressions and are useful with proofs.

Operations are defined in a precondition/post-condition style. However, the precondition is implicitly defined within the operation, i.e., it is not separated out as in standard VDM. Each operation has an associated proof obligation to ensure that if the precondition is true, then the operation preserves the system invariant. The initial state itself is, of course, required to satisfy the system invariant. Post-conditions employ a logical predicate which relates the pre-state to the post-state, and the post-state of a variable v is given by priming, e.g., v'. Various conventions are employed, e.g., $v?$ indicates that v is an input variable and $v!$ indicates that v is an output variable. The symbol $\Xi\ Op$ operation indicates that this operation does not affect the state, whereas $\Delta\ Op$ indicates that this operation affects the state.

Many data types employed in Z have no counterpart in standard programming languages. It is therefore important to identify and describe the concrete data structures that will ultimately represent the abstract mathematical structures. The operations on the abstract data structures may need to be refined to yield operations on the concrete data structure that yield equivalent results. For simple systems, direct refinement (i.e., one step from abstract specification to implementation) may be possible; in more complex systems, deferred refinement is employed, where a sequence of increasingly concrete specifications are produced to eventually yield the executable specification.

Z has been successfully applied in industry, and one of its well-known successes is the CICS project at IBM Hursley in England. Z is described in more detail in Chap. 17.

16.11   The B Method

The B-Technologies [18] consist of three components: a method for software development, namely the B-Method; a supporting set of tools, namely, the B-Toolkit; and a generic program for symbol manipulation, namely, the B-Tool (from which the B-Toolkit is derived). The B-Method is a model-oriented approach and is closely related to the Z specification language. Abrial developed the

B specification language, and every construct in the language has a set theoretic counterpart, and the method is founded on Zermelo set theory. Each operation has an explicit precondition.

A key role of the *abstract machine* in the *B*-Method is to provide encapsulation of variables representing the state of the machine and operations that manipulate the state. Machines may refer to other machines, and a machine may be introduced as a refinement of another machine. The abstract machines are specification machines, refinement machines, or implementable machines. The *B*-Method adopts a layered approach to design where the design is gradually made more concrete by a sequence of design layers. Each design layer is a refinement that involves a more detailed implementation in terms of the abstract machines of the previous layer. The design refinement ends when the final layer is implemented purely in terms of library machines. Any refinement of a machine by another has associated proof obligations, and proof is required to verify the validity of the refinement step.

Specification animation of the Abstract Machine Notation (AMN) specification is possible with the *B*-Toolkit, and this enables typical usage scenarios to be explored for requirements validation. This is, in effect, an early form of testing, and it may be used to demonstrate the presence or absence of desirable or undesirable behaviour. Verification takes the form of a proof to demonstrate that the invariant is preserved when the operation is executed within its precondition, and this is performed on the AMN specification with the *B*-Toolkit.

The *B*-Toolkit provides several tools that support the *B*-Method, and these include syntax and type checking, specification animation, proof obligation generator, auto prover, proof assistor, and code generation. Thus, in theory, a complete formal development from initial specification to final implementation may be achieved, with every proof obligation justified, leading to a provably correct program.

The *B*-Method and toolkit have been successfully applied in industrial applications, including the CICS project at IBM Hursley in the United Kingdom [19]. The automated support provided has been cited as a major benefit of the application of the *B*-Method and the *B*-Toolkit.

16.12   Predicate Transformers and Weakest Preconditions

The precondition of a program S is a predicate, i.e., a statement that may be true or false, and it is usually required to prove that if the precondition Q is true then execution of S is guaranteed to terminate in a finite amount of time in a state satisfying R. This is written as $\{Q\}\ S\ \{R\}$.

The weakest precondition of a command S with respect to a post-condition R [20] represents the set of all states such that if execution begins in any one of these states, then execution will terminate in a finite amount of time in a state with R true. These set of states may be represented by a predicate Q', so that $wp(S,R) = wp_S\ (R) = Q'$, and so wp_S is a predicate transformer: i.e., it may be regarded as a function on predicates. The weakest precondition is the precondition that places the fewest constraints on the state than all of the other preconditions of (S,R). That is, all the other preconditions are stronger than the weakest precondition.

The notation $Q\{S\}R$ is used to denote partial correctness, and indicates that if execution of S commences in any state satisfying Q, and if execution terminates, then the final state will satisfy R. Often, a predicate Q which is stronger than the weakest precondition $wp(S,R)$ is employed, especially where the calculation of the weakest precondition is nontrivial. Thus, a stronger predicate Q such that $Q \rightarrow wp$ (S,R) is often employed.

There are many properties associated with the weakest preconditions, and these may be used to simplify expressions involving weakest preconditions, and in determining the weakest preconditions of various program commands such as assignments, iterations, etc. Weakest preconditions may be used in developing a proof of correctness of a program in parallel with its development [21].

An imperative program F may be regarded as a predicate transformer. This is since a predicate P characterizes the set of states in which the predicate P is true, and an imperative program may be regarded as a binary relation on states, which, leads to the Hoare triple $P\{F\}Q$. That is, the program F acts as a predicate transformer with the predicate P regarded as an input assertion, i.e., a Boolean expression that must be true before the program F is executed, and the predicate Q is the output assertion, which is true if the program F terminates (where F commenced in a state satisfying P).

16.13 The Process Calculii

The objectives of the process calculi [22] are to provide mathematical models which provide insight into the diverse issues involved in the specification, design, and implementation of computer systems which continuously act and interact with their environment. These systems may be decomposed into sub-systems that interact with each other and their environment.

The basic building block is the *process*, which is a mathematical abstraction of the interactions between a system and its environment. A process that lasts indefinitely may be specified recursively. Processes may be assembled into systems; they may execute concurrently or communicate with each other. Process communication may be synchronized, and this takes the form of one process outputting a message simultaneously to another process inputting a message. Resources may be shared among several processes. Process calculi such as CSP [22] and CCS [23] have been developed and they enrich the understanding of communication and concurrency, and they obey several mathematical laws.

The expression $(a \ ? \ P)$ in CSP describes a process which first engages in event a, and then behaves as process P. A recursive definition is written as $(\mu X) \cdot F(X)$ and an example of a simple chocolate vending machine is:

$$\text{VMS} = \mu X : \{coin, choc\} \cdot (coin?(choc?X))$$

The simple vending machine has an alphabet of two symbols, namely, *coin* and *choc*. The behaviour of the machine is that a coin is entered into the machine, and then a chocolate selected and provided, and the machine is ready for further use. CSP processes use channels to communicate values with their environment, and input on channel c is denoted by $(c?.x\,P_x)$. This describes a process that accepts any value x on channel c, and then behaves as process P_x. In contrast, $(c!e\ P)$ defines a process which outputs the expression e on channel c and then behaves as process P.

The π-calculus is a process calculus based on names. Communication between processes takes place between known channels, and the name of a channel may be passed over a channel. There is no distinction between channel names and data values in the π-calculus. The output of a value v on channel a is given by $\bar{a}v$; i.e., output is a negative prefix. Input on a channel a is given by $a(x)$ and is a positive prefix. Private links or restrictions are denoted by $(x)P$.

16.14 Finite State Machines

Warren McCulloch and Walter Pitts published early work on finite state automata in 1943. They were interested in modelling the thought process for humans and machines. Moore and Mealy developed this work further, and these machines are referred to as the "*Moore machine*" and the "*Mealy machine*". The Mealy machine determines its outputs through the current state and the input, whereas the output of Moore's machine is based upon the current state alone.

Definition 16.2 (*Finite State Machine*)
A finite state machine (FSM) is an abstract mathematical machine that consists of a finite number of states. It includes a start state q_0 in which the machine is in initially; a finite set of states Q; an input alphabet Σ; a state transition function δ; and a set of final accepting states F (where F $\subseteq$, Q).

The state transition function takes the current state and an input and returns the next state. That is, the transition function is of the form:

$$\delta : Q \times \Sigma \rightarrow Q$$

The transition function provides rules that define the action of the machine for each input, and it may be extended to provide output as well as a state transition. State diagrams are used to represent finite state machines, and each state accepts a finite number of inputs. A finite state machine may be deterministic or non-deterministic, and a *deterministic machine* (Fig. 16.1) changes to exactly one state for each input transition, whereas a *non-deterministic machine* may have a choice of states to move to for a particular input.

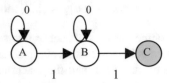

Fig. 16.1 Deterministic finite state machine

Finite state automata can compute only very primitive functions and are not an adequate model for computing. There are more powerful automata such as the *Turing machine* [14] that is essentially a finite state automaton with a potentially infinite storage (memory). Anything that is computable is computable by a Turing machine.

The memory of the Turing machine is a tape that consists of a potentially infinite number of one-dimensional cells. The Turing machine provides a mathematical abstraction of computer execution and storage, as well as providing a mathematical definition of an algorithm.

16.15 The Parnas Way

Parnas has been influential in the computing field, and his ideas on the specification, design, implementation, maintenance, and documentation of computer software remain important. He advocates a solid engineering approach and argues that the role of the engineer is to apply scientific principles and mathematics to design and develop products. He argues that computer scientists need to be educated as engineers to ensure that they have the appropriate background to build software correctly. His contributions to software engineering include (Table 16.2).

16.16 Usability of Formal Methods

There are practical difficulties associated with the industrial use of formal methods. It seems to be assumed that programmers and customers are willing to become familiar with the mathematics used in formal methods, but this is true in only some domains.[11] Customers are concerned with their own domain and speak the technical

---

[11] The domain in which the software is being used will influence the willingness or otherwise of the customers to become familiar with the mathematics required. There appears to be little interest in mainstream software engineering, and their perception is that formal methods are unusable. However, in there is a greater interest in the mathematical approach in the safety critical field.

Table 16.2   Parnas's contributions to software engineering

Area	Contribution
Tabular expressions	These are mathematical tables for specifying requirements and enable complex predicate logic expressions to be represented in a simpler form
Mathematical documentation	He advocates the use of precise mathematical documentation for requirements and design
Requirements specification	He advocates the use of mathematical relations to specify the requirements precisely
Software design	He developed *information hiding* that is used in object-oriented design[a], and allows software to be designed for change. Every information-hiding module has an interface that provides the only means to access the services provided by the modules. The interface hides the module's implementation
Software inspections	His approach requires the reviewers to take an active part in the inspection. They are provided with a list of questions by the author and their analysis involves the production of mathematical table to justify the answers
Predicate logic	He developed an extension of the predicate calculus to deal with partial functions, and it preserves the classical two-valued logic when dealing with undefined values

[a] It is surprising that many in the object-oriented world seem unaware that information hiding goes back to the early 1970s and many have never heard of Parnas

language of that domain.[12] Often, the use of mathematics is an alien activity that bears little resemblance to their normal work. Programmers are interested in programming rather than in mathematics and are generally not interested in becoming mathematicians.[13]

However, the mathematics involved in most formal methods is reasonably elementary, and, in theory, if both customers and programmers are willing to learn the formal mathematical notation, then a rigorous validation of the formal specification can take place to verify its correctness. It is usually possible to get a developer to learn a formal method, as a programmer has some experience of mathematics and logic; however, in practice, it is more difficult to get a customer to learn a formal method.

This often means that often a formal specification of the requirements and an informal definition of the requirements using a natural language are maintained. It is essential that both are consistent and that there is a rigorous validation of the formal specification. Otherwise, if the programmer proves the correctness of the code with respect to the formal specification, and the formal specification is incorrect, then the formal development of the software is incorrect. There are several techniques to validate a formal specification (Table 16.3) and these are described in more detail in [24].

---

[12] Most customers have a very limited interest and even less willingness to use mathematics. There are exceptions to this especially in the regulated sector.

[13] Mathematics that is potentially useful to software engineers is discussed in [14].

Table 16.3 Techniques for validation of formal specification

Technique	Description
Proof	This involves demonstrating that the formal specification satisfies key properties of the requirements. The implementation will need to preserve these properties
Software Inspections	This involves a Fagan like inspection to compare an informal set of requirements (unless the customer has learned the formal method) with the formal specification, and to ensure consistency between them
Specification Animation	This involves program (or specification) execution to validate the formal specification. It is like testing
Tools	Tools provide some limited support in validating a formal specification

16.16.1 Why are Formal Methods Difficult?

Formal methods are perceived as being difficult to use, and of providing limited value in mainstream software engineering. Programmers receive education in mathematics as part of their studies, but many never use formal methods or mathematics again once they take an industrial position.

It may well be that the very nature of formal methods is such that it is suited only for specialists with a strong background in mathematics. Some of the reasons why formal methods are perceived as being difficult are listed in Table 16.4.

16.16.2 Characteristics of a Usable Formal Method

It is important to investigate ways by which formal methods can be made more usable to software engineers. This may involve designing more usable notations

Table 16.4 Why are formal methods difficult?

Factor	Description
Notation/intuition	The notation employed differs from that employed in mathematics. Many programmers find the notation in formal methods to be unintuitive
Formal specification	It is easier to read a formal specification than to write one
Validation of formal specification	The validation of a formal specification using proof techniques or a Fagan like inspection is difficult
Refinement[a]	The refinement of a formal specification into more concrete specifications with proof of each refinement step is difficult and time consuming
Proof	Proof can be difficult and time consuming
Tool support	Many of the existing tools are difficult to use

[a] The author doubts that refinement is cost effective for mainstream software engineering. However, it may be useful in the regulated environment

Table 16.5 Characteristics of a usable formal method

Characteristic	Description
Intuitive	A formal method should be intuitive
Teachable	A formal method needs to be teachable to the average software engineer. The training should include writing practical formal specifications
Tool support	Good tools to support formal specification, validation, refinement, and proof are required
Adaptable to change	Change is common in a software engineering environment. A usable formal method should be adaptable to change
Technology transfer path	The process for software development needs to be defined to include formal methods. The migration to formal methods needs to be managed
Cost[a]	The use of formal methods should be cost effective with a return on investment (e.g., benefits in time, quality, and productivity)

[a] A commercial company will expect a return on investment from the use of a new technology. This may be reduced software development costs, improved quality and improved timeliness of projects, and improvements in productivity. A company does not go to the trouble of deploying a new technology just to satisfy academic interest

and better tools to support the process. Practical training and coaching to employees can help. Some of the characteristics of a usable formal method are listed in Table 16.5.

16.17   Review Questions

1. What are formal methods and describe their potential benefits? How essential is tool support?
2. What is stepwise refinement and how realistic is it in mainstream software engineering?
3. Discuss Parnas's criticisms of formal methods and discuss whether his views are valid.
4. Discuss the applications of formal methods and which areas have benefited most from their use? What problems have arisen?
5. Describe a technology transfer path for the deployment of formal methods in an organization.
6. Explain the difference between the model-oriented approach and the axiomatic approach.
7. Discuss the nature of proof in formal methods and tools to support proof.
8. Discuss the Vienna Development Method and explain the difference between standard VDM and VDM✦.
9. Discuss Z and B. Describe the tools in the B-Toolkit.
10. Discuss process calculi such as CSP, CCS or π–calculus.

16.18   Summary

This chapter discussed formal methods which offers a mathematical approach to the development of high-quality software. Formal methods employ mathematical techniques for the specification and development of software and are useful in the safety critical field. They consist of a formal specification language; a methodology for formal software development; and a set of tools to support the syntax checking of the specification, as well as the proof of properties of the specification.

The model-oriented approach includes formal methods such as VDM, Z and B, whereas the axiomatic approach includes the process calculi such as CSP, CCS and the π calculus. VDM was developed at the IBM lab in Vienna, and it has been used in academia and industry. CSP was developed by C.A.R Hoare, and CCS by Robin Milner.

Formal methods allow questions to be asked and answered about what the system does independently of the implementation. They offer a way to debug the requirements, and to show that certain desirable properties are true of the specification, whereas certain undesirable properties are absent.

The use of formal methods generally leads to more robust software and to increased confidence in its correctness. There are challenges involved in the deployment of formal methods, as the use of these mathematical techniques may be a culture shock to many staff.

The usability of existing formal methods was considered, and reasons for their perceived difficulty considered. The characteristics of a usable formal method was explored.

There are various tools to support formal methods including syntax checkers; specialized editors; tools to support refinement; automated code generators that generate a high-level language corresponding to the specification; theorem provers; and specification animation tools where the execution of the specification can be simulated.

References

1. J.M. Spivey, *The Z Notation. A Reference Manual* (Prentice Hall International Series in Computer Science, 1992)
2. M.J.D. Brown, Rational for the development of the U.K. Defence Standards for Safety Critical software, in Compass Conference (1990)
3. M. Hinchey, J. Bowen, *Applications of Formal Methods* (Prentice Hall International Series in Computer Science, 1995)
4. 00-55 (PART 1) *I* Issue 1, The Procurement of Safety Critical software in Defence Equipment, PART 1: Requirements. Ministry of Defence, Interim Defence Standard, U.K., 1991
5. 00-55 (PART 2) *I* Issue 1, The Procurement of Safety Critical software in Defence Equipment, PART 2: Guidance. Ministry of De fence, Interim Defence Standard, U.K., 1991
6. M. Tierney, The Evolution of Def Stan 00-55 and 00-56: An Intensification of the "Formal Methods debate" in the UK (Research Centre for Social Sciences, University of Edinburgh, 1991)

7. S. Gerhart, D. Craighen, T. Ralston, *Experience with Formal Methods in Critical Systems* (IEEE Software, 1994, January)
8. M.M.A. Airchinnigh, D. Belsnes, G. O'Regan, Formal Methods and Service Specification, in International Conference on Intelligence in Services and Networks (Springer, Berlin, 1994), pp. 563–572
9. J. Woodcock, P.G. Larsen, J. Bicarregui, J. Fitzgerald, *Formal Methods: Practice and Experience* (ACM Computer Surveys, 2009)
10. T. Kuhn, *The Structure of Scientific Revolutions* (University of Chicago Press, 1970)
11. G. O'Regan, *Concise Guide to Formal Methods* (Springer, Berlin, 2017)
12. D. Bjorner, C. Jones, The Vienna Development Method. The meta language. *Lecture Notes in Computer Science*, vol. 61 (Springe, Berlin, 1978)
13. D. Bjorner, C. Jones, *Formal Specification and software Development* (Prentice Hall International Series in Computer Science, 1982)
14. G. O' Regan, *Guide to Discrete Mathematics* (Springer, Berlin, 2016)
15. M.M.A. Airchinnigh, PhD thesis. Conceptual Models and Computing. Department of Computer Science. University of Dublin. Trinity College. Dublin, 1990
16. G. Polya, *How to Solve It. A New Aspect of Mathematical Method* (Princeton University Press, 1957)
17. I. Lakatos, *Proof and Refutations. The Logic of Mathematical Discovery* (Cambridge University Press, 1976)
18. E. McDonnell, MSc thesis. Department of Computer Science. Trinity College, Dublin, 1994
19. J.P. Hoare, Application of the B-method to CICS, in *Applications of Formal Method,.* ed by M. Hinchey, J.P. Bowen (Prentice Hall International Series in Computer)
20. D. Gries, *The Science of Programming* (Springer, Berlin, 1981)
21. G. O' Regan, *Mathematical Approaches to Software Quality* (Springer, Berlin, 2006)
22. C.A.R. Hoare, *Communicating Sequential Processes* (Prentice Hall International Serien in Computer Science, 1985)
23. R. Milner et al., *A Calculus of Mobile Processes (Part 1)*. LFCS Report Series. ECS-LFCS-89-85. (Department of Computer Science, University of Edinburgh, 1989)
24. B.A. Wickmann, *A Personal View of Formal Methods* (National Physical Laboratory, 2000, March)

Z Specification Language

17

Abstract

This chapter presents the Z specification language, which is one of the most widely used formal methods. Z is a formal specification language based on Zermelo set theory. It was developed at the Programming Research Group at Oxford University in the early 1980s. Z specifications are mathematical and employ a classical two-valued logic. The use of mathematics ensures precision and allows inconsistencies and gaps in the specification to be identified. Theorem provers may be employed to demonstrate that the software implementation meets its specification.

Keywords

Sets, relations and functions · Bags and sequences · Precondition · Postcondition · Invariant · Data reification · Refinement · Schema calculus · Proof in Z

17.1 Introduction

Z is a formal specification language based on Zermelo set theory. It was developed at the Programming Research Group at Oxford University in the early 1980s [1] and became an ISO standard in 2002. Z specifications are mathematical and employ a classical two-valued logic. The use of mathematics ensures precision and allows inconsistencies and gaps in the specification to be identified. Theorem provers may be employed to prove properties of the specification, and to demonstrate that the software implementation meets its specification.

Z is a '*model oriented*' approach with an explicit model of the state of an abstract machine given, and operations are defined in terms of this state. Its mathematical notation is used for formal specification, and its schema calculus is used to structure

© Springer Nature Switzerland AG 2022
G. O'Regan, *Concise Guide to Software Engineering*,
Undergraduate Topics in Computer Science,
https://doi.org/10.1007/978-3-031-07816-3_17

the specification. The schema calculus is visually striking, and consists essentially of boxes, with these boxes or schemas used to describe operations and states. The schemas may be used as building blocks and combined with other schemas. The simple schema below (Fig. 17.1) is the specification of the positive square root of a real number.

The schema calculus is a powerful means of decomposing a specification into smaller pieces or schemas. This helps to make Z specifications highly readable, as each individual schema is small and self-contained. Exception handling is addressed by defining schemas for the exception cases. These are then combined with the original operation schema. Mathematical data types are used to model the data in a system, and these data types obey mathematical laws. These laws enable simplification of expressions and are useful with proofs.

Operations are defined in a precondition/postcondition style. A precondition must be true before the operation is executed, and the postcondition must be true after the operation has executed. The *precondition is implicitly defined* within the operation. Each operation has an associated proof obligation to ensure that if the precondition is true, then the operation preserves the system invariant. The system invariant is a property of the system that must be always true. The initial state itself is, of course, required to satisfy the system invariant.

The precondition for the specification of the square root function above is that $num? \geq 0$; i.e., the function *SqRoot* may be applied to positive real numbers only. The postcondition for the square root function is $root!^2 = num?$ and $root! \geq 0$. That is, the square root of a number is positive, and its square gives the number. Postconditions employ a logical predicate which relates the pre-state to the post-state, with the post-state of a variable being distinguished by priming the variable, e.g., v'.

Z is a typed language and whenever a variable is introduced its type must be given. A type is simply a collection of objects, and there are several standard types in Z. These include the natural numbers $\mathbb{N}$, the integers $\mathbb{Z}$ and the real numbers $\mathbb{R}$. The declaration of a variable x of type X is written $x : X$. It is also possible to create your own types in Z.

Various conventions are employed within Z specification: for example, $v?$ indicates that v is an input variable, and $v!$ indicates that v is an output variable. The variable $num?$ is an input variable and $root!$ is an output variable in the square root

$$
\begin{array}{|l}
\text{--SqRoot}\text{------} \\
num?, root! : \mathbb{R} \\
\hline
num? \geq 0 \\
root!^2 = num? \\
root! \geq 0 \\
\hline
\end{array}
$$

Fig. 17.1 Specification of positive square root

$$
\begin{array}{|l}
\hline
\textit{--Library}\text{---} \\
\textit{on-shelf, missing, borrowed}: \mathbb{P} \ \textit{Bkd-Id} \\
\hline
\textit{on-shelf} \cap \textit{missing} = \emptyset \\
\textit{on-shelf} \cap \textit{borrowed} = \emptyset \\
\textit{borrowed} \cap \textit{missing} = \emptyset \\
\hline
\end{array}
$$

Fig. 17.2 Specification of a library system

schema above. The notation Ξ Op in a schema indicates that the operation Op does not affect the state, whereas the notation Δ Op in the schema indicates that Op is an operation that affects the state.

Many of the data types employed in Z have no counterpart in standard programming languages. It is therefore important to identify and describe the concrete data structures that ultimately will represent the abstract mathematical structures. As the concrete structures may differ from the abstract, the operations on the abstract data structures may need to be refined to yield operations on the concrete data that yield equivalent results. For simple systems, direct refinement (i.e., one step from abstract specification to implementation) may be possible; in more complex systems, deferred refinement[1] is employed, where a sequence of increasingly concrete specifications are produced to yield the executable specification. There is a calculus for combining schemas to make larger specifications, and this is discussed later in the chapter.

Example 17.1 The following is a Z specification to borrow a book from a library system. The library is made up of books that are on the shelf; books that are borrowed; and books that are missing. The specification models a library with sets representing books on the shelf, on loan or missing. These are three mutually disjoint subsets of the set of books *Bkd-Id*. The system state is defined in the *Library* schema (Fig. 17.2), and operations such as *Borrow* and *Return* affect the state. The *Borrow* operation is specified in Fig. 17.3.

The notation $\mathbb{P}$*Bkd-Id* is used to represent the power set of *Bkd-Id* (i.e., the set of all subsets of *Bkd-Id*). The disjointness condition for the library is expressed by the requirement that the pair wise intersection of the subsets *on-shelf, borrowed, missing* is the empty set.

The precondition for the *Borrow* operation is that the book must be available on the shelf to borrow. The postcondition is that the borrowed book is added to the set of borrowed books and is removed from the books on the shelf.

---

[1] Stepwise refinement involves producing a sequence of increasingly more concrete specifications until eventually the executable code is produced. Each refinement step has associated proof obligations to prove that the refinement step is valid.

$$\begin{array}{|l}
\hline
\textit{--Borrow}\text{------} \\
\Delta\,\textit{Library} \\
b?\,:\textit{Bkd-Id} \\
\hline
b? \in \textit{on-shelf} \\
\textit{on-shelf'} = \textit{on-shelf} \setminus \{b?\} \\
\textit{borrowed'} = \textit{borrowed} \cup \{b?\} \\
\hline
\end{array}$$

Fig. 17.3 Specification of borrow operation

Z has been successfully applied in industry including the CICS project at IBM Hursley in the UK.[2] Next, we describe key parts of Z including sets, relations, functions, sequences, and bags.

17.2 Sets

A set is a collection of well-defined objects, and this section focuses on their use in Z. Sets may be enumerated by listing all of their elements. Thus, the set of all even natural numbers less than or equal to 10 is:

$$\{2,4,6,8,10\}$$

Sets may be created from other sets using set comprehension: i.e., stating the properties that its members must satisfy. For example, the set of even natural numbers less than or equal to 10 is given by set comprehension as:

$$\{n : \mathbb{N} \mid n \neq 0 \wedge n \leq 10 \wedge n \bmod 2 = 0 \cdot n\}$$

There are three main parts to the set comprehension above. The first part is the signature of the set and this is given by $n : \mathbb{N}$. The first part is separated from the second part by a vertical line. The second part is given by a predicate, and for this example the predicate is $n \neq 0 \wedge n \leq 10 \wedge n \bmod 2 = 0$. The second part is separated from the third part by a bullet. The third part is a term, and for this example it is simply n. The term is often a more complex expression: e.g., $\log(n^2)$.

In mathematics, there is just one empty set $\emptyset$. However, there is an empty set for each type of set in Z (as Z is a typed language), and so there are an infinite number of empty sets in Z. The empty set is written as $\emptyset\,[X]$ where X is the type of the empty set. However, in practice, X is omitted when the type is clear.

Various set operations such as union, intersection, set difference, and symmetric difference are employed in Z. The power set of a set X is the set of all subsets of X, and it is denoted by $\mathbb{P}\,X$. The set of non-empty subsets of X is denoted by $\mathbb{P}_1 X$ where

---

[2] This project claimed a 9% increase in productivity attributed to the use of formal methods.

$$\mathbb{P}_1 X == \{U : \mathbb{P}X \mid U \neq \varnothing \, [X]\}$$

A finite set of elements of type X (denoted by F X) is a subset of X that cannot be put into a one-to-one correspondence with a proper subset of itself. That is:

$$F X == \{U : \mathbb{P}X \mid \neg \exists V : \mathbb{P}U \cdot V \neq U \wedge (\exists f : V \rightarrowtail U)\}$$

The expression $f: V \rightarrowtail U$ denotes that f is a bijection from U to V, and injective, surjective, and bijective functions are discussed in [2].

The fact that Z is a typed language means that whenever a variable is introduced (e.g., in quantification with $\forall$ and $\exists$) it is first declared. For example, $\forall j{:}J \mid P \cdot Q$. There is also the unique existential quantifier $\exists_1 j: J \mid P$ which states that there is exactly one j of type J that has property P.

17.3 Relations

Relations are used extensively in Z and a relation R between X and Y is any subset of the Cartesian product of X and Y, i.e., $R \subseteq (X \times Y)$. A relation in Z is denoted by $R: X \leftrightarrow Y$, and the notation $x \mapsto y$ indicates that the pair $(x,y) \subset R$.

Consider, the relation *home_owner*: *Person* ↔ *Home* that exists between people and their homes. An entry *daphne* ↦ *mandalay* ∈ *home_owner* if *daphne* is the owner of *mandalay*. It is possible for a person to own more than one home:

$$rebecca \mapsto nirvana \in home\_owner$$
$$rebecca \mapsto tivoli \in home\_owner$$

It is possible for two people to share ownership of a home:

$$rebecca \mapsto nirvana \in home\_owner$$
$$lawrence \mapsto nirvana \in home\_owner$$

There may be some people who do not own a home, and there is no entry for these people in the relation *home_owner*. The type *Person* includes every possible person, and the type of *Home* includes every possible home. The domain of the relation *home_owner* is given by:

$$x \in \text{dom } home\_owner \Leftrightarrow \exists h : Home \cdot x \mapsto h \in home\_owner.$$

The range of the relation *home_owner* is given by:

$$h \in \text{ran } home\_owner \Leftrightarrow \exists x : Person \cdot x \mapsto h \in home\_owner.$$

The composition of two relations *home_owner*: *Person* $\leftrightarrow$ *Home* and *home_-value*: *Home* $\leftrightarrow$ *Value* yields the relation *owner_wealth*: *Person* $\leftrightarrow$ *Value* and is given by the relational composition *home_owner*; *home_value* where:

$$p \mapsto v \in home\_owner\,;home\_value \Leftrightarrow$$

$$(\exists h : Home \cdot p \mapsto h \in home\_value \land h \mapsto v \in homevalue)$$

The relational composition may also be expressed as:

$$owner\_wealth = home\_value \circ home\_owner$$

The union of two relations often arises in practice. Suppose a new entry *aisling* $\mapsto$ *muckross* is to be added. Then this is given by.

$$home\_owner' = home\_owner \cup \{aisling \mapsto muckross\}$$

Suppose that we are interested in knowing all females who are house owners. Then we restrict the relation *home_owner* so that the first element of all ordered pairs must be female. Consider *female*: $\mathbb{P}$ *Person* with $\{aisling, rebecca\} \subseteq female$.

$$home\_owner = \{aisling \mapsto muckross, rebecca \mapsto nirvana,$$
$$lawrence \mapsto nirvana\}$$

$$female \lhd home\_owner = \{aisling \mapsto muckross, rebecca \mapsto nirvana\}$$

That is, *female* $\lhd$ *home_owner* is a relation that is a subset of *home_owner*, such that the first element of each ordered pair in the relation is female. The operation $\lhd$ is termed domain restriction and its fundamental property is:

$$x \mapsto y \in U \lhd R \Leftrightarrow (x \in U \land x \mapsto y \in R\}$$

where R: X $\leftrightarrow$ Y and U: $\mathbb{P}$ X.

There is also a domain anti-restriction (subtraction) operation, and its fundamental property is:

$$x \mapsto y \in U \ntriangleleft R \Leftrightarrow (x \notin U \land x \mapsto y \in R\}$$

where R: X $\leftrightarrow$ Y and U: $\mathbb{P}$X.

There are also range restriction (the $\lhd$ operator) and the range anti-restriction operator (the $\not\triangleright$ operator). These are discussed in [1].

17.4 Functions

A function is an association between objects of some type X and objects of another type Y such that given an object of type X, there exists only one object in Y associated with that object [1]. A function is a set of ordered pairs where the first element of the ordered pair has at most one element associated with it. A function is therefore a special type of relation, and a function may be *total* or *partial*.

A total function has exactly one element in Y associated with each element of X, whereas a partial function has at most one element of Y associated with each element of X (there may be elements of X that have no element of Y associated with them). A partial function from X to Y ($f: X \nrightarrow Y$) is a relation $f: X \leftrightarrow Y$ such that:

$$\forall x: \mathbf{X}; y, z: \mathbf{Y} \cdot (x \mapsto y \in f \wedge x \mapsto z \in f \Rightarrow y = z)$$

The association between x and y is denoted by $f(x) = y$, and this indicates that the value of the partial function f at x is y. A total function from X to Y (denoted $f: X \rightarrow Y$) is a partial function such that every element in X is associated with some value of Y.

$$f: X \rightarrow Y \Leftrightarrow f: X \nrightarrow Y \wedge \operatorname{dom} f = X$$

Clearly, every total function is a partial function but not vice versa.

```
 - TempMap--------
CityList : ℙ City
temp : City ⇸ Z

------

dom temp = CityList

------------------
```

One operation that arises quite frequently in specifications is the function override operation. Consider the specification of a temperature map above and an example temperature map given by $temp = \{Cork \mapsto 17, Dublin \mapsto 19, London \mapsto 15\}$. Then consider the problem of updating the temperature map if a new temperature reading is made in Cork: e.g., $\{Cork \mapsto 18\}$. Then the new temperature chart is obtained from the old temperature chart by function override to yield $\{Cork \mapsto 18, Dublin \mapsto 19, London \mapsto 15\}$. This is written as:

$$temp' = temp \oplus \{Cork \mapsto 18\}$$

The function override operation combines two functions of the same type to give a new function of the same type. The effect of the override operation is that the entry $\{Cork \mapsto 17\}$ is removed from the temperature chart and replaced with the entry $\{Cork \mapsto 18\}$.

Suppose f, $g: X \nrightarrow Y$ are partial functions then $f \oplus g$ is defined and indicates that f is overridden by g. It is defined as follows:

$$(f \oplus g)(x) = g(x) \text{ where } x \in \text{dom } g$$
$$(f \oplus g)(x) = f(x) \text{ where } x \notin \text{dom } g \wedge x \in \text{dom } f$$

This may also be expressed (using domain anti-restriction) as:

$$f \oplus g = ((\text{dom } g) \ntriangleleft f) \cup g$$

There is notation in Z for injective, surjective and bijective functions. An injective function is one to one: i.e.,

$$f(x) = f(y) \Rightarrow x = y$$

A surjective function is onto i.e.,

$$\text{Given } y \in Y, \exists x \in X \text{ such that } f(x) = y$$

A bijective function is one to one and onto, and it indicates that the sets X and Y can be put into one-to-one correspondence with one another. Z includes lambda calculus notation (λ-calculus is discussed in [2]) to define functions. For example, the function cube = $\lambda x{:}N \cdot x * x * x$. Function composition f; g is similar to relational composition.

17.5 Sequences

The type of all sequences of elements drawn from a set X is denoted by seq X. Sequences are written as $\langle x_1, x_2, \dots x_n \rangle$ and the empty sequence is denoted by $\langle \rangle$. Sequences may be used to specify the changing state of a variable over time, with each element of the sequence representing the value of the variable at a discrete time instance.

Sequences are functions and a sequence of elements drawn from a set X is a finite function from the set of natural numbers to X. A finite partial function f from X to Y is denoted by $f: X \nrightarrow\!\!\!\!+ Y$.

A finite sequence of elements of X is given by $f: \mathbf{N} \nrightarrow\!\!\!\!+ X$, and the domain of the function consists of all numbers between 1 and $\#f$ (where $\#f$ is the cardinality of f). It is defined formally as:

$$\text{seq } X == \{f : \mathbf{N} \nrightarrow\!\!\!\!+ X \mid \text{dom} f = 1 .. \#f \cdot f\}$$

The sequence $\langle x_1, x_2, \ldots x_n \rangle$ above is given by:

$$\{1 \mapsto x_1, 2 \mapsto x_2, \ldots \ldots \ldots n \mapsto x_n\}$$

There are various functions to manipulate sequences. These include the sequence concatenation operation. Suppose $\sigma = \langle x_1, x_2, \ldots x_n \rangle$ and $\tau = \langle y_1, y_2, \ldots y_m \rangle$ then:

$$\sigma^\frown \tau = \langle x_1, x_2, \ldots x_n, y_1, y_2, \ldots y_m \rangle$$

The head of a non-empty sequence gives the first element of the sequence.

$$\text{head } \sigma = \text{ head } \langle x_1, x_2, \ldots x_n \rangle = x_1$$

The tail of a non-empty sequence is the same sequence except that the first element of the sequence is removed.

$$\text{tail } \sigma = \text{tail}\langle x_1, x_2, \ldots x_n \rangle = \langle x_2, \ldots x_n \rangle$$

Suppose $f: X \rightarrow Y$ and a sequence σ: seq X then the function map applies f to each element of σ:

$$\text{map } f \ \sigma = \text{map } f \langle x_1, x_2, \ldots x_n \rangle = \langle f(x_1), f(x_2), \ldots f(x_n) \rangle$$

The map function may also be expressed via function composition as:

$$\text{map } f \ \sigma = \sigma; f$$

The reverse order of a sequence is given by the rev function:

$$\text{rev } \sigma = \text{rev}\langle x_1, x_2, \ldots x_n \rangle = \langle x_n, \ldots x_2, x_1 \rangle$$

17.6 Bags

A bag is like a set except that there may be multiple occurrences of each element in the bag. A bag of elements of type X is defined as a partial function from the type of the elements of the bag to positive whole numbers. The definition of a bag of type X is:

$$\text{bag } X = X \nrightarrow \mathbb{N}_1.$$

For example, a bag of marbles may contain 3 blue marbles, 2 red marbles, and 1 green marble. This is denoted by B = [|b, b, b, g, r, r]. The bag of marbles is thus denoted by:

$$\text{bag } Marble = Marble \nrightarrow \mathbb{N}_1.$$

The function count determines the number of occurrences of an element in a bag. For the example above, count *Marble b* = 3, and count *Marble y* = 0 since there are no yellow marbles in the bag. This is defined formally as:

$$\text{count bag} Xy = 0 \qquad\qquad y \notin \text{bag} X$$
$$\text{count bag} Xy = (\text{bag} X)(y) \quad y \in \text{bag} X$$

An element y is in bag X if and only if y is in the domain of bag X.

$$y \text{ in bag } X \Leftrightarrow y \in \text{dom}(\text{bag} X)$$

The union of two bags of marbles B_1 = [|b, b, b, g, r, r] and B_2 = [| b, g, r, y] is given by $B_1 \uplus B_2$ = [| b, b, b, b, g, g, r, r, r, y]. It is defined formally as:

$$(B_1 \uplus B_2)(y) = B_2(y) \qquad\qquad y \notin \text{dom} B_1 \wedge y \in \text{dom} B_2$$
$$(B_1 \uplus B_2)(y) = B_1(y) \qquad\qquad y \in \text{dom} B_1 \wedge y \notin \text{dom} B_2$$
$$(B_1 \uplus B_2)(y) = B_1(y) + B_2(y) \qquad y \in \text{dom}_1 \wedge y \in \text{dom} B_2$$

A bag may be used to record the number of occurrences of each product in a warehouse as part of an inventory system. It may model the number of items remaining for each product in a vending machine (Fig. 17.4).

The operation of a vending machine would require other operations such as identifying the set of acceptable coins, checking that the customer has entered sufficient coins to cover the cost of the good, returning change to the customer, and updating the quantity on hand of each good after a purchase. A detailed account is in [1].

$$
\begin{array}{|l}
\hline
\text{--}\Delta Vending\ Machine\text{------} \\
stock : \text{bag } Good \\
price : Good \rightarrow \mathbb{N}_1 \\
\hline
\text{dom } stock \subseteq \text{dom } price \\
\hline
\end{array}
$$

Fig. 17.4 Specification of vending machine using bags

17.7 Schemas and Schema Composition

The Z specification is presented in visually striking boxes called schemas. These are used for specifying states and state transitions, and they employ notation to represent the before and after state (e.g., s and s' where s' represents the after state of s). They group all relevant information that belongs to a state description.

There are several useful schema operations such as schema inclusion, schema composition, and the use of propositional connectives to link schemas together. The Δ convention indicates that the operation affects the state, whereas the Ξ convention indicates that the state is not affected. These conventions allow complex operations to be specified concisely and assist with the readability of the specification. Schema composition is analogous to relational composition and allows new schemas to be derived from existing schemas.

A schema name S_1 may be included in the declaration part of another schema S_2. The effect of the inclusion is that the declarations in S_1 are now part of S_2 and the predicates of S_1 are S_2 are joined together by conjunction. If the same variable is defined in both S_1 and S_2, then it must be of the same type in both.

$$
\begin{array}{|l}
- S_1 \\
x, y : \mathbb{N} \\
\hline
x + y > 2 \\
\end{array}
\qquad
\begin{array}{|l}
- S_2----- \\
S_1 ; z : \mathbb{N} \\
\hline
z = x + y \\
\end{array}
$$

The result is that S_2 includes the declarations and predicates of S_1 (Fig. 17.5).

Two schemas may be linked by propositional connectives such as $S_1 \wedge S_2$, $S_1 \vee S_2$, $S_1 \Rightarrow S_2$, and $S_1 \Leftrightarrow S_2$. The schema $S_1 \vee S_2$ is formed by merging the declaration parts of S_1 and S_2, and then combining their predicates by the logical $\vee$ operator. For example, $S = S_1 \vee S_2$ yields (Fig. 17.6).

$$
\begin{array}{|l}
-S_2 \\
x, y : \mathbb{N} \\
z : \mathbb{N} \\
\hline
x + y > 2 \\
z = x + y \\
\end{array}
$$

Fig. 17.5 Schema inclusion

$$
\begin{array}{|l}
-S \\
x, y : \mathbb{N} \\
z : \mathbb{N} \\
\hline
x + y > 2 \vee z = x + y \\
\end{array}
$$

Fig. 17.6 Merging schemas ($S_1 \vee S_2$)

Schema inclusion and the linking of schemas use normalization to convert sub-types to maximal types, and predicates are employed to restrict the maximal type to the sub-type. This involves replacing declarations of variables (e.g., u: 1..35 with $u : Z$, and adding the predicate $u > 0$ and $u < 36$ to the predicate part). The Δ and Ξ conventions are used extensively, with the notation Δ *TempMap* is used in the specification of schemas that involve a change of state.

$$\Delta\ TempMap = TempMap \wedge TempMap'$$

The longer form of Δ *TempMap* is written as:

$$
\begin{array}{|l}
-\ \Delta\ TempMap\text{----------} \\
CityList, CityList' : \mathbb{P}\ City \\
temp, temp' : City \nrightarrow Z \\
\text{dom}\ temp = CityList \\
\text{dom}\ temp = CityList' \\
\text{------------------}
\end{array}
$$

The notation Ξ *TempMap* is used in the specification of operations that do not involve a change to the state.

$$
\begin{array}{|l}
-\ \Xi\ TempMap\text{----------} \\
\Delta TempMap \\
\text{------} \\
CityList = CityList' \\
temp = temp' \\
\text{------------------}
\end{array}
$$

Schema composition is analogous to relational composition, and it allows new specifications to be built from existing ones. It allows the after-state variables of one schema to be related with the before variables of another schema. The composition of two schemas S and T (S; T) is described in detail in [1], and involves 4 steps (Table 17.1).

The example below should make schema composition clearer. Consider the composition of S and T where S and T are defined as follows:

Table 17.1 Schema composition

Step	Procedure
1	Rename all *after* state variables in S to something new: S [s⁺/s']
2	Rename all *before* state variables in T to the same new thing: i.e., T [s⁺/s]
3	Form the conjunction of the two new schemas: S [s⁺/s'] ∧T [s⁺/s]
4	Hide the variable introduced in step 1 and 2 S; T = (S [s⁺/s'] ∧T [s⁺/s]) \ (s⁺)

$$\begin{array}{|l} -S\ \text{---------} \\ x, x', y? : \mathbb{N} \\ \text{---------} \\ x' = y? - 2 \\ \text{---------} \\ \end{array}$$

$$\begin{array}{|l} -T\ \text{---------} \\ x, x' : \mathbb{N} \\ \text{---------} \\ x' = x \mid 1 \\ \text{---------} \\ \end{array}$$

$$\begin{array}{|l} -S_1\ \text{---------} \\ x, x^+, y? : \mathbb{N} \\ \text{---------} \\ x^\vdash = y? - 2 \\ \text{---------} \\ \end{array}$$

$$\begin{array}{|l} -T_1\ \text{---------} \\ x^+, x' : \mathbb{N} \\ \text{---------} \\ x' = x^+ + 1 \\ \text{---------} \\ \end{array}$$

S_1 and T_1 represent the results of step 1 and step 2, with x' renamed to x^+ in S, and x renamed to x^+ in T. Step 3 and step 4 yield (Fig. 17.7).

Schema composition is useful as it allows new specifications to be created from existing ones.

$$\begin{array}{|l} -S_1 \wedge T_1\ \text{------} \\ x, x^+, x', y? : \mathbb{N} \\ \hline x^+ = y? - 2 \\ x' = x^+ + 1 \\ \hline \end{array}$$

$$\begin{array}{|l} -S\ ;\ T\ \text{------} \\ x, x', y? : \mathbb{N} \\ \hline \exists x^+ : \mathbb{N}\ \bullet \\ \quad (x^+ = y? - 2 \\ \quad x' = x^+ + 1) \\ \hline \end{array}$$

Fig. 17.7 Schema composition

17.8 Reification and Decomposition

A Z specification involves defining the state of the system and then specifying the required operations. The Z specification language employs many constructs that are not part of conventional programming languages, and a Z specification is therefore not directly executable on a computer. A programmer implements the formal specification, and mathematical proof may be employed to prove that a program meets its specification.

Often, there is a need to write an intermediate specification that is between the original Z specification and the eventual program code. This intermediate specification is more algorithmic and uses less abstract data types than the Z specification. The intermediate specification needs to be correct with respect to the specification, and the program needs to be correct with respect to the intermediate specification. The intermediate specification is a refinement (reification) of the state of the specification, and the operations of the specification have been decomposed into those of the intermediate specification.

The representation of an abstract data type such as a set by a sequence is termed data reification, and data reification is concerned with the process of transforming an abstract data type into a concrete data type. The abstract and concrete data types are related by the retrieve function, and the retrieve function maps the concrete data type to the abstract data type. There are typically several possible concrete data types for a particular abstract data type (i.e., refinement is a relation), whereas there is one abstract data type for a concrete data type (i.e., retrieval is a function). For example, sets are often refined to unique sequences; however, more than one unique sequence can represent a set whereas a unique sequence represents exactly one set.

The operations defined on the concrete data type are related to the operations defined on the abstract data type. That is, the commuting diagram property is required to hold (Fig. 17.8). That is, for an operation $\boxdot$ on the concrete data type to correctly model the operation $\odot$ on the abstract data type the commuting diagram property must hold. That is, it is required to prove that:

$$ret\,(\sigma \boxdot \tau) = (ret\,\sigma) \odot (ret\,\tau)$$

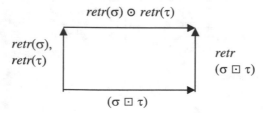

Fig. 17.8 Refinement commuting diagram

In Z, the refinement and decomposition is done with schemas. It is required to prove that the concrete schema is a valid refinement of the abstract schema, and this gives rise to several proof obligations. It needs to be proved that the initial states correspond to one another, and that each operation in the concrete schema is correct with respect to the operation in the abstract schema, and that it is applicable (i.e., whenever the abstract operation may be performed the concrete operation may also be performed).

17.9 Proof in Z

Mathematicians perform rigorous proof of theorems using technical and natural language. Logicians employ formal proofs to prove theorems using propositional and predicate calculus. Formal proofs generally involve a long chain of reasoning with every step of the proof justified. Rigorous proofs involve precise reasoning using a mixture of natural and mathematical language. Rigorous proofs [1] have been described as analogous to high level programming languages, with formal proofs analogous to machine language.

A mathematical proof includes natural language and mathematical symbols, and often many of the tedious details of the proof are omitted. Many proofs in formal methods such as Z are concerned with crosschecking on the details of the specification, or on the validity of the refinement step, or proofs that certain properties are satisfied by the specification. There are often many tedious lemmas to be proved, and tool support is essential as proof by hand often contain errors or jumps in reasoning. Machine proofs are lengthy and largely unreadable; however, they provide extra confidence as every step in the proof is justified. The proof of various properties about the programs increases confidence in its correctness.

17.10 Review Questions

1. Describe the main features of the Z specification language.
2. Explain the difference between $\mathbb{P}1\ X$, $\mathbb{P}\ X$ and FX.
3. Explain the three main parts of set comprehension in Z. Give examples.
4. Discuss the applications of Z. What problems have arisen?
5. Give examples to illustrate the use of domain and range restriction operators and domain and range anti-restriction operators with relations in Z.
6. Give examples to illustrate relational composition.
7. Explain the difference between a partial and total function, and give examples to illustrate function override.

8. Give examples to illustrate the various operations on sequences including concatenation, head, tail, map and reverse operations.
9. Give examples to illustrate the various operations on bags.
10. Discuss the nature of proof in Z and tools to support proof.
11. Explain the process of refining an abstract schema to a more concrete representation, the proof obligations, and the commuting diagram property.

17.11 Summary

Z is a formal specification language that was developed in the early 1980s at Oxford University in England. It has been employed in both industry and academia, and it was used successfully on the IBM's CICS project at Hursley. Its specifications are mathematical, and this allows properties to be proved about the specification, and any gaps or inconsistencies in the specification may be identified.

Z is a model oriented' approach and an explicit model of the state of an abstract machine is given, and the operations are defined in terms of their effect on the state. Its main features include a mathematical notation that is similar to VDM, and the schema calculus. The latter consists essentially of boxes that are used to describe operations and states.

The schemas are used as building blocks to form larger specifications, and they are a powerful means of decomposing a specification into smaller pieces. This helps with the readability of Z specifications, since each schema is small in size and self-contained.

Z is a highly expressive specification language, and it includes notation for sets, functions, relations, bags, sequences, predicate calculus, and schema calculus. Z specifications are not directly executable, as many of its data types and constructs are not part of modern programming languages. A programmer implements the formal specification, and mathematical proof may be employed to prove that a program meets its specification.

Often, there is a need to write an intermediate specification that is between the original Z specification and the eventual program code. This intermediate specification is more algorithmic and uses less abstract data types than the Z specification. The intermediate specification needs to be correct with respect to the specification, and the program needs to be correct with respect to the intermediate specification. The intermediate specification is a refinement (reification) of the state of the specification, and the operations of the specification have been decomposed into those of the intermediate specification.

Therefore, there is a need to refine the Z specification into a more concrete representation and prove that the refinement is valid. The refinement and decomposition is done with schemas, and it is required to prove that the concrete schema is a valid refinement of the abstract schema. This gives rise to several proof obligations, and it needs to be shown that each operation in the concrete schema is correct with respect to the operation in the abstract schema.

References

1. A. Diller, *Z. An Introduction to Formal Methods* (Wiley, England, 1990)
2. G. O' Regan, *Guide to Discrete Mathematics* (Springer, Berlin, 2016)

Unified Modelling Language

18

Abstract

This chapter presents the Unified Modelling Language (UML), which is a visual modelling language for software systems, and it is used to present several views of the system architecture. It was developed at Rational Corporation as a notation for modelling object-oriented systems. We present various UML diagrams such as use case diagrams, sequence diagrams and activity diagrams.

Keywords

Use case diagrams · Classes and objects · Sequence diagrams · Activity diagrams · State diagrams · Collaboration diagrams · Object constraint language · Rational unified process

18.1 Introduction

The unified modelling language (UML) is a visual modelling language for software systems. It was developed by Rumbaugh et al. [1] at Rational Corporation (now part of IBM), as a notation for modelling object-oriented systems. It provides a visual means of specifying, constructing, and documenting object-oriented systems, and it facilitates the understanding of the architecture of the system, and in managing the complexity of a large system.

The language was strongly influenced by three existing methods: the *Object Modelling Technique* (OMT) developed by Rumbaught; the *Booch Method* developed by Booch; and *Object-Oriented Software Engineering* (OOSE) developed by Jacobson. UML unifies and improves upon these methods, and it has become a popular formal approach to modelling software systems.

© Springer Nature Switzerland AG 2022
G. O'Regan, *Concise Guide to Software Engineering*,
Undergraduate Topics in Computer Science,
https://doi.org/10.1007/978-3-031-07816-3_18

Models provide a better understanding of the system to be developed, and a UML model allows the system to be visualized prior to its implementation, and it simplifies the underlying reality. Large complex systems are difficult to understand in their entirety, and the use of a UML model is an aid to abstracting and simplifying complexity. The choice of the model is fundamental, and a good model will provide a good insight into the system. Models need to be explored and tested to ensure their adequacy as a representation of the system. Models simplify the reality, but it is important to ensure that the simplification does not exclude any important details. The chosen model affects the view of the system, and different roles require different viewpoints of the proposed system.

An architect will design a house prior to its construction, and the blueprints will contain details of the plan of each room, as well as plans for electricity and plumbing. That is, the plans for a house include floor plans, electrical plans, and plumping plans. These plans provide different viewpoints of the house to be constructed and are used to provide estimates of the time and materials required to construct it.

A database developer will often focus on entity-relationship models, whereas a systems analyst may focus on algorithmic models. An object-oriented developer will focus on classes and on the interactions of classes. Often, there is a need to view the system at different levels of detail, and no single model is sufficient for this. This leads to the development of a small number of interrelated models.

UML provides a formal model the system, and it allows the same information to be presented in several ways, and at different levels of detail. The requirements of the system are expressed in terms of use cases; the design view captures the problem space and solution space; the process view models the systems processes; the implementation view addresses the implementation of the system; and the deployment view models the physical deployment of the system.

There are several UML diagrams providing different viewpoints of the system, and these provide the blueprint of the software.

18.2 Overview of UML

UML is an expressive graphical modelling language for visualizing, specifying, constructing, and documenting a software system. It provides several views of the software's architecture, and it has a clearly defined syntax and semantics. Each stakeholder (e.g., project manager, developers, and testers) has a different perspective, and looks at the system in different ways at different times during the project. UML is a way to model the software system before implementing it in a programming language.

A UML specification consists of precise, complete, and unambiguous models. The models may be employed to generate code in a programming language such as Java or C++. The reverse is also possible, and so it is possible to work with either the graphical notation of UML, or the textual notation of a programming language.

UML expresses things that are best expressed graphically, whereas a programming language expresses things that are best expressed textually, and tools are employed to keep both views consistent. UML may be employed to document the software system, and it has been employed in several domains including the banking sector, defence, and telecommunications.

The use of UML requires an understanding of its basic building blocks, the rules for combining the building blocks, and the common mechanisms that apply throughout the language. There are three kinds of building blocks employed:

- Things,
- Relationships,
- Diagrams.

Things are the object-oriented building blocks of the UML. They include *structural things, behavioural things, grouping things* and *annotational things* (Table 18.1). Structural things are the nouns of the UML models; behavioural things are the dynamic parts and represent behaviour and their interactions over time; grouping things are the organization parts of UML; and annotation things are the explanatory parts. Things, relationships, and diagrams are all described graphically and are discussed in detail in [1].

Table 18.1 Classification of UML things

Thing	Kind	Description
Structural	Class	A class is a description of a set of objects that share the same attributes and operations
	Interface	An interface is a collection of operations that specify a service of a class or component. It specifies externally visible behaviour of the element
	Collaboration	A collaboration defines an interaction between software objects
	Use case	A use case is a set of actions that define the interaction between an actor and the system to achieve a particular goal
	Active class	An active class is used to describe concurrent behaviour of a system
	Component	A component is used to represent any part of a system for which UML diagrams are made
	Node	A node is used to represent a physical part of the system (e.g., server, network, etc.)
Behavioural	Interaction	These comprise interactions (message exchange between components) expressed as sequence diagrams or collaboration diagrams
	State machine	A state machine is used to describe different states of system components
Grouping	Packages	These are the organization parts of UML models. A package organizes elements into groups and is a way to organize a UML model
Annotation		These are the explanatory parts (notes) of UML

There are four kinds of relationship in UML:

- Dependency,
- Association,
- Generalization,
- Extensibility.

Dependency is used to represent a relationship between two elements of a system, in which a change to one thing affects the other thing (dependent thing). *Association* describes how elements in the UML diagram are associated and describes a set of connections among elements in a system. *Aggregation* is an association that represents a structural relationship between a whole and its parts. A *generalization* is a parent/child relationship in which the objects of the specialized element (child) are substituted for objects of the generalized element (the parent). *Extensibility* refers to a mechanism to extend the power of the language to represent extra behaviour of the system. Next, we describe the key UML diagrams.

18.3   UML Diagrams

The UML diagrams provide a graphical visualization of the system from different viewpoints, and we present several key UML diagrams in Table 18.2.

Table 18.2 UML diagrams

Diagram	Description
Class	A class is a key building block of any object-oriented system. The class diagram shows the classes, their attributes and operations, and the relationships between them
Object	This shows a set of objects and their relationships. An object diagram is an instance of a class diagram
Use Case	These show the actors in the system, and the different functions that they require from the system
Sequence	These diagrams show how objects interact with each other, and the order in which the interactions occur
Collaboration	This is an interaction diagram that emphasizes the structural organization of objects that send and receive messages
State chart	These describe the behaviour of objects that act differently according to the state that they are in
Activity	This diagram is used to illustrate the flow of control in a system (it is like a flow chart)
Component	This diagram shows the structural relationship of components of a software system, and their relationships/interfaces
Deployment	This diagram is used for visualizing the deployment view of a system and shows the hardware of the system and the software on the hardware

The concept of class and objects are taken from object-oriented design, and classes are the most important building block of any object-oriented system. A class is a set of objects that share the same attributes, operations, relationships, and semantics [1]. Classes may represent software things and hardware things. For example, walls, doors, and windows are all classes, whereas individual doors and windows are objects. A class represents a set of objects rather than an individual object.

Automated bank teller machines (ATMs) include two key classes: customers and accounts. The class definition includes both the data structure for customers and accounts, and the operations on customers and accounts. These include operations to add or remove a customer, operations to debit or credit an account, or to transfer from one account to another. There are several instances of customers and accounts, and these are the actual customers of the bank and their accounts.

Every class has a name (e.g., Customer and Account) to distinguish it from other classes. There will generally be several objects associated with the class. The class diagram describes the name of the class, its attributes, and its operations. An attribute represents some property of the class that is shared by all objects; for example, the attributes of the class 'Customer' are name and address. Attributes are listed below the class name, and the operations are listed below the attributes. The operations may be applied to any object in the class. The responsibilities of a class may also be included in the definition (Table 18.3).

Class diagrams typically include various relationships between classes. In practice, very few classes are stand alone, and most collaborate with others in various ways. The relationship between classes needs to be considered, and these provide different ways of combining classes to form new classes. The relationships include dependencies (a change to one thing affects the dependent thing); generalizations (these link generalized classes to their specializations in a subclass/superclass relationship); and associations (these represent structural relationships among objects).

A dependency is a relationship that states that a change in the specification of one thing affects the dependent thing. It is indicated by a dashed line (—>). Generalizations allow a child class to be created from one or more parent classes (single or multiple inheritance). A class that has no parents is termed a base class (e.g., consider the base class Shape with three children: Rectangle, Circle and Polygon, and where Rectangle has one child namely Square). Generalization is indicated by a solid directed line that points to the parent (—▶). Association is a

Table 18.3 Simple class diagram

Customer	Account
Name: String	Balance:Real
Address: String	Type:String
Add()	Debit()
Remove()	Credit()
	CheckBal()
	Transfer()

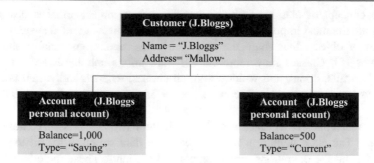

Fig. 18.1 Simple object diagram

structural relationship that specifies that objects of one thing are connected to objects of another thing. It is indicated by a solid line connecting the same or different classes.

The object diagram (Fig. 18.1) shows a set of objects and their relationships at a point of time. It is related to the class diagram in that the object is an instance of the class. The ATM example above had two classes (customers and accounts), and the objects of these classes are the actual customers and their corresponding accounts. Each customer may have several accounts, and the names and addresses of the customers are detailed as well as the corresponding balance in the customer's accounts. There is one instance of the customer class and two instances of the account class in this example.

An object has a state that has a given value at each time instance. Operations on the object will often (except for query operations) change its state. An object diagram contains objects and links to other objects and gives a snapshot of the system at a particular moment of time.

A use case diagram models the dynamic aspects of the system, and it shows a set of use cases and actors and their relationships. It describes scenarios (or sequences of actions) in the system from the user's viewpoint (actor) and shows how the actor interacts with the system. An actor represents the set of roles that a user can play, and the actor may be human or an automated system. Actors are connected to use cases by association, and they may communicate by sending and receiving messages.

A use case diagram shows a set of use cases, with each use case representing a functional requirement. Use cases are employed to model the visible services that the system provides within the context of its environment, and for specifying the requirements of the system as a black box. Each use case carries out some work that is of value to the actor, and the behaviour of the use case is described by the flow of events in text. The description includes the main flow of events for the use case and the exceptional flow of events. These flows may also be represented graphically. There may also be alternate flows as well as the main flow of the use case. Each sequence is termed a scenario, and a scenario is one instance of a use case.

Use cases provide a way for the end users and developers to share a common understanding of the system. They may be applied to all or part of the system (subsystem), and the use cases are the basis for development and testing. A use case is represented graphically by an ellipse. The benefits of use cases include:

- Enables the stakeholders (e.g., domain experts, developers, testers, and end users) to share a common understanding of the functional requirements.
- Models the requirements (specifies what the system should do).
- Models the context of a system (identifies actors and their roles).
- May be used for development and testing.

Figure 18.2 presents a simple example of the definition of the use cases for an ATM application. The typical user operations at an ATM machine include the balance inquiry operation, cash withdrawal, and the transfer of funds from one account to another. The actors for the system include 'customer' and 'admin', and these actors have different needs and expectations of the system.

The behaviour from the user's viewpoint is described, and the use-cases include "withdraw cash", "balance enquiry", "transfer" and "maintain/reports". The use case view includes the actors who are performing the sequence of actions.

The next UML diagram considered is the sequence diagram which models the dynamic aspects of the system and shows the interaction between objects/classes in the system for each use case. The interactions model the flow of control that characterizes the behaviour of the system, and the objects that play a role in the interaction are identified. A sequence diagram emphasizes the time ordering of messages, and the interactions may include messages that are dispatched from object to object, with the messages ordered in sequence by time.

The example in Fig. 18.3 considers the sequences of interactions between objects for the "Balance Enquiry" use case. This sequence diagram is specific to the case of a valid balance enquiry, and a sequence diagram is also needed to handle the exception cases.

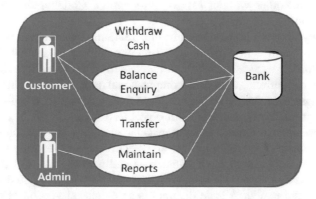

Fig. 18.2 Use-case diagram of ATM machine

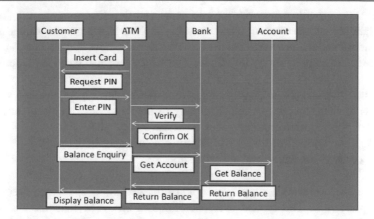

Fig. 18.3 UML sequence diagram for balance enquiry

The behaviour of the "balance enquiry" operation is evident from the diagram. The customer inserts the card into the ATM machine and the PIN number is requested by the ATM. The customer then enters the number, and the ATM machine contacts the bank for verification of the number. The bank confirms the validity of the number, and the customer then selects the balance enquiry operation. The ATM contacts the bank to request the balance of the account, and the bank sends the details to the ATM machine. The balance is displayed on the screen of the ATM machine. The customer then withdraws the card. The actual sequence of interactions is evident from the sequence diagram.

The example has four objects (Customer, ATM, Bank and Account) and these are laid out from left to right at the top of the sequence diagram. Collaboration diagrams are interaction diagrams that consist of objects and their relationships. However, while sequence diagrams emphasize the time ordering of messages, a collaboration diagram emphasizes the structural organization of the objects that send and receive messages. Sequence diagrams and collaboration diagrams may be converted to the other without loss of information. Collaboration diagrams are described in more detail in [1].

The activity diagram is considered in Fig. 18.4, and this diagram is essentially a flow chart showing the flow of control from one activity to another. It is used to model the dynamic aspects of a system, and this involves modelling the sequential and possibly concurrent steps in a computational process. It is different from a sequence diagram in that it shows the flow from activity to activity, whereas a sequence diagram shows the flow from object to object.

State diagrams (also known as state machine diagrams or state charts) show the dynamic behaviour of a class, and how an object behaves differently depending on the state that it is in. There is an initial state and a final state, and the operation generally results in a change of state, with the operations resulting in different states being entered and exited. A state diagram is an enhanced version of a finite state machine (as discussed in Chap. 16) (Fig. 18.5).

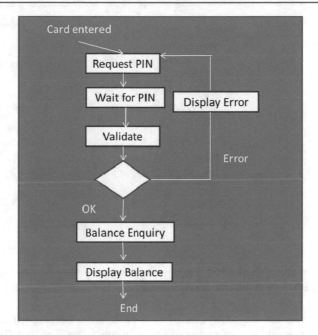

Fig. 18.4 UML activity diagram

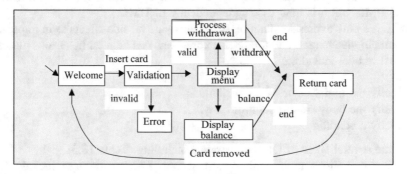

Fig. 18.5 UML state diagram

There are several other UML diagrams including component and deployment diagrams. The reader is referred to [1].

Advantages of UML

UML offers a rich notation to model software systems, and to understand the proposed system from different viewpoints. Its main advantages are (Table 18.4).

Table 18.4 Advantages of
UML

Advantages of UML
Visual modelling language with a rich expressive notation
Mechanism to manage complexity of a large system
Enables the proposed system to be studied before implementation
Visualization of architecture design of the system
It provides different views of the system
Visualization of system from different viewpoints
Use cases allow the description of typical user behaviour
Better understanding of implications of user behaviour
Use cases provide a mechanism to communicate the proposed behaviour of the software system
Use cases are the basis of development and testing

18.4 Object Constraint Language

The object constraint language (OCL) is a declarative language that provides a
precise way of describing rules (or expressing constraints) on the UML models.
OCL was originally developed as a business modelling language by Jos Warmer at
IBM, and it was developed further by the Object Management Group (OMG), as
part of a formal specification language extension to UML. It was initially used as
part of UML, but it is now used independently of UML.

OCL is a pure expression language: i.e., there are no side-effects as in imperative
programming languages, and the OCL expressions can be used in various places in
the UML model including:

- Specify the initial value of an attribute.
- Specify the body of an operation.
- Specify a condition.

There are several types of OCL constraints including (Table 18.5).

There are various tools available to support OCL, and these include OCL
compilers (or checkers) that provide syntax and consistency checking of the OCL
constraints, and the USE specification environment is based on UML/OCL.

18.5 Tools for UML

There are many tools that support UML (mainly developed by IBM/Rational), and a
small selection is listed in Table 18.6.

Table 18.5 OCL constraints

OCL constraint	Description
Invariant	A condition that must always be true. An invariant may be placed on an attribute in a class, and this has the effect of restricting the value of the attribute. All instances of the class are required to satisfy the invariant. An invariant is a predicate, and is introduced after the keyword **inv**
Precondition	A condition that must be true before the operation is executed. A precondition is a predicate and is introduced after the keyword **pre**
Postcondition	A condition that must be true when the operation has just completed execution. A postcondition is a predicate and is introduced after the keyword **post**
Guard	A condition that must be true before the state transition occurs

Table 18.6 UML tools

Tool	Description
Requisite Pro	Requirements and use case management tool. It provides requirements management and traceability
Rational Software Modeler (RSM)	RSM is a visual modelling and design tool that is used by systems architects/systems analysts to communicate processes, flows, and designs
Rational Software Architect (RSA)	RSA is a tool that is used by software architects to enable a good architectures to be created
Clearcase/Clearquest	These are configuration management/change control tools that are used to manage change in the project

18.6   Rational Unified Process

Software projects need a well-structured software development process to achieve their objectives, and the *Rational Unified Development Software Process* (RUP) [2] is a way to mitigate risk in software development projects. RUP and UML are often used together, and RUP is:

- Use case driven,
- Architecture centric,
- Iterative and incremental.

It includes iterations, phases, workflows, risk mitigation, quality control, project management, and configuration control. Software projects may be complex, and there are risks that requirements may be missed in the process, or that the interpretation of a requirement may differ between the customer and developer. RUP gathers requirements as use cases, which describe the functional requirements from the point of view of the users of the system.

The use case model describes what the system will do at a high-level, and there is a focus on the users in defining the scope the project. Use cases drive the development process, and the developers create a series of design and implementation models that realize the use cases. The developers review each successive model for conformance to the use-case model. The testers verify that the implementation model correctly implements the use cases.

The software architecture concept embodies the most significant static and dynamic aspects of the system. The architecture grows out of the use cases and factors such as the platform that the software is to run on, deployment considerations, legacy systems, and non-functional requirements.

A commercial software product is a large undertaking, and the work is decomposed into smaller slices or mini-projects, where each mini-project is a manageable chunk. Each mini project is an iteration that results in an increment to the product (Fig. 18.6).

Iterations refer to the steps in the workflow, and an increment leads to the growth of the product. If the developers need to repeat the iteration, then the organization loses only the misdirected effort of a single iteration, rather than the entire product. Therefore, the unified process is a way to reduce risk in software engineering. The early iterations implement the areas of greatest risk to the project.

RUP consists of four phases, and these are inception, elaboration, construction, and transition (Fig. 18.7). Each phase consists of one or more iterations, where each iteration consists of several workflows. The workflows may be requirements, analysis, design, implementation, and test. Each phase terminates in a milestone with one or more project deliverables.

The inception identifies and prioritizes the most important project risks, and it is concerned with initial project planning, cost estimation and early work on the architecture and functional requirements for the product. The elaboration phase specifies most of the use cases in detail. The construction phase is concerned with building the product and implements all agreed use cases. The transition phase covers the period during which the product moves into the customer site and includes activities such as training customer personnel, providing help-line assistance and correcting defects found after delivery.

The waterfall lifecycle has the disadvantage that the risk is greater towards the end of the project, where it is costly to undo mistakes from earlier phases. The iterative process develops an increment (i.e., a subset of the system functionality

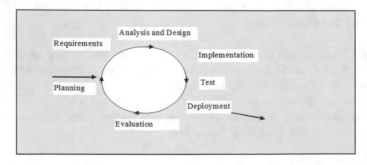

Fig. 18.6 Iteration in rational unified process

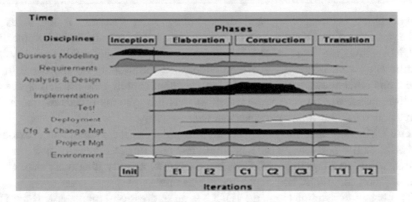

Fig. 18.7 Phases and workflows in rational unified process

with the waterfall steps applied in the iteration), then another, and so on, and avoids developing the whole system in one step as in the waterfall methodology. That is, the RUP approach is a way to mitigate risk is software development projects.

18.7   Review Questions

1. What is UML? Explain its main features.
2. Explain the difference between an object and a class.
3. Describe the various UML diagrams.
4. What are the advantages and disadvantages of UML?
5. What is the Rational Unified Process?
6. Describe the workflows in a typical iteration of RUP.
7. Describe the phases in the Rational Unified Process.
8. Describe OCL and explain how it is used with UML.
9. Investigate and describe tools to support UML.

18.8   Summary

The unified modelling language is a visual modelling language for software systems, and it facilitates the understanding of the architecture, and management of the complexity of large systems. It was developed by Rumbaugh, Booch, and Jacobson as a notation for modelling object-oriented systems, and it provides a visual means of specifying, constructing, and documenting such systems. It facilitates the understanding of the architecture of the system, and in managing its complexity.

UML allows the same information to be presented in several different ways and at different levels of detail. The requirements of the system are expressed in use cases; and other views include the design view that captures the problem space and solution space; the process view which models the systems processes; the implementation view and the deployment view.

The UML diagrams provide different viewpoints of the system and provide the blueprint of the software. These include class and object diagrams, use case diagrams, sequence diagrams, collaboration diagrams, activity diagrams, state charts, collaboration diagrams, and deployment diagrams.

The object constraint language (OCL) is an expression language, and the OCL expressions may be used in various places in a UML model to specify the initial value of an attribute, the body of an operation or a condition.

RUP consists of four phases, and these are inception, elaboration, construction, and transition. Each phase consists of one or more iterations, and the iteration consists of several workflows. The workflows may be requirements, analysis, design, implementation, and test. Each phase terminates in a milestone with one or more project deliverables. The RUP approach is a way to mitigate risk is software development projects.

References

1. I. Jacobson, G. Booch, J. Rumbaugh, *The Unified Software Modelling Language User Guide* (Addison-Wesley, 1999)
2. J. Rumbaugh et al., *The Unified Software Development Process* (Addison Wesley, 1999)

Software Process Improvement

19

Abstract

This chapter discusses software process improvement. It begins with a discussion of a software process, and discusses the benefits that may be gained from a software process improvement initiative. Various models that support software process improvement are discussed, and these include the Capability Maturity Model Integration (CMMI), ISO 9000, Personal Software Process (PSP) and Team Software Process (TSP).

Keywords

Software process · Software process improvement · Process mapping · Benefits of software process improvement · CMMI · ISO/IEC 15504 (SPICE) · ISO 9000 · PSP and TSP · Root cause analysis · Six sigma

19.1 Introduction

The success of business today is highly influenced by the functionality and quality of the software that it uses. It is essential that the software is safe, reliable, of a high quality and fit for purpose. Companies may develop their own software internally, or they may acquire software solutions off-the-shelf or from bespoke software development. Software development companies need to deliver high-quality and reliable software consistently on time to their customers.

Cost is a key driver in most organizations, and it is essential that software is produced as cheaply and efficiently as possible, and that waste is reduced or eliminated in the software development process. In a nutshell, companies need to produce software that is *better, faster, and cheaper* than their competitors in order to survive in the marketplace. Another words, companies need to continuously

© Springer Nature Switzerland AG 2022

G. O'Regan, *Concise Guide to Software Engineering*,

Undergraduate Topics in Computer Science,

https://doi.org/10.1007/978-3-031-07816-3_19

work smarter to improve their businesses, and to deliver superior solutions to their customers.

Software process improvement initiatives are aligned to business goals and play a key role in helping companies achieve their strategic goals. It is invaluable in the implementation of best practice in organizations and allows companies to focus on fire prevention rather than firefighting. It allows companies to problem solve key issues to eliminate quality problems, and to critically examine their current processes to determine the extent to which they meet its needs, as well as identifying how the processes may be improved, and identifying where waste can be minimized or eliminated.

It allows companies to identify the root causes of problems (e.g., using the *five why tool*), and to determine appropriate solutions to the problems. The benefits of successful process improvement include the consistent delivery of high-quality software, improved financial results and increased customer satisfaction.

Software process improvement initiatives lead to a focus on the process and on ways to improve it. Many problems are caused by a defective process rather than people, and a focus on the process helps to avoid the blame culture that arises when blame is apportioned to individuals rather than the process. The focus on the process leads to a culture of openness in discussing problems and their solutions, and in instilling process ownership among the process practitioners.

Software process improvement (SPI) allows companies to mature their software engineering processes, and to achieve their business goals more effectively. It helps software companies to improve performance and to deliver high-quality software on time and on budget, as well, reducing the cost of development, and improving customer satisfaction. It has become an indispensable tool for software engineers and managers to achieve their goals, and it provides a return on investment to the organization.

19.2 What is a Software Process?

A software development process is the process used by software engineers to design and develop computer software. It may be an undocumented ad hoc process as devised by the team for a particular project, or it may be a standardized and documented process used by various teams on similar projects. The process is seen as the glue that ties people, technology, and procedures coherently together.

The processes employed in software development include processes to determine the requirements; processes for the design and development of the software; processes to verify that the software is fit for purpose; and processes to maintain the software.

A *software process* is a set of activities, methods, practices, and transformations that people use to develop and maintain software and the associated work products.

Definition 19.1 (*Software Process*)
A *process* is a set of practices or tasks performed to achieve a given purpose. It may include tools, methods, material, and people.

An organization will typically have many processes in place for doing its work, and the object of process improvement is to improve these to meet business goals more effectively.

The Software Engineering Institute (SEI) believes that there is a close relationship between the quality of the delivered software and the quality and maturity of the underlying processes employed to create the software. The SEI adopted and applied the principles of process improvement used in the manufacturing field to develop process maturity models such as the CMM and its successor the CMMI. These maturity models are invaluable in maturing the software processes in software intensive organizations.

The process is an abstraction of the way in which work is done in the organization, and it is seen as the glue that ties people, procedures, and tools together (Fig. 19.1).

A process is often represented by a process map which details the flow of activities and tasks. The process map will typically include the inputs to each activity as well as the output from an activity. Often, the output from one activity will become an input to the next activity. A simple example of a process map for creating the system requirements specification is described in Fig. 19.2. The input to the activity to create the systems requirements specification will typically be the business (user) requirements, whereas the output is the systems requirements specification document itself.

As a process matures it is defined in more detail and documented. It will have clearly defined entry and exit criteria, inputs and outputs, an explicit description of the tasks, verification of the process and consistent implementation throughout the organization.

Fig. 19.1 Process as glue for
people, procedures and tools

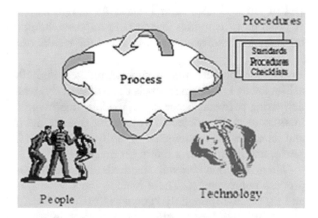

Fig. 19.2 Sample process map

19.3   What is Software Process Improvement?

The origins of the software process improvement field go back to Walter She-whart's work on statistical process control in the 1930s. Shewhart's work was later refined by Deming and Juran, who argued that high-quality processes are essential to the delivery of a high-quality product. They argued that the quality of the end product is largely determined by the processes used to produce and support it, and that therefore there needs to be an emphasis on the process as well as on the product.

These quality gurus argued that product quality will improve as variability in process performance is reduced [1], and their approach was effective in trans-forming manufacturing companies with quality problems to companies that would consistently deliver high-quality products. Further, the improvements to quality led to cost reductions and higher productivity, as less time was spent in reworking defective products.

The ideas of Deming and Juran was later applied to the software quality field by Watt Humphries and others at the Software Engineering Institute (SEI) leading to the birth of the software process improvement field. Software process improvement is concerned with practical action to improve the software processes in the orga-nization to improve performance, and to ensure that business goals are achieved more effectively. For example, the business goals may be to deliver projects faster and with higher quality.

Definition 19.2 (*Software Process Improvement*)
A program of activities designed to improve the performance and maturity of the organization's software processes and the results of such a program.

Software process improvement initiatives (Fig. 19.3) support the organization in achieving its key business goals more effectively, where the business goals could be delivering software faster to the market, improving quality, and reducing or elim-inating waste. The objective is to work smarter and to build software better, faster, and cheaper than competitors. Software process improvement makes business sense, and it provides a return on investment.

There are international standards and models available to support software process improvement. These include the CMMI Model, the ISO 90001 standard, and ISO 15504 (popularly known as SPICE). The SEI developed the CMMI model, and it includes best practice for processes in software and systems engineering.

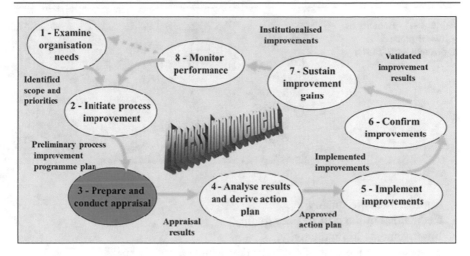

Fig. 19.3 Steps in process improvement

The ISO 9001 standard is a quality management system that may be employed in hardware, software development or service companies. The ISO 15504 standard is an international standard for software process improvement and process assessment, and it is popular in the automotive sector.

Software process improvement is concerned with defining the right processes and following them consistently. It involves training all staff on the new processes, refining the processes, and continuously improving the processes. The need for a process improvement initiative often arises due to the realization that the organization is weak in some areas in software engineering, and that it needs to improve to achieve its business goals more effectively. The starting point of any improvement initiative is an examination of the business needs of the organization, and these may include goals such as delivering high-quality products on time or delivering products faster to the market.

19.4   Benefits of Software Process Improvement

It is a challenge to deliver high-quality software consistently on time and on-budget. There are problems with budget and schedule overruns, late delivery of the software, spiralling costs, quality problems with the delivered software, customer complaints, and staff morale.

Software process improvement can assist in dealing with these problems. There are costs involved but it provides a return on the investment made. Specifically, the benefits from software process improvement include:

Table 19.1 Benefits of software process improvement (CMMI)

Improvements	Median	#Data points	Low	High
Cost	20%	21	3%	87%
Schedule	37%	19	2%	90%
Productivity	62%	17	9%	255%
Quality	50%	20	7%	132%
Customer satisfaction	14%	6	−4%	55%
ROI	4.7:1	16	2:1	27:1

- Improvements to quality,
- Reductions in the cost of poor quality,
- Improvements in productivity,
- Reductions to the cost of software development,
- Improvements in on-time delivery,
- Improved consistency in budget and schedule delivery,
- Improvements to customer satisfaction,
- Improvements to employee morale.

The Software Engineering Institute maintains data on the benefits that organizations have achieved from using the CMMI. These include improvements in several categories such as cost, schedule, productivity, quality, customer satisfaction, and the return on investment.

Table 19.1 presents results in software process improvement collaborations of twenty-five organizations taken from conference presentations, published papers and individual [2].

For example, *Northrop Grumman Defense Systems* met every milestone (25 in a row) with high-quality and customer satisfaction; *Lockheed Martin* reported an 80% increase in software productivity over a five-year period when it achieved CMM level 5, and obtained further increases in productivity as it moved to CMMI level 5. *Siemens (India)* reported an improved defect removal rate from over 50% before testing to over 70% before testing, and a post- release defect rate of 0.35 defects per KLOC. *Accenture* reported a 5:1 return on investment from software process improvement activities.

19.5 Software Process Improvement Models

A process model[1] such as the CMMI defines best practice for software processes in an organization. It describes what the processes should do rather than how they should be done, and this allows the organization to use its professional judgement in

---
[1] There is the well-known adage "All models are wrong, some are useful".

the implementation of processes to meet its needs. The process model will need to be interpreted and tailored to the organization.

A process model provides a place to start an improvement initiative, and it provides a common language and shared vision for improvement. It provides a framework to prioritize actions, and it allows the benefits of the experience of other organizations to be shared. The popular process models used in software process improvement include:

- Capability Maturity Model Integration (CMMI),
- ISO 9001 Standard,
- ISO 15504,
- PSP and TSP,
- Six sigma,
- Root cause analysis (RCA),
- Balanced Scorecard.

The CMMI was developed by the Software Engineering Institute, and it is the successor to the older software CMM which was released in the early 1990s. The latter is specific to the software field, and it was influenced by Watt Humphrey's work at IBM [3]. The CMMI is a suite of products used for improving processes, and it includes models, appraisal methods and training material. The CMMI models address three areas of interest:

- CMMI for development (CMMI-DEV),
- CMMI for services (CMMI-SVC),
- CMMI for acquisition (CMMI-ACQ).

The CMMI Development Model is discussed in Chap. 20, and it provides a structured approach to improvement, which allows the organization to set its improvement goals and priorities. The CMMI framework allows organizations to improve their maturity by improvements to their underlying processes. It provides a clearly defined roadmap for improvement, and it allows the organization to improve at its own pace. Its approach is evolutionary rather than revolutionary, and it recognizes that a balance is required between project needs and process improvement needs. It allows the processes to evolve from ad hoc immature activities to disciplined mature processes.

The CMMI practices may be used for the development, acquisition and maintenance of products and services. A SCAMPI appraisal determines the actual process maturity of an organization, and a SCAMPI class A appraisal allows the organization to benchmark itself against other organizations.

ISO 9001 is an internationally recognized quality management standard (Fig. 19.4), and it is customer and process focused. It applies to the processes that an organization uses to create and control products and services, and it emphasizes

Fig. 19.4 ISO 9001 quality
management system

continuous improvement.[2] The standard is designed to apply to any product or
service that the organization supplies.

The implementation of ISO 9001 involves understanding the requirements of the
standard, and how the standard applies to the organization. It requires the organization to identify its quality objectives, define a quality policy, produce documented
procedures, and carry out independent audits to ensure that the processes and
procedures are followed. An organization may be certified against the ISO 9001
standard to gain recognition on its commitment to quality and continuous
improvement. The certification involves an independent assessment of the organization to verify that it has implemented the ISO 9001 requirements properly, and
that the quality management system is effective. It will also verify that the processes
and procedures defined are consistently followed, and that appropriate records are
maintained. The ISO 9004 standard provides guidance for continuous
improvement.

The ISO/IEC 15504 standard (popularly known as ISO SPICE) is an international standard for process assessment. It includes guidance for process improvement and for process capability determination, as well as guidance for performing
an assessment. It uses the international standard for software and systems lifecycle
processes (ISO/IEC 12207) as its process model.

The ISO 12207 standard distinguishes between several categories of software
processes including the primary life cycle processes for developing and maintaining
software; supporting processes to support the software development lifecycle; and
organization life cycle processes. There is a version of SPICE termed "*Automotive
SPICE*" that is popular in the automotive sector. ISO/IEC 15504 can be used in a
similar way to the CMMI, and its process model (i.e., ISO 12207) may be employed
to implement best practice in the definition of processes. Assessments may be
performed to identify strengths and opportunities for improvement.

---

[2] The ISO 9004 standard provides guidance on continuous improvement.

The Personal Software Process (PSP) is a disciplined data driven software development process that is designed to help software engineers understand and to improve their personal software process performance. It was developed by Watt Humphrey at the SEI, and it helps engineers to improve their estimation and planning skills, and to reduce the number of defects in their work. This enables them to make commitments that they can keep and to manage the quality of their projects.

The Team Software Process (TSP) was developed by Watt Humphries at the SEI, and is a structured approach designed to help software teams understand and improve their quality and productivity. Its focus is on building an effective software development team, and it involves establishing team goals, assigning team roles as well as other teamwork activities. Team members must already be familiar with the PSP.

Six Sigma (6σ) was developed by Motorola to improve quality and reduce waste. Its approach is to identify and remove the causes of defects in processes by reducing process variability. It uses quality management techniques and tools such as the five whys, business process mapping, statistical techniques, and the DMAIC and DMADV methodologies. There are several roles involved in six sigma initiatives such as Champions, Black Belts and Green Belts, and each role requires knowledge and experience, and is awarded on merit subject to training and certification. Sponsorship and leadership is required from top management to ensure the success of a 6σ initiative, and 6σ was influenced by earlier quality management techniques developed by Shewhart, Deming and Juran. A 6σ project follows a defined sequence of steps and has quantified targets (e.g., financial, quality, customer satisfaction, and cycle time reduction).

19.6 Process Mapping

The starting point for improving a process is first to understand the process as it is currently performed, and to determine the extent to which it is effective. The process stakeholders reach a common understanding of how the process is performed, and the process (as currently performed) is then sketched pictorially, with the activities and their inputs and outputs recorded graphically. This graphical representation is termed a *"process map"* and is an abstract description of the process *"as is"*.

The process map is an abstraction of the way that work is done, and it may be critically examined to determine how effective it really is, and to identify weaknesses and potential improvements. This critical examination by the process practitioners leads to modifications to its definition, and the proposed definition is sketched in a new process map to yield the process *"to be"*.

Each activity has an input and an output, and these are recorded in the process map. Once the team has agreed the definition of new process, the supporting templates required become clear from an examination of the input and output of the various activities. There may be a need for standards to support the process (e.g., procedures and templates), and the procedures or guidelines will be documented to provide the details on how the process is to be carried out, and they will detail the tasks and activities, and the roles required to perform them.

19.7 Process Improvement Initiatives

The need for a software process improvement initiative often arises from the realization that the organization is weak in some areas in software engineering, and that it needs to improve to achieve its business goals more effectively. The starting point of any improvement initiative is an examination of the business goals of the organization, and these may include:

- Delivering high-quality products on time,
- Delivering products faster to the market,
- Reducing the cost of software development,
- Improving software quality.

There is more than one approach to the implementation of an improvement program. A small organization has fewer resources available and team members involved in the initiative will typically be working part time. Larger organizations may be able to assign people full time on the improvement activities. The software process improvement initiative is designed to enable the organization to achieve its business goals more effectively.

Once the organization goals have been defined the improvement initiative commences. This involves conducting an appraisal (Fig. 19.6) to determine the current strengths and weaknesses of the processes; analysing the results to formulate a process improvement plan; implementing the plan; piloting the improved processes and verifying that they are effective; training staff and rolling out the new processes. The improvements are monitored for effectiveness and the cycle repeats. The software process improvement philosophy is:

- The improvement initiative is based on business needs.
- Improvements should be planned based on the strengths and weaknesses of the processes in the organization.
- The CMMI Model (or an alternate model) is the vehicle for improvement.
- The improvements are prioritized (it is not possible to do everything at once).
- The improvement initiative needs to be planned and managed as a project.
- The results achieved need to be reviewed at the end of the period, and a new improvement cycle started for continuous improvement.
- Software process improvement requires people to change their behaviour, and so organization culture (and training) needs to be considered.

- There needs to be a process champion/project manager to drive the process improvement initiative in the organization.
- Senior management need to be 100% committed to the success of the initiative.
- Staff need to be involved in the improvement initiative, and there needs to be a balance between project needs and the improvement activities.

19.8 Barriers to Success

Software process improvement initiatives are not always successful, and occasionally are abandoned. Some of the reasons for failure are:

- Unrealistic expectations,
- Trying to do too much at once,
- Lack of senior management sponsorship,
- Focusing on a maturity level,
- Poor project management of the initiative,
- Not run as a standard project,
- Insufficient involvement of staff,
- Insufficient time to work on improvements,
- Inadequate training on software process improvement,
- Lack of pilots to validate new processes,
- Inadequate training/rollout of new processes.

It is essential that a software process improvement initiative be treated as a standard project with a project manager assigned to manage the initiative. Senior management need to be 100% committed to the success of the initiative, and they need to make staff available to work on the improvement activities. It needs to be clear to all staff that the improvement initiative is a priority to the organization. All employees need to receive appropriate training on software process improvement and on the process maturity model.

The CMMI project manager needs to consider the risks of failure of the initiative and to manage them accordingly.

19.9 Setting Up an Improvement Initiative

The implementation of an improvement initiative is a project, and it needs good planning and management to ensure its success. Once an organization decides to embark on such an initiative, a project manager needs to be appointed to manage the project. The project manager will treat the implementation as a standard project, and plans are made to implement the initiative within the approved schedule and budget. The improvement initiative will often consist of several improvement cycles, with each improvement cycle implementing one or more process areas. Small improvement cycles may be employed to implement findings from an appraisal or improvement suggestions from staff.

One of the earliest activities carried out on any improvement initiative is to determine the current maturity of the organization with respect to the model. This will usually involve an appraisal conducted by one or more experienced appraisers. The findings will indicate the current strengths and weaknesses of the processes, as well as gaps with respect to the practices in the model. This initial appraisal is important, as it allows management in the organization to understand its current maturity with respect to the model, and to communicate where it wants to be, as well as how it plans to get there. The initial appraisal assists in prioritizing improvements for the first improvement cycle.

The project manager will then prepare a project plan and schedule. The plan will detail the scope of the initiative, the budget, the process areas to be implemented, the teams and resources required, the initial risks identified, the key milestones, the quality and communication plan, and so on. The project schedule will detail the deliverables to be produced, the resources required and the associated timeline for delivery. Project management was discussed in Chap. 4.

The software process improvement initiative is designed to support the organization in achieving its business goals more effectively. The steps include examining organization needs; conducting an appraisal to determine the current strengths and weaknesses; and analysing the results to formulate an improvement plan. The improvement plan is then implemented; the improvements monitored and confirmed as being effective; and the improvement cycle repeats. The continuous improvement cycle is described in Fig. 19.5 and Table 19.2.

The teams involved in implementation are discussed in Table 19.3.

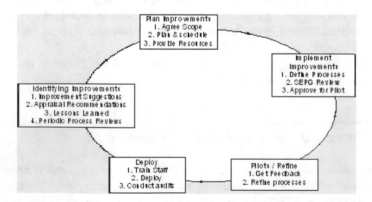

Fig. 19.5 Continuous improvement cycle

Table 19.2 Continuous improvement cycle

Activity	Description
Identify improvements to be made	The improvements to be made during an improvement cycle come from several sources: • Improvement suggestions from staff • Lessons learned by projects • Periodic process reviews • Recommendations from appraisals
Plan improvements	A project plan and schedule are prepared for a large improvement cycle (involving the implementation of several process areas). An action plan (with owners and target completion dates) is sufficient for small improvement initiatives
Implement improvements	The improvements will consist of new processes, standards, templates, procedures, guidelines checklists, and tools (where appropriate) to support the process
Pilots/refine	Selected new processes and standards will often be piloted[a] prior to their deployment to ensure that they are fit for purpose
Deploy	• Staff are trained on the new processes and standards • Staff receive support during the deployment • Audits are conducted
Do it all again	Improvement is continuous and as soon as an improvement cycle is complete its effectiveness is considered, and a new improvement cycle is ready to commence

[a]The result from the pilot may be that the new process is not suitable to be deployed in the organization or that it needs to be significantly revised prior to deployment

Table 19.3 Teams in improvement program

Role/team	Members	Responsibility
Project manager	Project manager	Project manage the improvement project Provides leadership on process improvement
Steering group (project board)	Senior manager(s)/project manager	Provides management sponsorship of initiative Provides resources and funding for the initiative Uses influence to remove any roadblocks that arise with the improvement activities
SEPG team	Managers, technical and PROJECT manager	Coordinate day-to-day improvement activities Provides direction and support to improvement terms Review and approve new processes & coordinate pilots, training, and rollout of new processes
Improvement teams	Process users/project manager	Focus on specific process area(s) Review the current process "as is" and define the new process "to be" Obtain feedback on new process, conduct pilots, refine process, provide training, and conduct rollout of new process
Staff	All affected staff	Participate in improvement teams Participate in pilots Participate in training on new processes Adhere to new processes
External consultancy	External consultant	Conduct appraisal to determine initial maturity and assist in planning of first improvement cycle Provide expertise/training on the maturity model Conduct periodic process reviews Conduct appraisal at end of each improvement cycle

19.10 Appraisals

Appraisals (Fig. 19.6) play an essential role in the software process improvement program. They allow an organization to understand its current software process maturity, including the strengths and weaknesses in its processes. An initial appraisal is conducted at the start of the initiative to allow the organization to understand its current process maturity, and to plan and prioritize improvements for the first improvement cycle. Improvements are then implemented, and an appraisal is typically conducted at the end of the cycle to confirm that progress has been made in the improvement initiative.

An appraisal is an independent examination of the software engineering and management practices in the organization, and is conducted using an appraisal methodology (e.g., SCAMPI). It will identify strengths and weaknesses in the processes, and any gaps that exist with respect to the maturity model.

The appraisal leader kicks off the appraisal with an opening presentation, which introduces the appraisal team, and presents the activities that will be carried out during the appraisal. These will include presentations, interviews, reviews of project documentation, and detailed analysis to determine the extent to which the practices in the model have been implemented.

The appraisal leader will present the appraisal findings, and this may include a presentation and an appraisal report. The appraisal output summarizes the strengths and weaknesses, and ratings of the process areas will be provided (where this is part of the appraisal). The appraisal findings are valuable and will allow the project manager to plan and schedule the next improvement cycle. They allow an organization to:

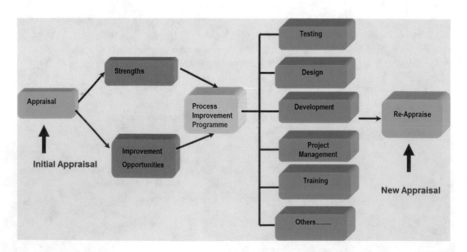

Fig. 19.6 Appraisals

Table 19.4 Phases in an appraisal

Phase	Description
Planning and preparation	This involves identifying the sponsor's objectives and the requirements for the appraisal. A good appraisal plan is essential to its success
Conducting the appraisal	The appraisal team interviews the participants and examines data to judge the extent to which the CMMI is implemented in the organization
Reporting the results	The findings (including a presentation and an appraisal report).are reported to the sponsor

- Understand its current process maturity (including strengths and weaknesses),
- Relate its strengths and weaknesses to the improvement model,
- Prioritize its improvements for the next improvement cycle,
- Benchmark itself against other organizations.

There are three phases in an appraisal (Table 19.4).

19.11 Review Questions

1. What is a software process?
2. What is software process improvement?
3. What are the benefits of software process improvement?
4. Describe the various models available for software process improvement?
5. Draw the process map for the process of cooking your favourite meal.
6. Describe how a process improvement initiative may be run?
7. What are the main barriers to successful software process improvement initiatives and how can they be overcome?
8. Describe the three phases in an appraisal.

19.12 Summary

The success of business is highly influenced by software, and companies may develop their own software internally, or they may acquire software solutions off-the-shelf or from bespoke software development.

Software process improvement plays a key role in helping companies to improve their software engineering capability, and to achieve their strategic goals. It enables organizations to implement best practice in software engineering, and to achieve improved results. It allows companies to focus on fire prevention rather than firefighting, by critically examine their processes to determine the extent to which they are fit for purpose. It helps in identifying how the process may be improved and how waste may be eliminated.

Software process improvement initiatives lead to a focus on the process, which is important since many problems are caused by defective processes rather than by people. This leads to a culture of openness in discussing problems and instils process ownership among the process practitioners.

Software process improvement helps software companies to deliver the agreed software on-time and on-budget, as well as improving the quality of the delivered software, reducing the cost of development, and improving customer satisfaction.

It has become an indispensable tool for software engineers and managers to achieve their goals, and it provides a return on investment to the organization. The next chapter introduces the Capability Maturity Model Integration (CMMI), which has become a useful framework in maturing software engineering processes.

References

1. W. Edwards Deming, *Out of Crisis* (M.I.T. Press, 1986)
2. Software Engineering Institute, in *CMMI Executive Overview* (Presentation by the SEI, 2006)
3. W. Humphry. *Managing the Software Process* (Addison Wesley, 1989)

Capability Maturity Model Integration

20

Abstract

This chapter gives an overview of the CMMI model and discusses its five maturity levels and their constituent process areas. We discuss both the staged and continuous representations of the CMMI, and SCAMPI appraisals that indicate the extent to which the CMMI has been implemented in the organization, as well as identifying opportunities for improvement.

Keywords

CMMI maturity levels · CMMI capability levels · CMMI staged representation · CMMI continuous representation · CMMI process areas · Appraisals

20.1 Introduction

The Software Engineering Institute[1] developed the Capability Maturity Model (CMM) in the early 1990s as a framework to help software organizations improve their software process maturity. The CMMI is the successor to the older CMM, and its implementation brings best practice in software and systems engineering into the

---

[1] The SEI was founded by the US Congress in 1984 and has worked successfully in advancing software engineering practices in the US and worldwide. It performs research to find solutions to key software engineering problems, and its proposed solutions are validated through pilots. These solutions are then disseminated to the wider software engineering community through its training program. The SEI's research and maturity models have played an important role in helping companies to deliver high-quality software consistently on time and on budget.

© Springer Nature Switzerland AG 2022
G. O'Regan, *Concise Guide to Software Engineering*,
Undergraduate Topics in Computer Science,
https://doi.org/10.1007/978-3-031-07816-3_20

organization. The SEI and many other quality experts believe that there is a close relationship between the maturity of software processes and the quality of the delivered software product.

The CMM built upon the work of quality gurus such as Edwards Deming [1], Juran [2] and Crosby [3]. These quality gurus were effective in transforming struggling manufacturing companies with quality problem to companies that could consistently produce high quality products. Their success was due to the focus on improving the manufacturing process and in reducing variability in the process. The work of these quality experts is discussed in [4].

Similarly, software companies need to have quality software processes to deliver high-quality software to their customers. The SEI has collected empirical data to suggest that there is a close relationship between software process maturity and the quality of the delivered software. Therefore, there is a need to focus on the software process as well as on the product.

The CMM was released in 1991 and its successor, the CMMI® model, was released in 2002 [5]. The CMMI is a framework to assist an organization in the implementation of best practice in software and systems engineering. It is an internationally recognized model for process improvement and is used world-wide by thousands of organizations.

The focus of the CMMI is on improvements to the software process to ensure that they meet business needs more effectively. A *process* is a set of practices or tasks performed to achieve a given purpose. It may include tools, methods, material, and people. An organization will typically have many processes in place for doing its work, and the object of process improvement is to improve these to meet business goals more effectively.

The process is an abstraction of the way in which work is done in the organization and is seen as the glue (Fig. 20.1) that ties people, procedures, and tools together.

It may be described by a process map which details the flow of activities and tasks. The process map will include the input to each activity and the output from each activity. Often, the output from one activity will become the input to the next activity. A simple example of a process map for creating the system requirements specification was described in Fig. 19.2.

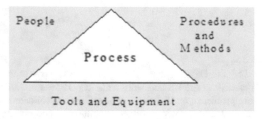

Fig. 20.1 Process as glue for people, procedures and tools

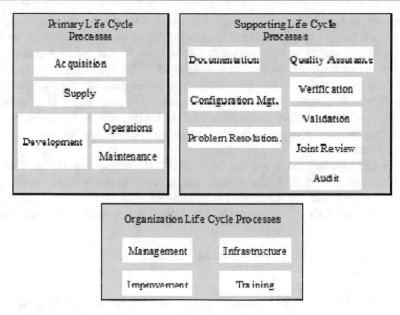

Fig. 20.2 ISO/IEC 12207 standard for software engineering processes

The ISO/IEC 12207 standard for software processes distinguishes between several categories of software processes, including the primary life cycle processes for developing and maintaining software; supporting processes to support the software development lifecycle; and organization life cycle processes. These are summarized in Fig. 20.2.

Watt Humphries began applying the ideas of Deming, Juran and Crosby to software development, and he published the book "*Managing the Software Process*" in the late 1980s [6]. He moved to the SEI to work on software process maturity models with the other SEI experts, and the SEI released the Capability Maturity Model in the early 1990s. This process model has proved to be effective in assisting companies in improving their software engineering practices and in achieving consistent results and high-quality software.

The CMM is a process model, and it defines the characteristics or best practices of good processes. It does not prescribe how the processes should be defined, and it allows the organization the freedom to interpret the model to suit its context and business needs. It also provides a roadmap for an organization to get from where it is today to a higher level of maturity. The advantage of model-based improvement is that it provides a place to start process improvement, as well as a common language and a shared vision.

The CMM consists of five maturity levels with the higher maturity levels representing advanced software engineering capability. The lowest maturity level is level one and the highest is level five. The SEI developed an assessment methodology (CBA IPI) to determine the maturity of software organizations, and initially most organizations were assessed at level one maturity. However, over time companies embarked on improvement initiatives, and matured their software processes, and today many companies are performing at the higher maturity levels.

The first company to be assessed at CMM level 5[2] was the Motorola plant in Bangalore in India. The success of the software CMM led to the development of other process maturity models such as the systems engineering capability maturity mode (CMM/SE) which is concerned with maturing systems engineering practices, and the people capability maturity model (P-CMM) which is concerned with improving the ability of the software organizations to attract, develop, and retain talented software engineering professionals.

The SEI commenced work on the CMMI® [5] in the late 1990s. This is a replacement for the older CMM model, and its development involved merging the software CMM and the systems CMM and ensuring that the new model was compatible with ISO 15504 standard.[3] The CMMI is described in the next section.

20.2 The CMMI

The CMMI consists of five maturity levels (Fig. 20.4) with each maturity level (except level one) consisting of several process areas. Each process area consists of a set of goals, and these must be implemented by a set of related practices for the process area to be satisfied. The practices specify what is to be done rather than how it should be done. Processes are activities associated with carrying out certain tasks, and they need to be defined and documented. The users of the process need to receive appropriate training to enable them to carry out the process, and process discipline need to be enforced by independent audits. Process performance needs to be monitored and improvements made to ineffective processes.

The emphasis for level two of the CMMI is on maturing management practices such as project management, requirements management, configuration management, and so on. The emphasis on level three of the CMMI is on maturing engineering and organization practices. Maturity level three is concerned with defining standard organization processes, and it also includes process areas for the various engineering activities needed to design and develop the software. Level four is concerned with ensuring that key processes are performing within strict quantitative limits, and adjusting processes, where necessary, to perform within these limits. Level five is concerned with continuous process improvement. Maturity levels may not be skipped in the staged implementation of the CMMI, as each maturity level is the foundation for work on the next level.

---

[2] Of course, the fact that a company has been appraised at a certain CMM or CMMI rating is no guarantee that it is performing effectively as a commercial organization. For example, the Motorola plant in India was appraised at CMM level 5 in the late 1990s while Motorola lost business opportunities in the GSM market.

[3] ISO 15504 (popularly known as SPICE) is an international standard for software process assessment.

Table 20.1 Motivation for CMMI implementation

Motivation for CMMI implementation
Enhances the credibility of the company
Marketing benefit of CMMI maturity level
Implementation of best practice in software and systems engineering
Clearly defined roadmap for improvement
It increases the capability and maturity of an organization
It improves the management of subcontractors
It provides improved technical and management practices
It leads to higher quality of software
It leads to increased timeliness of projects
It reduces the cost of maintenance and incidence of defects
It allows the measurement of processes and products
It allows projects/products to be quantitatively managed
It allows innovative technologies to be rigorously evaluated to enhance process performance
It improves customer satisfaction
It changes the culture from firefighting to fire prevention
It leads to a culture of improvement
It leads to higher morale in company

There is also a continuous representation[4] of the CMMI (like ISO 15504) that allows the organization to focus its improvements on the key processes that are closely related to its business goals. This allows it the freedom to choose an approach that should result in the greatest business benefit rather than proceeding with the standard improvement roadmap of the staged approach. However, in practice it is often necessary to implement several of the level two process areas before serious work can be done on maturing a process to a higher capability level. Table 20.1 presents motivations for the implementation of the CMMI.

The CMMI model covers both the software engineering and systems engineering disciplines. Systems engineering is concerned with the development of systems that may or may not include software, whereas software engineering is concerned with the development of software systems. The model contains extra information relevant to a particular discipline, and this is done by discipline amplification.[5] The CMMI has been updated in recent years to provide support for the Agile methodology.

---

[4] Our focus is on the implementation of the staged representation of the CMMI rather than the continuous representation. This provides a clearly defined roadmap to improvement, and it also allows benchmarking of organizations. Appraisals against the staged representation are useful since a CMMI maturity level rating is awarded to the organization, and the company may use this to publicize its software engineering capability.

[5] Discipline amplification is a specialized piece of information that is relevant to a particular discipline. It is introduced in the model by text such as "For Systems Engineering".

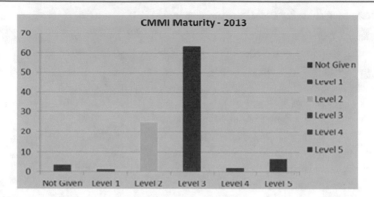

Fig. 20.3 CMMI worldwide maturity 2013

The CMMI allows organizations to benchmark themselves against similar organizations (Fig. 20.3). This is generally done by a formal SEI SCAMPI Class A appraisal[6] conducted by an authorized SCAMPI lead appraiser. The results will generally be reported back to the SEI, and there is a strict qualification process to become an authorized lead appraiser. The qualification process helps to ensure that the appraisals are conducted fairly and objectively and that the results are consistent. An appraisal verifies that an organization has improved, and it enables the organization to prioritize improvements for the next improvement cycle. Small organizations will often prefer a SCAMPI Class B or C appraisal, as these are less expensive and time consuming.[7]

The time required to implement the CMMI in an organization depends on its size and current maturity. It generally takes one to two years to implement maturity level two, and a further one to two years to implement level 3. The implementation of the CMMI needs to be balanced against the day-to-day needs of the organization in delivering products and services to its customers (Fig. 20.4).

The SEI has gathered empirical data (Table 20.2) on the benefits gained from the implementation of the CMMI [7]. The table shows the median results reported to the SEI.

---

[6] A SCAMPI Class A appraisal is a systematic examination of the processes in an organization to determine the maturity of the organization with respect to the CMMI. An appraisal team consists of a SCAMPI lead appraiser, one or more external appraisers, and usually one internal appraiser. It consists of interviews with senior and middle management and reviews with project managers and project teams. The appraisers will review documentation and determine the extent to which the processes defined are effective, as well as the extent to which they are institutionalized in the organization. Data will be gathered and reviewed by the appraisers, ratings produced, and the findings presented.

[7] Small organizations may not have the budget for a formal SCAMPI Class A appraisal. They may be more interested in an independent SCAMPI Class B or C appraisal, which is used to provide feedback on their strengths and opportunities for improvement. Feedback allows the organization to focus its improvement efforts for the next improvement cycle.

Fig. 20.4 CMMI maturity levels

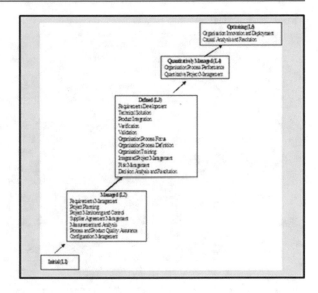

Table 20.2 Benefits of CMMI implementation

Benefit	Actual saving
Cost	34%
Schedule	50%
Productivity	61%
Quality	48%
Customer satisfaction	14%
Return on investment	4:1

The processes implemented during a CMMI initiative will generally include:

- Developing and Managing Requirements,
- Design and Development,
- Project Management,
- Selecting and managing Subcontractors,
- Managing change and Configurations,
- Peer reviews,
- Risk Management and Decision Analysis,
- Testing,
- Audits.

20.3   CMMI Maturity Levels

The CMMI is divided into five maturity levels (Table 20.3) with each maturity level (except level one) consisting of several process areas. The maturity level is a predictor of the results that will be obtained from following the software process,

Table 20.3 CMMI maturity levels

Maturity level	Description
Initial	Processes are often ad hoc or chaotic with performance often unpredictable. Success is often due to the heroics of people rather than having high-quality processes in place. The defined process is often abandoned in times of crisis, and there are no audits to enforce the process
	It is difficult to repeat previous success since success is due to heroic efforts of its people rather than processes. These organizations often over-commit, as they often lack an appropriate estimation process on which to base project commitments
	Firefighting is a way of life in these organizations. High-quality software might be produced, but at a cost including long hours, high level of rework, over budget and schedule and unhappy staff and customers. Projects do not perform consistently as their success is dependent on the people involved
	They may have few processes defined and poor change control, poor estimation and project planning, and weak enforcement of standards
Managed	A level two organization has good project management practices in place and planning and managing new projects is based on experience with similar previous projects
	The process is planned, performed, and controlled. A level two organization is disciplined in following processes, and the process is enforced with independent audits
	The status of the work products produced by the process is visible to management at major milestones, and changes to work products are controlled. The work products are placed under appropriate configuration management control
	The requirements for a project are managed and changes to the requirements are controlled. Project management practices are in place to manage the project, and a set of measures are defined for budget, schedule, and effort variance. Subcontractors are managed
	Independent audits are conducted to enforce the process. The processes in a level two organization are defined at the project level
Defined	A maturity level three organization has standard processes defined that support the whole organization
	These standard processes ensure consistency in the way that projects are conducted across the organization. There are guidelines defined that allow the organization process to be tailored and applied to each project
	There are standards in place for design and development and procedures defined for effective risk management and decision analysis
	Level 3 processes are generally defined more rigorously than level 2 processes, and the definition includes the purpose of the process, inputs, entry criteria, activities, roles, measures, verification steps, exit criteria and output. There is also an organization wide training program and improvement data is collected
Quantitatively managed	A level 4 organization sets quantitative goals for the performance of key processes, and these processes are controlled using statistical techniques
	Processes are stable and perform within narrowly defined limits. Software process and product quality goals are set and managed

(continued)

Table 20.3 (continued)

Maturity level	Description
	A level 4 organization has predictable process performance, with variation in process performance identified and the causes of variation corrected
Optimizing	A level 5 organization has a continuous process improvement culture in place, and processes are improved based on a quantitative understanding of variation
	Defect prevention activities are an integral part of the development lifecycle. New technologies are evaluated and introduced (where appropriate) into the organization. Processes may be improved incrementally or through innovative process and technology improvements

and the higher the maturity level of the organization, the more capable it is and the more predictable its results. The current maturity level acts as the foundation for the improvements to be made in the move to the next maturity level.

The maturity levels provide a roadmap for improvements in the organization, and maturity levels are not skipped in the staged implementation. A particular maturity level is achieved only when all process areas belonging to that maturity level (and all process areas belonging to lower maturity levels) have been successfully implemented and institutionalized[8] in the organization.

The implementation of the CMMI generally starts with improvements to processes at the project level. The focus at level two is on improvements to managing projects and suppliers, and improving project management, supplier selection and management practices, and so on.

The improvements at level 3 involve a shift from the focus on projects to the organization. It involves defining standard processes for the organization, and projects may then tailor the standard process (using tailoring guidelines) to produce the project's software process. Projects are not required to do everything in the same way as the tailoring of the process allows the project's defined software process to reflect the unique characteristics of the project: i.e., a degree of variation is allowed as per the tailoring guidelines to reflect the unique characteristics of the project.

The implementation of level three involves defining procedures and standards for engineering activities such as design, coding, and testing. Procedures are defined for peer reviews, testing, risk management and decision analysis.

The implementation of level four involves achieving process performance within defined quantitative limits. This involves the use of metrics and setting quantitative goals for project and process performance and managing process performance. The implementation of level 5 is concerned with achieving a culture of continuous

---

[8] Institutionalization is a technical term and means that the process is ingrained in the way in which work is performed in the organization. An institutionalized process is defined, documented, and followed in the organization. All employees have been appropriately trained in its use and process discipline is enforced via audits. It is illustrated by the phrase "*That's the way we do things around here*".

improvement in the company. The causes of defects are identified, and resolution actions implemented to prevent a reoccurrence.

20.3.1   CMMI Representations

The CMMI is available in the staged and continuous representations. Both representations use the same process areas as well as the same specific and generic goals and practices.

The staged representation was described in Fig. 20.4, and it follows the well-known improvement roadmap from maturity level one through improvement cycles until the organization has achieved its desired level of maturity. The staged approach is concerned with organization maturity, and it allows statements of organization maturity to be made, whereas the continuous representation is concerned with individual process capability.

The continuous representation is illustrated in Fig. 20.5, and it has been influenced by ISO 15504 (the standard for software process assessment). It is concerned with improving the capability of those selected processes, and it gives the organization the freedom to choose the order of improvements that best meet its business needs (Fig. 20.6). The continuous representation allows statements of

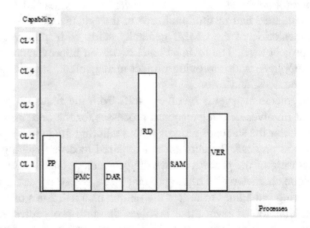

Fig. 20.5 CMMI capability levels

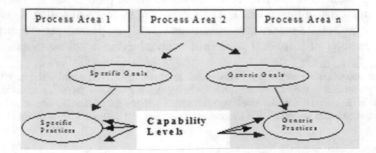

Fig. 20.6 CMMI—continuous representation

Table 20.4 CMMI capability levels for continuous representation

Capability level	Description
Incomplete (0)	The process does not implement all the capability level one generic and specific practices. The process is either not performed or partially performed
Performed (1)	A process that performs all the specific practices and satisfies its specific goals. Performance may not be stable
Managed (2)	A process at this level has infrastructure to support the process. It is managed: i.e., planned and executed in accordance with policy, its users are trained; it is monitored and controlled and audited for adherence to its process description
Defined (3)	A process at this level has a defined process: i.e., a managed process that is tailored from the organization's set of standard processes. It contributes work products, measures, and other process improvement information to the organization's process assets
Quantitatively managed (4)	A process at this level is a quantitatively managed process: i.e., a defined process that is controlled by statistical techniques. Quantitative objectives for quality and process performance are established and used to control the process
Optimizing (5)	A process at this level is an optimizing process: i.e., a quantitatively managed process that is continually improved through incremental and innovative improvements

individual process capability to be made. It employs six capability levels, and a process is rated at a particular capability level.

Each capability level consists of a set of specific and generic goals and practices, and the capability levels provide a path for process improvement within the process area. Process improvement is achieved by the evolution of a process from its current capability level to a higher capability level. For example, a company may wish to mature its project planning process from its current process rating of capability level 2 to a rating of capability level 3. This requires the implementation of practices to define a standard project planning process as well as collecting improvement data. The capability levels are shown in Table 20.4.

An incomplete process is a process that is either partially performed or not performed at all. A performed process carries out the expected practices and work products. However, such a process may not be adequately planned or enforced. A managed process is planned and executed with appropriately skilled and trained personnel. The process is monitored and controlled and periodically enforced via audits.

A defined process is a managed process that is tailored from the standard process in the organization using tailoring guidelines. A quantitatively managed process is a defined process that is controlled using quantitative techniques. An optimizing process is a quantitatively managed process that is continuously improved through incremental and innovative improvements.

The process is rated at a particular capability level provided it satisfies all the specific and generic goals of that capability level, and it also satisfies the specific and generic goals of all lower capability levels.

We shall be concerned with the implementation of the staged representation of the CMMI rather than the continuous representation. The reader is referred to [5] for more information on both representations.

20.4 Categories of CMMI Processes

The process areas on the CMMI can be divided into four categories. These are (Table 20.5).

Table 20.5 CMMI process categories

Maturity level	Description
Process management	The process areas in this category are concerned with activities to define, plan, implement, deploy, monitor, control, appraise, measure, and improve the processes in the organization: They include • Organization process focus • Organization process definition • Organization training • Organization process performance • Organization innovation and deployment
Project management	These process areas are concerned with activities to create and maintain a project plan, tailoring the standard process to produce the project's defined process, monitoring progress with respect to the plan, taking corrective action, the selection and management of suppliers, and the management of risk. They include • Project planning • Project monitoring and control • Risk management • Integrated project management • Supplier agreement management • Quantitative project management
Engineering	These process areas are concerned with engineering activities such as determining and managing requirements, design, and development, testing and maintenance of the product. They include • Requirements development • Requirements management • Technical solution • Product integration • Verification • Validation
Support	This includes activities that support product development and maintenance • Configuration management • Process and product quality assurance • Measurement and analysis • Decision analysis and resolution

20.5 CMMI Process Areas

This section provides a brief overview of the process areas of the CMMI model. All maturity levels (except for level one) contain several process areas. The process areas are described in more detail in [5] (Table 20.6).

Table 20.6 CMMI process areas

Maturity level	Process area	Description of process area
Level 2	REQM	*Requirements management* This process area is concerned with managing the requirements for the project and ensuring that the work products are kept consistent with the requirements
	PP	*Project planning* This process area is concerned with estimation for the project, developing and obtaining commitment to the project plan and maintaining the plan
	PMC	*Project monitoring and control* This process area is concerned with monitoring progress against the plan and taking corrective action when project performance deviates from the plan
	SAM	*Supplier agreement management* This process area is concerned with the selection of suppliers, documenting the (legal) agreement/statement of work with the supplier and managing the supplier during the execution of the agreement
	MA	*Measurement and analysis* This process area is concerned with determining management information needs and measurement objectives. Measures are then specified to meet these objectives, and data collection and analysis procedures defined
	PPQA	*Process and product quality assurance* This process area is concerned with providing visibility to management on process compliance. Non-compliance issues are documented and resolved by the project team
	CM	*Configuration management* This process area is concerned with setting up a configuration management system; identifying the items that will be subject to change control and controlling changes to them
Level 3	RD	*Requirements development* This process area is concerned with specifying the user and system requirements and analysing and validating them
	TS	*Technical solution* This process area is concerned with the design, development, and implementation of an appropriate solution to the customer requirements
	PI	*Product integration* This process area is concerned with the assembly of the product components to deliver the product and verifying that the assembled components function correctly together

(continued)

Table 20.6 (continued)

Maturity level	Process area	Description of process area
	VER	*Verification* This process area is concerned with ensuring that selected work products satisfy their specified requirements. This is achieved by peer reviews and testing
	VAL	*Validation* This process area is concerned with demonstrating that the product or product component is fit for purpose and satisfies its intended use
	OPF	*Organization process focus* This process area is concerned with planning and implementing process improvements based on a clear understanding of the current strengths and weakness of the organization's processes
	OPD	*Organization process definition* This process area is concerned with creating and maintaining a usable set of organization processes. This allows consistent process performance across the organization
	OT	*Organization training* This process area is concerned with developing the skills and knowledge of people to enable them to perform their roles effectively
	IPM	*Integrated project management* This process area is concerned with tailoring the organization set of standard processes to define the project's defined process. The project is managed according to the project's defined process
	RSKM	*Risk management* This process area is concerned with identifying risks and determining their probability of occurrence and impact should they occur. Risks are identified and managed throughout the project
	DAR	*Decision analysis and resolution* This process area is concerned with formal decision making. It involves identifying options, specifying evaluation criteria and method, performing the evaluation, and recommending a solution
Level 4	OPP	*Organization process performance* This process area is concerned with obtaining a quantitative understanding of the performance of selected organization processes to quantitatively manage projects in the organization
	QPM	*Quantitative project management* This process area is concerned with quantitatively managing the project's defined process to achieve the project's quality and performance objectives
Level 5	OID	*Organization innovation and deployment* This process area is concerned with incremental and innovative process improvements
	CAR	*Causal analysis and resolution* This process area is concerned with identifying causes of defects and taking corrective action to prevent a re-occurrence in the future

20.6   Components of CMMI Process Areas

The maturity level of an organization indicates the expected results that its projects will achieve and is a predictor of future project performance. Each maturity level consists of several process areas, and each process area consists of specific and generic goals, and specific and generic practices. Each maturity level is the foundation for improvements for the next level.

The specific goals and practices are listed first and then followed by the generic goals and practices. The specific goals and practices are unique to the process area being implemented and are concerned with what needs to be done to perform the process. The specific practices are linked to a particular specific goal, and they describe activities that when performed achieve the associated specific goal for the process area (Fig. 20.7).

The generic goals and practices are common to all process areas for that maturity level and are concerned with process institutionalization at that level. The generic practices are organized by four common features:

- Commitment to perform,
- Ability to perform,
- Directing implementation,
- Verifying implementation.

They describe activities that when implemented achieve the associated generic goal(s) for the process area. The commitment to perform practices relate to the creation of policies and sponsorship of process improvement; the ability to perform

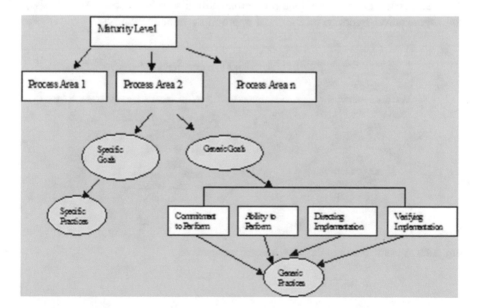

Fig. 20.7 CMMI staged model

practices are related to the provision of appropriate resources and training to perform the process; the directing implementation practices relate to activities to control and manage the process; and verifying practices relate to activities to verify adherence to the process.

The implementation of the generic practices institutionalizes the process and makes it ingrained in the way that work is done. Institutionalization means that the process is defined, documented, and understood. Process users are appropriately trained, and the process is enforced by independent audits. Institutionalization helps to ensure that the process is performed consistently and is more likely to be retained during times of stress. The degree of institutionalization is reflected in the extent to which the generic goals and practices are satisfied. The generic practices ensure the sustainability of the specific practices over time.

There is one specific goal associated with the Requirements Management process area (Fig. 20.8), and it has five associated specific practices:

SG 1—Manage Requirements

Requirements are managed and inconsistencies with project plans and work products are identified.

The components of the CMMI model are grouped into three categories: namely, required, expected, and informative components. The *required category* is essential to achieving goals in a particular area and includes the *specific* and *generic goals* that must be implemented and institutionalized for the process area to be satisfied. The *expected category* includes the *specific and generic practices* that an organization will typically implement to perform the process effectively. These are intended to guide individuals or groups who are implementing improvements, or who are performing appraisals to determine the current maturity of the organization. They state what needs to be done rather than how it should be done, thereby giving the organization freedom on the most appropriate implementation.

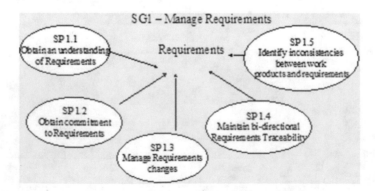

Fig. 20.8 Specific practices for SG1—manage requirements

The informative category includes information to guide the implementer on how best to approach the implementation of the specific and generic goals and practices. These include *sub-practices*, *typical work products*, *discipline amplifications,* and so on. This information assists with the implementation of the process area.

The implementation and institutionalization of a process area involves the implementation of the specific and generic practices. The specific practices are concerned with process implementation and are described in detail in [8]. The generic practices are concerned with process institutionalization and are summarized in Table 20.7.

Table 20.7 CMMI generic practices

Generic goal	Generic practice	Description of generic practice
GG 1 Performed process	GP 1.1	*Perform base practices* The purpose of this generic practice is to produce the work products and services associated with the process (i.e., as detailed in the specific practices). These practices may be done informally without following a documented process description and success may be dependent on the individuals performing the work. That is, the basic process is performed but it may be immature
GG 2 Managed process	GP 2.1	*Organization policy* The organization policy is established by senior management and defines the management expectations of the organization
	GP 2.2	*Plan the process* A plan is prepared to perform the process and it will assign responsibilities and document the resources needed to perform the process as well as any training requirements. The plan is revised as appropriate
	GP 2.3	*Provide resources* This is concerned with ensuring that the resources required to perform the process (as specified in the plan) are available when required
	GP 2.4	*Assign responsibility* The purpose of this generic practice is to assign responsibility for performing the process
	GP 2.5	*Train people* This generic practice is concerned with ensuring that people receive the appropriate training to enable them to perform and support the process
	GP 2.6	*Manage configurations* This generic practice is concerned with identifying the work products created by the process that will be subject to configuration management control
	GP 2.7	*Identify and involve relevant stakeholders* This is concerned with ensuring that the stakeholders are identified (as described in the plan) and involved appropriately during the execution of the process

(continued)

Table 20.7 (continued)

Generic goal	Generic practice	Description of generic practice
	GP 2.8	*Monitor and control the process* This generic practice is concerned with monitoring process performance and taking corrective action
	GP 2.9	*Objectively evaluate adherence* This is concerned with conducting audits to verify that process execution adheres to the process description
	GP 2.10	*Review status with higher level management* This is concerned with providing higher level management with appropriate visibility into the process
GG 3 Defined process	GP 3.1	*Establish a defined process* This is concerned with tailoring the organization set of standard processes to produce the project's defined process
	GP 3.2	*Collect improvement information* This generic practice is concerned with collecting improvement information and work products to support future improvement of the processes
GG 4 Quantitatively managed process	GP 4.1	*Establish quantitative objectives* This is concerned with agreeing quantitative objectives (e.g., quality/performance) for the process with the stakeholders
	GP 4.2	*Stabilize sub-process performance* This generic practice is concerned with stabilizing the performance of one or more key sub-processes of the process using statistical techniques. This enables the process to achieve its objectives
GG 5 Optimizing process	GP 5.1	*Ensure continuous process improvement* This generic practice is concerned with systematically improving selected processes to meet quality and process-performance targets
	GP 5.2	*Correct root cause of problems* This generic practice is concerned with analysing defects encountered to correct the root cause of these problems and to prevent re-occurrence

The generic goals support an evolution of process maturity, and the implementation of each generic goal provides a foundation for further process improvements. That is, a process rated at a particular maturity level has all the maturity of a process at the lower levels and the additional maturity of its rated level. In other words, a defined process is a managed process; a quantitatively managed process is a defined process, and so on.

Several of the CMMI process areas support the implementation of the generic goals and practices. These process areas contain one or more specific practices that when implemented may either fully implement a generic practice or generate a work product that is used in the implementation of the generic practice. The implementation of the generic practices is supported by the following process areas (Table 20.8).

Table 20.8 Implementation of generic practices

Generic goal	Generic practice	Process area supporting implementation of generic practice
GG 2 Managed process	GP 2.2 Plan the process	Project planning
	GP 2.5 Train the people	Organization training Project planning
	GP 2.6 Manage configurations	Configuration management
	GP 2.7 Identify/involve relevant stakeholders	Project planning
	GP 2.8 Monitor and control the process	Project monitoring and control
	GP 2.9 Objectively evaluate adherence	Process and product quality assurance
GG 3 Defined process	GP 3.1 Establish defined process	Integrated project management Organization process definition
	GP 3.2 Improvement information	Integrated project management Organization process focus Organization process definition
GG 4 Quantitatively managed process	GP 4.1 Establish quantitative objectives for process	Quantitative project management Organization process performance
	GP 4.2 Stabilize sub-process performance	Quantitative project management Organization process performance
GG 5 Optimizing process	GP 5.1 Ensure continuous Process improvement	Organization innovation and deployment
	GP 5.2 Correct root cause of problems	Causal analysis and resolution

20.7 SCAMPI Appraisals

SCAMPI appraisals are conducted to enable an organization to understand its current software process maturity, and to prioritize future improvements [9]. The appraisal is an independent examination of the processes used in the organization against the CMMI model, and its objective is to identify strengths and weaknesses in the processes, which are then used to prioritize improvements in the next improvement cycle.

The SCAMPI methodology is the appraisal methodology used with the CMMI, and there are three distinct classes of appraisal (SCAMPI Class A, B, and C) [10] These classes vary in formality, the cost, effort, and timescales involved, the rating of the processes, and the reporting of results.

The scope of the appraisal includes the process areas to be examined, and the projects and organization unit to be examined. It may be limited to the level 2 process areas, or the level 2 and level 3 process areas, and so on. The scope depends on how active the organization has been in process improvement.

The appraisal will identify any gaps that exist with respect to the implementation of the CMMI practices for each process area within the scope of the appraisal. The appraisal team will conduct interviews and review project documentation, and they will examine the extent to which the practices are implemented.

The appraisal findings are presented and are used to plan and prioritize the next improvement cycle. SCAMPI appraisals are discussed in more detail in [4].

20.8 Review Questions

1. Describe the CMMI Model.
2. Describe the staged and continuous representations of the CMMI.
3. What are the advantages and disadvantages of each CMMI representation?
4. Describe the CMMI maturity levels and the process areas in each level.
5. What is the purpose of the CMMI specific and generic practices?
6. Describe how the generic practices are implemented?
7. What is the difference between implementation and institutionalization?
8. What is the purpose of SCAMPI appraisals?
9. How do appraisals fit into the software process improvement cycle?

20.9 Summary

The Capability Maturity Model Integration is a framework to assist an organization in the implementation of best practice in software and systems engineering. It was developed at the Software Engineering Institute and is used by many organizations around the world.

The SEI and other quality experts believe that there is a close relationship between the quality of the delivered software, and the maturity of the processes used to create the software. Therefore, there needs to be a focus on the process as well as on the product, and the CMMI contains best practice in software and systems engineering to assist in the creation of high-quality processes.

The process is seen as the glue that ties people, technology, and procedures coherently together. Processes are activities associated with carrying out certain tasks, and they need to be defined and documented. The users of the process need to receive appropriate training on their use, and process discipline need to be enforced with independent audits. Process performance needs to be monitored and improvements made to ineffective processes.

The CMMI consists of five maturity levels with each maturity level (except level one) consisting of several process areas. Each maturity level acts as a foundation for improvement for the next improvement level, and each increase in maturity level represents more advanced software engineering capability. The higher the maturity level of the organization, the more capable it is, and the more predictable its results. The lowest level of maturity is maturity level 1, and the highest level is maturity level 5.

Each process area consists of a set of specific and generic goals, and these must be implemented by an associated set of specific and generic practices. The practices specify what is to be done rather than how it should be done, and the organization is given freedom in choosing the most appropriate implementation to meet its needs.

The SCAMPI appraisal methodology is used to determine the maturity of software organizations. It is a systematic examination of the processes used in the organization against the CMMI model, and it includes interviews and reviews of documentation. A successful SCAMPI Class A appraisal allows the organization to report its maturity rating to the SEI and to benchmark itself against other companies. Appraisals are a part of the improvement cycle, and improvement plans are prepared after the appraisal to address the findings and to prioritize improvements.

References

1. W. Edwards Deming, *Out of Crisis* (M.I.T. Press, 1986)
2. J. Juran, *Juran's Quality Handbook* (McGraw Hill 1951)
3. P. Crosby, *Quality is Free. The Art of Making Quality Certain* (McGraw Hill, 1979)
4. G. O' Regan, *Introduction to Software Quality* (Springer, 2014)

5. M.B. Chrissis, M. Conrad, S. Shrum, *CMMI for Development. Guidelines for Process Integration and Product Improvement*, 3rd edn. SEI Series in Software Engineering (Addison Wesley, 2011)

6. W. Humphry, *Managing the Software Process* (Addison58 Wesley, 1989)

7. *CMMI Impact. Presentation by Anita Carleton* (Software Engineering Institute, 2009)

8. G. O'Regan, *Introduction to Software Process Improvement* (Springer, London, 2010)

9. *Standard CMMI Appraisal Method for Process Improvement*. CMU/SEI-2006-HB-002. V1.2 (2006)

10. Appraisal Requirements for CMMI V1.2. (ARC V1.2). SCAMPI Upgrade Team. TR CMU/SEI-2006-TR-011 (2006)

Software Engineering Tools

21

Abstract

This chapter discusses various tools to support the various software engineering activities. The focus is first to define the process, and then to find tools to support the process. Tools to support project management are discussed as well as tools to support requirements engineering, configuration management, design and development activities and software testing.

Keywords

Microsoft project · COCOMO · Planview Enterprise · IBM Rational DOORS · Rational Software Modeler · LDRA Testbed · Integrated development environment · Sparx Enterprise Architect · HP Quality Center · Jira

21.1 Introduction

The goal of this chapter is to give a flavour of a selection of tools[1] that can support the performance of the various software engineering activities. Tools for project management, requirements management, configuration management, design and

---

[1] The list of tools discussed in this chapter is intended to give a flavour of what tools are available, and the inclusion of a particular tool is not intended as a recommendation of that tool. Similarly, the omission of a particular tool should not be interpreted as disapproval of that tool.

© Springer Nature Switzerland AG 2022
G. O'Regan, *Concise Guide to Software Engineering*,
Undergraduate Topics in Computer Science,
https://doi.org/10.1007/978-3-031-07816-3_21

Table 21.1 Tool evaluation table

	Tool 1	Tool 2	...	Tool k
Requirement 1	8	7		9
Requirement 2	4	6		8
...				
...				
Requirement n	3	6		8
Total	35	38	...	45

development, testing, and so on are considered. The approach is generally to choose tools to support the process, rather than choosing a process to support the tool.[2]

Mature organizations will employ a structured approach to the introduction of new tools. First, the requirements for a new tool are specified, and the options to satisfy the requirements are considered. These may include developing a tool internally; outsourcing the development of a tool to a third-party supplier; or purchasing an off the shelf solution from a vendor.

The sample tool evaluation process (Table 21.1) lists all the requirements vertically that the test tool is to satisfy, and the candidate tools that are to be evaluated and rated against each requirement are listed horizontally. Various rating schemes may be employed, and a simple numeric mechanism is employed for the example below. The tool evaluation criteria are used to rate the effectiveness of each candidate tool, and to indicate the extent to which the tool satisfies the defined requirements. The chosen tool in this example is Tool k as it is the most highly rated of the evaluated tools.

Several candidate tools will be identified and considered prior to selection, and each candidate tool will be evaluated to determine the extent to which it satisfies the specified requirements. An informed decision is then made, and the proposed tool will be piloted prior to its deployment. The pilot provides feedback on its suitability, and the feedback will be considered prior to a decision on full deployment, and whether any customization is required prior to roll out.

Finally, the users are trained on the tool, and the tool is rolled out throughout the organization. Support is provided for a period post deployment. First, we consider a selection of tools for project management.

21.2 Tools for Project Management

There are several tools to support the various project management activities such as estimation and cost prediction, planning and scheduling, monitoring risks and issues, and managing a portfolio of projects. These include tools such as Microsoft Project, which is a powerful project planning and scheduling tool that is widely used in industry. Small projects may employ a simpler tool such as Microsoft Excel for their project scheduling activities.

---

[2] That is, the process normally comes first then the tool rather than the other way around.

The Constructive Cost Model (Cocomo) is a cost prediction model developed by Boehm [1], and it is used to estimate effort, schedule, and cost for small and medium projects. It is based on an effort estimation equation that calculates the software development effort in person-months from the estimated project size. The effort estimation calculation is based on the estimate of a project's size in thousands of *source lines of code* (SLOC[3]). The accuracy of the tool is limited, as there is a great deal of variation among teams due to differences in the expertise and experience of the personnel in the project team.

There are several commercial variants of the tool including the Cocomo Basic, Intermediate and Advanced Models. The Intermediate Model includes several cost drivers to model the project environment, and each cost driver is rated. There are over fifteen cost drivers used, and these include product complexity, reliability, and experience of personnel as well as programming language experience. The Cocomo parameters need to be calibrated to reflect the actual project development environment. The effort equation used in Cocomo is given by:

$$\text{Effort} = 2.94 * \text{EAF} * (\text{KSLOC})^{E} \tag{21.1}$$

In this equation, EAF refers to the effort adjustment factor that is derived from the cost drivers, and E is the exponent that is derived from the five scale drivers.[4] The Costar tool is a commercial tool that implements the Cocomo Mode, and it may be used on small or large projects. It needs to be calibrated to reflect the software engineering environment, and this will enable more accurate estimates to be produced.

Microsoft Project (Fig. 4.2) is a project management tool that is used for planning, scheduling, and charting project information. It enables a realistic project schedule to be created, and the schedule is updated regularly during the project to reflect the actual progress made, and the project is re-planned as appropriate. We discussed project management in Chap. 4.

A project is defined as a series of steps or tasks to achieve a specific goal. The amount of time that it takes to complete a task is termed its duration, and tasks are performed in a sequence determined by the nature of the project. Resources such as people and equipment are required to perform a task. A project will typically consist of several phases such as planning and requirements; design; implementation; testing and closing the project.

The project schedule (Fig. 4.2) shows the tasks and activities to be carried out during the project; the effort and duration of each task and activity; the percentage complete of each task, and the resources needed to carry out the various tasks. The schedule shows how the project will be delivered within the key project parameters such as time, cost, and functionality without compromising quality in any way.

---

[3] SLOC includes delivered source lines of code created by project staff (excluding automated code generated and code comments).
[4] The five scale drivers are factors contributing to duration and cost and they determine the exponent used in the Effort equation. Examples include team cohesion and process maturity.

The project manager is responsible for managing the schedule and will take corrective action when project performance deviates from expectations. The project schedule will be updated regularly to reflect actual progress made, and the project re-planned appropriately.

The project manager may employ tools for recording and managing risks and issues, and this may be as simple as using an excel spreadsheet. The project manager may maintain a lessons-learned log to record the lessons learned during a project, and these will be analysed towards the end of a project and the lessons learned report prepared. The project reporting may be done with a tool or with a standard Microsoft word report.

Project portfolio management (PPM) is concerned with managing a portfolio of projects, and it allows the organization to choose the mix and sequencing of its projects to yield the greatest business benefit to the organization.

PPM tools analyse the project's total expected cost, the resources required, the schedule, the benefits that will be realized as well as interdependencies with other projects in the portfolio. This allows project investment decisions to be made methodically to deliver the greatest benefit to the organization. The approach moves away from the normal once off analysis of an individual project proposal, to the analysis of a portfolio of projects. PPM tools aim to manage the continuous flow of projects from concept all the way to completion.

There are several commercial portfolio management tools available from various vendors. These include Clarity PPM from Computer Associates; Change Point from Compuware; RPM from IBM Rational; PPM Center from HP; and Planview Enterprise from Planview. We limit our discussion in this section to the Planview Enterprise tool.

Planview Enterprise Portfolio Management allows organizations to manage projects and resources across the enterprise, and to align their initiatives for maximum business benefit. It provides visibility into and control of project portfolios and allows the organization to prioritize and manage its projects and resources. This allows it to make better investment decisions, and to balance its business strategy against its available resources. Planview helps an organization to optimize its business through eight key capabilities (Table 21.2).

Planview allows key project performance indicators to be closely tracked, and these include dashboard views of variances of cost, effort, and schedule, which are used for analysis and reporting (Fig. 21.1).

Planview includes Process Builder (Fig. 21.2), which allows modelling and management of enterprise-wide processes. It provides tracking, control, and audit capabilities in key process areas such as requirements management and product development, as well as satisfying key regulatory requirements.

The organization may define and model its processes in Process Builder, and this includes process adoption, compliance, and continuous improvement. The functionality includes:

Table 21.2 Key capabilities of Planview Enterprise

Capability	Description
Strategic planning	Define mission, objectives, and strategies Allocate funding/staffing for chosen strategy Automate and manage strategic process
Investment analysis	Devise strategic long-term plans Identify key criteria to evaluate initiatives Optimze strategic and project investments to maximize business benefit
Capacity management	Balance resources with business demands Ensure capacity supports business strategy Align top down and bottom-up planning Forecast resource capacity
Demand management	Request work & Check status Review lifecycles
Project management	Scope, schedule, and execution of work Track/report time worked against projects Track and manage risks and issues Track/display performance & trend analysis
Financial management	Collaborate to better forecast cost Monitor spending
Resource management	Balance portfolios/assign people efficiently Improve forecasting Keep staff productive
Change management	Determine impact of change on schedule/cost Effectively manage change

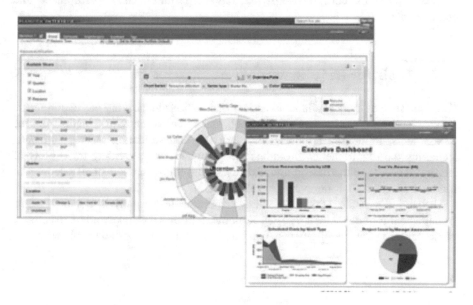

Fig. 21.1 Dashboard views in Planview Enterprise

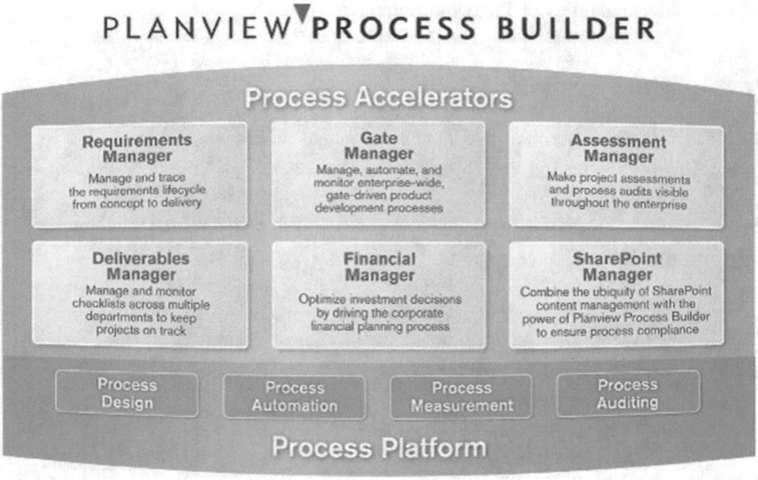

Fig. 21.2 Planview process builder

- Process Design.
- Process Automation.
- Process Measurement.
- Process Auditing.

Next, we will consider tools to support requirements development and management.

21.3   Tools for Requirements

There are several tools available to assist organizations in carrying out requirements development and management. These tools assist in eliciting requirements from the stakeholders; modelling requirements; verifying and validating the requirements; managing the requirements throughout the lifecycle; and providing traceability of the requirements to the design and test cases. The following is a small selection of some of the tools that are available (Table 21.3).

Doors® (Dynamic Object-Oriented Requirements System) is a requirements management tool developed by IBM Rational. It allows the stakeholders to actively participate in the requirements process, and aims to optimize requirements

Table 21.3 Tools for requirements development and management

Tool	Description
DOORS (IBM/Rational)	This is a Requirements Management tool developed by Telelogic (which is now part of IBM/Rational)
Requisite Pro (IBM/Rational)	This is a Requirements Management and Use Case management tool developed by IBM/Rational
Enterprise Architect (Sparx Systems)	This is a UML analysis and design tool that covers requirements gathering, analysis and design, and testing and maintenance. It was developed by Sparx Systems and integrates requirements management with the other software development activities
CORE (Vitech)	This is a requirements tool developed by Vitech, which may be used for modelling and simulation
Integrity (MKS)	This tool was developed by MKS and enables organizations to capture and validate software requirements, and to link them to downstream development and testing activities

communication, collaboration, and verification. High-quality requirements help the organization in reducing costs,[5] and in meeting their business objectives.

The tool can capture, link, trace, analyse, and manage changes to the requirements. It enhances communication and collaboration to ensure that the project conforms to the customer requirements, as well as compliance to regulations and standards.

Requirements are documented in a way that is easy to interpret and navigate. It is easy to locate information within the database, and the user requirements are recorded in a document style showing each individual requirement. It provides views of the list with assigned identifiers and an Explorer-like navigation tree.

The tool employs links to support traceability of the requirements, and these are traversed with a simple click of the mouse to the corresponding object. The links are easy to create by dragging and dropping, e.g., a new link from the user requirements to the system requirements is created in this way. The tool provides dynamic reporting on traceability, and filters may be employed to ensure that traceability is complete. Traceability is essential in demonstrating that the requirements have been implemented and tested.

The management of change is an important part of the requirements process. The DOORS tool supports changes to requirements and allows an impact analysis of the proposed changes to be performed. It allows changes that could impact other requirements or design items and test cases to be tagged. The DOORS® tool (Fig. 21.3) provides:

---

[5] A good requirements process will enable high-quality requirements to be consistently produced, and the cost of poor quality is reduced as wastage and rework is minimized. The requirements are the foundation of the system and if they are incorrect then the delivered system will not be fit for purpose.

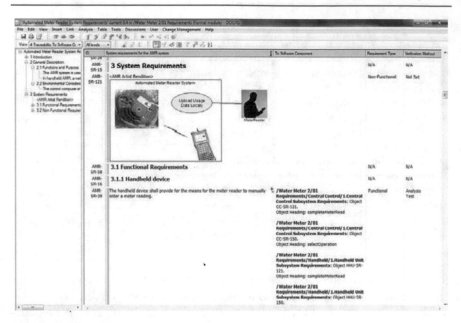

Fig. 21.3 IBM Rational Doors tool

- A comprehensive requirements management environment.
- Web browser access to the requirements database.
- Manages changes to requirements.
- Scalable solution for managing project scope and cost
- Traceability to design items, test plans and test cases.
- Active engagement from stakeholders.
- Integrates with other IBM Rational tools.

There are several other IBM Rational tools that may be integrated with Doors®.
These include the IBM Rational System Architect, Requirements Composer,
Rhapsody, and Quality Manager.

IBM Rational RequisitePro is a requirements management tool that allows
requirements to be documented with familiar document-based methods, and it
provides capabilities such as requirements traceability and impact analysis.
Requirements are managed throughout the lifecycle, and changes to the requirements controlled.

The Core product suite was developed by Vitech, and it has functionality for
requirements management, modelling and simulation, and verification and validation. It supports UML activity and sequence diagrams, which are used to describe
the desired behaviour and flow of control, as well as allowing analysis to be carried
out. The tool provides:

- Comprehensive end-to-end system traceability.
- Change impact analysis.
- Multiple modelling notations with integrated graphical views.
- System simulation based on behavioural models.
- Generation of Documentation from the database.

The Integrity tool was developed by MKS and it enables organizations to capture and validate software requirements. It enables them to link the requirements to downstream development and testing activities, and to manage changes to the requirements. Next, we will consider tools to support software design and development.

21.4 Tools for Design and Development

This section describes various tools to support software design and development activities. The software design includes the high-level architecture of the system, as well as the lower-level design and algorithms. There are various tools available including (Table 21.4).

IBM Rational Software Modeler® (RSM) is a UML-based visual modelling and design tool (Fig. 21.3). It promotes communication and collaboration during design and development and allows information about development projects to be specified and communicated from several perspectives. It is used for model-driven development and aligns the business needs with the product (Fig. 21.4).

It gives the organization control over the evolving architecture and provides an integrated analysis and design platform. Abstract UML specifications may be built with traceability and impact analysis shown.

It has an intuitive user interface and a diagram editor to create expressive and interactive diagrams. The tool may be integrated with other IBM Rational tools such as Clearcase, Clearquest and Requisite Pro.

Table 21.4 Tools for software design

Tool	Description
Microsoft Visio	This tool is used to create many types of drawings such as flowcharts, workflow diagrams and network diagrams
IBM Rational Software Modeler	This is a UML based visual modelling and software design tool
IBM Rational Rhapsody	This modelling environment tool is based on UML and provides a visual development environment for software engineers. It uses graphical models and generates code in C, C++, and Java
IBM Rational Software Architect	This modelling and development tool uses UML for designing architecture for C++ and Java applications
Enterprise Architect (Sparx Systems)	This UML analysis and design tool is used for modelling systems with traceability from requirements to design and testing. It supports code generation

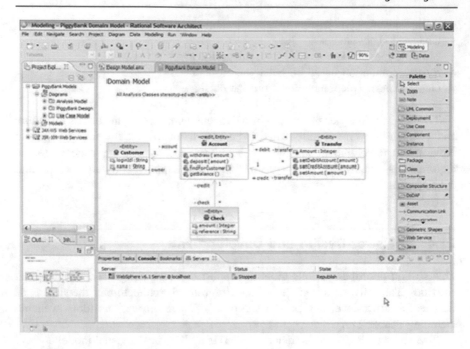

Fig. 21.4 IBM Rational Software Modeler

IBM Rational Rhapsody® is a visual development environment used in real-time or embedded systems. It helps teams collaborate to understand and elaborate requirements; abstract complexity using modelling languages such as UML; validate functionality early in development; and automate code generation to speed up the development process.

Sparx Enterprise Architect (Fig. 21.5) is a UML analysis and design tool used for modelling business and IT systems. It was developed by the Australian company, Sparx Systems, and it covers the full product development lifecycle, including business modelling, requirements management, software design, code generation, and testing. It supports automated document generation, code generation and reverse engineering of source code. Its reverse engineering feature allows a visual representation of the software application to be provided.

It is a multi-user graphical tool with built in reporting and documentation. It can model, manage and trace requirements to the design, test cases and deployment, and it can trace the implementation of the system requirements to model elements. It can search and report on requirements and perform an impact analysis on proposed changes to the requirements.

The tool allows deployments scripts to be built, debugged, and tested and executed from within its development environment. UML and modelling are integrated into the development process and debugging capabilities are provided. This includes run time examination of the executing code for several programming languages, and NUnit and JUnit test classes (used as part of test-driven development) may be generated and integrated directly into the test process.

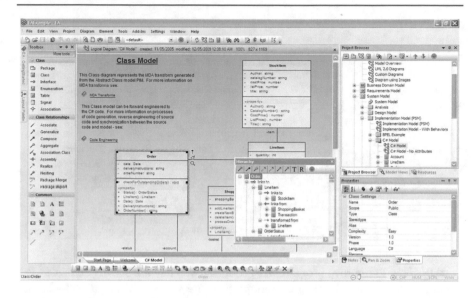

Fig. 21.5 Sparx Enterprise Architect

An integrated development environment (IDE) is a software application that provides comprehensive support facilities to software developers. It includes specialized text editors; a compiler; build automation; and debugging capabilities. The features of an IDE are described in Table 21.5.

Table 21.5 Integrated development environment

Item	Description
Source code editor	This is a specialized text editor (e.g., Microsoft Visual Studio) designed for editing the source code. It includes features to speed up the input of source code, including syntax checking of the code while the programmer types
Compiler or interpreter	A compiler is a computer program that translates the high-level programming language source code into object code to produce the executable code. A compiler carries out lexical analysis, parsing and code generation An interpreter is a program that executes instructions written in a programming language. It may involve the direction execution of the code; translation of the code into an intermediate representation and immediate direct execution; or execution of stored precompiled code made by a compiler which is part of the Interpreter System
Build automation tools	Build automation involves scripting to automate the build process. This includes tasks such as compiling the source code; linking the object code and building the executable software; performing automated tests and reporting results; reporting the build status; and generating release notes
Debugger	A debugger is a software application that is used to debug and test other software programs. Debuggers offer step by step execution of the code, or execution to breakpoints in the code. Examples include IBM Rational Purify and Microsoft Visual Studio Debugger

Table 21.6 Features of Jira for Agile project management

Item	Description
Customizable scrum boards	The scrum boards are customizable as per project needs and the team's workflow and it may be used to visualize all of the work in a sprint
Flexible Kanban boards	A Kanban board is an agile project management tool designed to help visualize work, as well as limiting work in progress and maximizing efficiencies. It helps in ensuring that the team commits to the right amount of work and gets it done
Agile reporting	Jira reports provide critical insights for the scrum team including sprint reports, burnout charts, release burndown, and velocity charts. Jira agile reports enable Kanban teams to predict future performance and spot bottlenecks
Customizable workflows	Jira has its own built-in workflows such as Task Management that gets tasks done as soon as possible. It is easy to customize workflows (e.g., adding screens to the workflow transitions)

IDEs help to improve programmer productivity. They are usually dedicated to a specific programming language, although there are some multi-language tools such as Eclipse and Microsoft Visual Studio. There are many IDEs for languages such as Pascal, C, C++, and Java. The next section is concerned with tools to support Agile Development.

21.5 Tools for Agile Development

There are several tools to support Agile software development and we discuss one of the more popular tools in this section. Atlassian Jira is one of the most popular project management tools used by Agile teams in software development. The tool was originally developed as an issue tracking tool in 2002, but today, it is used for Agile project management, and includes features such as (Table 21.6)

21.6 Tools for Configuration Management and Change Control

Configuration management is concerned with identifying the work products that are subject to change control and controlling changes to them. It involves creating and releasing baselines, maintaining their integrity, recording and reporting the status of the configuration items and change requests, and verifying the correctness and completeness of the configuration items with configuration audits.

Visual Source Safe (VSS) is a version control management system for source code and binary files. It was developed by the Microsoft Corporation and is used mainly by small software development organizations. It allows multiple users to place their source code and work products under version control management. It is easy to use and may be integrated with the Microsoft Visual Studio tool. Microsoft has replaced VSS with its Visual Studio Team System tool.

Polytron Version Control System (PVCS) is a version control system for software code and binary files. It was developed by Serena Software Inc. and is suitable for use by large or small teams. It allows multiple users to place their source code and project deliverables under version control management and it allows files to be checked in and checked out; baselines to be controlled; roll-back of code; and tracking of check-ins. It includes functionality for branching, merging, and labelling. It includes the PV Tracker tool for tracking defects, and the PV Builder tool for performing builds and releases.

The PV Tracker tool automates the capture and communication of issues and change requests. This is done throughout the software development lifecycle for project teams, and the tool allows the developers to link the affected source code files with issues and changes. It allows managers to determine and report on team progress, and to prioritize tasks. PV Builder maintains an audit trail of the files included in the build as well as their versions.

IBM Rational Clearcase and Clearquest are popular configuration management tools with a rich feature set. Clearcase allows software code and other software deliverables to be placed under version control management, and it may be employed in large or medium projects. It can handle many files and supports standard configuration management tasks such as checking in and checking out of the software assets as well as labelling and branching. Objects are stored in repositories called VOBs.

Clearquest may be linked to Clearcase as well as to other IBM Rational tools. It allows the defects in a project to be tracked, and it allows the versions of source code modules that were changed to be linked to a defect number in Clearquest.

21.7 Tools for Code Analysis and Code Inspections

Static code analysis is the analysis of software code without the actual execution of the code. It is usually performed with automated tools and the analysis performed depends on the sophistication of the tools. Some tools may analyse individual statements or declarations, whereas others may analyse the whole source code. The objective of the analysis is to highlight potential coding errors early in the development lifecycle.

The LDRA Tools automatically determine the complexity of the source code and provide metrics that give an indication of the maintainability of the code. A useful feature of LDRA is that it gives a visual picture of system complexity, and it has a re-factoring tool to assist with its reduction. It generates code assessment reports listing all the files examined, and providing metrics of the clarity, maintainability and testability of the code. Other LDRA tools may be used for code coverage analysis (Fig. 21.6).

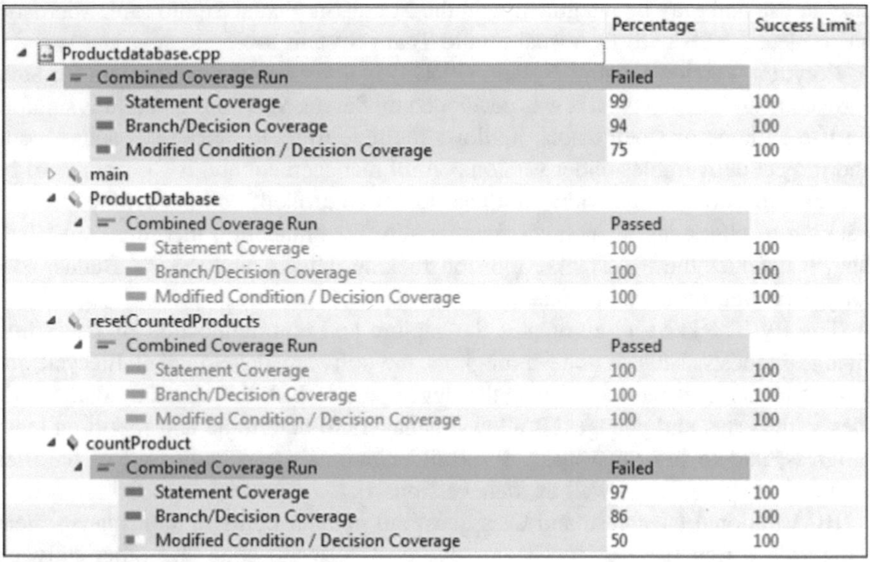

	Percentage	Success Limit
◢ 📄 Productdatabase.cpp		
◢ ▱ Combined Coverage Run	Failed	
▪ Statement Coverage	99	100
▪ Branch/Decision Coverage	94	100
▪ Modified Condition / Decision Coverage	75	100
▷ ◈ main		
◢ ◈ ProductDatabase		
◢ ▱ Combined Coverage Run	Passed	
▪ Statement Coverage	100	100
▪ Branch/Decision Coverage	100	100
▪ Modified Condition / Decision Coverage	100	100
◢ ◈ resetCountedProducts		
◢ ▱ Combined Coverage Run	Passed	
▪ Statement Coverage	100	100
▪ Branch/Decision Coverage	100	100
▪ Modified Condition / Decision Coverage	100	100
◢ ◈ countProduct		
◢ ▱ Combined Coverage Run	Failed	
▪ Statement Coverage	97	100
▪ Branch/Decision Coverage	86	100
▪ Modified Condition / Decision Coverage	50	100

Fig. 21.6 LDRA code coverage analysis report

Compliance to coding standards is important in producing readable code and in preventing error-prone coding styles. There are several tools available to check conformance to coding standards including the LDRA TBvision tool, which has reporting capabilities to show code quality as well as fault detection and avoidance measures. It provides intuitive functionality to view the results in various graphs and reports.

Some static code analysis tools (e.g., tools for formal methods) aim to prove properties about a particular program. This may include reasoning about program correctness or that of a program meeting its specification. These tools often provide support for assertions, and a precondition is the assertion placed before the code fragment, and this predicate is true before execution of the code. The post-condition is the assertion placed after the code fragment, and this predicate is true after the execution of the code.

There are several open-source tools available for static code analysis, and these include the RATS tools which provide multi-language support for C, C++, Perl and PHP, and the PMD tool for Java. There are several commercial tools available, and these include the LDRA Testbed tool which provides support for C, C++ and Java; The Fortify tool helps developers to identify security vulnerabilities in C, C++ and Java; and the Parasoft tool helps developers to identify coding issues that lead to security, reliability, performance, and maintainability issues later.

21.8 Tools for Testing

Testing plays a key role in verifying that the software system satisfies the requirements and is fit for purpose. There are various tools to support testing such as test management tools; defect tracking tools; regression test automation tools; performance tools; and so on [2]. The tools considered in this section include:

- Test Director (HP Quality Center).
- Winrunner.
- Load Runner.

Test Director (now called HP Quality Center) is a web-based test management tool developed by HP Mercury.[6] It provides a consistent repeatable process for gathering requirements; planning and scheduling tests; analysing results; and managing defects. It consists of four modules namely:

- Requirements.
- Test Plan.
- Test Lab.
- Defect Management.

The Requirements module supports requirements management and traceability of the test cases to the requirements. The Test Plan module supports the creation and update of test cases. The Test Lab module supports execution of the test cases defined in the Test Plan module. The Defect Management module supports the logging of defects, and these defects can be linked back to the test cases that failed.

HP Quality Center supports a high-level of collaboration and communication between the stakeholders. It allows the business analysts to define the application requirements and testing objectives. The test managers and testers may then design test plans, test cases and automated scripts. The testers then run the manual and automated tests, report results and log the defects. The developers review and correct the logged defects. Project and test managers can create status reports and manage test resources. Test and product managers decide objectively whether the application is ready to be released.

The HP Quality Center™ tool (Fig. 21.7) standardizes and manages the entire test and quality process and is a web-based system for automated software quality management and testing. It employs dashboard technology to give visibility into the process.

Mercury developed the Winrunner tool that automatically captures, verifies, and replays user interactions. It is used mainly used to automate regression testing, which improves productivity and allows defects to be identified in a timely manner.

---

[6] Mercury is now part of HP.

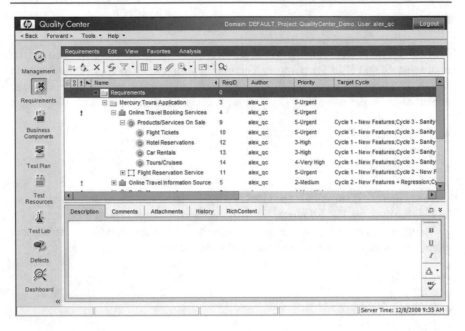

Fig. 21.7 HP Quality Center

This provides confidence that enhancements to the software have had no negative impact on the integrity of the system. The Winrunner tool has been replaced by HP Unified Functional Testing Software, which includes HP Quick Test Professional and HP Service Test.

Mercury developed the LoadRunner performance testing tool, which allows a software application to be tested with thousands of concurrent users to determine its performance under heavy loads. It allows the scalability of the software system to be determined, and whether it can support future predicted growth.

21.9 Review Questions

1. Why are tools used in software engineering?
2. How should a tool be selected?
3. What is the relationship between the process and the tool?
4. What tools would you recommend for project management?
5. Describe how you would go about selecting a tool for requirements development.

6. Describe various tools that are available for design and development.
7. What tools would you recommend for testing?
8. What tools would you recommend for configuration management?

21.10 Summary

The objective of this chapter was to give a flavour of various tools available to support the organization in engineering software. These included tools for project management, configuration management, design and development, test management, and so on. The tools are chosen to support the process.

The project management tools included a discussion of the Cocomo Cost Model, which may be employed to estimate the cost and effort for a project; and the Microsoft Project tool, which is used extensively by project managers to schedule and track their projects. The Planview Portolio Management Tool was also discussed, and this tool allows an organization to manage a portfolio of projects.

The tools to support requirements development and management included IBM Rational Doors, Requisite Pro and Core. The Doors tool allows all stakeholders to actively participate in the requirements process, and aims to optimize requirements communication, collaboration and verification.

The tools to support design and development included the IBM Rational Software Modeler tool, the Sparx Enterprise Architect tool and Integrated Developer Environments to support software developers. The Rational Software Modeler® (RSM) is a UML-based visual modelling and design tool. Enterprise Architect is a UML analysis and design tool, and provides traceability from requirements to design, testing and deployment. The tools discussed to support configuration management included PVCS and Clearcase.

The tools to support testing included Quality Center™, Winrunner and Loadrunner tools. HP Quality Center™ standardizes and manages the entire test process. It has modules for requirements management, test planning, test lab and defect management.

Tool selection is done in a controlled manner. First, the organization needs to determine its requirements for the tool. Various candidate tools are evaluated and a decision on the proposed tool is made. Next, the tool is piloted to ensure that it meets the needs of the organization, and feedback from the pilot may lead to changes or customizations of the tool. Finally, the end users are trained on the use of the tool and it is rolled out throughout the organization.

References

1. B. Boehm, *Software Engineering Economics* (Prentice Hall, New Jersey, 1981)
2. G. O'Regan, *Concise Guide to Software Testing* (Springer, 2019)

A Miscellany of Innovation

22

Abstract

This chapter discusses innovation in the software field including miscellaneous topics such as distributed systems, service-oriented architecture, software as a service, cloud computing and embedded systems. We discuss the need for innovation in software engineering and discuss some recent innovations including aspect-oriented software engineering.

Keywords

Distributed systems · Service-oriented architecture · Software as a service · Cloud computing · Aspect-oriented software engineering · Embedded systems · Innovation in software engineering

22.1 Introduction

The objective of this chapter is to give a flavour of several topics that have become relevant to the software engineering field in recent times. The software field is highly innovative and continually evolving, and this has led to the development of many new technologies and systems. This includes distributed systems, service-oriented architecture (SOA), software as a service (SaaS), cloud computing, embedded systems, and many more. Software engineering needs to continually respond to the emerging technology trends with innovative solutions and methodologies to support the latest developments.

A distributed system is a collection of computers that appears to be a single system, and many large computer systems used today are distributed systems. A distributed system allows hardware and software resources to be shared, and it supports concurrency with multiple processors running on different computers on the network.

© Springer Nature Switzerland AG 2022   383
G. O'Regan, *Concise Guide to Software Engineering*,
Undergraduate Topics in Computer Science,
https://doi.org/10.1007/978-3-031-07816-3_22

Service-oriented architecture (SOA) is a way of developing a distributed system consisting of stand-alone web services that may be executing on distributed computers in different geographic regions. Software as a service (SaaS) allows software to be hosted remotely on a server (or servers), and the user can access the software over the Internet through a web browser. Cloud computing is a type of internet-based computing that provides computing resources and various other services on demand.

An embedded system is a computer system within a larger electrical or mechanical system, and it is *embedded* as part of a complete system that includes hardware and mechanical parts. An embedded system is usually designed to do a specific task rather than as a general-purpose device, and it may be subject to real time performance constraints.

Many innovative software engineering practices have been developed since the birth of software engineering. We discuss aspect-oriented software engineering (AOSE), which is based on the principle of separation of concerns. It states that software should be organized so that each program element does exactly one thing and one thing only. AOSE has been applied to requirements engineering, software design and programming, with the goal is to make it easier to maintain and reuse the software.

22.2 Distributed Systems

A distributed system (Fig. 22.1) is a collection of computers, interconnected via a network, which can collaborate on a task. It appears to be a single integrated computing system to the user, and most large computer systems today are distributed systems. The components (or nodes) of a distributed system are located on networked computers and interact to achieve a common goal.

The communication and coordination of action is via message passing. A distributed system is not centrally controlled, and as a result the individual computers may behave differently at different times, and each computer has a limited and incomplete view of the system.

Fig. 22.1 A distributed system

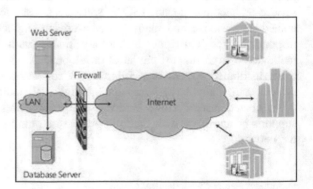

A distributed system allows hardware and software resources (e.g., printers and files) to be shared, and information may be shared between people and processes located in distant geographical regions. It supports concurrency with multiple processors running on different computers on the network. The processors in a distributed system run concurrently in parallel, and each computer is running on its own local operating system.

A distributed system is designed to tolerate failures on individual computers, and the system is designed to be reliable and to continue service when a node fails. Another words, a distributed system needs to be designed to be fault tolerant, and it must remain available even if there are hardware, software, or network failures. This requires recovery and redundancy features such as the duplication of information on several computers to be built in. The fault tolerant design allows continuity of service (possibly a degraded service) when failures occur.

The design of distributed systems is more complex than a centralized system, as there may be complex interactions between its components and the system infrastructure. The performance of the distributed system is dependent on the network bandwidth and load, as well on the speed of the computers that are on the network. This differs from a centralized system, which is dependent on the speed of a single processor. The performance and response time of a distributed system may vary (and be unpredictable) depending on the network load and network bandwidth, and so the response time may vary from user to user.

The nodes in a distributed system are often independent systems with no central control, and the network connecting the nodes is a complex system, which is not controlled by the systems using the network. There are many applications of distributed system in the telecommunication domain, such as fixed line, mobile and wireless networks, company intranets, the Internet, and the World Wide Web. Next, we describe service-oriented architecture and how it is used in distributed systems.

22.3 Service-Oriented Architecture

The objective of this section is to give a brief introduction to service-oriented architecture (SOA), which is a way of developing a distributed system using stand-alone web services executing on distributed computers in different geographic regions. It is an approach to create an architecture based upon the use of services, where a service may carry out some small function such as producing data or validating a customer.

A web service is a computational or information resource that may be used by another program, and it allows a service provider to provide a service to an application (*service requestor*) that wishes to use the service. The web service may be accessed remotely and is acted upon independently. The *service provider* is responsible for designing and implementing the services and specifying the interface to the service.

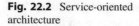

Fig. 22.2 Service-oriented architecture

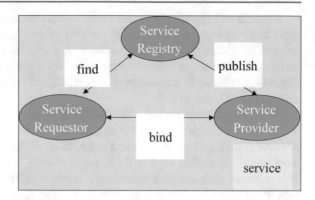

The service is platform and implementation language independent, and it is designed and implemented by the service provider with the interface to the service specified. Information about the service is published in an accessible registry, and service clients (requestor) can locate the service provider and link their application with the specific service and communicate with it. The idea of a SOA is illustrated in Fig. 22.2.

There are several standards that support communication between services, as well as standards for service interface definition. These are discussed in [1].

22.4   Software as a Service

The idea of software as a service (SaaS) is that the software may be hosted remotely on a server (or servers), and access provided to it over the Internet through a web browser. The functionality is provided at the remote server with client access provided through the web browser.

The cost model for traditional software is made up of an up-front cost for a perpetual license and optional on-going support fees. SaaS is a software licensing and delivery model where the software is licensed to the user on a subscription basis. The software provider owns and provides the service, whereas the software organization that is using the service will pay a subscription for its use. Occasionally, the software is free to use with funding for the service provided using advertisements, or there may be a free basic service provided with charges applied for the more advanced version.

A key benefit of SaaS is that the cost of hosting and management of the service is transferred to the service provider, with the provider responsible for resolving defects and installing upgrades of the software. Consequently, the initial set up costs for users is significantly less than for traditional software.

The disadvantages to the user are that data must be transferred at the speed of the network, and the transfer of a large amount of data may take a lot of time. The subscription charges may be monthly or annual, with extra charges possibly due depending on the amount of data transferred.

22.5   Cloud Computing

Cloud computing is a type of Internet-based computing that provides computing processing resources on demand. It provides access to a shared pool of configurable computing resources such as networks, servers and applications on-demand, and such resources may be provided and released with minimal effort. It provides users and organizations with capabilities to store and process their data in third party data centres that may be in distant geographical locations.

A key advantage of cloud computing is that it allows companies to avoid large up-front infrastructure costs such as purchasing hardware and servers, and it also allows organizations to focus on their core business. Further, it allows companies to get their applications operational in a shorter period, as well as providing an efficient way for companies to adjust resources to deal with fluctuating demand. Companies can scale up as computing needs increase and scale down as demand decreases. Cloud providers generally use a "pay as you go" model (Fig. 22.3).

Among the well-known cloud computing platforms are Amazon's Elastic Compute Cloud, Microsoft's Azure and Oracle's cloud. The main enabling technology for cloud computing is virtualization, which separates a physical computing device into one or more virtual devices. Each of the virtual devices may be easily used and managed to perform computing tasks, and this leads to the creation of a

Fig. 22.3 Cloud computing.
Creative Commons

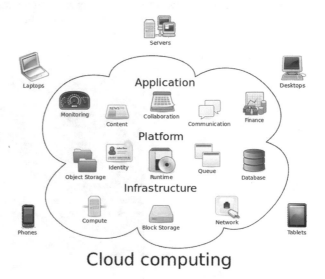

Cloud computing

scalable system of multiple independent computing devices that allows the idle physical resources to be allocated and used more effectively.

Cloud computing providers offer their services according to different models. These include infrastructure as a service (IaaS) where computing infrastructure such as virtual machines and other resources are provided as a service to subscribers. Platform as a service (Paas) provides capability to the consumer to deploy infrastructure related or application related that are supported by the provider onto the cloud. PaaS vendors offer a development platform to application developers. Software as a service (SaaS) provides capability to the consumer to use the provider's applications running on a cloud infrastructure through a web browser or a program interface. Cloud providers manage the infrastructure and platforms that run the applications.

22.6 Embedded Systems

An embedded system is a computer system within a larger electrical or mechanical system that is usually subject to real time constraints. The computer system is *embedded* as part of a complete system that includes hardware and mechanical parts. Embedded systems vary from personal devices such as MP3 players and mobile phones, to household devices such as dishwashers and cookers, to the automotive sector, and to traffic lights. An embedded system is usually designed to do a specific task rather than as a general-purpose device, and it may be subject to real time performance constraints (Fig. 22.4).

Some embedded systems are termed *reactive systems* as they react to events that occur in their environment, and so their design is often based on a stimulus–response model. An event (or condition) that occurs in the system environment that causes the system to respond in some way is termed a stimulus, and a response is a signal sent by the software to its environment. For example, in the automotive

Fig. 22.4 Example of an embedded system

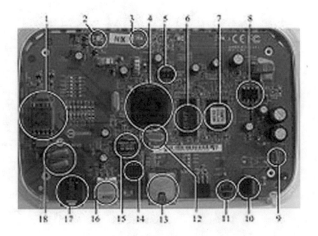

sector there are sensors in a car that detect when the temperature in the engine goes too high, and the response may be an audio alarm and visual warning to the driver.

One of the earliest embedded system was the guidance computer developed for the Minuteman II missile [2] in the mid-1960s. Embedded systems are ubiquitous today, and they control many devices that are in common use such as microwave ovens, washing machines, coffee makers, clocks, DVD players, mobile phones and televisions.

Embedded systems became more popular following the introduction of the microprocessor in the early 1970s, as cheap microprocessors were able to fulfil the same role as many components. Most microprocessors produced today are used as components of embedded systems.

22.7 Software Engineering and Innovation

The software field is highly innovative, and many new technologies and systems have been developed. We have discussed a sample of these innovations in this chapter, and the software engineering field needs to continually respond to these emerging technology trends with innovative solutions and methodologies to support the latest developments.

There have been many innovations in software engineering since its birth in the late 1960s. These include the waterfall and spiral lifecycle models, the Rational Unified Process, and iterative development; the Agile methodology; software inspections and reviews; software testing and test-driven development; information hiding, object-oriented design and development; formal methods and UML; software process improvement, the CMM, CMMI and ISO SPICE.

There is also the need to focus on best practice in software engineering, as well as emerging technologies from various research programs. Piloting or technology transfer of innovative technology is an important part of continuous improvement. We discuss aspect-oriented software engineering to illustrate innovation in software engineering.

22.7.1 Aspect-Oriented Software Engineering

The objective of this section is to give a brief introduction to aspect-oriented software engineering (AOSE), which is an innovation in software engineering based on the principle of separation of concerns. This principle states that software should be organized so that each program element does exactly one thing and one thing only. It is an important way to think about and structure software systems and makes it easier to maintain and reuse the software. Aspect-oriented software engineering may be applied to requirements engineering, software design and programming.

Concerns reflect system requirements and examples of concerns are specific functionality, performance requirements, security requirements, and so on. In most systems, the mapping between the requirements (concerns) and components is not one to one, and this means that the implementation of a change to the requirements may involve changes to more than one component. AOSE is an approach that aims to address this problem, and it is based on the idea of an aspect, which is a program abstraction that encapsulates functionality based on the separation of concerns. Programs that have been designed with the principle of separation of concerns have clear traceability to the requirements.

The principle of separation of concerns is a key principle in software engineering and requires that the software be organized in such a way that each element in the program (e.g., class, procedure) does exactly one thing. Another words, it is a design principle that separates a computer program into distinct sections such that each section addresses a separate concern.

A modular program implements the principle of separation of concerns through information hiding, where access to the module is through a well-defined interface with the information inside the module hidden. The value of the principle of separation of concerns is that individual sections of programs may be reused or modified independently without needing to be familiar with or modifying other sections of the program.

22.8   Review Questions

1. What is a distributed system?
2. What is service-oriented architecture?
3. What is software as a service?
4. What is cloud computing?
5. What is embedded software engineering?
6. Describe the various models that are used in cloud computing.
7. What is aspect-oriented software engineering?

22.9   Summary

This chapter gave a brief introduction to distributed systems, service-oriented architecture, software as a service, cloud computing, embedded systems, and aspect-oriented software engineering.

A distributed system is a collection of interconnected computers that appears to be a single system. Service-oriented architecture is a way of developing a distributed system consisting of stand-alone web service executing on distributed computers in different geographic regions. Software as a service allows software to be hosted remotely on a server (or servers), and access is provided to it over the Internet through a web browser. Cloud computing is a type of internet-based computing that provides computing resources and various other services on demand.

An embedded system is a computer system within a larger electrical or mechanical system, and it is usually designed to do a specific task rather than as a general purpose device, and it may be subject to real time performance constraints.

Aspect-oriented software engineering is based on the principle of separation of concerns, and it has been applied to requirements engineering, software design and programming, with the goal is to make it easier to maintain and reuse the software.

References

1. I. Sommerville, *Software Engineering*, 9th edn. (Pearson, 2011)
2. G. O'Regan, *Introduction to the History of Computing* (Springer, 2016)

Legal Aspects of Software Engineering

23

Abstract

This chapter is concerned with the application of the legal system to the computing field. This includes the protection of intellectual property such as patents, copyright, trademarks and trade secrets, and the resolution of disputes between parties.

Keywords

Law of tort · Lawsuits · Professional responsibility · Professional negligence · Outsourcing · Software licenses

23.1 Introduction

The legal system consists of a set of laws and rules that guides human behaviour by permitting some actions and forbidding others. Laws are made by the state, and a particular act is either permitted or not. There are consequences (enforced by the state) for those who do not follow the rules. A good law is generally moral, but law has no necessary basis in morality, and immoral laws could be part of the legal system.

There are two broad classes of the legal system namely criminal law and civil law. Criminal law refers to the laws governing crimes against the state, whereas civil law is used to resolve disputes that arise between two parties.

Morality does not directly tell us what we should or shouldn't do, and it is in a sense a set of standards to evaluate good or bad behaviour. An individual needs to be conscious of ethical concerns in situations that arise in human existence, and to use their moral compass and values to do what he or she believes to be the right thing. Moral standards are important for the proper functioning of society.

Modern society is governed by various rules of behaviour such as rules of etiquette, rules from religion, rules of membership of an organization, and laws (legal rules) of behaviour. Laws are made by the legislature of the state and may be enforced by the various organs of the state with fines or imprisonment.

The origin of civil law is from the Roman world, and this is a codified system that specifies the rules and regulations for the purpose of providing civil order in a society. They specify what may be brought to court as well as the applicable procedures and punishment. These laws are generally produced by legislation in parliaments, and judges interpret the law and the intentions of parliament. They may interpret the law literally or modify the interpretation (e.g., extending the definition in a statue or considering what problem the legislators were attempting to solve) to prevent absurd results. The role of the judge is to establish the facts and to apply the applicable code.

English common law developed in England from the twelfth century, when King Henry II developed a single system of justice for the entire country that would be under the control of the king. Judges play an important role in making the law in that their decisions establish legal principles, and the system operates on the principle of *binding precedent* where the judge in a particular case must follow the decision of judges in previous similar cases.

Legal aspects of computing are concerned with the application of the legal system to the computing field. This includes the protection of intellectual property such as patents, copyright, trademarks and trade secrets, and the resolution of disputes between parties. Patents provide legal protection for intellectual ideas such as inventions; copyright law protects the expression of an idea such as the software code; and trademarks provide legal protection of names or symbols (e.g., Apple or Amazon).

There are potential legal consequences to an organization that has developed software that has had serious quality problems causing harm or damages to others, and where the software has been inadequately developed and tested, or where the development and testing practices are deemed to be inadequate or negligent.

The use of software is generally subject to a license, where a software license is a legal agreement between the copyright owner and the licensee that governs the use or distribution of software to the user. The two most common categories of software licenses that may be granted under copyright law are those for proprietary software and those for free open-source software. The software license agreement provides limited warranties on the quality of the software, and limited remedies when the software is defective.

There are potential legal implications on both parties during bespoke software development and test outsourcing, where a legal contract is prepared between the supplier and the customer. This will generally include a statement of work that stipulates the deliverables to be produced, and it may also include a service level agreement and an Escrow agreement. Such contracts specify what will be delivered and when as well as quality expectations, and the milestone payments are generally linked to the completion of the agreed deliverables and acceptance of them at key project milestones. Such agreements often provide greater legal remedy than software that has been provided under license, as there is a clear contract between both parties.

Computer crime includes the unauthorized access of computer resources, the theft of personal information, cyber extortion, and denial of service attacks. The problem of hacking is where a hacker uses his (or her) computer skills to gain unauthorized access to a computer system. We distinguish between ethical white hat hackers and malicious black hat hackers, where white hat hackers play a role in improving system security, whereas black hat hackers seek to exploit vulnerabilities for financial or malicious gain.

Electronic commerce includes transactions to place an order, the acknowledgement of the order, the acceptance of the order where a legal contract now exists between both parties, and order fulfilment. The contract specifies the terms and places responsibilities on both parties, and such contracts generally have a cooling off period, where the buyer may cancel the contract without penalty (but the buyer would be subject to the costs involved in returning the goods in the case of cancellation).

23.2 Intellectual Property

Intellectual property law deals with the rules that apply in protecting inventions, designs, and artistic work, and in enforcing such rights. Intangible assets such as software designs or inventions may be protected in a similar way to the protection of private property, and the inventor is generally granted exclusive rights to the invention for a defined period. This gives the inventor the incentive to develop creative works that may benefit society, as it allows the owner of the invention to profit from their work without fear of misappropriation by others.

The main forms of intellectual property are patents, copyright, and trademarks. Patents give inventors exclusive rights to their invention for a specified period (possibly up to 20 years), or to profit from the invention by transferring the right to another party. A *patent* protects innovative ideas and concepts, and the invention itself must be novel and more than an obvious next step from existing technology. The patent needs to be filed at the Patent Office, and the patent gives the inventor protection against patent infringement in a specific country or region of the world.

A *copyright* applies to original writing, music, motion pictures and other original intellectual and artistic expressions. It does not protect the underlying idea as such, and what is protected is the expression of the idea. Copyrights are exclusive rights to making copies of the expression, where the ways of expressing ideas is copyrightable. Copyright law protects computer software source code from being copied by third parties without obtaining the required permission. The term *"fair use"* refers to the permitted limited use of copyrightable material without acquiring permission from the copyright owner.

A *trademark* protects names or symbols that are used to identify goods or services, and their purpose is to avoid confusion and to help customers to distinguish one brand from another.

A *trade secret* is information that provides competitive advantage over others, and it is of value only if it is kept secret. It applies in the computer sector where programs may use algorithms that are unknown to others.[1]

23.2.1 Patents

Patents are the strongest part of intellectual property, and they provide much stronger protection than copyright or trademarks. They protect the implementation of innovative ideas and inventions for a period (often up to 20 years), but the time interval of protection is much shorter than with copyrights (70 years after the life of the author) or trademarks (often indefinite). They are expensive to apply for and costly to obtain/defend, but they in effect give the inventor a monopoly (or exclusive rights) to exploit the invention during the lifetime of the patent, and all others need the permission of the patent holder to use the invention. At the end of the lifetime of the patent the invention becomes public domain with unrestrictive use.

A patent may be for an innovative idea for a product or a process for making something in a new way. There are several types of patents such as *utility patents* that are patents for a novel, useful and functional invention. These are the most common type of patent and are the most useful and profitable. There is a variation termed the *utility model* for small useful functional innovations. These patents are narrow in focus and so do not merit a utility patent as such, and they often refer to something small in the manufacturing process. These tend to be inexpensive and fast to obtain, and they are often called petty or minor patents. *Design patents* protect the beauty or design of a manufactured product, and so it is essentially like the copyright of the design of the manufactured product. It protects the appearance of the product but not its functionality (Fig. 23.1).

A utility patent protects the idea or function (the way it works) of something useful such as the invention of a product or a process, whereas a design pattern protects the expression of the idea such as the appearance of the product. For example, the *iPhone* has over 2000 utility patents protecting how various parts of the phone work, but it only has a small number of design patents that protect its appearance. Often utility patents apply to sub-elements of the product rather than to the product itself, and so instead many functions of the product are patented, as the product itself is too big to patent.

The benefits of patents to society are that they encourage investment and the development of useful products and foster a culture of innovation in the state as the inventor and wider society benefits from the exploitation of the invention. Trade secrets were a common way to protect inventions prior to the widespread use of

---

[1] It is not illegal to use reverse engineering to try to discover the trade secret.

Fig. 23.1 Patent for an invention

patents, but their disadvantage is that other companies were unaware of the latest developments. The granting of exclusive rights to the inventor for a temporary time period (the lifetime of the patent) fosters the publication of inventions and encourages their commercial exploitation as the inventor has exclusive (or monopoly rights) for a period of time. This is especially important in situations where there are large costs and major risks involved in bringing a product to market such as in the pharmaceutical sector. Further, the invention or technology may be licensed (for a fee) to other companies during the lifetime of the patent. For example, there are many patents on mobile phones, and companies may license their patents to the manufacturers that make the phones.

The disadvantage of patents is that they may impact competition as they act as a barrier to market entry. A market participant may be reluctant to enter the market due to the high charges incurred for each licensed patent, and existing participants may be discouraged and depart the market. It may also lead to higher charges for consumers, as there are significant legal costs involved in both lodging and defending patents, and this means that the cost of the product is higher than it would otherwise be due to the legal overhead.

Table 23.1 Process for obtaining a patent

Step	Description
Obtaining a provisional patent	This starts the clock on the patent application, as the date of first application is extremely relevant in patent law, as priority is given to the party that is first to file. The provisional patent is easy to obtain and gives the right to the inventor to say: "*patent pending*"
Formal application	The formal patent application may be filed up to one year from the provisional application, and it requires a lot of technical detail, and is expensive (up to $100 k) and time consuming. Most patents filed will be rejected
Review and appeal	The third step involves working through the patent review and appeal process (average 2.5 years) at the patent office
Defending patent	Once a patent is granted there may be a need to go to court to defend it (e.g., a party might dispute the validity of the patent) anytime during its lifetime, or to take legal action against a party for patent infringement (e.g., where a party uses a patent without permission)

Patents are difficult and expensive to apply for, and it is time consuming for both companies and the government patent office. Further, lawsuits are expensive in both taking a lawsuit for patent infringement and in defending a lawsuit alleging patent violation. And so, the question is sometimes asked as to whether the benefits of the patent process are worth the costs, with some computer scientists such as Richard Stallman arguing against intellectual property law [1]. The process for obtaining a utility patent involves (Table 23.1).

The patent application must show that the invention is *novel*[2] (i.e., the invention is new, and the inventor is the first to discover it). Next, it must be more than an obvious next step from existing technology (i.e., the invention is *not obvious* and is a significant advance over the existing *prior art*[3]). Further, the invention must have *utility*, and so it must be useful and of practical benefit to the public and society. That is, the requirements for a patent on an invention are that it is:

- Novel,
- Utility,
- Not obvious.

The process for obtaining a design patent is easy and quick to get as it is just protecting appearance, and all that it required is to show that it is new or original, that the person who is filing the patent is its creator and has not copied it from someone else, and that it is ornamental. The process for obtaining a utility model patent is short and quick, but it is not as strong as a utility patent.

---

[2] The invention must not have been publicly disclosed to the public (e.g., described in a publication or presented at a conference).
[3] Prior art refers to the existing state of knowledge of a field.

The general rule is one patent one country, and the patent can only be enforced in the country or jurisdiction where it was issued. Another words, a patent issued in Malaysia is not valid in the United States and vice versa, and so there is a need for the company or individual to apply for a patent in every country that is important. Further, if the patent is issued to a company or individual in Malaysia then it can be only enforced with a lawsuit in Malaysia, and the courts will not consider patents from other countries.

Patent litigation is where the patent owner takes a lawsuit against another party for infringing the exclusive rights that the patent holder has with respect to the invention. The defendant may be as selling a technology that uses the patented invention, and the plaintiff will need to show that:

- It has a patent for the invention
- The patent has not expired
- The patent is valid in the country where the infringement took place
- The defendant used the invention
- The defendant did not have a license to use the invention
- The defendant's actions led to loss to the plaintiff.

Often, the parties will reach a settle (e.g., licensing) rather than going through the expense of the legal process.

23.2.2 Copyright

Copyrights apply to original writing and to original intellectual and artistic expressions, and it protects the expression of the idea rather than facts or the idea itself. Copyright law protects literary, musical, and artistic works such as poetry, songs, books, painting, dance, movies, music, information in news media and computer software. It provides exclusive rights to making copies of the expression (subject to copyright law and fair use), where the ways of expressing ideas is copyrightable.

One of the earliest disputes in copyright law occurred during early Irish Christianity in the late sixth century A.D., where there is a story of a dispute between St. Columba and St. Finnian over the right to copy part of the bible. St. Jerome had created a Latin copy of the bible called the Vulgate, and St. Jerome's Psalter refers to the Book of Psalms in the bible. St. Columba had borrowed the Psalter from St. Finnian and made a copy that he called the *Cathach*. St. Finnian disputed St. Columba's right to make a copy, and he claimed ownership of the copy. King Diarmuid Mac Cerbhaill intervened to resolve the dispute, and he ruled that *"To every cow belongs her calf, therefore to every book belongs its copy"*, and so established the principle of copyright law in early Christian Ireland (Fig. 23.2).

A copyright gives the copyright owner rights to exclude others from using or copying the finished work, and most copyrights are generally valid for the creator's lifetime plus 70 years (the exact period depends on the jurisdiction as copyright

Fig. 23.2 St. Colomba's
Cathach

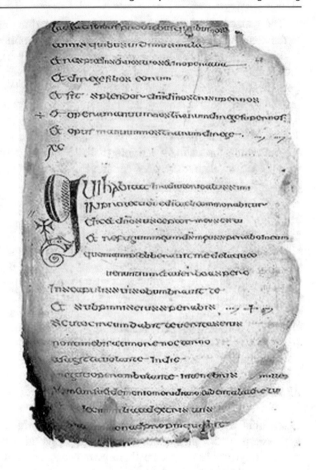

laws vary between countries). The original reason why copyright developed was to motivate artists to produce more artistic work thereby encouraging creative art, and so artists are rewarded for creating more music, art, and so on. Over time, the period for protection has increased in a major way, and today the purpose of copyright is more about protecting the artistic creations of business and large corporations.

The creator of an original work may obtain a copyright, and the work needs to be recorded (e.g., on paper, art, laptops, and mobile phones). Copyright is automatic in most countries although a small number of countries require registration. Registration gives extra benefits as often it allows the copyright owner to sue for a larger amount, and so it may be useful to get registered. Copyrights are

- Original
- Recorded
- Registration is useful
- Mainly corporate owned.

Copyrights do not protect ideas or concepts, as copyrights protect expression and not the idea itself. Sometimes in a copyright dispute one party may be alleging that the expression protected in the copyright was violated, with the other party arguing that it was the idea that was used to create a derivative work and that no copyright violation took place. Names and common phrases may not be protected, and similarly with facts and data. Methods of operation or equipment maintenance instructions are excluded under copyright law, as are most manufactured goods (exceptions include books and DVDs). Useful things are not protected by copyright as patents protect most of these, but there are some exceptions such as dictionaries and software where expression is protected.

The copyright holder has several rights including the right to *prevent others from making copies* of the work, as well as the rights to *stop others from making a derivative work*, i.e., something that is based upon the work. The copyright owners have the *right to distribute the work*, and to display the work anywhere and anytime they like. The owners of a copy have limited rights and may display the copy in one location only. The original *copyright owner has performance rights*, and the *right to exclude others from performing the work*. The performance right is limited in the case of music, where others have the right to perform the music in public in return for a royalty payment to the original author of the song.

There are several limitations of copyright and the most important of these is *"fair use"* (or right to copy), which refers to the permitted limited use of copyrighted material without obtaining permission from the copyright owner. Fair use is not a right as such: rather, it is more of a defence that the defendant makes to the judge, and it is the rationale for why the use of the copyrighted material is viewed as fair by the defendant. Fair use is a little subjective and there are several factors that the judge will need to consider in coming to an informed and balanced view on whether it is reasonable to apply fair use in the case. These factors include:

- Purpose of use
- Amount used
- Nature of work
- Commercial impact.

The purpose of use is the reason why the material has been used, and it is easier to justify fair use for non-profit purposes such as educational use (especially in face-to-face education rather than on-line education). Other areas that are used to justify fair use include literature, criticism, parody, and news reporting. The amount or proportion of material used is important, as it is easier to justify the use of a small portion of the work, or a small proportion of the amount used to the whole of the copyrighted work. There may be complications if the amount used is the core part of the copyrighted material.

The nature of the work is important as some types are better protected than others, and so if the work is mainly facts and data, it may not be so well protected, whereas if it is a good story about a wizard called "Harry Potter" it will be well protected. The commercial impact involves determining the financial costs and the effect on the market or the commercial value from using the material, and if the costs are minimal, it is easier to justify fair use. The defendant bears the burden of proving fair use in any litigation on copyright infringement.

A *copyright infringement* is where the rights of the copyright owner have been violated, and where there may be grounds to sue another party for infringing the rights. An indirect infringement is where a person indirectly and illegally uses copyrighted work (without being aware of it), as in the unconscious plagiarism of the song "He's so fine" that was written by Ronnie Mack and recorded by the Chiffons in 1963, by George Harrison in his 1970 song "My Sweet Lord". A direct infringement is where a person distributes, displays, or performs copyrighted work, or prepares a derivative work without permission. A contributory infringement is where a person has contributed in some material way to the copyright infringement.

The copyright owner will need to convince the judge that a copyright infringement has occurred, and the plaintiff must first show that it is the copyright owner of the original work. Often, there may be no direct evidence of infringement, and so the judge often considers circumstantial evidence, as this may assist in determining on the balance of probability that it is more likely than not that an infringement took place. The judge will consider whether copying took place, and if so, whether that copying was legal (e.g., fair use, ideas, public domain) or not. Further, the more the works differ, the higher the standard of proof required to show infringement. The damages claimed could include the economic damage such as loss of sales and profit, or the plaintiff may be looking for statutory damages which are a high fixed amount as defined in law, or in the case of a blatant violation of copyright the damages sought could include personal liability including major costs for the individual or even that of a criminal offence.

It is permitted to create a derivative work if permission has been obtained from the author of the original work, and the agreement will often include a financial settlement or licensing to create the derivative work (e.g., creating a movie based upon a book will generally include a payment to the author). In many countries the translation of a book creates a derivative work, and so it requires the permission of the copyright holder, and similarly for audio books (China is an exception as it considers translation as transformative fair use). The recording of sheet music is a derivative work and needs permission, as are arrangements of a work.

23.2.3 Copyright of Software

Software code is protected automatically without copyright registration in most countries, and software copyright law is part of global copyright law. A copyright protects expression (i.e., the way in which something is said), and a registered copyright is inexpensive and easy to get, although court cases for copyright violation are expensive. Software patents protect function (not the expression of the function) and provide stronger protection, but they are costly, time consuming and difficult to obtain.

The same function may be expressed in multiple ways by different programs, but if the function is protected (as in a software patent) then nobody else can do that thing without permission or licensing from the patent holder. That is, copyright law protects one expression of the function, and as a different program could implement the same function in a different way, the function itself is not protected. Another words, copyright law protects just the expression of the function, whereas patent law protects the function itself.

Computer software source code was granted protection by copyright law from the mid-1970s, which means that the reproduction of the computer software created by software developers and software companies is protected. This protection includes that of the deliverables created as part of the software development process (e.g., the specification, design, code, testing and other artefacts). The work of an employee automatically belongs to the company (i.e., the company owns the creative work of its employees), and if an employee moves to a new company, then the intellectual creations of the employee's previous employment belong to the previous employer and should not be disclosed to the new employer. The employee may have signed a non-disclosure agreement with the previous employer, and so the employee must respect any confidential information from previous employment.

Further, if a software contractor produces the software code for a company, then this generally belongs to the company (there is usually a signed legal agreement to that effect). All such work is protected by copyright, which means that if a software contractor is implementing the same function in another company and uses the same software code that he/she previously developed for a former client, then the contractor and the new company would be in breach of copyright law, unless permission has been obtained for its use.

The copyright grants the author the right to exclude others from making copies, and the owners of the copies have the right to make additional copies (for archival purposes) without the authorization of the copyright owner. Further, owners of copies have the right to sell their copies.

This has led the software sector to move towards licensing their software rather than selling it. There is some software code that is freely available, and this includes software created by the free software movement (which began in the mid-1980s), the open-source initiative (which began in the late 1990s as a move that wished to highlight the benefits of freely available source code), or software that is in the public domain and that is therefore not subject to copyright. Open-source software (OSS) is software that is freely available under an open-source license to study, change and distribute to anyone for any purpose.

The 1998 US Digital Millennium Copyright Act (DMCA) is an extension of copyright law for the United States, and one of its motivations was a response to the rise of e-commerce in the late 1990s, and the desire of lawmakers to protect and support the digital economy, and to enhance protections for US copyright law. There are three main areas of protection in the act:

- Safe harbour
- Digital Rights Management (DRM)
- Prohibit Copy Protection Circumvention.

DMCA provides safe harbour protections to Internet Service businesses in the US, and in it does this by adding extra provisions to makes fair use far wider for these businesses. It is designed to protect online service providers (OSP) from copyright claims from conduct of their end users that copyright holders claim is infringing their copyright. The EU has rejected the safe harbour provisions in DMCA.

Digital Rights Management (DRM) refers to using digital coding to enact rights like fair trial version or limited version or restrictions on use, and it essentially involves the use of digital code to assign digital assess rights to users. That is, users are stopped from doing certain things using digital code, and DMCA is a legal tool to make DRM stronger in its protections of these rights, and it makes violation of these rights a criminal offence.

Finally, the prohibition of copy protection circumvention makes it a criminal offence to break encryption algorithms to gain access and does not provide a fair use exception. DMCA remains unique to the United States, but any individual or company around the world that breaks encryption could be sued and even jailed in the United States. That is, DMCA poses risks to international companies, and while copyright violations are mainly civil lawsuits DMCA creates criminal liability for violations.

23.2.4 Software Licensing

A software license is a legal agreement between the copyright owner and the licensee, which governs the use or distribution of software to the user (licensee). Computer software code is protected under copyright law in most countries, and a typical software license grants the user permission to make one or more copies of the software, where the copyright owner retains exclusive rights to the software under copyright law.

The two most common categories of software licenses that may be granted under copyright law are those for *proprietary software*, and those for *free open-source software* (FOSS). The rights granted to the licensee are quite different for each of these categories, where the user has the right to copy, modify and distribute (under the same license) software that has been supplied under an open-source license, whereas proprietary software typically does not grant these rights to the user.

The *licensing of proprietary software* typically gives the owner of a copy of the software the right to use it (including the rights to make copies for archival purposes). The software may be accompanied with an end-user license agreement (EULA) that may place further restrictions on the rights of the user. There may be restrictions on the ownership of the copies made, and on the number of installations allowed under the term of the distribution. The ownership of the copy of the software often remains with the copyright owner, and the end user must accept the license agreement to use the software.

The most common licensing model is per single user, and the customer may purchase a certain number of licenses over a fixed period. Another model employed is the license per server model (for a site license), or a license per dongle model, which allows the owner of the dongle use the software on any computer. A license may be perpetual (it lasts forever), or it may be for a fixed period (typically one year).

The software license often includes maintenance for a period (typically one year), and the maintenance agreement generally includes updates to the software during that time and it may also cover a limited amount of technical support. The two parties may sign a service level agreement (SLA), which stipulates the service that will be provided by the service provider. This will generally include timelines for the resolution of serious problems, as well as financial penalties that will be applicable where the customer service performance does not meet the levels defined in the SLA.

Free and open-source licenses are often divided into two categories depending on the rights to be granted in distribution of the modified software. The first category aims to give users unlimited freedom to use, study and modify the software, and if the user adheres to the terms of an open-source license such as GNU or General Public License (GPL), the freedom to distribute the software and any changes made to it. The second category of open-source licenses give the user permission to use, study and modify the software, but not the right to distribute it freely under an open source license (it could be distributed as part of a proprietary software license).

23.3 Lawsuits

A lawsuit is a proceeding taken by one party (or several parties) against another party in a civil court. The basic principles of litigation are where the plaintiff sues another person(s) for being negligent, where the negligence of the defendant caused injury or damage to the property of the plaintiff, and the plaintiff is seeking compensation for her loss. It involves proving in a court of law that:

- The defendant had a duty of care
- The defendant breached this duty of care
- The breach caused harm to the plaintiff or the property of the plaintiff.

The plaintiff is entitled to compensation of the full value of the injury or the damage to the property if the case is successfully proved. Further, if there is clear evidence that the defendant acted maliciously, or fraudulently then punitive damages may be awarded to the plaintiff to punish the defendant. Punitive damages are generally awarded in a small percentage of lawsuits, and they may be appealed to a higher court.

Table 23.2 Types of lawsuits

Type	Description
Criminal	This type of lawsuit is brought by the state against the software company or individuals (e.g., developers or testers) for committing a criminal act (e.g., tampering with a computer or loading a virus onto a computer)
Tort	This type of lawsuit is brought by an individual(s) against a company or individual(s) (e.g., developers or testers) for committing some wrong to him or his computer (e.g., releasing a virus onto his computer)
Negligence	The company has a duty of care to take all reasonable measures to make the product safe, so that the public may not suffer personal injuries or damage or loss of their property. The company could be judged to be negligence if it employed inadequate software development and testing practices
Malpractice	This is where the quality of service is judged against a professional standard and deemed to be negligent, with mistakes made in the delivery of the service that would not be made by an ordinary professional in the field
Strict Liability	A product defect caused a personal injury or damage to property, and the burden of proof required is to demonstrate that the program was defective and that the defect caused the accident (e.g., the failure of the program controlling the breaks in the car led to the car crash)
Fraud	The company made a statement of fact to you when it knew that the statement was false, and where you relied on the statement to make an economic decision such as buying a defective product
Regulatory	The regulatory sector (e.g., FDA) places requirements on how software should be developed and tested so that it is safe for the public to use
Breach of contract	A software contract specifies the obligations that both parties have to each other (as well as implied terms such as implied warranty)
Intellectual property infringement	This type of litigation is where one party takes civil action against another for copyright or patent infringement

There are several types of lawsuits that may be brought against a software company (the defendant) including (Table 23.2).

23.3.1 Tort in Software Engineering

The *law of tort* refers to a civil wrong where one party (the *defendant*) is held accountable for their actions (by the *plaintiff*). There are several actions that the defendant could be held accountable: e.g., negligence, trespass, misstatement, product liability, defamation, and so on. For example, the defendant may be accused of negligence and a breach of his duty of care, where damage that was reasonably foreseeable was caused by his negligence.

The impact of a flaw in software may be catastrophic, and so a software development organization must take all reasonable precautions to prevent the occurrence of defects (as otherwise it could be sued for negligence). This is especially true in the safety critical domain, where defects could cause major damage or even loss of life among the public. This requires reasonable precautions such as having appropriate software engineering practices in place to allow the organization to consistently produce high quality software, and for stringent processes to validate the requirements and to verify that the implementation satisfies the specification.

A quality management system indicates that the organization takes software quality seriously, and that it has a sound software development process in place that serves the needs of the organization and its customers. Modem quality assurance systems include processes for software inspections, testing, quality audits, customer satisfaction, software development, project planning, etc.

The organization will need to provide evidence that it took all reasonable steps in the design, development and testing of the software to ensure that a quality product was produced. This will generally include records of the various quality assurance activities that took place during the project and showing that there is a sound quality management system in place, and that it is appropriate and fully operational within the organization.

It is important to maintain records and an audit trail of the various quality assurance activities for a period after the project, so that the organization may defend itself should a customer decide to take legal action for negligence against it following a serious problem in the software at the customer site. The records will allow the organization to prepare a legal defence to show that it took all reasonable steps during the software development and testing, and that its behaviour was always professional.

That is, the presence of records may be used to demonstrate that all reasonable steps were taken, and the records typically include lists of all the deliverables in the project; minutes of project meetings; records of risk and issue logs, records of reviews of requirements, design, and software code, records of test plans and test results; and so on.

23.3.2 Software Licenses and Failure

Software developers and testers often employ dedicated tools for various parts of software development and testing process, and the use of tools is generally subject to a licensing agreement. The tools may be developed in-house, but it is more common to employ proprietary tools or open-source tools.

A software license is a legal agreement between the copyright owner and the licensee, which governs the use or distribution of software to the user (licensee). The license may cover the entire site, several users, or a single user. The organization must satisfy the licensing agreement and must have sufficient licenses for the deployed version of the tool on site.

Computer software code is protected under copyright law in most countries, and a typical software license grants the user permission to make one or more copies of the software, where the copyright owner retains exclusive rights to the software under copyright law. We discussed licensing in more detail in Sect. 23.2.4.

Software license agreements generally include limited warranties on the quality of the licensed software, and they often provide limited remedies to the customer when the software is defective. The software vendor typically promises that the software will conform to the software documentation for a specified period (the warranty period), and the software warranty generally excludes problems that are not caused by the software, or problems that are beyond the software vendor's control.

The customers are generally provided with limited remedies in the case of defective software. For example, the remedy provided may be an offer to replace the defective software with a corrected version, or termination of the user's right to use the defective software and a partial refund of the license fee. There is generally no financial compensation for loss or damage, and this is generally excluded in the software licensing agreement.

Software licensing agreements are generally accompanied by a comprehensive disclaimer that protects the software vendor from any liability (however remote) that might result from the use of the software. It may include statements such as "*the software is provided 'as is', and that the customers use the software at their own risk*".

A limited warranty and disclaimer limit the customer's rights and remedies if the licensed software is defective, and so the customer may need to consider how best to manage the associated risks. Table 23.2 discussed various lawsuits that could potentially be launched against a software provider.

23.3.3   Legal Aspects of Outsourcing

The bespoke development or testing of software has become popular in the software engineering field. This may involve the outsourcing of the complete project (including development and testing), or perhaps just the outsourcing of the software testing to an independent external organization. Bespoke (or custom) software is software that is developed for a specific customer or organization, and it needs to satisfy the defined customer requirements.

The organization will need to be rigorous in its selection of the appropriate supplier, as it is essential that the supplier selected has the capability of delivering high-quality and reliable software on time and on budget. The contract should not be awarded on costs alone, as this is just one criterion among several other important criteria.

This means that the capability of the supplier is clearly understood, and the associated risks with the supplier are known prior to selection. The selection is based on objective criteria such as cost, previous working experience (if any) with the supplier, the planned approach to develop the solution, the ability of the supplier

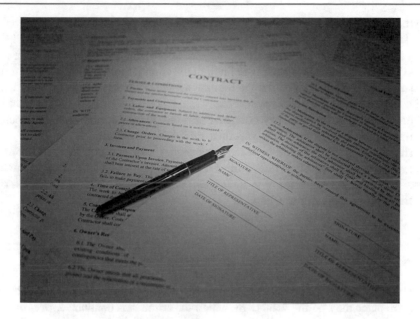

Fig. 23.3 Legal contract Creative Commons

to deliver the required solution, and the supplier capability. Although, cost is an important factor in the selection, it is just one among several other important factors to consider. Often, weightings will be employed to reflect the relative importance of the criteria.

Once the selection of the supplier is finalized a legal agreement is drawn up between the contractor and supplier, which states the terms and condition of the contract, as well as the statement of work (Fig. 23.3). The *statement of work* (SOW) details the work to be carried out, the deliverables to be produced, when they will be produced, the personnel involved, their roles and responsibilities, any training to be provided, and the standards to be followed. The agreement will need to be signed by both parties, and may (depending on the type of agreement) include a warranty period, a service level agreement, training, user guides and manuals, customer support, and an escrow agreement.

Sometimes, it will be just the testing part of a project that is outsourced, and so this is concerned with the selection and management of an appropriate supplier to perform the testing. It is essential that the selected test organization can carry out the required testing to the defined quality standard, as well as being capable of completing the testing within the budget and schedule constraints.

The legal contract specifies the obligations on both the supplier and the organization and should either party fail to honour their commitments they may well be in breach of contract. For example, the contract places obligations on the supplier to deliver various deliverables at various times during the project, and that they will need to satisfy certain quality standards. Further, the contract will detail milestone payments to be made by the organization to the supplier provided defined deliverables have been produced to the right standard by a certain date.

It may be that one or more parties does not honour their agreement or there may be a dispute as to whether what is defined in the contract has been honoured or not. The organization may claim that the binding agreement has not been honoured, and there may be a need to seek legal remedy if a *material* breach of the contract has occurred, and the supplier may counter-claim that the organization is in breach of contract for failing to make the specified milestone payments.

The first step is dialogue between both parties with the objective of finding a reasonable resolution, but if both parties are unable to agree a way forward the first party may seek a legal remedy in a civil court. We discussed the legal breach of a contract for outsourcing in Chap. 11.

23.4 Computer Crime

Computer crime (or *cybercrime*) is a crime that involves a computer and a network. The computer may be the vehicle by which the crime was conducted, or it may be the target of the crime. Today, more and more individuals and companies are online, and networking systems and computers have become quite complex. There has been a major growth in attacks on businesses and individuals, and so it is essential to consider computer and network security. The introduction of the World Wide Web in the early 1990s transformed the world of computing, and it later led to an explosive growth in attacks on computers and systems. The Internet was developed based on trust with security features added later as a response to various types of attacks, as hackers and malicious software sought to exploit known security vulnerabilities. It is therefore essential to develop secure systems that can deal with and recover from such external attacks.

One of the earliest Internet attacks was back in 1988 when a graduate student from Carnegie Mellon University released a program on the Internet (an Internet Worm) that exploited security vulnerability in the mail software to automatically replicate itself locally and on remote machines. It affected lots of machines and effectively shut down the Internet for 1–2 days.

Humans face danger on some streets or neighbourhoods in urban areas, and such dangers need to be managed (Fig. 23.4). Similarly, the Internet has dangers with hackers, scammers, and web predators lurking in the shadows, and ready to pounce on those who are not well prepared or defended. There are several threats associated with network connectivity such as *unauthorized access* (a break-in by an unauthorized person), *disclosure of sensitive information* to people who should not have access to the information, and *denial of service* (DoS), where there is a degradation of service that makes it impossible to access the web site and perform productive work. The threats facing a user include:

Fig. 23.4 Dandy
Pickpockets (1818)

DANDY PICKPOCKETS diving

- Unauthorized access
- Disclosure of sensitive information
- Denial of service
- Theft of credit card data
- Bank fraud
- Defacement of web sites
- Phishing emails
- Virus
- Cyberextortion
- Ransomware
- Various Internet scams.

A hacker may be accessing a computer resource without authorization with the intention of committing an unlawful act. The hacker's activities may be limited to *cavesdropping* (listening to a conversation), or it may be an active *man-in-the-middle* attack, where the hacker may possibly alter the conversation between two parties.

There may be attacks that lead to defacement of the web sites, bank fraud, theft of credit card numbers, hoax (scam) letters, phishing emails that appear to come from legitimate parties but contain links to a site that is different from the one that the user expects to go to, intercepting of packets and password sniffing. *Phishing* is an attempt to obtain sensitive information such as usernames, passwords, and credit card details with the intention of committing fraud.

A computer *virus* is a self-replicating computer program that is installed on the user's computer without consent. It is malicious software in that when it is executed it replicates itself and infects other computer programs by modifying them. A virus often performs some type of harmful activity on the infected computers such as accessing private information, spamming email contacts, or corrupting data. It is not a crime per se to write a computer virus or malicious software. However, if that software or other malware spreads to other computers, then it could be considered a crime.

Cyberextortion is a crime that involves an attack, or threat of an attack, accompanied by a demand for money to stop the attack. They are often initiated through malware in an email attachment. These may include denial of service attacks or *ransomware* attacks that encrypts the victim's data. The victim is then offered the private key to resolve the encryption in return for payment. Companies need to manage the risks associated with cyberextortion, and to ensure that end users are properly educated on malware and phishing.

Another form of computer crime is Internet fraud where one party is intent on deceiving another. Among these are hoax email scams, which are designed to deceive, and fraud the email recipient. These may include the *Nigeria 419* scams, where the email recipient is offered a share of a large amount of money trapped in their country, if the recipient will help in getting the money out of the country. The recipient may be asked for their bank account details to help them to transfer the money (this information will later be used by them to steal funds), or the request may be to pay fees or taxes to release payment with further fees requested. Of course, the money will never arrive, and if a recipient receives a message that sounds too good to be true then in all probability it is a scam.

The unauthorized access to a computer system and the theft of confidential data and disruption of its services is unlawful and may be subject to prosecution and the full rigour of the law.

23.5 Review Questions

1. What is intellectual property law?
2. Describe the behaviours of the ethical software tester.
3. How can a software company demonstrate that it took all reasonable steps to deliver a high-quality software product, and that the testing was fit for purpose.
4. Explain the different types of software licensing.
5. Explain the legal aspects of bespoke software development.
6. What happens when one party in a test-outsourcing project believes that a material breach of the contract has occurred?
7. What types of lawsuits could be brought against a software company?
8. Explain the difference between ethical and malicious hackers.

23.6 Summary

Legal aspects of computing are concerned with the application of the legal system to the computing field. It includes intellectual property law including patents, copyright, trademarks, and trade secrets; bespoke software development; test outsourcing; licensing of software; professional negligence in the development and testing of software; and computer crime.

A lawsuit is a proceeding by a party against another party in a civil court where the plaintiff sues another person for being negligent, where the negligence of the defendant caused injury or damage to the property of the plaintiff

Bespoke software (or custom software) is software that is developed for a specific customer or organization and needs to satisfy specific customer requirements. The legal contract specifies the obligations of the supplier, and should the supplier fail to honour its commitments it may well be in breach of contract. This may result in the first party seeking a legal remedy in a civil court.

A software license is a legal agreement between the copyright owner and the licensee, which governs the use or distribution of software to the user (licensee). Computer software code is protected under copyright law, and the license grants the user permission to make one or more copies of the software. Software license agreements generally provide limited remedies to the customer when the software defective. However, there may be legal implications if the software has been inadequately developed and tested.

A hacker is a person who uses his (or her) computer skills to gain unauthorized access to computer files or networks. Hackers may probe parts of the system for weaknesses, and system vulnerabilities may lead to attackers gaining unauthorized access to the system.

Reference

1. G. O' Regan, *Giants of Computing* (Springer, 2013)

Cybersecurity and Cybercrime

24

Abstract

This chapter discusses cybersecurity and cybercrime. Computer crime (or cybercrime) is a crime that involves a computer and a network. The computer may be the vehicle by which the crime was conducted, or it may be the target of the crime. Cybersecurity is the protection of information through good security practices, including the protection of confidentiality, integrity, and availability of data. It is achieved through policies that ensure consistency in employee behaviour in the use of computer resources, as well as training and awareness of security in the workplace.

Keywords

Computer crime · Scam · Malware · Hacking · Cyberextortion · Cybersecurity · Phishing · Trojan horse

24.1 Introduction

Computer crime (or cybercrime) is a crime that involves a computer and a network. The computer may be the vehicle by which the crime was conducted, or it may be the target of the crime. It is common in the major urban areas to encounter dangers in some streets or neighbourhoods, and such dangers need to be managed. Similarly, the Internet has dangers with hackers, scammers, and web predators lurking in the shadows. A hacker may be accessing a computer resource without authorization with the intention of committing an unlawful act. The hacker's activities may be limited to *eavesdropping* (listening to a conversation), or it may be an active *man-in-the-middle* attack, where the hacker may possibly alter the conversation between two parties.

One of the earliest computer crimes that occurred in the United States was in the late 1950s, and this was a financial crime that involved the alteration of bank records to embezzle cents from the interest earned on long-term accounts. The trial took place several years later in 1966, and this was the first prosecuted computer crime case in the US. One of the earliest Internet attacks was in 1988, when a graduate student from Carnegie Mellon University released a program on the Internet (an Internet Worm), which exploited security vulnerability in the mail software to automatically replicate itself locally and on remote machines. It affected lots of machines and effectively shut down the Internet for 1–2 days.

The legal system evolves as technology evolves and an accepted legal principle is that a person cannot or should not face criminal punishment for an act that was not a criminal offence before he or she committed the act (*nullum crimen sine lege*). Another words, the principle says that there is no punishment without law, and this protects the perpetrators from punishment outside of the law. That is, there was very little law dealing with computer crime in the early days of computing, and so there was minimal punishment of offenders, as the probability of conviction in the absence of law was very low. Prosecutors attempted to use the existing law to bring perpetrators to justice, but often there were loopholes that could be exploited by the defence.

The number of computers and computer users in the early days of computing was extremely small, and the introduction of time-sharing systems in the 1960s was a way to share scarce computer resources among several users. This led to an increase in the number of computer users, but most of the population had no access to computer technology. Most computer crimes that occurred involved some form of theft, with unauthorized access regarded more as an abuse of computer resources rather than a crime. This was since computer resources were still quite rare at that time, and so unauthorized access to computer resources was more socially acceptable that it is today, as in the modern age computer resources are everywhere, and it is not acceptable for others to gain unauthorized access to computer resources.

Most developed countries introduced laws criminalizing computer crime from the early 1970s, and these laws have evolved as technology evolves. Often new problems arise from the introduction of new technology that need to be addressed by the legal system. For example, the introduction of the Internet and World Wide Web has transformed computer crime to the global stage, with billions of users accessing web sites around the world, and this has created a whole new set of problems and challenges for the legal system to deal with.

Today, more and more individuals and companies are online, and networking systems and computers have become quite complex. There has been a major growth in attacks on businesses and individuals, and so it is essential to consider computer and network security. The Internet was developed based on trust with security features added as a response to different types of attacks.

There are several threats associated with network connectivity such as *unauthorized access* (a break-in by an unauthorized person), *disclosure of sensitive information* to people who should not have access to the information, and *denial of service* (DoS), where there is a degradation of service that makes it impossible to access the web site and perform productive work. Table 24.1 presents several examples of computer crimes:

There are many possible computer crimes varying from attacks that lead to defacement of the web sites, to bank fraud and the theft of credit card numbers, the sending of hoax (scam) letters and phishing emails that appear to come from

Table 24.1 Computer crimes

Crime	Description
Intellectual property	Infringements of intellectual property are usually civil matters rather than criminal, but the deliberate violation of intellectual property for commercial gain may be a criminal matter
Spam	This is where unsolicited messages are sent to many people usually for commercial purposes such as in advertisements for products, but possibly for fraudulent purposes such as phishing
Phishing	Phishing is the fraudulent activity that aims to obtain sensitive personal information such as user-ids and passwords, bank account and credit card information, etc., by deceiving users that communication is coming from legitimate parties
Identity theft	This is where someone obtains and deliberately uses another person's personal information (e.g., bank account or credit card information) to commit fraud
Scams	A scam is an illegal or dishonest scheme designed to steal or commit fraud, where the scheme is designed to get the victim part with her money. The scam may appear very convincing to the victim
Cyberextortion	This is a crime that involves an attack, or threat of an attack, accompanied by a demand for money to stop the attack
Ransomware	This cyberextortion attack encrypts the victim's data and threatens to perpetually block access to the data unless a ransom is paid
Cyberbullying	Cyberbullying (or online bullying) is a form of bullying or harassment by electronic means, where someone harasses another over the Internet (especially on social media sites)
Fraud	Fraud is intentional deception with the intention of gaining financial gain at the expense of the victim. The fraud may be a civil or a criminal matter
Malware	Malware is malicious software that is designed to create harm or cause damage to a computer or network, and they include viruses and Trojan horses
Theft of corporate data	This is where information that is stored on corporate databases or servers is stolen and may occur because of an employee's account being compromised or due to an unsecured network
Denial of service	This attack essentially shuts down a machine or network or where there is a degradation of service that makes it inaccessible to its users or prevents them from performing productive work
Unauthorized access	Unauthorized access is where someone gains access to a website or server without permission. It may be due to a security breach, where someone gained access by using another person's account, or through guessing their password

legitimate parties but contain links to a site that is different from the one that the user expects to go to and so attempt to steal from the use. Other crimes include the interception of packets and password sniffing. Next, we discuss some of the cybercrimes in more detail.

24.1.1 Scams

A scam is a scheme where one party is intent on deceiving another for financial gain, and it generally involves persuading the victim to part with his/her money. The scam may be extremely convincing, and the communication may appear to come from a legitimate source. A scam is often sent by a hoax email that is designed to deceive, and fraud the email recipient.

For example, the victim may receive an email from a party that appears to be her bank that advises her that she is overdrawn on her current account, or that there is a suspicious transaction on her account. She is requested to login with the link provided in the email, and once she has clicked on the link and provided her financial details to what appears to be her bank, she suffers immediate financial loss.

Phishing is an attempt to obtain sensitive information such as usernames, passwords, and credit card details with the intention of committing fraud. The scam may take the form of a phishing email designed to persuade the victim to reveal personal information such as name, address, date of birth, phone number, financial details, login details, passwords for *identity theft*, and the goal may be to use the information gained to access bank accounts, or to sell on the personal information to other criminal groups.

The *cold call* scam is where somebody claiming to be from the technical department of a computer company contacts the recipient and advises her that their computer is infected with a virus or hacked. They offer to remotely connect to the computer to solve the problem for a fee, and as the victim may be in a state of shock or fear they may well agree to a remote connection. The scammer may simulate a virus on the remote machine and just take the fee, or their actions may be more sinister where they encrypt all the data on the machine, and demand payment for resolution.

The infamous *Nigeria 419* scam is where the email recipient is offered a share of a large amount of money trapped in the sender's country, if the recipient will help in getting the money out of the country. The recipient may be asked for their bank account details to help them to transfer the money (this information will later be used by them to steal funds), or the request may be to pay fees or taxes to release payment, with further fees requested as time goes on. Of course, the money will never arrive, and *if an email looks like it really is too good to be true then it has a high probability of being a scam.*

24.1.2 Malware

Malware is malicious software that is designed to negatively impact the victim's computer, and it may delete files, change user settings, spy on the user, and open the computer to attacks. It installs itself on the victim's computer without their consent, and it may install itself without the victim's knowledge by exploiting vulnerabilities in operating systems or browsers, or it may install itself after a user downloads and runs an infected program.

A computer *virus* is a self-replicating computer program that is installed on the user's computer without their consent. This malicious program replicates itself on execution and infects other computer programs by modifying them. A virus often performs some type of harmful activity on the infected computers such as accessing private information, spamming email contacts, or corrupting data. It is not a crime per se to write a computer virus or malicious software. However, if that software or other malware spreads to other computers, then it could be considered a crime.

A *Trojan horse* is a type of malware that is disguised as legitimate software, and it misleads the user on its true intent. Hackers often use this type of software to gain access to the victim's computer system. The origin of the term is from the deceptive Trojan horse that led to the fall of Troy during the Trojan War. The wooden horse contained Odysseus and several other Greeks, and it was left as a victory gift for the Trojans when the Greeks sailed away. The Trojans brought the horse inside their city, and Odysseus and the Greeks later opened the gates of Troy for the returning Greeks, leading to the slaughter of the citizens of Troy and their exodus led to the founding of the city of Rome, as described in Virgil's Aeneid. This well-known event in Greek mythology led to the well-known aphorism *"Beware of Greeks bearing gifts"* (Fig. 24.1).

24.1.3 Cyberextortion and Ransomware

Cyberextortion is a crime that involves an attack, or threat of an attack, accompanied by a demand for money to stop the attack. It may involve an individual or group sending a threatening email to a company advising them that they are able to seriously harm them, and that they will exploit security vulnerabilities or breaches to launch an immediate attack on the company unless they receive a payment to prevent the attack. The attack could be to threaten to expose private personal information of customers obtained because of a security breach, or it could be a direct attack on the data and information held on databases and servers.

A *ransomware* attack is an even more sinister form of extortion that involves encrypting the victim's files and making them inaccessible, and a ransom payment is demanded to decrypt the victim's data. The victim is unable to recover the files without the decryption key as decryption is an intractable problem, and so the only way to recover the files is to make the payment and pay the ransom. The victim will

Fig. 24.1 Trojan horse at Troy

usually be required to make payment with Bitcoin or another digital currency, and so tracing the perpetrator of the attack is extremely difficult. Once payment is made the victim will be provided with the decryption key and will be able to access the files.

Ransomware attacks are often initiated through malware in an email attachment, which contains a Trojan horse that looks like a legitimate file, and the victim unwittingly opens it. Care is always required when opening an attachment even if it appears to be from a legitimate source.

The *denial-of-service attack* is when a web site is overloaded by a malicious attack, and where users are therefore unable to access the web site for an extended period. That is, this attack is where the perpetrator attempts to make a computer or network unavailable for use by disrupting the services of a host connected to the Internet. It is achieved by flooding the target computer or server with requests with the goal of overloading the system and preventing normal operation. The attack may be conducted to blackmail the victim for a financial payment, or it may be carried out as an act of revenge.

There are other forms of extortion such as *sextortion*, where the victim is blackmailed into providing sexual favours to the perpetrator, where the latter has obtained indiscreet images of her that he is threatening to share on social media. This type of coercion involves the abuse of the power that the perpetrator has over the victim.

24.2 Hacking

A *hacker* is a person who uses his (or her) computer skills to gain unauthorized access to computer files or networks. A hacker may enjoy experimenting with computer technology (the original meaning of the term), but some hackers enjoy breaking into systems and causing damage (the modern meaning of the word). Ethical (*white hat*) hackers are former hackers who play an important role in the security industry in testing network security, and in helping to create secure products and services. Malicious (*black hat*) hackers (also called *crackers*) are generally motivated by personal gain, and they exploit security and system vulnerabilities to steal, exploit or sell data (Fig. 24.2).

Many computer systems in use today have vulnerabilities that may be exploited by a determined hacker to gain unauthorized entry to the system, and access to unauthorized information. It is vital that best practice in software and system engineering is employed to develop safe and secure systems, and that known vulnerabilities in system security are addressed promptly by updates to the system software. Further, it is essential to educate staff on security, and to define (and follow) the appropriate procedures to prevent security breaches.

The early hackers were mainly young students without malicious intent who were exploring the university computer systems. These included students at Massachusetts Institute of Technology in the late 1950s who were interested in exploring the IBM 704 computer, and they would enter areas of the system without authorization and gain access to privileged resources.

They were motivated by knowledge and wished to have a deeper understanding of the systems that they had access to. The idea of a hacker ethic was formulated in a book by Steven Levy in the mid-1980s [1], and he outlined several ethical principles including free access to computers and information and improvement to quality of life. His six key tenets are:

Fig. 24.2 Hacker at work on blacklit keyboard. Creative Commons

- Access to computers should be unlimited and total,
- All information should be free,
- Mistrust authority,
- Hackers should be judged by their hacking and not by bogus criteria such as race and religion,
- Art and beauty can be created on a computer,
- Computers can change your life for the better.

The *free software movement* arose in the early 1980s from followers of the hacker ethic, with Richard Stallman (its founder) often referred to as "the last true hacker" [2]. Today, ethical hackers need to obtain permission prior to acting, as their actions may potentially cause major disruption to an organization. Responsible (white hat) hackers can provide useful information on security vulnerabilities and may assist by testing and improving computer security.

Hackers will often attempt to steal confidential data and to disrupt the services being offered by a system. Security engineering is concerned with the development of systems that can prevent such malicious attacks and recover from them. It has become an important part of software and system engineering, and software developers need to be aware of the threats facing a system and develop solutions to manage them.

Hackers may probe parts of the system for weaknesses, and system vulnerabilities may lead to attackers gaining unauthorized access to the system. The security of the system refers to its ability to protect itself from accidental or deliberate external attacks, which are common today since most computers are networked and connected to the Internet. The introduction of the world wide web in the early 1990s transformed the world of computing, but it led to an explosive growth in attacks on computers and systems, as hackers and malicious software sought to exploit known security vulnerabilities. It is therefore essential to develop secure systems that can deal with and recover from such external attacks.

There are various security threats in any networked system including threats to the confidentiality and integrity of the system and its data, and threats to the availability of the system. Therefore, controls are required to enhance security and to ensure that attacks are unsuccessful. There is a need to conduct a risk assessment of the security threats facing a system early in the software development process, and this will lead to several security requirements for the system. The system needs to be designed for security, as it is difficult to add security after the system has been implemented. Security loopholes may be introduced in the development of the system, and so care needs to be taken to prevent these as well as preventing hackers from exploiting security vulnerabilities.

Encryption is one way to reduce system vulnerability, as encrypted data is unreadable to the attacker. There may be controls that detect and repel attacks, and these controls may be used to monitor the system and to take appropriate action to shut down parts of the system or restrict access in the event of an attack. There may be controls that limit exposure (e.g., insurance policies and automated backup strategies) that allow recovery from the problems introduced.

The choice of architecture and how the system is organized is fundamental to the security of the system, and different types of systems will require different technical solutions to provide an acceptable level of security to its users. The following guidelines for designing secure systems are described in [3]:

- Security decisions should be based on the security policy,
- A security critical system should fail securely,
- A secure system should be designed for recoverability,
- A balance is needed between security and usability,
- A single point of failure should be avoided,
- A log of user actions should be maintained,
- Redundancy and diversity should be employed,
- Organization of information in system into compartments.

Security testing of the software is important, and it is essential to identify security vulnerabilities and any flaws in the security mechanisms of the computer system, and to verify that the security requirements such as confidentiality, availability, and integrity are satisfied. However, the successful completion of security testing does not guarantee that there are no remaining security vulnerabilities in the system, and it is important to remain vigilant. Further, it is important that users be educated on security, and their role in preventing breaches of security to minimize the risks of becoming victims of computer crime.

The unauthorized access to a computer system and the theft of confidential data and disruption of its services is unlawful and may be subject to prosecution and the full rigour of criminal law.

24.3 Cybersecurity

The introduction of the Internet led to a major growth in attacks on businesses and individuals. The Internet was developed based on trust with security features added as a response to different types of attacks. Today, good cybersecurity is an essential part of modern electronic systems. The consequences of poor security are potentially very serious including the theft of personal information and credit cards of customers, resulting in a loss of trust and damage to the reputation and credibility of the company. The security of the system refers to its ability to protect itself from attacks, and there are several characteristics of security such as:

- Confidentiality,
- Integrity,
- Availability.

Confidentiality means that the information may be viewed and accessed only by those authorized, and encryption may be employed to ensure that the unauthorized access of information is meaningless to anyone other than the intended parties.

Other approaches include access controls where only those with the appropriate access privileges may access the data. *Integrity* means that the data may only be modified by those authorized to do so, and *availability* refers to the fact that the system and its data are always available for use (i.e., it is not subject to a denial-of-service attack).

Security is holistic and it is essential to identify any security vulnerabilities and to correct them. There may be vulnerabilities with respect to the security of the subcontractors of a company, and it is important that their access privileges to the company's computer network be limited. It is important to be able to limit the access that malicious software may have within the company's network. There may be controls that detect and repel attacks such that parts of the system are shut down or access restricted to prevent the malicious software from moving around the network. Hackers may use phishing emails to install malicious software to get credentials and steal passwords. They are often motivated by personal gain, and they exploit security and system vulnerabilities to steal, exploit or sell data or intellectual property. Attacks may be from internal or external to the company and the attacks may lead to:

- Unauthorized data access and usage,
- Unauthorized data theft and deletion,
- Unauthorized data manipulation.

The system needs to be designed for security, as it is difficult to add security after the system has been implemented. Examples of best practice for the implementation of good security includes:

- Apply need to know principle (only those that need to know have access),
- Apply minimal user rights principle (level of access restricted to task),
- Update systems regularly,
- Design systems with security and privacy in mind.

Security loopholes may be introduced in the development of the system, and so care needs to be taken to prevent these as well as preventing hackers from exploiting security vulnerabilities. Early risk analysis is conducted to determine what needs to be protected, and the threats and vulnerabilities of the current system are analysed as well as their probability and impacts, which leads to a risk profile of the system. The high-risk areas lead to the security requirements including the required security measures and supporting technologies. There is a trade-off between security risks and the cost of security measures, and this is a continuous process due to continued changes in technology. A comprehensive security system requires a range of measures such as:

- Preventive measures,
- Detective measures,
- Administrative measures.

Preventive measures are used to stop unauthorized attacks from occurring before they succeed and do any harm, *detective measures* are used to discover any unauthorized attacks that may be on-going or completed, and *administrative measures* which are used to clarify processes, rules, and standards within an organization. Organizational and administrative measures are as important as technical measures in securing a system.

The administrative measures include identifying the technical measures, actions and enforcement mechanisms that are needed, and defining the responsibilities for carrying out the measures. The policies and procedures as defined in the Information Security Management System of ISO/IEC 27001 provide guidance on what should be implemented in security management.

Preventive measures often involve the use of encryption for communication and stored data, and these measures mean that the data is meaningless to anyone who is not authorized to see it. The encryption and decryption are performed with keys, where the same secret key is used for symmetric cryptography and different keys (public and private) are used for asymmetric cryptography with digital certificates used to verify the authenticity of the key owner.

Preventive measures also include access control mechanisms for *authentication* to verify if the person is who she claims to be, and a range of measures such as user id and password, smart card and biometric data may be used for verification. The next step is to ensure that those authenticated have the appropriate level of *authorization* to access the data, and an authorization matrix may be used to specify the roles and the level of access for each role.

The goal of detective measures is to monitor whether a system is secure, and to detect attacks. Security audits may be conducted to verify that the planned security measures have been implemented, for example, which recommended measures have been implemented, as well as verifying that all planned measures have been implemented. Penetration testing are a way to find and remove security weaknesses, and it involves experts (e.g., white hat hackers) playing the role of attackers trying to find vulnerabilities in a system, and improvement actions are then taken to improve any identified weakness in the system.

The system needs to be designed for security, and the protection of privacy in the electronic age requires good security practices to be in place. Security is holistic and it is essential to identify any security vulnerabilities and to correct them. It is important to be able to limit the access that malicious software may have within the company's network, and this may include controls that detect and repel attacks such as shutting down parts of the system or restricting access thereby preventing the malicious software from moving around the network.

Cybersecurity is the protection of information through good security practices, and it protects the confidentiality, integrity and availability of data. It is achieved through policies that ensure consistency in employee behaviour in the use of computer resources, as well as training and awareness of security in the workplace. Technology (e.g., firewalls) plays an important role in the implementation of security. The implementation of security is achieved through:

- Policy,
- Training,
- Awareness,
- Technology.

The cybersecurity policy regulates the behaviour of employees to ensure consistency in what they can or cannot do to prevent the misuse of computer resources, or damage or destruction of information. It is essential to develop, implement and manage the cyber security policy, and there may be specific policies for particular systems as well as an organization wide security policy. The policy defines the vision, sets the direction and scope of security, and provides detailed instructions for its conduct.

The implementation of the security policy leads to an effective intrusion detection and prevention system, and includes the day-to-day operations risk management, monitoring of security problems, incidence management to handle incidents, disaster recovery management, and business continuity planning.

Training and awareness programs are concerned with teaching employees and raising awareness on the good use of information assets, and on how to use technology responsibly in the workplace. Training helps in improving employee behaviour and in ensuring compliance with the security policy.

Technology plays an important role in the implementation of security policy, with the use of technology often invisible to the user as it is implemented by IT staff. Users will be familiar with technology that enforces periodic changing of passwords and the security of passwords. The technology may include firewalls that are computer hardware or software that act as a gatekeeper to keep unwanted data out and prevents unwanted data such as malware from reaching inside the trusted network. That is, firewalls control the flow of information between the outside world (un-trusted network) to the inside world (trusted network). There is a need to employ up to date versions of anti-virus software to protect computers from viruses.

Encryption is a way to protect information by enciphering it so that it is unreadable to others who do not possess a security key to decipher it. A virtual private network (VPN) uses encryption technology to create a secured connection between two points. Other technical controls include access controls with authentication and authorization, where the identity of the user is authenticated by password, and a user is assigned a level of access corresponding to her role. Audit logs are maintained to record who and when accessed various parts of the system.

Sun Tzu Wu's description of warfare in "The Art of War" c. 500 B.C. is analogous to security (Fig. 24.3).

- He who knows the enemy and himself will not be in danger in 100 battles,
- He who knows himself but not the enemy will win some and lose some battles,
- He who neither knows himself or the enemy will be in danger in all battles.

Computer security began with the development of early computers, and security for these large expensive machines was physical where access to sensitive locations was protected. The threats in the early days of computing were theft of equipment,

Fig. 24.3 Sun Tzu Wu

espionage, and sabotage. The development of the ARPANET network of computers in the late 1960s led to new security challenges, as there were security problems with ARPANET. These included insufficient controls and safeguards to protect data from unauthorized remote users.

The weaknesses in ARPANET security included the poor structure of passwords, the lack of security protocols for phone-based phone connections, and the lack of user based identification and authentication methods. This meant that hackers had easy access to ARPANET due to the network insecurity. TCP/IP became the protocol for ARPANET in the early-1980s.

ARPANET evolved into the Internet during the 1980s and virtually all computers could now be interconnected by phone line and modem, and the Internet became pervasive in all corners of globe. The Internet consists of the interconnection of millions of networks and billions of computers. Early Internet deployment treated security as a low priority, and many security problems today are due to this lack of security (e.g., email). The Internet brings millions of unsecured computer networks and billions of unsecured computers into continuous communication with each other.

The security of information of a particular computer is dependent on the security of every other computer that it is connected to, or another words there is a clear and present danger from others when connected online. This means that there is a need to be conscious of cybersecurity, and to improve security practices to prevent cyber-attacks. The goal is to avoid being the victim of information warfare, which could arise if one is undefended. A security breach may be an intentional act by a hostile party, or it could occur accidentally because of clicking a link in an email.

There may be cybersecurity attacks such as phishing and ransomware attacks that may impact public and private system users. The software on a web site runs on the web server, and it may store personal customer data in a database on the hard drive of a server or in the cloud. Hackers will exploit any vulnerabilities to gain access, and the unauthorized activities may include an attack on the data either damaging or compromising information. The goal may be to steal personal customer data such as credit card information.

The modern world is digital and there has been a transformation in technology and communication, with technologies such as the Internet of Things, social media, and AI. There have been privacy and security breaches with digital technology allowing personal and confidential data to be compromised.

Poor security may lead to cybercrime, theft of confidential data such as credit cards or personal data, identity theft with the goal of financial fraud, financial loss, ransomware attacks, disruption due to a virus attack or where the user is unable to access their data. There may be legal and privacy violations and negative publicity. Human error is the major cause of cybersecurity breaches, and so education needs to be provided to employees and the public to ensure their awareness of cybersecurity.

Users should choose strong passwords and change them regularly. They should think carefully before clicking on a link or opening an attachment, and to beware of phishing emails that encourage them to give out personal information such as login information for banks.

The World Wide Web consists of unknown users and suppliers with un-predictable behaviour operating in unknown countries around the world. These users and web sites may be friendly or hostile and the issue of trust arises:

- Is the other person whom they claim to be?
- Can the other person be relied upon to deliver the goods on-payment?
- Can the other person be trusted not to inflict malicious damage?
- Is financial information kept confidential on the server?

Hostility may manifest itself in various acts of destruction. For example, malicious software may attempt to format the hard disc of the local machine, and if successful all local data will be deleted. Other malicious software may attempt to steal confidential data from the local machine including bank account or credit card details.

The display of web pages on the local client machine may involve the downloading of programs from the server and running the program on the client machine. Standard HTML allows the static presentation of a web page, whereas many web pages include active content. There is a danger that a Trojan horse may be activated during the execution of active content.

Security threats may be from anywhere (e.g., client side, server side, transmission) in an e-commerce environment, and therefore a holistic approach to security is required. Internal and external security measures need to be considered, with internal security generally implemented with good processes and procedures and assigning appropriate access privileges.

It is essential that the user is confident in the security provided as otherwise they will be reluctant to pass credit card details over the web for purchases. Technologies such as secure-socket layer (SSL) and secure HTTP (S-HTTP) help to ensure security.

There is a need for care with wifi as it may not be possible to determine its security, and it may not even be the desired network as it could be an evil twin. There is a need to apply security patches whenever they become available.

24.4 Review Questions

1. What is cybercrime?
2. What are the main computer crimes?
3. What is a scam?
4. What is identity theft?
5. What is malware?
6. Explain the difference between cyberextortion and ransomware.
7. What is a hacker?
8. What is cybersecurity?
9. Explain the analogy between Sun Wu's description of warfare and cybersecurity.
10. Explain the difference between "white hat" and "black hat" hackers.

24.5 Summary

Computer crime is a crime that involves a computer and a network. The computer may be the vehicle by which the crime was conducted, or it may be the target of the crime. The Internet has dangers with hackers, scammers, and web predators lurking in the shadows. A hacker may be accessing a computer resource without authorization with the intention of committing an unlawful act including to eavesdropping, or it may be an active man-in-the-middle attack, where the hacker may possibly alter the conversation between two parties.

Many developed countries introduced laws criminalizing computer crime from the early 1970s, and new laws have been introduced as technology evolves. The introduction of the Internet and World Wide Web has transformed computer crime to the global stage, with billions of users accessing web sites around the world, and this has created a whole new set of problems and challenges for the legal system to deal with.

Today, more and more individuals and companies are online, and networking systems and computers have become quite complex. There has been a major growth in attacks on businesses and individuals, and so it is essential to consider computer and network security.

References

1. S. Levy, *Hackers: Heroes of the Computer Revolution* (O'Reilly Media, 1984)
2. G. O'Regan, *Pillars of Computing* (Springer, 2015)
3. I. Sommerville, *Software Engineering*, 9th edn. (Pearson, 2011)

Epilogue

25

Abstract

This chapter is the concluding chapter in which we summarize the journey that we have travelled in this book.

We embarked on a long journey is this book and set ourselves the objective of providing a concise introduction to the software engineering field to students and practitioners. The book was based on the author's experience at leading industrial companies, and it covered both theory and practice. The objective was to give the reader a grasp of the fundamentals of the software engineering field, as well as guidance on how to apply the theory in an industrial environment.

Customers today have very high expectations on quality and expect high-quality software to be consistently delivered on time and on budget. The focus on quality requires that sound software engineering practices be employed to enable quality software to be consistently produced. Further, it is an accepted view in the software quality field that the quality of the delivered software is closely related to the quality of the underlying processes used to build the software, and on adherence to them.

Many processes are employed in the design and development of software, and companies need to determine the extent to which the underlying processes used to design, develop, test, and manage software projects are fit for purpose. The process will need to be continuously improved, and often model-based improvement using a framework such as the CMMI is employed. There is also the need to focus on best practice in software engineering, as well as emerging technologies from various research programs. Piloting or technology transfer of innovative technology is an important part of continuous improvement. Companies need to focus on customer satisfaction and software quality, and they need to ensure that the desired quality is built into the software product.

We discussed project planning and tracking, software lifecycles, software inspections and testing, configuration management, software quality assurance, etc. The capability maturity model integrated was discussed, and it provides a

© Springer Nature Switzerland AG 2022
G. O'Regan, *Concise Guide to Software Engineering*,
Undergraduate Topics in Computer Science,
https://doi.org/10.1007/978-3-031-07816-3_25

framework that assists organizations in software process improvement. The appraisal of an organization against the CMMI allows the organization to determine the current capability or maturity of selected software processes and to prioritize improvements.

We discussed the professional responsibility of software engineers, where engineers have a professional responsibility to behave ethically with their clients. The professional engineering body requires its member to adhere to the code of ethics of the profession.

We discussed ethical software engineering including the ethical impacts of technical decisions as part of the software engineering process. The ethical software engineer needs to examine both the technical and the ethical dimensions of decisions that affect wider society.

We introduced project management, and discussed project estimation; project planning and scheduling, project monitoring and control, risk management, and managing project quality.

We discussed requirements engineering including activities such as requirements gathering, requirements elicitation, requirements analysis, requirements management, and requirements verification and validation.

We then discussed design and development, including the high-level architectural design, the low-level design of individual programs, and software development and reuse. The views of Hoare and Parnas on software design were discussed, and we discussed the historical function-oriented design and object-oriented design. We discussed software development topics such as software reuse, customized-off-the-shelf software, and open-source software development.

We discussed software inspections including Fagan inspections, as well as the less formal review and walkthrough methodologies. Software testing was then discussed, including the various types of testing that may be carried out, and we discussed test planning, test case definition, test tracking, test metrics, test reporting, and testing in an e-commerce environment.

We then discussed ethics and privacy where professional ethics are a code of conduct that governs how members of a profession deal with each other and with third parties. It expresses ideals of human behaviour, and the fundamental principles of the organization, and is an indication of its professionalism. Privacy is defined as "the right to be left alone", and specifies there should be no intrusion upon seclusion, and no public disclosure of private facts or false information.

We then discussed metrics and problem solving, including the balanced score card and GQM, as well as presenting a collection of sample metrics for an organization.

We then discussed outsourcing including the selection and management of a software supplier, and we described how candidate suppliers may be formally evaluated, selected, and managed during the project.

We then discussed software configuration management including the concept of a baseline. Configuration management is concerned with identifying those deliverables that are subject to change control and controlling changes to them.

We discussed software quality assurance and the importance of process quality, and the discussion included audits and described how they are carried out.

We discussed the Agile methodology which is has become the dominant paradigm in software engineering. It is a popular lightweight approach to software development that has a strong collaborative style of working. It advocates adaptive planning and evolutionary development.

We then discussed software reliability and dependability, and covered topics such as software reliability and software reliability models; the Cleanroom methodology; system availability; safety and security critical systems, and dependency engineering.

We discussed formal methods, which are often employed in the safety critical and security critical fields. These consist of a set of mathematical techniques to specify and derive a program from its specification. Formal methods may be employed to rigorously state the requirements of the proposed system; they may be employed to derive a program from its mathematical specification; and they provide a rigorous proof that the implemented program satisfies its specification.

We discussed the Z specification language, which was developed at the Programming Research Group at Oxford University in the early 1980s. Z specifications are mathematical, and the use of mathematics ensures precision, and allows inconsistencies and gaps in the specification to be identified. Theorem provers may be employed to demonstrate that the software implementation meets its specification

We then discussed the unified modelling language, which is a visual modelling language for software systems, and it is used to present several views of the system architecture. We presented various UML diagrams such as use case diagrams, sequence diagrams and activity diagrams.

We then discussed the important field of software process improvement, and discussed the idea of a software process, and discussed the benefits that may be gained from software process improvement.

We gave an overview of the CMMI model and discussed its five maturity levels and their constituent process areas. We discussed both the staged and continuous representations of the CMMI.

We then discussed a selection of tools to support various software engineering activities, including tools to support project management, requirements engineering, configuration management, design and development activities and software testing.

We then discussed some innovative developments in the computer field, such as distributed systems, service-oriented architecture, software as a service, cloud computing and embedded systems. This led to a discussion of the many innovations in the software engineering, and the need for continuous innovation.

We then discussed legal aspects of computing including the application of the legal system to the computing field. This includes the protection of intellectual property such as patents, copyright, trademarks and trade secrets, and the resolution of disputes between parties.

Finally, we discussed cybersecurity and cybercrime. Computer crime (or cybercrime) is a crime that involves a computer and a network. The computer may be the vehicle by which the crime was conducted, or it may be the target of the crime. Cybersecurity is the protection of information through good security practices, including the protection of confidentiality, integrity, and availability of data. It is achieved through policies that ensure consistency in employee behaviour in the use of computer resources, as well as training and awareness of security in the workplace.

25.1   The Future of Software Engineering

Software engineering has come a long way since the 1950s and 1960s, when it was accepted that the completed software would always contain lots of defects, and that the coding should be done as quickly as possible, to enable these defects to be quickly identified and corrected.

The software crisis in the late 1960s highlighted problems with budget and schedule overruns, as well as problems with the quality and reliability of the delivered software. This led to the birth of software engineering as a discipline, and the realization that programming is quite distinct from science and mathematics.

The software engineering field is highly innovative, and many new technologies and systems have been developed over the decades. These include object-oriented design and development; formal methods and UML; the waterfall and spiral models; software inspections and software testing; software process improvement and the CMMI; and the Agile methodology.

Software engineering will continue to be fundamental to the success of projects. There is not a one size that fits all: some companies (e.g., in the safety critical or security critical fields) are likely to focus on formal methods and software process maturity models such as the CMMI. For other areas, the lightweight Agile methodology may be the appropriate software development methodology.

Companies are likely to measure the cost of poor quality in future, as driving down the cost of poor quality will become more important. Software components and the verification of software components is likely to become important, to speed up software development and to shorten time to market. Software reuse and open-source software development is likely to grow in popularity, and continuous innovation will continue in the software engineering field.

Glossary

ACM Association of Computing Machinery

AECL Atomic Energy of Canada Ltd.

AMN Abstract Machine Notation

AOSE Aspect Oriented Software Engineering

ATM Automated Teller Machine

BCS British Computer Society

BRS Business Requirements Specification

BSC Balanced Score Card

CAR Causal Analysis and Resolution

CBA IPI CMM Based Assessment Internal Process Improvement

CCB Change Control Board

CCS Calculus Communicating Systems

CICS Customer Information Control System

CM Configuration Management

CMM® Capability Maturity Model

CMMI® Capability Maturity Model Integration

COCOMO Constructive Cost Model

COPQ Cost of Poor Quality

COTS Customized Off the Shelf

CR Change Request

CSP Communicating Sequential Processes

CSR Corporate Social Responsibility

DAR Decision Analysis and Resolution

DMAIC Define, Measure, Analyse, Improve, Control

DMADV Define, Measure, Analyse, Design, Verify

DMCA Digital Millennium Copyright Act

DOORS Dynamic Object-Oriented Requirements System

DPIA Data Protection Impact Assessment

DRM Digital Rights Management

DSDM Dynamic Systems Development Method

EAF Effort Adjustment Factor

EDSAC Electronic Delay Storage Automatic Calculator

ESA European Space Agency

ESI European Software Institute

EULA End User License Agreement

FDA Food and Drug Administration

FIPPs Fair Information Practice Principles

FOSS Free Open-Source Software

FSF Free Software Foundation

FSM Finite State Machine

GDPR General Data Protection Regulation

GG Generic Goal

GNU GNU's Not Unix15

GP Generic Practice

GPL General Public License

GQM Goal, Question, Metric

GUI Graphical User Interface

HP Hewlett Packard

HR Human Resources

HTML Hyper Text Mark-up Language

HTTP Hypertext Transfer Protocol

IaaS Infrastructure as a Service

IBM International Business Machines

IDE Integrated Development Environment

IEC International Electro technical Commission

IEEE Institute of Electrical and Electronic Engineers

IoT Internet of Things

IP Internet Protocol

IPM Integrated Project Management

ISEB Information System Examination Board

ISO International Standards Organization

ISP Internet Service Provider

ISTQB International Software Testing Qualifications Board

JAD Joint Application Development

JVM Java Virtual Machine

KLOC Thousand Lines of Code

LCL Lower Control Limit

LDRA Liverpool Data Research Associates

LPF Logic of Partial Functions

LOC Lines of Code

MA Measurement and Analysis

MOD Ministry of Defence

MTBF Mean Time Between Failure

MTTF Mean Time to Failure

MTTR Mean Time to Repair

NATO North Atlantic Treaty Organization

OCL Object Constraint Language

ODC Orthogonal Defect Classification

OID Organization Innovation and Deployment

OMG Object Management Group

OMT Object Modelling Technique

OOD Object-Oriented Design

OOSE Object-Oriented Software Engineering

OPD Organization Process Definition

OPF Organization Process Focus

OPP Organization Process Performance

OSP Online Service Provider

OSS Open-Source Software

OT Organization Training

PaaS Platform as a Service

PCE Phase Containment Effectiveness

P-CMM People Capability Maturity Model

PI Product Integration

PL/1 Programming Language

PMBOK Project Management Book of Knowledge

PMI Project Management Institute

PMC Project Monitoring and Control

PMO Project Management Office

PMP Project Management Professional

PP Project Planning

PPM Project Portfolio Management

PPQA Process and Product Quality Assurance

Prince Projects In a Controlled Environment

PSP Personal Software Process

PVCS Polytron Version Control System

QPM Quantitative Project Management

RAD Rapid Application Development

RAG Red, Amber, Green

RCA Root Cause Analysis

RD Requirements Development

REQM Requirements Management

RFP Request for Proposal

ROI Return on Investment

RPM Rational Portfolio Manager

RSM Rational Software Modeler

RSKM Risk Management

RUP Rational Unified Process

SaaS Software as a Service

SAM Supplier Agreement Management

SCAMPI Standard CMMI Appraisal Method for Process Improvement

SCM Software Configuration Management

SDI Strategic Defence Initiative

SEI Software Engineering Institute

SEPG Software Engineering Process Group

SG Specific Goal

SIG Special Interest Group

SIG AI AI Special Interest Group

SIG SOFT Software Engineering Special Interest Group

SLA Service Level Agreement

SLOC Source lines of code

SOA Service Oriented Architecture

SOW Statement of Work

SP Specific Practice

SPC Statistical Process Control

SPI Software Process Improvement

SPICE Software Process Improvement Capability dEtermination

SQA Software Quality Assurance

SRB Solid Rocket Booster

SRS System Requirements Specification

SSADM Structured Systems Analysis and Design Method

SSL Secure Socket Layer

TCP Transport Control Protocol

TDD Test Driven Development

TDI Turbo Charged Direction Injection

TS Technical Solution

TSP Team Software Process

UAT User Acceptance Testing

UCL Upper Control Limit

UK United Kingdom

UML Unified Modelling Language

URS User Requirements Specification

VAL Validation

VDM Vienna Development Method

VDM♣ Irish School of VDM

VER Verification

VOB Version Object Base

VPN Virtual Private Network

VSS Visual Source Safe

XP Extreme Programming

Y2K Year 2000

Index

Printed in the United States
by Baker & Taylor Publisher Services